B.R. 45(2), ADMIRALTY MANUAL OF NAVIGATION, VOL. II

Revised 1973, superseding the edition of 1960

December 1973   *By Command of the Defence Council*

MINISTRY OF DEFENCE
Director of Naval Warfare
D/CS(PS)3/3/6/9/4

RECORD OF CHANGES

CHANGE NO.	AUTHORITY	DATE OF INSERTION	INITIALS

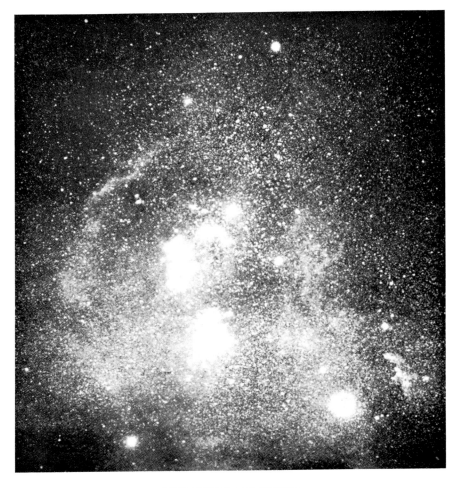

THE FIELD OF ORION

The whole constellation, showing Nebulosities. This
photograph was taken at the Yerkes Observatory of the
University of Chicago in 1927, Jan. 6, with a 3-in. lens, focal
length 21 in., exp. 5 hours, and is reproduced by courtesy
of the Director of Yerkes Observatory.

[*See* Chapter 15

MINISTRY OF DEFENCE (NAVY)

Admiralty
Manual of Navigation

VOLUME II

B.R. 45(2)

Revised 1973

LONDON
HER MAJESTY'S STATIONERY OFFICE

HER MAJESTY'S STATIONERY OFFICE

Government Bookshops

49 High Holborn, London WC1V 6HB
13a Castle Street, Edinburgh EH2 3AR
41 The Hayes, Cardiff CF1 1JW
Brazennose Street, Manchester M60 8AS
Southey House, Wine Street, Bristol BS1 2BQ
258 Broad Street, Birmingham B1 2HE
80 Chichester Street, Belfast BT1 4JY

Government publications are also available
through booksellers

Printed in Scotland by Her Majesty's Stationery Office
at HMSO Press, Edinburgh

Dd 716841 C40 6/82 (200697)

ISBN 0 11 771467 4

Preface

The *Admiralty Manual of Navigation* consists of four volumes:

Volume I (1964) is a practical guide for seaman officers covering the syllabus laid down for examination in Navigation and Pilotage for the rank of Lieutenant, but omitting the study of nautical astronomy and meteorology.

Volume II (revised 1973) is the textbook of nautical astronomy and off-shore navigation completing the above syllabus. This volume also covers the syllabus of meteorology for officers qualifying in Navigation. This revision contains examples worked from the *Nautical Almanac* of 1971. The Rapid Sight Reduction Method and the Astroplot have been included as Chapter 23 of this revision.

Volume III (1954) is based on the navigation syllabus for officers qualifying in Navigation and deals with advanced subjects and mathematical proofs not included in Volumes I and II. It will be unnecessary for seaman officers in general to study this volume. (Out of print)

Volume IV (1962) is intended to provide data on certain navigational equipment and techniques used by HM ships and details of the handling qualities of various classes of HM ships. It is not available for the Press or public.

Thanks are due to the Hydrographic Department, the Naval Weather Service, the Admiralty Compass Observatory, the Astronomer Royal, the Institute of Navigation, the Director of the Yerkes Observatory, Wisconsin, the Royal Astronomical Society, London, and various instrument manufacturers. Acknowledgements are also due to Messrs. Hutchinson and Co. (Publishers) Limited for use of the extracts from *On the Bridge*, by Vice-Admiral Sir James A. G. Troup, KBE, CB, and to Messrs. Imray, Laurie, Norie and Wilson Limited for use of the extract from *Norie's Tables*.

Contents

CONTENTS

CONTENTS

CONTENTS

CONTENTS

xi

CONTENTS

CONTENTS

Introduction

The part of navigation which is concerned with 'pilotage', or the conduct of a ship in the vicinity of dangers, such as rocks and shoals, and in narrow waters, is fully explained in Volume I.

The purpose of this volume is to describe off-shore navigation, or the passages of ships across the open sea where, in general, position lines cannot be obtained by observations of terrestrial objects except by means of radio waves.

Under these conditions, the navigator's problem is to conduct the ship from one point to another, the two points being defined by their latitude and longitude. He will need to know the course or courses to steer to achieve this. He will also need to be able to obtain his position by observation of heavenly bodies (or by the various radio navigational aids described in Volume I), so that he can tell if he is on the track that he has planned and adjust his course as necessary if he is not. He needs to be able to calculate the distances between points of departure and arrival, so that he can adjust his speed or time of departure in order to arrive at the destination at a predetermined time or to forecast his time of arrival.

The first three chapters of Volume II are concerned mainly with distances, courses, tracks and charts. In subsequent chapters the various methods of obtaining position lines and positions from astronomical observations are explained.

A knowledge of elementary spherical trigonometry is assumed, though all formulae used are established in Appendix 1.

Considerations common to both pilotage and off-shore navigation are discussed mainly in Volume I, with the exception of elementary meteorology, which is treated in the present volume.

CHAPTER 1

The Rhumb Line

The most convenient course for a ship to steer is a steady course; one along which the bearing of her head remains constant. Her track must then cut all meridians at the same angle, and in general it will spiral towards the nearer pole.

The Rhumb Line

A line on the earth's surface which cuts all meridians at the same angle is called a *rhumb line*. In Figs. 1a and 1b, $FABCT$ is the rhumb line joining F to T. The angles PFA, PAB, PBC and PCT are all equal, and any one of them may be taken as the course.

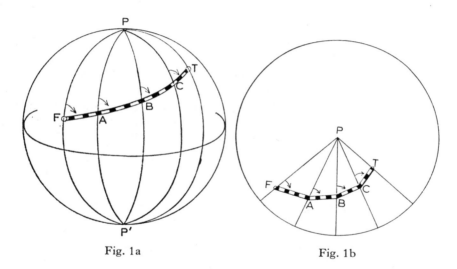

Fig. 1a   Fig. 1b

When this constant angle is 90°, the rhumb line is either a parallel of latitude or the equator itself (Fig. 2). When the angle is 0°, the rhumb line coincides with the meridian. The track of a ship steering a steady course is thus either a rhumb line or a meridian, and except at the poles (where the meridians cut at angles ranging from 0° to 180°) a meridian may be considered to be a rhumb line.

The 'rhumb-line course' is always referred to as *the course*, and mention of the course that must be followed in order to go from one place to another will always refer to the angle between any meridian and the rhumb line joining the two places.

Distance along a Parallel of Latitude

In order to find the course and distance along a rhumb line it is necessary to know the distance along a parallel of latitude between two given points, because the formulae for rhumb-line sailing are constructed by considering a large number of small right-angled triangles, in each of which one side lies along a parallel of latitude.

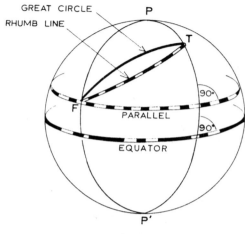

Fig. 2

In Fig. 3a, *FT* is the arc of the parallel of latitude, the length of which is to be found. *FT* is thus the distance along the parallel between the meridians through *F* and *T*. *AB* is the distance along the equator between the same meridians; that is, the d.long between *F* and *T*.

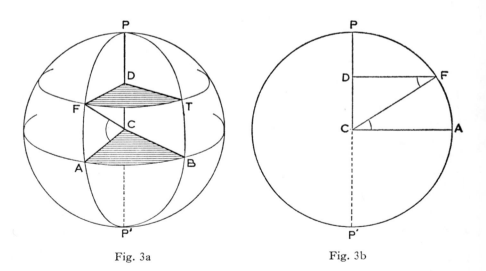

Fig. 3a   Fig. 3b

It is apparent that the nearer the parallel is to the pole – in other words, the higher the latitude – the shorter *FT* becomes. But the d.long does not alter.

FT must therefore bear to AB some relation depending on the latitude. To find this relation, consider the sections DFT and CAB. They are parallel and equiangular. Hence:

$$\frac{FT}{AB} = \frac{DF}{CA}$$

But, from the triangle DCF in Fig. 3b:

$$DF = CF \cos (\text{latitude})$$
$$= CA \cos (\text{latitude})$$

since CF is equal to CA, each being a radius of the Earth. Therefore:

$$\frac{FT}{AB} = \frac{CA \cos (\text{latitude})}{CA}$$

i.e., $FT = AB \cos (\text{latitude})$

The distance along a parallel of latitude in nautical miles is thus equal to the d.long, expressed in minutes of arc, multiplied by the cosine of the latitude.

Suppose, for example, that the latitude of the parallel is 40°N, and that the longitudes F and T are 15°E and 60°E respectively. Then the d.long is 45° or, in minutes of arc which are also nautical miles at the equator, 2,700'.

$$\therefore \quad FT = 2,700' \times \cos 40°$$
$$= 2,068'\cdot3$$

Had the latitude been 60° instead of 40°, the distance along this new parallel would have been 2,700' × cos 60°, which is 1,350'.

Departure

The distance along a parallel of latitude is a particular example of what is called *departure*.

Departure is the distance made good in an east–west direction in sailing from one place to another along a rhumb line.

Suppose that a navigator goes from F to T in Fig. 4. The distance he moves in an east–west direction in doing so cannot be greater than FT', the distance along the parallel through F, because the two meridians FF' and $T'T$ converge north of FT'. For the same reason it cannot be less than $F'T$.

The distance he moves in an east–west direction in going from F to T must therefore be equal to the distance along some parallel, MN, lying between the parallels through F and T.

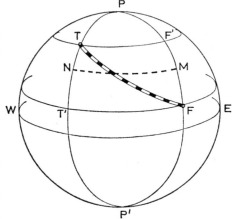

Fig. 4

Middle Latitude

The latitude of this parallel *MN* is called the *middle latitude* between *F* and *T*. Hence, by the formula just established:

departure = d.long cos (middle latitude)

The mathematical theory by which this middle latitude is found is given in Volume III. An approximation, however, suggests itself.

Mean Latitude

Except when the difference of latitude is large or the latitudes themselves are high, the middle latitude may be taken, without appreciable error, as the arithmetic mean of the two latitudes. The accurate formula:

departure = d.long cos (middle latitude)

then becomes the approximate one:

departure = d.long cos (mean latitude).

When the two places are close to the equator, but on opposite sides of it, the departure can be taken as being equal to the d.long. If they are not sufficiently close for this assumption to be made, the arithmetic mean of the latitudes is no longer an approximation to the middle latitude, and the methods of Mercator sailing (Chapter 3) must be used.

In general, the use of a mean instead of a middle latitude suffices up to distances of 600′, the limit of the traverse tables described in this chapter.

To find the Middle Latitude

When the positions involved suggest that the middle latitude should be used, it can be found by adding a small correction (Fig. 5) to the mean latitude. This correction is given in *Norie's Tables*.

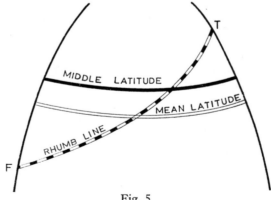

Fig. 5

If, for example, a ship steams from a position *F* in latitude 30°N, longitude 40°W, to a position *T* in latitude 34°N, longitude 36°W, her departure (easterly) by the approximate formula would be:

$$(40° - 36°) \cos \tfrac{1}{2} (34° + 30°)$$
$$= 240' \cos 32°$$
$$= 203'·5$$

The correction from *Norie's Tables*, which is applied to the mean latitude of 32° in order to give the middle latitude, is −26′. The accurate formula therefore gives the ship's departure as:

$$240' \cos 31° 34'$$
$$= 204'·5$$

The difference between these two results is small, but if the ship had steamed from 50°N, 20°W, to 70°N, 8°W, say, it would have been appreciable. Her departure by the approximate formula would have been:

$$(20° − 8°) \cos \tfrac{1}{2} (70° + 50°)$$
$$= 720' \cos 60°$$
$$= 360'$$

The accurate formula gives it as:

$$(20° − 8°) \cos (60° + 1° 09')$$
$$= 720' \cos 61° 09'$$
$$= 347'·4$$

THE RHUMB-LINE FORMULAE

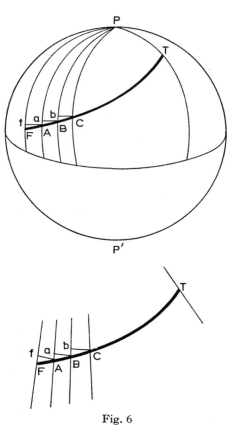

With his knowledge of the distance along a parallel of latitude and the departure between two places, the navigator can find the course he must steer in order to follow the rhumb line joining the two places, and also the distance he will travel while doing so.

In Fig. 6, *FT* is the rhumb line divided into a large number of equal parts *FA*, *AB*, *BC* . . .

Af, *Ba*, *Cb* . . . are the arcs of parallels drawn through *A*, *B*, *C* . . . and the angles at *f*, *a*, *b* . . . are therefore right angles. If the divisions of *FT* are made sufficiently small, the triangles *FAf*, *ABa*, *BCb* . . . are themselves small enough to be treated as plane triangles. Also, since the course angle at *F*, *A*, *B*, *C* . . . remains constant by the definition of a rhumb line, these small triangles are equal.*

Fig. 6

---

* It should be clearly understood that to regard certain small triangles as plane is not to disregard the initial decision to consider the Earth as a sphere. The triangles are merely assumed to be sufficiently small to lie flat on the Earth's surface.

DEPARTURE = DISTANCE × SIN (COURSE)

In covering the length *AB*, say, the navigator makes good in the west–east direction a distance which may be taken as being equal to *aB* since *AB* itself is small. The smaller the triangles *FAf*, *ABa*, *BCb* . . . are taken, the more nearly does *aB* approximate to the departure between *A* and *B*.

The departure between *F* and *T* is therefore the sum of all these small arcs of parallels, *fA*, *aB*, *bC* . . .

But:
$$fA = FA \sin (\text{course})$$
$$aB = AB \sin (\text{course})$$
$$bC = BC \sin (\text{course})$$

Therefore, by addition:
$$fA + aB + bC + \ldots = (FA + AB + BC + \ldots) \sin (\text{course}),$$
i.e. departure = distance sin (course)

D.LAT = DISTANCE × COS (COURSE)

This, the second rhumb-line formula, is found by considering the lengths of the sides of these small triangles that lie along the meridians. Thus:
$$Ff = FA \cos (\text{course})$$
$$Aa = AB \cos (\text{course})$$
$$Bb = BC \cos (\text{course})$$

But *Ff* is the d.lat between *F* and *A*, *Aa* between *A* and *B*, . . . so that *Ff* + *Aa* + *Bb* + . . . is the total d.lat between *F* and *T*. Therefore, by addition:
$$Ff + Aa + Bb + \ldots = (FA + AB + BC + \ldots) \cos (\text{course}),$$
i.e. d.lat = distance cos (course)

Short-distance sailing

By the term 'short-distance sailing' is meant the following of a rhumb-line track for a distance not greater than 600'. Within this limiting distance, the navigator can obtain all he wants to know about the track from the three formulae:

departure = d.long cos (mean latitude) . . . . . *formula* (1)

departure = distance sin (course) . . . . . . *formula* (2)

d.lat = distance cos (course) . . . . . . *formula* (3)

The course is given by (2) divided by (3). Thus:

$$\frac{\text{departure}}{\text{d.lat}} = \tan (\text{course})$$ . . . . *formula* (4)

In short-distance sailing, the navigator's problem usually takes one of two forms:

1. *To find the course and distance when the positions of the starting-point and destination are given.*
Since the d.long and the mean latitude are known, the departure can be

found from formula (1). Formula (4) now gives the course, and either (2) or (3) gives the distance.

2. *To find the position after a given rhumb-line track has been followed for a given distance.*

In this problem, course and distance are known, and the departure and d.lat can be found at once from formulae (2) and (3). With this d.lat, the mean latitude is found, and formula (1) gives the d.long.

THE TRAVERSE TABLE

It should be apparent, from their construction, that these formulae for short-distance sailing do no more than solve an ordinary right-angled triangle, the hypotenuse of which is the distance, the vertical side the d.lat, and the horizontal one the departure (Fig. 7). To enable the navigator to solve this triangle quickly, he is provided with a *Traverse Table*.

Norie's Tables include a traverse table in which the d.lat and departure are given for any distance up to 600′ and for any course. The layout of the table is shown in the extract printed here of the upper and lower portions of a right-hand page.

333° ↑ 207°		**TRAVERSE TABLE** 27 DEGREES.							027° ↑ 153°	1h 48m	**27°**
D Lon	Dep.		D Lon	Dep.		D Lon	Dep.		D Lon	Dep.	
Dist	D. Lat	Dep.	Dist	D. Lat	Dep.	Dist	D. Lat	Dep.	Dist	D. Lat	Dep.
301	268·2	136·7	361	321·7	163·9	421	375·1	191·1	481	428·6	218·4	541	482·0	245·6
302	269·1	137·1	362	322·5	164·3	422	376·0	191·6	482	429·5	218·8	542	482·9	246·1
303	270·0	137·6	363	323·4	164·8	423	376·9	192·0	483	430·4	219·3	543	483·8	246·5
304	270·9	138·0	364	324·3	165·3	424	377·8	192·5	484	431·2	219·7	544	484·7	247·0
305	271·8	138·5	365	325·2	165·7	425	378·7	192·9	485	432·1	220·2	545	485·6	247·4
306	272·6	138·9	366	326·1	166·2	426	379·6	193·4	486	433·0	220·6	546	486·5	247·9
307	273·5	139·4	367	327·0	166·6	427	380·5	193·9	487	433·9	221·1	547	487·4	248·3
308	274·4	139·8	368	327·9	167·1	428	381·4	194·3	488	434·8	221·5	548	488·3	248·8
309	275·3	140·3	369	328·8	167·5	429	382·2	194·8	489	435·7	222·0	549	489·2	249·2
310	276·2	140·7	370	329·7	168·0	430	383·1	195·2	490	436·6	222·5	550	490·1	249·7
311	277·1	141·2	371	330·6				195·7	491	437·5	222·9	551	490·9	
312	278·0	141·6								438·4	223·4			
			414	368·0	187·5	473	421·4							269·2
355	316·3	161·2	414	368·9	188·0	474	422·3	215·2	534	475·8	242·4	594	529·3	269·7
356	317·2	161·6	415	369·8	188·4	475	423·2	215·6	535	476·7	242·9	595	530·1	270·1
357	318·1	162·1	416	370·7	188·9	476	424·1	216·1	536	477·6	243·3	596	531·0	270·6
358	319·0	162·5	417	371·5	189·3	477	425·0	216·6	537	478·5	243·8	597	531·9	271·0
359	319·9	163·0	418	372·4	189·8	478	425·9	217·0	538	479·4	244·2	598	532·8	271·5
360	320·8	163·4	419	373·3	190·2	479	426·8	217·5	539	480·3	244·7	599	533·7	271·9
			420	374·2	190·7	480	427·7	217·9	540	481·1	245·2	600	534·6	272·4
Dist	Dep.	D.Lat	Dist	Dep.	D.Lat	Dist	Dep.	D.Lat	Dist	Dep.	D.Lat	Dist	Dep.	D.Lat
D Lon		Dep.	D Lon		Dep.	D Lon		Dep.	D Lon		Dep.	D Lon		Dep.
297° ↑ 243°				**63 DEGREES.**					063° ↑ 117°	4h 12m	**63°**

The traverse table is arranged on openings of two facing pages, tabulated on the left-hand page for 1′ to 300′ distance and on the right-hand page for 301′ to

600′ distance. Each opening gives a value for angle F (Fig. 7) and also its complementary angle, values between 0° and 45° appearing at the top of the page and the complement, 45° to 90°, at the bottom. The value denotes the course in relation to the appropriate cardinal points. The equivalent of the angle in 000° to 360° notation is shown for each quadrant of the compass at the top of the page, and similarly at the bottom for the complementary angle.

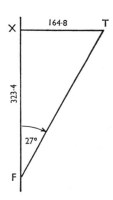

Fig. 7

The navigator who runs 363′ on a course 027°, for example, can see at once that his d.lat is 323′·4 and his departure 164′·8 and as he is moving north and east his d.lat is north and his departure east.

Had his course been 063°, the complementary angle, he would have read his departure and d.lat in the columns named at the bottom of the page instead of at the top and he would have found his d.lat to be 164′·8 north and his departure 323′·4 east. That is because the triangle has been turned round, as shown in Figs. 8a and 8b.

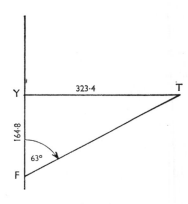

Fig. 8a   Fig. 8b

As a further example, a run of 536′ on course 207° would give a d.lat of 477′·6 south and a departure of 243′·3 west.

When using the traverse table to solve problems of the type just described, the required opening is most quickly found by mentally converting the course, if necessary, to its cardinal equivalent which is printed boldly in the margin of each page.

To find the course and distance when d.lat and departure are known the table must be searched for a page containing the set of columns in which the known quantities occur on the same line or nearly so. It will be seen in the extract that a d.lat of 246′ north and a departure of 483′ west would give a distance of 542′ and a course of 297°.

Further use of the traverse table

Since the traverse table solves an ordinary right-angled triangle, the sides and 'included' angle can be conveniently renamed to enable the table to be used for changing departure into d.long or d.long into departure. If cardinal course is treated as mean latitude, distance as d.long and d.lat as departure it will be seen that by renaming the quantities shown in Fig. 7 the following formulae can be used:

$$\text{departure} = \text{d.long cos (mean latitude)}$$
$$\text{d.long} = \text{departure sec (mean latitude)}.$$

The traverse table provides solutions to these formulae.

To change departure into d.long or d.long into departure

To find the opening required the table is entered with mean latitude in the place of cardinal course. The distance column is then used for d.long and the d.lat column for departure. The expressions 'D Lon' and 'Dep.' are shown bracketed together in their appropriate columns at the top and bottom of the page.

It will be seen in the extract that in mean latitude 27° a d.long of 361′ is equivalent to a departure of 321′·7. In mean latitude 63° a departure of 190′·7 gives a d.long of 420′.

It should be borne in mind that, whereas the d.long is fundamentally an angle measured in minutes of arc, departure is a distance measured in nautical miles. Also, when either conversion is made, the number expressing the departure can never be greater than the number expressing the d.long, since the d.long is equal to the departure multiplied by the secant of an angle. When the angle given by the mean latitude is zero, the departure is equal to the d.long, but for all other values of the mean latitude, the departure is less than the d.long.

It is a good plan to use the traverse table as often as possible, because a facility in using it can be acquired only by practice and the table lends itself to the solution of many problems involving a right-angled triangle.

Method of using the traverse table in short-distance sailing

The following examples illustrate the method of using the rhumb-line formulae for short-distance sailing:

EXAMPLE 1

A ship leaves a position F in latitude 41° 05′N, longitude 2° 12′E, and steams a distance of 305′ on a course of 115°. What is her position (T) at the end of the run?

A course of 115° is a cardinal course of S65°E.

By traverse table:

$$(\text{arguments: } 65° \text{ and } 305′)$$
$$\text{d.lat} = 128′·9S, \text{ dep} = 276′·4E$$
$$\text{mean lat.} = 41° 05′N - \frac{128′·9}{2}$$
$$= 41° 05′N - 64′·5S$$
$$= 40° 00′·5N$$

(arguments: mean lat. (cardinal course) 40° and dep. 276'·4)
d.long = 360'·9E

latitude F	41° 05'·0N		longitude F	2° 12'·0E
d.lat	2° 08'·9S		d.long	6° 00'·9E
latitude T	38° 56'·1N		longitude T	8° 12'·9E

The position at the end of the run is thus: $\left\{ \begin{array}{l} 38°\ 56'·1N \\ 8°\ 12'·9E \end{array} \right.$

EXAMPLE 2

A ship is required to steam from a position F in latitude 35° 52'N, longitude 3° 06'W, to a position T in latitude 38° 38'N, lontigude 1° 42'E. What course must she steer, and what distance will she cover?

latitude F	35° 52'N		longitude F	3° 06'W
latitude T	38° 38'N		longitude T	1° 42'E
d.lat	2° 46'N		d.long	4° 48'E
	= 166'N			= 288'E

By traverse table:

(arguments: mean lat. (cardinal course) 37° 15' and d.long 288')
dep. = 229'E
(arguments: dep. 229' and d.lat 166')
course = N54°E = 054°
distance = 283'

Dead Reckoning by traverse table

The use of a traverse table for giving the ship's position at the end of a straight run is explained above. If the ship alters course from time to time, the traverse table can still be used to give her final position.

EXAMPLE

A ship in position 50° 14'N, 16° 11'W at 0800 and steaming 132° at 15 knots, makes the following alterations of course:

(1) *at 0840, new course 246°*
(2) *at 0956   ,,   ,,   302°*
(3) *at 1032   ,,   ,,   010°*
(4) *at 1144   ,,   ,,   090°*

What is her DR position at noon?

TIME	INTERVAL IN MINUTES	CARDINAL COURSE	DIS-TANCE RUN	D.LAT		DEPARTURE	
				N	S	E	W
0800–0840	40	S48°E	10′	—	6′·7	7′·4	—
0840–0956	76	S66°W	19′	—	7′·7	—	17′·4
0956–1032	36	N58°W	9′	4′·8	—	—	7′·6
1032–1144	72	N10°E	18′	17′·7	—	3′·1	—
1144–1200	16	E	4′	—	—	4′·0	—
				22′·5	14′·4	14′·5	25′·0
				14′·4			14′·5
				d.lat 8′·1N		dep. 10′·5W	

lat.*F*	50° 14′·0N	mean lat. 50° 18′N	long.*F*	16° 11′·0W
d.lat	8′·1N		d.long	16′·4W
lat.*T*	50° 22′·1N		long.*T*	16°27′·4W

DR position at noon $\begin{cases} 50° \ 22′·1N \\ 16° \ 27′·4W \end{cases}$

Estimated Position by traverse table

If, in the previous example, the navigator estimated that the tidal stream experienced had set the ship 4′ in a direction 062°, an extra line in the working of the traverse would be necessary. The set is treated as another course and distance, and the line would read:

Cardinal Course	Distance	D.Lat	Departure
N62°E	4′	1′·9N	3′·5E

The total d.lat is now 10′N, the total departure 7′W, and the d.long 11′W.

CHAPTER 2

The Great Circle

A straight line is the shortest distance between two points, and when the two points lie on the surface of a sphere, the arc of the great circle joining them is the curve that most nearly approaches the straight line, because it has the greatest radius and therefore the least curvature. The shorter arc of the great circle joining two places on the Earth's surface is thus the shortest route between them. In Fig. 9, *FT* is such an arc, and its length is the shortest distance between

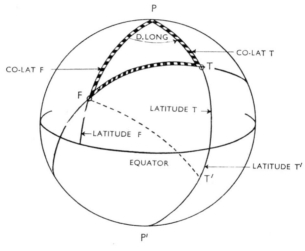

Fig. 9

the two points on the Earth's surface, *F* and *T*. *PF* and *PT* are arcs of the meridians passing through *F* and *T* and are also arcs of great circles. The triangle *PFT* is therefore a spherical triangle, and the problem of finding the shortest distance between two points is the problem of finding the length of the side opposite the pole in this triangle.

The navigator very often requires to know the 'true bearing' of one point from another. The true bearing of *T* from *F* is the angle between the meridian through *F* and the great circle joining *F* and *T*, measured clockwise from the meridian, that is, the angle *PFT*. This angle represents the initial course to be steered by a ship sailing on a great circle from *F* to *T*. Radio waves also travel along great circles near the Earth's surface, and the angle *PFT* is thus the bearing of *T* from *F* as it would be given by MF DF (Figs. 10a and 10b).

In Fig. 10a, at any intermediate point *G*, between *F* and *T*, the true bearing of *T* is the angle *PGT*, and this is not equal to the angle *PFT*. To an observer moving along the great circle from F to T, the true bearing of T changes continuously. Only when T is close to F may this change be neglected. The area

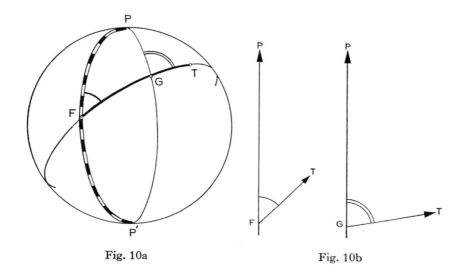

Fig. 10a   Fig. 10b

of the Earth's surface traversed by FT is then sufficiently small to be considered as a plane or flat surface, on which great circles appear as straight lines.

Great-circle Distance and Bearing

The length of the side FT (Fig. 9) and the true bearing PFT are found by solving the spherical triangle FPT. In this triangle the angle FPT is clearly the d.long between F and T. The lengths of the sides PF and PT depend upon the latitudes of F and T. When these latitudes have the same name – both F and T are north in Fig. 9 – PF is (90° − latitude F) and PT is (90° − latitude T). The distance (90° − latitude) is known as the 'co-latitude' of the place concerned.

When the destination is in the opposite hemisphere – T' has south latitude in Fig. 9 – the length of the side PT' is (90° + latitude T'). Therefore:

For latitudes of the same name:

$$PF = 90° - \text{latitude } F = \text{co-latitude } F$$
$$PT = 90° - \text{latitude } T = \text{co-latitude } T$$
$$\text{angle } FPT = \text{d.long.}$$

For latitudes of the opposite name:

$$PF = 90° - \text{latitude } F = \text{co-latitude } F$$
$$PT' = 90° + \text{latitude } T'$$
$$\text{angle } FPT' = \text{d.long.}$$

When *F* is also in southern latitudes, as in Fig. 11, the same relations hold if *P′* is substituted for *P*, so that for either hemisphere:

$$PF = 90° \pm \text{lat.}F$$
$$PT = 90° \pm \text{lat.}T$$

the sign being determined by the name of the pole and by the latitude of the place (*same names, subtract; opposite names, add*).

The solution of the spherical triangle *FPT* (or *FP′T*) is dealt with in Chapter 11. (*See also* Vol. III.) In practice the navigator normally plots great-circle tracks on a Mercator chart with the aid of a gnomonic chart or diagram, as shown in Chapter 3.

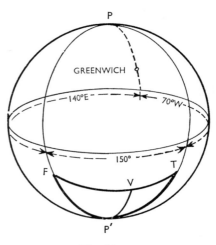

Fig. 11

Great-circle sailing

If a ship followed the great-circle track she would have to change course continually. In practice the great-circle track is divided into suitable lengths, successive points on the great circle being joined to form a succession of rhumb lines. This is known as 'approximate great-circle sailing', or, simply, 'great-circle sailing'.

Fig. 12 (which is a mercatorial drawing – *see* Chapter 3) illustrates any such approximate great circle. The navigator would alter course at *A*, *B* and *C*,

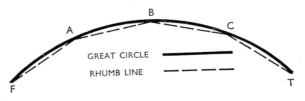

Fig. 12

and he would choose the lengths *FA*, *AB* . . . to suit his convenience. *FA*, for example, might be a twelve-hour run.

The Vertex

The point at which a great circle most nearly approaches the pole is called the *vertex* (of that great circle) – *V* in Fig. 11. At this point, the great circle ceases to approach the pole and begins to curve away. It must therefore cut the meridian through the vertex at right angles. The method of finding this position thus involves the use of right-angled spherical triangles and is given in Volume III.

The Composite Track

Since the great-circle track between two places not on the equator passes nearer to the pole than does the rhumb-line track, the ship may be carried into the ice region. When ice is likely to be encountered, the great-circle track must therefore be modified to avoid such high latitudes, while remaining the shortest possible safe track. This modified track is known as the 'composite track', and is formed by two great-circle arcs joined by an arc of the limiting or 'safe' parallel of latitude.

In Fig. 13, *FLVMT* is the great circle joining *F* and *T*. Latitudes higher than the *parallel* of *LM* are assumed to be dangerous. The ship cannot, there-

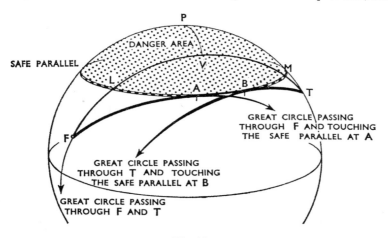

Fig. 13

fore, follow the great-circle arc *LVM*. Nor would she go from *F* to *L*, along to *M* and then down to *T*. The shortest route she can take is *FABT*, where *FA* and *BT* are great-circle arcs tangential to the safe parallel at *A* and *B*.

FABT is thus the composite track in this example. It is the shortest route because, if *L* and *M* are taken as any points on the parallel outside the part *AB*, (*FL* + *LA*) is greater than *FA* and (*BM* + *MT*) is greater than *BT*. Moreover, since *A* is the point nearest the pole on the great circle of which *FA* is an arc, any other great circle from *F* to a point between *A* and *B* would *cut* the parallel between *L* and *A* and so carry the ship into danger.

The composite track from *F* (43°S, 140°E) to *T* (56°S, 70°W), where the limiting latitude is 60°S, together with the great-circle and rhumb-line tracks for comparison, is shown on polar gnomonic and Mercator charts in Fig. 23.

CHAPTER 3

Charts

In the practice of navigation the navigator requires drawings of the Earth's surface on which to lay off his proposed course, fix the position of his ship, and find where he is in relation to the land. Moreover, since convenience demands that these drawings shall be flat, his problem is to show part of the surface of a sphere, which has three dimensions, as a plane or flat surface, which has only two. The sphere cannot be unrolled into a plane surface as can a cylinder or a cone. Distortion is therefore inevitable when a flat drawing of its surface is made, and if the area covered by the drawing is large, this distortion can be considerable. It is negligible only when the area is so small that the portion of the Earth's surface which it covers may be considered plane.

The Plan

A plane drawing of a small portion of the Earth is called a *plan*. It is useful

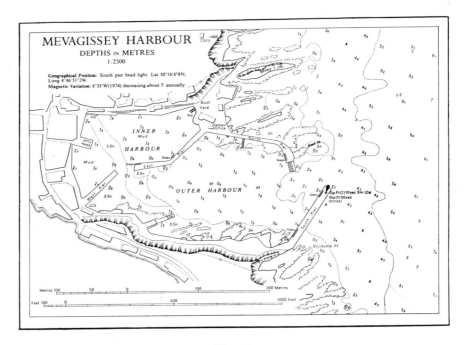

Fig. 14

when great detail has to be shown for a small area, such as a harbour or an intricate channel. Fig. 14 illustrates one such plan taken from a sheet of plans on Admiralty Chart No. 147. The position of any point in a plan is fixed in relation to some datum. In Fig. 14, this is the South pier head light in

$$\left\{ \begin{array}{l} 50°\ 16'\ 06''{\cdot}8N \\ 4°\ 46'\ 51''{\cdot}2W \end{array} \right.$$

Linear scales of metres and feet are given on all plans, and there is often a scale of cables. On some plans latitude and longitude are graduated round the border or given as separate linear scales. If the latitude scale only is given, the longitude scale can be constructed from it by the method explained in Volume I.

The 'natural scale' of the plan is the ratio of a length measured on the plan to the corresponding length measured on the Earth's surface.

The plan, which is really a gnomonic projection, is normally used for all charts of a natural scale 1/50,000 and larger.

The Plotting Chart

The navigator wishing to work out his position after manoeuvring in a limited area out of sight of land may do so by laying off distances and courses on a plan of his own making, called a *plotting chart*. On this, a convenient meridian and parallel of latitude are taken as axes, and the scale for latitude and distance is assumed to be the same everywhere on the chart. There is no separate scale for longitude. The change in longitude is found from the formula:

$$\text{d.long} = \text{departure} \times \sec (\text{mean latitude})$$

Fig. 15 shows the track of a ship as it would appear on a plotting chart if the ship steamed 6' on a course 075°, a distance and course indicated by OA; 4' on a course 340° (AB); and $3\frac{1}{2}'$ on a course 210° (BC). The position of C is then fixed in relation to O by its d.lat and departure.

d.lat (CX) = 2'·3N
departure (CY) = 2'·7E

If the position of O is 43°N, 15°W, the latitude of C is:

lat.O	43° 00'·0N
d.lat	2'·3N
lat.C	43° 02'·3N

By calculation (2'·7 × sec 43°), or from the tables (for departure 2'·7 and latitude 43°) the d.long is seen to be 3'·7E. The longitude of C is therefore:

long.O	15° 00'·0W
d.long	3'·7E
long.C	14° 56'·3W

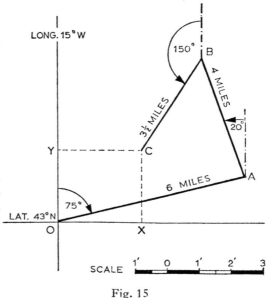

Fig. 15

Map projections

The distortion, which is inevitable when the area to be shown is large, takes different forms according to the different methods adopted for showing the area, and the cartographer's object is to arrange that the distortion resulting from a particular method shall serve a particular purpose. The graticule upon which the area is delineated is formed by the meridians and parallels passing through the area, and the term 'projection' is used to denote the type of graticule selected. It does not necessarily mean that the graticule is formed by the actual projection of meridians and parallels from a chosen point on to a particular plane.

THE MERCATOR CHART

To the navigator, the most useful chart is one on which he can show the track of his ship by drawing a straight line between his starting-point and his destination, and thus measure the steady course he must steer in order to arrive there. The Mercator chart (first published in 1569) permits him to do this because it is constructed so that:

1. rhumb lines on the Earth appear as straight lines on the chart;
2. the angles between these rhumb lines are unaltered, as between Earth and chart;

It therefore follows that:

1. the equator, which is a rhumb line as well as a great circle, appears on the chart as a straight line;
2. the parallels of latitude appear as straight lines parallel to the equator;
3. the meridians appear as straight lines perpendicular to the equator.*

In the general classification of graticules adopted by cartographers, the Mercator chart is described as a 'cylindrical orthomorphic projection'. The reason for this is explained fully in Volume III. The graticule, however, is *not* a true or a perspective projection of the meridians and parallels, formed by drawing straight lines from the centre of the sphere through certain points on the sphere and noting the corresponding points on a circumscribing cylinder: it is a graticule made according to certain mathematical laws, chosen because they give the chart the properties described.

Scale on the Mercator chart. Since the equator is shown on the chart as a straight line of definite length, and the meridians appear as straight lines

---

* Although a meridian is shown on the chart as a straight line and is therefore, by the principle of the chart's construction, a rhumb line over the length that appears on the chart, the definition of a meridian as a rhumb line breaks down at the pole. If there were not this mathematical discontinuity at the pole, it would be possible to steer a rhumb-line course between two places, F and T, differing by 180° in longitude, by proceeding up the meridian FP and then down the meridian PT. But the course along FP is *north*, whereas the course along PT is *south*. At P there has been a change of heading of 180°. The course from F to T is not therefore the same at all points, and FPT is not a rhumb-line track. This fact, however, is important only in the exact definition of the relation between a meridian and a rhumb line. It has no practical significance, because the pole can never be represented on a Mercator chart. In practice, then, a meridian is a rhumb line.

perpendicular to it, the *longitude* scale is fixed by that length and is constant in all latitudes. Let the scale of any Mercator chart be x millimetres to 1′ of d.long. Then, since departure = d.long cos (lat.), the departure on the chart represented by x millimetres is equal to 1′ cos (lat.): i.e. one mile in that particular latitude is represented by x sec (lat.) millimetres on the chart.

The scale of latitude and distance at any part of a Mercator chart, therefore, is proportional to the secant of the latitude of that part. For this reason, the amount of distortion in any latitude is governed by the secant of that latitude. Greenland, in 70°N, for example, appears as broad as Africa is drawn at the equator, although Africa is three times as broad as Greenland (sec 70° = 3). For a similar reason, Borneo, an island on the equator, appears about the same size as Iceland in 65°N, although in *area* Borneo is about five and a half times as large as Iceland.

Graduation of charts. Mercator charts are graduated along the left- and right-hand edges for latitude and distance, and along the top and bottom for longitude. *The longitude scale is used only for laying down or taking off the longitude of a place, never for measuring a distance.*

Measurement of distances on the chart. The length of the rhumb line between two places is referred to as the distance between them.

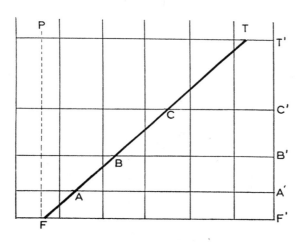

Fig. 16

In Fig. 16, *FABCT* is a rhumb line as it appears on the chart; *FF′*, *AA′*, *BB′* . . . are parallels of latitude.

The distance *FA* must be measured on the scale between *F′* and *A′*, the distance *AB* on the scale between *A′* and *B′*, and so on. If *FT* is not large – less than 100′ – no appreciable error is made by measuring it on the scale roughly either side of its middle point.

Meridional parts

Since the latitude and distance scale at any part of a Mercator chart is proportional to the secant of the latitude of that part, this scale continually increases as it recedes from the equator, until at the pole it becomes infinite. (For this reason, the complete polar regions cannot be shown on a Mercator chart.) The latitude scale thus affords no ready means of comparison with the fixed longitude scale. The tangent of the course-angle PFT, for example, is not PT divided by FP, where PT is measured on the longitude scale and FP on the latitude scale. For that ratio to be valid, PT and FP must be measured in the same fixed units. The fixed longitude scale provides this unit, which is the length of one minute of arc on that scale. This length is called a *meridional part*, and gives rise to the definition:

The meridional parts of any latitude are the number of longitude units in the length of a meridian between the parallel of that latitude and the equator.

The number of meridional parts of any latitude is tabulated in *Norie's Tables*, the quantities being calculated for the true shape of the Earth, an oblate spheroid. Meridional parts for the terrestrial spheroid are also given in *Burton's Nautical Tables*.*

If the longitude scale on the Mercator chart is 1 degree or 60 meridional parts to 10 mm, the length of the meridian between the parallel of 45°N and the equator, when measured on the chart, is not 450 mm but 502 mm, the length of 3013·38 meridional parts. Meridional parts thus involve chart lengths. They are not in any way connected with distance on the Earth's surface, which is expressed in nautical miles.

To find the meridional parts of any latitude

In Fig. 17, the upper half of which represents a part of the Earth's surface, F is a point on the equator, and FT the rhumb line joining it to T. The lower half of the figure shows this same rhumb line as the straight line ft on a Mercator chart.

If TQ is now divided into n small lengths, α, so that $(n\alpha)$ is equal to the latitude of T, the arcs of parallels drawn through the points of division are equally spaced and, with the meridians, form a series of small triangles FAX, ABY .... If, furthermore, α is so small that these triangles may be considered plane, they are equal in all respects, since:

$$FX = AY = \ldots = \alpha$$
$$\angle X = \angle Y = \ldots = \text{one right angle}$$
$$\angle F = \angle A = \ldots = \text{the course}$$

Therefore $AX = BY = \ldots$, and, since these small arcs recede in succession from the equator, the meridians which bound them are spaced successively farther apart. Hence:

$$FQ_1 < Q_1Q_2 < \cdots$$

---

* In *Inman's Tables* the meridional parts are tabulated for the perfect sphere. A small amount known as the 'reduction of the latitude' which is tabulated separately must be subtracted from the given latitude before the meridional parts are taken out.

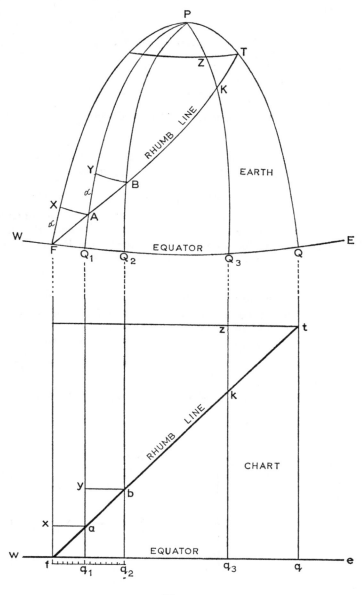

Fig. 17

A comparison of the two halves of the figure should make clear the relation
between the small triangles when they are drawn on the Earth and as they
appear when drawn on the chart. On the Earth they are all equal, but on the
chart they are only similar. They increase progressively as they recede from

C

the equator. This increase can be found by considering two similar and corresponding triangles. Thus:

$$\frac{fx}{FX} = \frac{ax}{AX} = \frac{FQ_1}{AX} \sec(\text{lat.}A)$$

$$fx = FX \sec(\text{lat.}A)$$

$$= \alpha \sec \alpha$$

Similarly, by considering the triangles ABY and aby:

$$ay = \alpha \sec 2\alpha$$

But qt, the length of the meridian between the parallel through t and the equator, is the sum of all the elements fx, ay ... kz. That is:

$$qt = \alpha(\sec\alpha + \sec 2\alpha + \sec 3\alpha + \ldots + \sec n\alpha)$$

The expression thus gives the number of meridional parts in the latitude of T for a perfect sphere. In *Norie's Tables*, as previously mentioned, the meridional parts are given allowing for the spheroidal shape of the Earth; the accurate formula for this, and its proof, are given in Volume III.

Difference of Meridional Parts (DMP)

When F does not lie on the equator, the latitude of F also has its meridional parts, a length referred to as 'mer-part F.' The number of meridional parts in the length of a meridian between the parallels through F and T will therefore be:

1. *F and T on the same side of the equator (Fig. 18a)* – mer-part T *minus* mer-part F.

2. *F and T on opposite sides of the equator (Fig. 18b)* – mer-part T *plus* mer-part F.

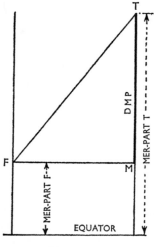

Fig. 18a

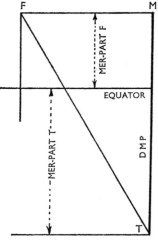

Fig. 18b

This length *MT* is always called the *difference of meridional parts* and written DMP.

MERCATOR SAILING

To find the course by Mercator sailing

From the triangle *FTM* in Figs. 18a and 18b, it is apparent that:

$$\tan(\text{course}) = \frac{FM}{MT} = \frac{\text{d.long}}{\text{DMP}}$$

The angle thus obtained is exact, irrespective of the length of *FT*. That length, as in plane sailing, is obtained from the formula:

$$\text{distance} = \text{d.lat} \sec(\text{course})$$

Fig. 19 shows the relation between the two methods of finding the course. In the mercatorial method the d.lat is stretched into DMP and the d.long remains unchanged; in the departure method, the d.lat remains unchanged and the d.long is compressed into departure. Hence:

$$\frac{\text{d.long}}{\text{DMP}} = \tan(\text{course}) = \frac{\text{dep.}}{\text{d.lat}}$$

The use of the departure formula, however, involves the labour of finding an accurate middle latitude, if an error in the course is to be avoided. For this reason, the mercatorial formula is preferable.

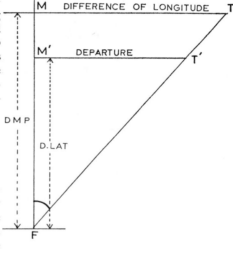

Fig. 19

Suppose, for example, that F *is 16° 00′S, 5° 55′W, and that* T *is 40° 28′N, 74° 00′W.*

To obtain the course and distance from *F* to *T* proceed thus:

lat.*F*	16° 00′S	mer-part *F*	966·28	long.*F* 5° 55′W
lat.*T*	40° 28′N	mer-part *T*	2,644·17	long.*T* 74° 00′W

d.lat   56° 28′N × 60 = 3,388′N   DMP   3,610·45   d.long 68° 05′W
                                                                    × 60
                                                                    4,085′W

$$\tan(\text{course}) = \frac{4,085}{3,610 \cdot 5}$$

log 4,085   3·611 19
log 3,610·5   3·557 57

log tan (course)   0·053 62

course = N48° 31'·7W

       = 311½°

distance = d.lat sec (course)   log 3,388   3·529 94

       = 3,388 sec 48° 31'·7   log sec 48° 31'·7   0·178 98

                                     log distance   3·708 92

distance = 5,115'·9

*Again, suppose that a ship leaves position 50°N, 17°W, and steams for 1,200'
on a course 260°. What is her position at the end of this run?*

The formula used now is:

d.lat = distance cos (course)

       = '1,200 cos 80° (S80°W)   log 1,200   3·079 18

                               log cos 80°   9·239 67

                               log d.lat   2·318 85

The d.lat is therefore 208'·4S, and hence the mer-parts of *F* and *T* and
the position of *T* are obtained:

lat.*F*	50° 00'·0N	mer-part *F*	3,456·53
d.lat	3° 28'·4S	mer-part *T*	3,144·26
lat.*T*	46° 31'·6N	DMP	312·27

d.long = DMP tan (course)

       = 312·27 tan 80°   log 312·27   2·494 53

                              log tan 80°   0·753 68

d.long = 1,771'W.   log d.long   3·248 21

long.*F*   17° 00'W

d.long   29° 31'W   The position of *T* is therefore 46° 31'·6N

                                               46° 31'·0W

To construct a Mercator chart of the World

Since there is no distortion at the equator, the base on which the chart is built
must be the line representing the equator, and convenience governs the length
of this line. Suppose it is 720 mm (about 28 in.). Then the longitude scale must
be:

$$\frac{\text{length of equator in degrees}}{\text{length of base in millimetres}} = \frac{360}{720}$$

that is, ½° of longitude or 30 meridional parts to 1 mm; more conveniently, 5°
of longitude or 300 meridional parts to 10 mm. Vertically the scale will be the
same, 300 meridional parts to 10 mm.

If it is required to draw the meridians for every 20°, for example, the
equatorial line must be divided into eighteen equal parts, 40 mm long. The
perpendiculars drawn through the points of division will be the meridians. The
one through the left-hand extremity will be the meridian of 180°W, the one
through the right-hand extremity the meridian of 180°E.

The table of meridional parts in *Norie's Tables* gives all the information necessary for deciding the positions of the parallels of latitude. The number of meridional parts between the parallel of 20° and the equator is 1,217·14, and, since these are drawn on a scale of 300 meridional parts to 10 mm, the parallels of 20° must be drawn 1,217·14 ÷ 30, or 40·6 mm, either side of the equatorial line on the chart.

The number of meridional parts between the parallel of 40° and the equator is 2,607·64. The parallels of 40° are therefore drawn 2,607·64 ÷ 30, or 86·9 mm from the equatorial line.

In the same way the other parallels are drawn, and on the graticule thus formed it is possible to insert the position of any place the latitude and longitude of which are known.

To construct a Mercator chart on a large scale

In order that small portions of the Earth may be shown in detail, it is necessary to employ a large scale and construct only the relevant portion of the chart. If it so happens that the equator is not included, the chart-lengths between successive parallels of latitude on the chart are found by reducing to millimetres, according to the scale employed, the difference between the corresponding meridional parts.

Suppose, for example, it is required to construct a chart from 142°E to 146°E, and 45°N to 49°N, the scale of the chart being 1° of longitude to 30 mm,

or 1′ of longitude to $\dfrac{30}{60} = 0\cdot5$ mm.

The difference of longitude between limiting meridians is 4°, and, since the scale of the chart is 1° of longitude to 30 mm, the line at the bottom of the chart representing the parallel of 45°N is 120 mm long, as shown in Fig. 20. The meridians of 142°, 143°, 144°, 145° and 146° will be perpendiculars erected on this line at its two ends and at the points dividing it into four equal parts.

The length in millimetres between the parallels of 45° to 49° can be deduced from the difference of meridional parts as shown in the table.

LATITUDE	MERIDIONAL PARTS	DMP	CHART-LENGTH BETWEEN PARALLELS $(DMP \times 0\cdot5)$
49°	3364·41		*mm*
		90·3	45·2
48°	3274·13		
		88·5	44·3
47°	3185·59		
		86·9	43·5
46°	3098·70		
		85·3	42·7
45°	3013·38		

In order to increase the accuracy with which positions can be plotted, the chart-lengths between meridians and between parallels are divided, if

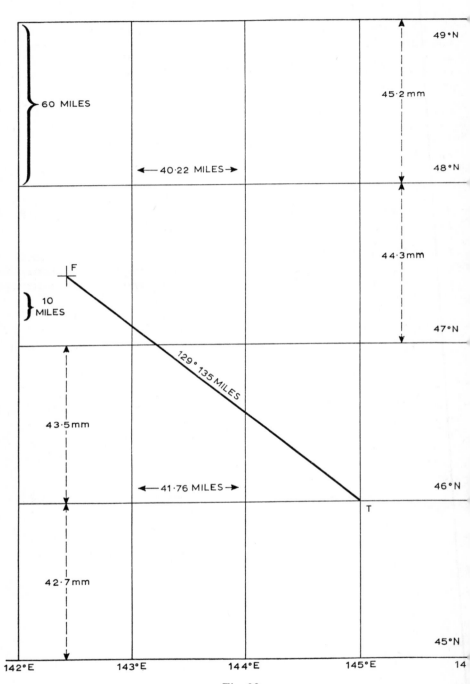

Fig. 20

necessary, into convenient units; 10' of longitude between meridians, and 10' of latitude between parallels. This division is easily effected on the longitude scale because that is fixed. On the latitude scale, however, it can be carried out only with the further aid of the table of meridional parts, which is now entered for every 10' between 45° and 49° instead of every degree.

Fig. 20 shows the complete graticule. Each rectangle, whatever its dimensions in millimetres, represents a part of the Earth's surface bounded by meridians 1° apart in longitude and parallels 1° apart in latitude; and, although the chart-lengths between these parallels vary from 42·7 mm to 45·2 mm as shown, each length represents a distance of 60 miles on the Earth's surface. The actual distance in miles between the meridians depends on the latitude in which it is measured on the chart.

As already explained, distances between places must be measured on the latitude scale on either side of the places. The distance between F and T, for example, is measured on the latitude scale between 46° and 48°, and is found to be 135 miles.

Great-circle tracks on a Mercator chart

Since only rhumb lines appear as straight lines on a Mercator chart, great circles will in general appear as curves.

Moreover, since the limiting great circles are the equator, which appears as a horizontal line, and any double meridian, which appears as two separate lines 180° apart and perpendicular to the equator, any other great circle passing through their points of intersection must appear as two curves whose vertices are towards the poles, as shown in Fig. 21. The great circle joining F and T

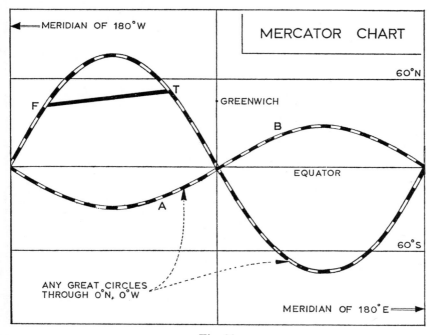

Fig. 21

will always lie, therefore, on the polar side of the rhumb line joining them, and when the difference of latitude between F and T is small and the difference of longitude large, it is seen that the difference between the two tracks is considerable. If, however, the two points lie on opposite sides of the equator, as at A and B, then the rhumb line almost coincides with the great circle.

GREAT-CIRCLE, OR GNOMONIC, CHARTS

In order to assist the navigator in finding the great-circle track between two places, charts are constructed so that any straight line drawn on them shall represent a great circle. These are known as *gnomonic charts*, and they are formed by projecting the Earth's surface from the Earth's centre on to the tangent plane at any convenient point.

Since a great circle is formed by the intersection of a plane through the Earth's centre with the Earth's surface, and as one plane will always cut another in a straight line, all great circles will appear on the chart as straight lines. But the meridians will not be parallel unless the tangent point is on the equator. Nor will rhumb lines be straight. Angles are also distorted, except at the tangent

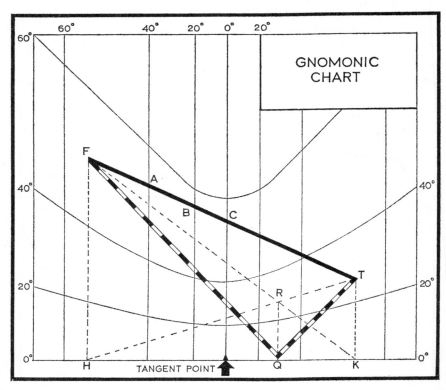

Fig. 22

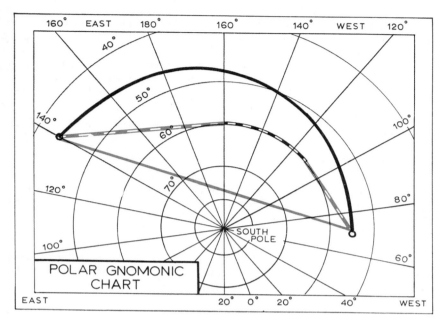

Fig. 23a

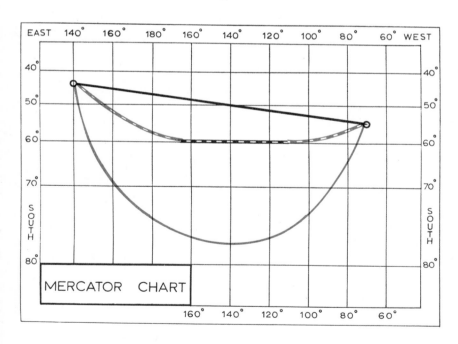

GREAT CIRCLE TRACK
RHUMB LINE ....
COMPOSITE ....

Fig. 23b

point. It is therefore impossible to take courses and distances from a gnomonic chart. The mathematical theory of this chart is explained in Volume III.

Fig. 22 shows the graticule of a gnomonic chart in which the tangent point is on the equator, and it will be noticed that the graticule is symmetrical about the meridian through this tangent point, which is independent of the longitude. The longitude scale can therefore be adjusted to suit the navigator's convenience. In the figure the tangent point is in longitude 0°.

The *Great-Circle Diagram*, as supplied to HM ships, is a graticule of this type.

To transfer a Great-circle track to a Mercator chart

The transference of a great-circle track, such as *FT* in Fig. 22, from a gnomonic to a Mercator chart, which is the normal navigational chart, is effected by noting the latitude and longitude of convenient points *A, B, C* . . . on the line *FT*, marking these points on the Mercator chart, and joining them by a smooth curve.

When *F* and *T* lie on opposite sides of the equator, *F* being north and *T* south, the same chart can be used because a gnomonic chart of both hemispheres when the tangent point is on the equator must be symmetrical about the equator. The following geometrical construction therefore suffices:

1. Mark the position of *T* as if it were in the northern hemisphere.

2. Join *F* to *K*, the point on the equator which has *T*'s longitude.

3. Join *T* to *H*, the point on the equator which has *F*'s longitude.

4. Drop a perpendicular *RQ* on the equator from *R*, the point where *FK* cuts *TH*.

5. Draw *FQ* and *QT*. Then *FQ* is the great-circle track in the northern hemisphere, and *QT* is the reflection of its continuation south of the equator. Points on *QT* may therefore be treated as if they were in the southern hemisphere.

The Polar Gnomonic chart

This is a gnomonic chart in which the pole is a tangent point. The meridians therefore radiate from the pole and parallels of latitude appear as concentric circles. It is thus an easy chart to read.

Figure 23a shows a polar gnomonic chart for the south polar regions on which are drawn the three tracks – rhumb-line, great-circle and composite – between Tasmania and Cape Horn, referred to on page 15. For comparison, the same tracks are shown (Fig. 23b) on a Mercator chart of the same area.

CHAPTER 4

The Celestial Sphere

To an observer on the Earth the sky has the appearance of an inverted bowl, so that the stars and other heavenly bodies, irrespective of their actual distance from the Earth, appear to be situated on the inside of a sphere of immense radius described about the Earth as centre. This is called the *celestial sphere.*

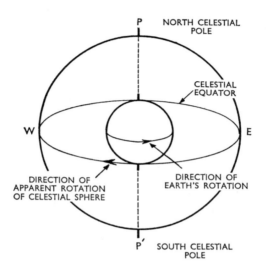

Fig. 24

The Celestial Poles. These are the points – P and P' in Fig. 24 – in which the Earth's axis, if produced, would cut the celestial sphere.

The Celestial Equator. This is the great circle in which the plane of the Earth's equator cuts the celestial sphere.

Apparent motion of the celestial sphere

Within the celestial sphere, which is fixed, the Earth rotates about its axis, turning eastward, but an observer on the Earth is not aware of this rotation unless he watches the movement of objects in no way connected with the Earth, just as a passenger in a railway train is not aware of its forward movement unless he watches the neighbouring countryside slipping backward across the carriage window. The celestial sphere therefore *appears* to rotate westward, and for this reason the Sun and the stars *appear* to rise east of, and to set west of, the observer's meridian.

31

Angular distance between the stars

The appearance of the stars on the celestial sphere conveys no idea of their actual distances from the Earth.

The star A, for example, in Fig. 25, may be ten times more remote than the star B, but the angle which the two subtend at C, the Earth's centre, is the same whether the stars are assumed to be at A' and B' or A'' and B''. To

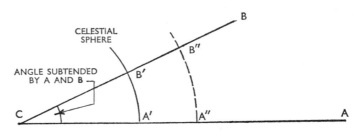

Fig. 25

an observer on the Earth, the distance between them (or between any other heavenly bodies) is thus an angular distance, and he can deal with all problems involving the measurement of that distance by the methods of spherical trigonometry. The actual distances, moreover, are so great that any movement which the stars have in space is lost to the casual observer on the Earth. Within ordinary limits of time the angle ACB thus remains constant except for the small variation which results from the Earth's orbital motion.

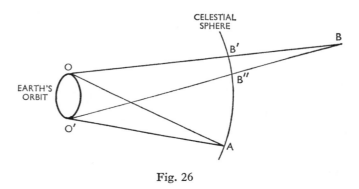

Fig. 26

Fig. 26, which is much exaggerated for the sake of clarity, shows how this variation can occur. A and B are two stars, the position of A being considered fixed in the celestial sphere. When the Earth is at O, the angle subtended by these stars is AOB, and B appears on the celestial sphere at B'; but when the Earth is at O', the other extremity of its orbit, the angle subtended is $AO'B$, and B appears on the celestial sphere at B''. The position of B therefore varies in relation to the position of *A*. This variation, however, is usually negligible because the length OO' is negligible in comparison with the distances of most stars.

Apparent path of the Sun in the celestial sphere

When a heavenly body such as the Sun is comparatively close to the Earth, its position in the celestial sphere changes considerably during a year relative

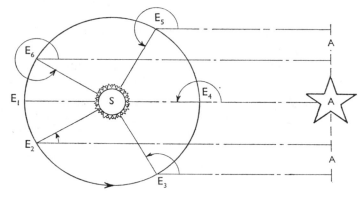

Fig. 27

to the Earth and a distant star lying in the plane of the Earth's orbit. The choice of such a star gives a fixed direction in space from which angles can be measured. In the practice of astronomy, however, it is convenient to choose not an actual star but the First Point of Aries (*see* page 35) and this is the point represented by *A* in Fig. 26.

In Fig. 27, the fixed direction of the point *A* is represented by the parallel lines E_1A, E_2A, etc. On 21st March the Earth is at E_1, in line with the Sun,

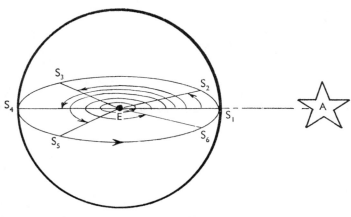

Fig. 28

S, and the First Point of Aries. A few weeks later, when the Earth has moved along its orbit to E_2, the angle subtended at the Earth by the Sun and the First Point of Aries is AE_2S, measured anti-clockwise.

When the Earth is at E_3, this angle has increased to AE_3S, and the increase continues steadily as the Earth moves through the positions E_4, E_5 and E_6, until, when the Earth is again at E_1, the angle reaches 360°. The motion is then repeated.

To an observer on the Earth this motion is revealed as a change in the Sun's position in the celestial sphere.

When the Earth is at E_1 (Fig. 27) A and S appear to coincide in the celestial sphere at a point S_1 in Fig. 28.

When the Earth has moved to E_2 (Fig. 27) the Sun, to this observer, appears at S_2 (Fig. 28), where the angles AE_2S (Fig. 27) and AES_2 (Fig. 28) are equal.

The Sun therefore passes through positions S_1, S_2 ... in the celestial sphere, corresponding to the positions E_1, E_2 ... actually passed through by the Earth during its orbit round the Sun; and since the angle itself increases from 0° to 360° during the year, the Sun, to an observer on the Earth, must appear to describe one complete circle in the celestial sphere during the same period.

The Ecliptic

This apparent path of the Sun in the celestial sphere is called the *ecliptic*. It is a great circle, and it makes an angle of 23° 27′ with the celestial equator because the Earth's axis of rotation is tilted that amount from the perpendicular to the plane of the Earth's orbit.

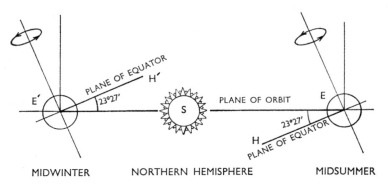

Fig. 29

Fig. 29 shows the tilt of the Earth's axis in relation to the Sun when the Earth is at those positions in its orbit which give rise to midsummer and midwinter to an observer in the northern hemisphere.

At the midsummer position, *E*, the Sun is raised above the plane of the equator by an amount equal to the tilt of the Earth's axis, which is 23° 27'. At the midwinter position, *E'*, the Sun is depressed an equal amount below the plane of the equator. The plane of the ecliptic is therefore inclined at an angle of 23° 27' to the plane of the equator, as shown in Fig. 30.

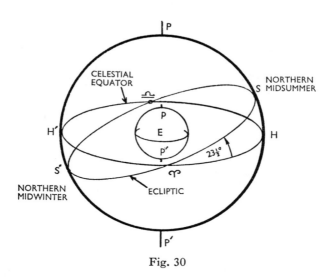

Fig. 30

The First Point of Aries

The ecliptic cuts the celestial equator in two points. The one through which the Sun passes on about 21st March is called the *First Point of Aries*, or the *vernal equinox*, and is denoted by ♈, the Ram's horns in the signs of the Zodiac; and the other, through which the Sun passes on about 23rd September, is called the *First Point of Libra*, or the *autumnal equinox*, and is denoted by ♎, the Scales.

The First Point of Aries takes its name from the constellation Aries through which the Sun appeared to pass when the early astronomers decided its path. There is, however, a slow backward movement of the actual point of intersection of the ecliptic and celestial equator along the ecliptic. The First Point of Aries therefore no longer coincides with the position of the constellation Aries in the celestial sphere.

The Celestial Meridians

These are semi-great circles joining the celestial poles, and they correspond exactly to the terrestrial meridians.

Position of heavenly bodies in the celestial sphere

For ordinary purposes the position of a heavenly body can be considered fixed in the celestial sphere in relation to the celestial equator and a particular celestial meridian, in the same way that the position of a place on the Earth is fixed in relation to the terrestrial equator and the particular meridian through Greenwich. The celestial meridian selected is the one through the First Point of Aries.

Sidereal Hour Angle (SHA)*

The sidereal hour angle of a heavenly body is the angle between the meridian through the First Point of Aries and the meridian through the body measured westwards from the former. It is thus the angle at the pole ♈ *PR*, or the angular distance along the equator, ♈ *R* in Fig. 31, and it is expressed in units of arc (degrees, minutes and tenths of minutes).

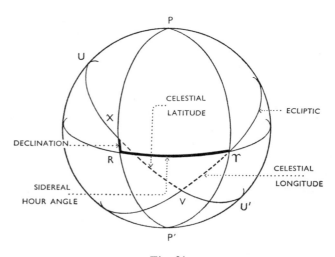

Fig. 31

The sidereal hour angles of 173 stars, including 57 selected stars, are tabulated for each month in the *Nautical Almanac*; no interpolation is required and the data may be used in precisely the same way as those for the selected stars on the daily pages. The stars are arranged in order of SHA. The 57 selected stars, arranged in alphabetical order, have been chosen for the daily pages of the *Nautical Almanac* because of their brightness and distribution in the sky. (*See* Appendix 2.)

---

* **Warning.** Although sidereal hour angle and declination strongly resemble terrestrial longitude and terrestrial latitude, they should not be looked upon as celestial counterparts. Celestial longitude and celestial latitude are quantities quite different from sidereal hour angle and declination. Celestial longitude is measured along the ecliptic from the First Point of Aries to the meridian through the pole of the ecliptic (♈ *V* in Fig. 31); and celestial latitude is measured from the ecliptic along this meridian (*VX* in Fig. 31). These quantities are not used in the theory of navigation.

The sidereal hour angles of the navigational planets are given in the *Nautical Almanac* for the middle day of the three days on the page. The sidereal hour angles of the Sun and Moon are not required and are not tabulated.

Right Ascension

When the angle between the meridian of the First Point of Aries and the meridian of the body is measured *eastwards* from Aries, it is known as the *Right Ascension* (RA) of the body. It is normally expressed in units of time (hours, minutes and seconds), 24 hours being equivalent to 360°.

$$RA = 360° - SHA$$

Right ascension is used by astronomers to define the position of a heavenly body in the celestial sphere, but for navigational purposes it has now been replaced by SHA.

Declination*

This corresponds to terrestrial latitude and is the angular distance of the heavenly body north or south of the celestial equator – *RX* in Fig. 31 – measured in units of arc (degrees, minutes and tenths of minutes usually).

The declinations of the stars change very slowly, and, like their sidereal hour angles, may be considered constant for up to one month. Declinations are tabulated in columns adjacent to sidereal hour angles in the *Nautical Almanac*.

The declination of the Sun, however, changes from $23\frac{1}{2}°$N to $23\frac{1}{2}°$S and back again during twelve months. The declinations of the four navigational planets, Venus, Mars, Jupiter and Saturn, also vary between wide limits. The declinations of the Sun and planets are therefore tabulated directly on the daily pages of the *Nautical Almanac* for every hour of GMT; to find their values at other times, interpolation is necessary. To aid interpolation, a quantity d is also tabulated at the foot of the column for the body concerned; d is equal to the mean hourly difference for that page, and the quantity to be added, or 'Corr^n', is given against the value of d in the right-hand column of the interpolation table for that minute of the GMT. The sign of the correction is positive or negative depending upon whether the declination is increasing or decreasing at the time. In practice, however, the interpolation for the Sun and planets can nearly always be carried out by inspection as d never exceeds $1'\cdot5$.

Because the Earth is turning continuously within the celestial sphere, the connection between sidereal hour angle and longitude is never more than instantaneous. Only once during the period of the Earth's rotation will the Greenwich meridian lie in the same plane as and also directly beneath, the meridian through the First Point of Aries, as in Fig. 32.

---

* See footnote on page 36.

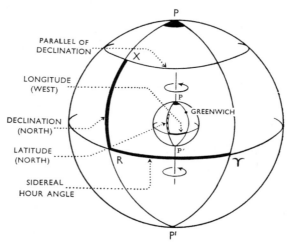

Fig. 32

EXAMPLE 1

What is the declination of Mars on 9th December 1971 at GMT $18^h\ 47^m\ 23^s$?

From the daily page for 9th December:

Declination at $18^h = 4°\ 57'·3S$ $d = 0'·7$

From the interpolation table for 47' (seconds of GMT do not matter here):

Corr^n for $d = 0'·7$ is $-\ 0'·6$ (minus because the declination is decreasing)

Therefore the declination at $18^h\ 47^m\ 23^s = 4°\ 57'·3 - 0'·6$
$$= 4°\ 56'·7S$$

The Moon's declination varies less uniformly and more quickly than that of the Sun and Planets and, although the declination is tabulated for every hour of GMT in the same way, the hourly difference has to be given for every hour. The correction is obtained from the interpolation table for the minutes of GMT in the same way as above.

EXAMPLE 2

What is the declination of the Moon on 9th December 1971 at GMT $18^h\ 47^m23^s$?

Declination at 18^h $= 1°\ 39'·2N$ $d = 13'·5$
Corr^n $= -10'·7$

Declination at $18^h\ 47^m\ 23^s = 1°\ 28'·5N$

Parallel of Declination

This corresponds to a parallel of latitude and is a small circle on the celestial sphere the plane of which is parallel to the plane of the celestial equator.

Polar Distance

This is the angular distance of a body from the elevated pole – the pole, that is, above the observer's horizon. It is *PX* in Fig. 32, if the observer is assumed to be in the north latitude.

When the elevated pole and the declination have the same names, the polar distance is clearly (90° − declination). When they have opposite names, it is equal to (90° + declination).

Geographical Position

If a line is drawn from a heavenly body to the Earth's centre, the point where this line cuts the Earth's surface is called the *geographical position* of the body. *XC* in Fig. 33 is such a line, and *x* is the geographical position of *X*. To an observer at *x*, the body would thus appear to be exactly overhead; that is, the body would be at the observer's zenith.

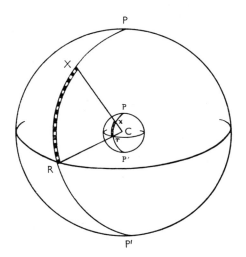

Fig. 33

The Observer's Zenith

This is the point where a straight line from the Earth's centre passing through the observer's position cuts the celestial sphere. The declination of the zenith (*ZQ* in Fig. 34) must therefore be equal to the observer's latitude (*Oq*).

The Celestial, or Rational, Horizon

The great circle on the celestial sphere, every point of which is 90° from the observer's zenith, is known as the *celestial*, or *rational, horizon*.

A plane through the centre of the Earth at right angles to the observer's radius, *CO*, would cut the celestial sphere in this great circle. The celestial horizon therefore divides the celestial sphere into hemispheres, the

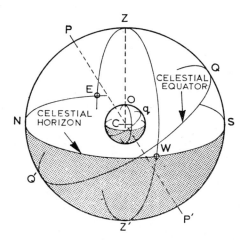

Fig. 34

upper one of which, containing Z, is known as the 'visible hemisphere' because, subject to certain small adjustments described in the next chapter, all heavenly bodies in this half of the celestial sphere are visible to the observer at O. Heavenly bodies in the lower hemisphere cannot be seen.

The Observer's Meridian

This is the celestial meridian which passes through the observer's zenith – $PZQSP'$ in Fig. 34. The meridian $PNQ'Z'P'$ differs from it by 180° in sidereal hour angle.

The points, N and S, in which these two meridians cut the celestial horizon are the *north* and *south points*, the north point being the one nearer the north pole.

The *east* and *west points*, E and W, lie on the celestial horizon midway between N and S.

The Plane of the Meridian

Fig. 34 is drawn on what is called the 'plane of the observer's meridian', or simply, the *plane of the meridian*, the observer being in north latitude, and it shows the Earth and the celestial sphere as they would appear if seen from the west. From the east they would appear as shown in Fig. 35a, in which, for convenience, the Earth and the observer are indicated by the single point O.

The Plane of the Celestial Horizon

When it is convenient to show the whole visible sky, the figure must be drawn on the *plane of the celestial horizon*, as if the celestial sphere were seen from a position directly above the observer's zenith. Z therefore appears as the centre of the circle that is the celestial horizon; the north–south and east–west

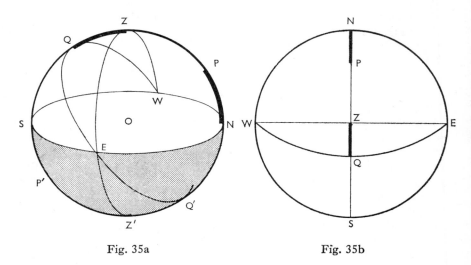

Fig. 35a   Fig. 35b

lines divide this circle into four equal parts, and the equator appears as a curve through W, Q and E as shown in Fig. 35b. The positions of P and Q are decided by simple proportion, and no attempt is made to insert them according to perspective.

In Fig. 35b, ZQ is the observer's latitude. But:

$$PZ + PN = 90° = PZ + ZQ$$
i.e. $$PN = ZQ$$

PN is therefore equal to the latitude, and the position of P is thus determined. If, for example, the observer's latitude is 35°N, P would be chosen so that, of the 90 equal parts into which NZ is divided, PN takes 35 and PZ the remainder.

Vertical Circles

All great circles passing through the observer's zenith are necessarily perpendicular to the celestial horizon and are known as *vertical circles*.

The Prime Vertical

The particular vertical circle passing through the east and west points is called the *prime vertical*.

The Principal Vertical Circle

The observer's meridian is sometimes called the *principal vertical circle* because it provides a fixed direction in the celestial sphere just as the observer's terrestrial meridian provides one on the Earth's surface.

The Azimuth of a heavenly body

This is the angle at the zenith between the observer's meridian and the vertical circle through the heavenly body, and it is measured east or west from his meridian from 0° to 180°, and named 'N' or 'S' from the elevated pole.

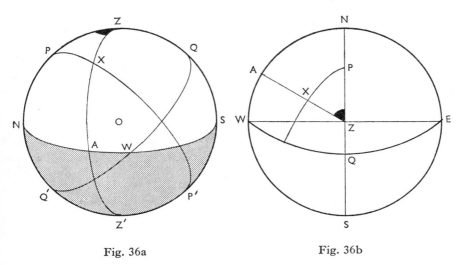

Fig. 36a   Fig. 36b

Figures 36a and 36b show this angle, PZX, and should make it clear that the azimuth can also be measured from the points N or S along the celestial horizon, just as the d.long can be expressed either as an angle at the pole or as an angular distance along the equator.

Since the azimuth of a heavenly body is measured east or west from the meridian and named from the elevated pole, it is not always the same as the true bearing of the heavenly body, which is measured clockwise from true north. The azimuth of X in Figs. 36a and 36b is N60°W, but the true bearing of X is 300°.

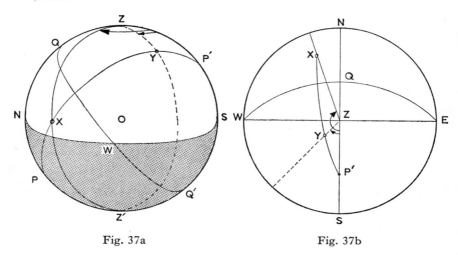

Fig. 37a   Fig. 37b

In Figs. 37a and 37b, which are drawn for an observer in south latitude, the azimuths of X and Y are respectively S160°W and S45°W, whereas their true bearings are 340° and 225°.

The azimuth cannot be greater than 180°.

It should be noted also that when a figure is drawn on the plane of the horizon, only the azimuth is shown correctly to scale. Everything else, though conveniently put in by simple proportion, is wrongly placed. For practical purposes, however, the figure suffices because accurate measurements are not required from it.

CHAPTER 5

Altitude and Zenith Distance

Although the position of a heavenly body is fixed in the celestial sphere by its declination and sidereal hour angle, these angular distances are measured from theoretical axes, and for his own convenience when he wishes to point out a particular heavenly body an observer will employ others – his own meridian and the horizon – and will decide the heavenly body's position by a bearing from the meridian and an altitude above the horizon. He will also make use of that altitude when finding his own position. He is therefore concerned not only with the altitude of the body above the horizon which he actually sees, but also with its altitude above the celestial horizon; having measured the altitude above the one, he applies certain corrections until it refers to the other.

True Altitude of a heavenly body

This is the angular distance of the body above the celestial horizon, measured along the vertical circle through the body and the observer's zenith. In Figs. 38a

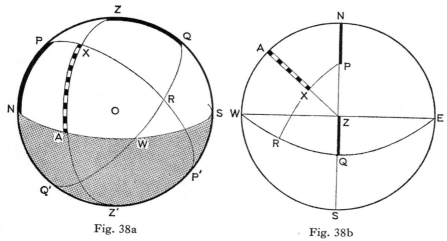

| Fig. 38a | Fig. 38b |

(on the plane of the meridian) and 38b (on the plane of the horizon) the *true* altitude of X is AX.

True Altitude of the Pole

It was shown on page 41 that PN is equal to ZQ, the observer's latitude. The 'true altitude of the pole' (which is PN) is therefore the latitude of the place from which the observation is made.

The observer's sea, or visible, horizon

This is the horizon – usually the small circle on the Earth's surface where the sea and sky appear to meet – above which the observer actually measures the altitude of a heavenly body.

In Fig. 39 the tangent from the observer to the Earth's surface decides the position of this small circle, but refraction alters it slightly because the path of a light ray from the horizon to the observer is not a straight line. (*See* page 47.)

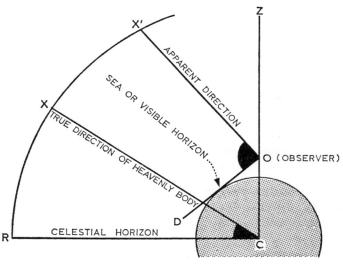

Fig. 39

The Observed Altitude

An altitude above the sea horizon (the angle *DOX'* in Fig. 39) is always known as an *observed altitude*, in order that it may not be confused with the true altitude (the angle *RCX*), which is obtained by correcting the observed altitude.

The Sextant Altitude

In practice, altitudes are measured with a sextant, and since most sextants give slightly erroneous readings the *sextant altitude* of a heavenly body will usually differ slightly from the observed altitude.

Corrections to the Sextant Altitude

In order to obtain the true altitude, five corrections must be applied to the sextant altitude:

> Index error
> Dip
> Refraction
> Semi-diameter
> Parallax.

For reasons which will be apparent, they are applied in that order.

Index Error

This is an instrumental error inherent in the particular sextant that is used for measuring the angle. The methods of finding it are explained in Chapter 17.

Index error is added to the sextant altitude when *plus*, and subtracted when *minus*.

Dip

Dip is the angle between the horizontal plane through the observer's eye and the apparent direction of the visible horizon. It is the angle *DOH* in Fig. 40.

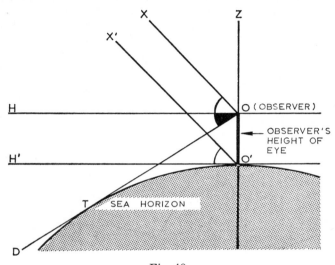

Fig. 40

Dip occurs because the observer's eye is always above sea-level and the observed altitude, *DOX*, is greater than the altitude would be to an observer at *O'* with no height of eye. The amount of dip therefore depends on the observer's height of eye, and it must be subtracted from the observed altitude.

In Fig. 40, it has been assumed that the heavenly body *X* is sufficiently distant for *O'X'* to be considered parallel to *OX*. This assumption, however, does not take refraction into account.

The Apparent Altitude

This is defined as the sextant altitude corrected for instrumental error and dip.

Refraction

Refraction is the bending of light from its path, and it occurs when the ray passes from one medium to another of different density. The optical law – illustrated in Fig. 41 – is that the ray is bent towards the normal on

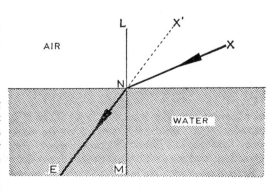

Fig. 41

entering a more dense medium, the normal being the line perpendicular to the surface of the medium at the point where the ray enters. A ray of light passing from an object at X and entering the water at N, for example, would be bent towards the normal LNM, so that the angle ENM is less than the angle XNL. But an observer always sees an object in the direction in which the ray from that object enters his eye. To an observer at E, the object at X would therefore appear in the direction ENX', and the altitude of X would appear to be increased.

Since the density of the air surrounding the Earth grows less as the distance from the Earth's surface increases, a ray of light from a heavenly body passes continually from one medium to another of greater density, from the moment it enters the surrounding envelope of air until it reaches the observer. Its path is therefore curved, as shown by the line $XTSRQO$ in Fig. 42. For this reason

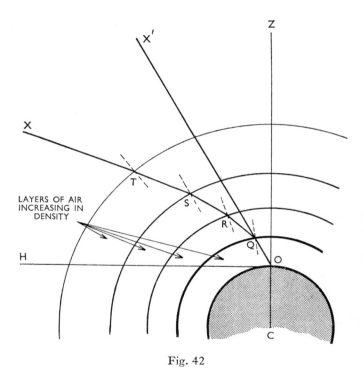

Fig. 42

an observer sees the heavenly body X as if it were at X', with an observed altitude HOX' which is greater than its actual altitude above the horizontal plane through O. The difference between these two altitudes is the angle of refraction, and it must be subtracted from the observed altitude.

Refraction varies with the altitude. It is greatest when the body is on the horizon. It vanishes altogether when the body is at the observer's zenith, because the ray of light then passes along the normal itself.

Effect of refraction on dip

Since the effect of refraction is to increase the apparent altitude of the body, the horizon that an observer actually sees will not be the horizon formed by drawing tangents from the position of his eye to the Earth's surface.

In Fig. 43, OT is the tangent from the observer to the Earth's surface, and T should mark the horizon. But the point which the observer actually sees is T', and, since the ray is bent as shown, the visible horizon appears in the direction OD, where OD is a tangent to $T'O$ at O. The dip is therefore the angle DOH, which is less than the theoretical angle of dip, TOH.

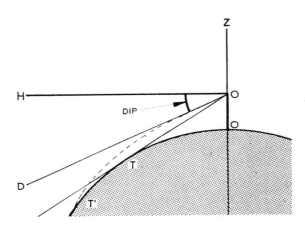

Fig. 43

The *Nautical Almanac* gives the values that the angle of dip, DOH, assumes for heights of eye up to 48 m (and 155 ft), so that in practice, the effect of refraction on the position of the visible horizon (an effect known as 'terrestrial refraction') is included in the tabulated dip and need not be considered.

Abnormal refraction

The formula giving the dip is based on the assumption that there is not a great difference between the air temperature and the sea temperature. If that difference is considerable the tables are unreliable. There is no way of determining the extent of the error introduced, and if its existence is suspected observations should be treated with caution.

Looming and mirage, phenomena described in Volume III, are signs of abnormal refraction, further remarks on which will also be found in Chapter 18 of the present volume.

Correction for Semi-diameter

Because of their size and nearness to the Earth, an observer sees the Sun and Moon not as points of light but as bodies that have an appreciable diameter; and when finding their altitudes, he measures the angles between the horizon and their lower or upper edges, and then arrives at the altitudes of their centres by adding or subtracting their semi-diameters. The positions of the Sun and Moon given in the *Nautical Almanac* are the positions of their centres.

The Sun's Semi-diameter

The point on the Sun's disc nearest the horizon is called the Sun's *lower limb* and denoted by LL or ⊙, and the point farthest from the horizon the *upper limb*, denoted by UL or ⊙̄. In practice, the altitude measured is generally that of the Sun's lower limb, and the Sun's semi-diameter is thus generally *added*.

The Sun's semi-diameter is measured by the angle TOS (Fig. 44), where OT is a tangent and therefore at right-angles to the radius ST. ST itself is roughly 430,000 miles, and OS, the distance of the observer from the Suns' centre, which may be taken as the average distance of the Earth's centre from the Sun's is 93,000,000 miles. Hence:

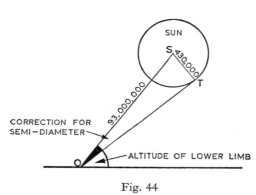

Fig. 44

$$\sin (TOS) = \frac{ST}{OS} = \frac{43}{9,300}$$

The average semi-diameter is thus 16′.

The *Nautical Almanac* gives the Sun's semi-diameter for the three days of each page. It varies from 15′·8 at the beginning of July, when the Earth is farthest from the Sun, to 16′·3 at the beginning of January, when the Earth is nearest.

The Moon's Semi-diameter

Unless the Moon is full, the observer usually has no choice but to measure the altitude of one limb, which may be either the upper or lower because at

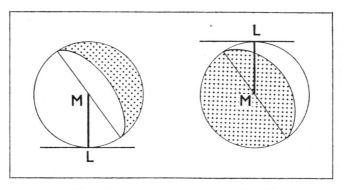

Fig. 45a   Fig. 45b

any phase other than the full, only a part of the Moon is visible, and the shape of that part is either gibbous or crescent, with, more often than not, a sloping diameter.

Fig. 45a shows a gibbous moon, only the lower limb of which can be observed; Fig. 45b a crescent moon, only the upper limb of which can be observed. In each figure ML is the semi-diameter, to be added to the altitude when the lower limb is observed and subtracted when the upper limb is observed. The Moon's visible limb is always that nearer the Sun.

The *Nautical Almanac* gives the Moon's semi-diameter for each day.

Parallax

By applying the corrections so far considered to the observed altitude of a heavenly body's upper or lower limb, an observer is able to find the altitude of the heavenly body's centre above the horizontal tangent plane. It remains for him to allow for the Earth's radius.

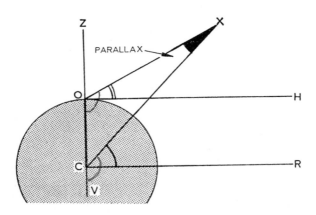

Fig. 46

In Fig. 46 the altitude above the horizontal tangent plane is HOX and the true altitude is RCX. From the triangle OCX, since the external angle is equal to the sum of the two internal and opposite angles:

$$\angle VCX = \angle COX + \angle OXC$$
$$\angle RCX + 90° = \angle HOX + 90° + \angle OXC$$
$$\angle RCX = \angle HOX + \angle OXC$$

The difference between the true altitude and the altitude above the horizontal plane is thus the angle OXC, which is the angle subtended at the heavenly body by the radius of the earth drawn to the observer's position. This angle is known as the *parallax in altitude*, or simply the *parallax*, and it is clearly a correction to be *added*.

By the rule of sines applied to the triangle OCX:

$$\frac{\sin(\text{parallax})}{OC} = \frac{\sin(COX)}{CX}$$

i.e. $\sin(\text{parallax}) = \dfrac{OC}{CX}\sin(90° + HOX)$

$$= \frac{OC}{CX}\cos(\text{altitude})$$

The parallax of a heavenly body therefore vanishes when the body is at the observer's zenith.

Horizontal Parallax

Since the greatest value of the cosine is unity, and this value is attained when the angle is nought, the parallax of a heavenly body is greatest when the heavenly body is on the horizon, and it is then known as the *horizontal parallax*.

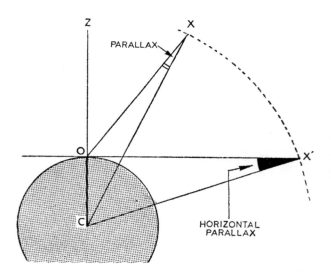

Fig. 47

From Fig. 47 it is seen that the horizontal parallax (HP) is given by:

$$\sin(\text{HP}) = \frac{OC}{CX'}$$

Hence the formula giving the parallax becomes:

$$\sin(\text{parallax}) = \sin(\text{HP})\cos(\text{altitude}),$$

or, as an approximation, since both the parallax and the horizontal parallax are small:

$$\text{parallax} = (HP) \cos (\text{altitude}).$$

Only in the case of the Moon is the horizontal parallax large, and that is because the Moon is close to the Earth in comparison with other heavenly bodies, and the horizontal parallax is, from the above formula, governed entirely by the distance of the heavenly body from the Earth. OC is constant, and therefore as CX' increases OC/CX' decreases.

For the Moon the horizontal parallax is about 60', and the correction for parallax to be applied to the observed altitude is therefore appreciable.

For the planets the maximum horizontal parallax is about 30", for the Sun about 8" and for the stars it is negligible.

Corrections for additional refraction in non-standard atmospheric temperatures and pressures

In addition to the altitude correction tables which include the effect of mean refraction, further tables are given in the *Nautical Almanac* which provide additional corrections for use when observing under non-standard conditions of temperature and pressure and when high accuracy is required. These tables provide for temperatures from $-30°C$ to $45°C$ and pressures from 970 to 1050 millibars, over the range of altitudes $0°$ to $50°$. In practice, however, these corrections are seldom applied because low-altitude observations can usually be avoided except in very high latitudes. If it is necessary to use an altitude of less than $20°$, these tables must be used in addition to the normal altitude-correction tables.

Correction of the Sun's altitude

The altitude correction tables for the Sun, given in the *Nautical Almanac*, cover all altitudes from $0°$ to $90°$ and heights of eye from 1 to 48 metres (and 2 to 155 feet). These tables give the corrections to be applied to both upper and lower limbs, and are in two parts: the first part contains the effects of refraction (calculated for a barometric pressure of 1010 millibars and a temperature of $10°C$), semi-diameter and parallax, and the second contains the dip correction.

In order to allow for the change in the Sun's semi-diameter throughout the year the first part is divided into two sections: the first section, based on a semi-diameter of $16'\cdot15$, is to be used during the period October–March and the second, based on a semi-diameter of $15'\cdot9$, is to be used during April–September. Both parts of the table are arranged critically, the first part with argument apparent altitude and the second with argument height of eye.

All corrections in the first part are applied positively to the apparent altitude when the lower limb is observed and negatively when the upper limb is observed. All corrections for height of eye are subtracted from the observed altitude.

Suppose, for example, that the sextant altitude of the Sun's lower limb is 36° 20'·0 on 1st January, and that the index error (IE) is −2'·7, and the observer's height of eye 9·7 m (32 ft).

Then the true altitude would be found thus:

Sextant Altitude (Sext.Alt.)	36° 20'·0
IE	− 2'·7
Observed Altitude	36° 17'·3
Dip	− 5'·5
Apparent Altitude	36° 11'·8
Sun's correction	+ 14'·9
True Altitude	36° 26'·7

Observation of the Sun's upper limb

If the observation in the previous example were taken of the Sun's upper limb, the altitude correction table for the upper limb would be used.

Sext.Alt.	36° 20'·0
IE	− 2'·7
Obs.Alt.	36° 17'·3
Dip	− 5'·5
Apparent Alt.	36° 11'·8
Sun's correction	− 17'·4
True Altitude	35° 54'·4

Correction of a star's altitude

Because it is so far from the Earth a star has no parallax. For the same reason it appears as a point-source of light and has no semi-diameter. The total correction to its altitude therefore consists of dip and refraction only and is negative.

Suppose that the sextant altitude of Sirius is 17° 49'·5, the IE being +3'·2 and the observer's height of eye 7·3 m (24 ft).

Then the true altitude is found thus:

Sext.Alt. Sirius	17° 49'·5
IE	+ 3'·2
Obs.Alt.	17° 52'·7
Dip	− 4'·8
Apparent Alt.	17° 47'·9
Star's correction	− 3'·0
True Alt.	17° 44'·9

Correction of a planet's altitude

Unless an accuracy is required greater than is normal for the practice of navigation, the planets are treated as stars and their altitudes corrected by means
of the total correction table for stars. Additional corrections for phase and parallax
for Venus and parallax for Mars are however given in the *Nautical Almanac*
in case this additional accuracy is needed.

Correction of the Moon's altitude

The Moon's correction table in the *Nautical Almanac* includes the effects of
semi-diameter, parallax, augmentation (*see below*) and refraction. It is in two
parts: the first part is taken from the top part of the table with argument
apparent altitude, and the second from the bottom part of the table with argument HP, *in the same column* as that from which the first correction was taken.
Separate corrections are given in the bottom table for lower (L) and upper (U)
limbs. All corrections are *added* to apparent altitude, but 30′ must be subtracted from the altitude of the upper limb after the other corrections have
been applied (an arbitrary 30′ having in fact been added to the second correction
for U in order to keep it positive and small).

The tables contain no correction for height of eye and this must be applied
separately from the table on the same page.

*Suppose the sextant altitude of the Moon's upper limb is 42° 30′·0 on 3rd July
1971, at 1700 GMT.*

From the daily pages of the *Nautical Almanac*:

horizontal parallax 55′·2

Suppose also that IE is −2′·5 and the height of eye 9·7 m (32 ft), then:

Sext.Alt.	42° 30′·0	
IE	− 2′·5	
Obs.Alt.	42° 27′·5	
Dip	− 5′·5	
Apparent Alt.	42° 22′·0	
Corrections (1)	+ 52′·2	(for apparent altitude 42° 22′)
(2)	+ 2′·4	(for HP 55′·2)
	43° 16′·6	
	− 30′·0	
True Altitude	42° 46′·6	

Augmentation of the Moon's semi-diameter

Since the Moon is relatively close to the Earth – the average distance between
the two centres is only 240,000′ – the distance between an observer and the
Moon varies appreciably with the Moon's altitude. The Moon's semi-diameter
therefore varies with its altitude.

D

The Moon's semi-diameter to an observer at O, Fig. 48, is given by:

$$\sin(MOL') = \frac{ML'}{OM}$$

where ML' is the Moon's radius and OM the distance of the observer from the Moon's centre, both lengths being measured in miles.

But to an observer situated at the Earth's centre, the Moon's semi-diameter would be given by:

$$\sin(MCL) = \frac{ML}{CM}$$

where ML is equal to ML', and CM is the distance between the Earth's centre and the Moon's centre. This value of the semi-diameter is the one tabulated in the *Nautical Almanac* for each day.

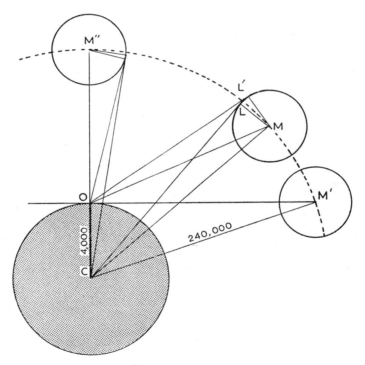

Fig. 48

Fig. 48 shows that, so long as the Moon is above the horizontal tangent plane, OM is less than CM. The Moon's apparent semi-diameter will therefore be greater than the one that is tabulated in the *Nautical Almanac*. The difference between them, known as the *augmentation of the Moon's semi-diameter*, is included in the Moon's correction table. The amount of this augmentation is given in *Norie's Tables*. Its greatest value, when the Moon is overhead (at M'') is 0'·3.

Zenith Distance

Once the true altitude of a heavenly body has been obtained by the use of the appropriate corrections, the distance of the body from the observer's zenith can be found – ZX in Figs. 49a and 49b. It is $(ZA - XA)$ or $(90° -$ altitude).

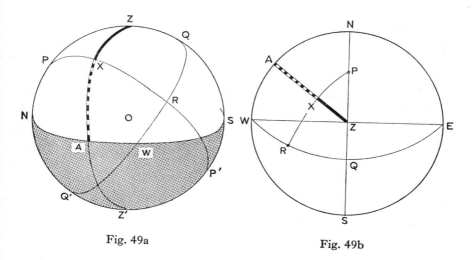

Fig. 49a   Fig. 49b

This distance ZX is known as the *zenith distance* and it is most important, because it is the third side of the spherical triangle PZX.

CHAPTER 6

The Hour Angle

In studying the spherical triangle *PZX*, the three sides and the angle at *Z* have been considered. Of the remaining angles, *X*, the bearing of the observer from the heavenly body, is unimportant. The other, the angle at the pole, is known as the *hour angle* and is most important.

The Hour Angle of a heavenly body

This is defined as the angle between the observer's meridian and the meridian through the heavenly body. It is called the 'hour angle' of the heavenly body because it is an expression of time; it is measured westwards from the observer's meridian in units of arc (0°–360°), or in units of time (0^h–24^h), as convenience suggests.

Since the hour angle is an angle at the pole, the angular length of the arc *AB* on the celestial equator (Fig. 50) also measures it.

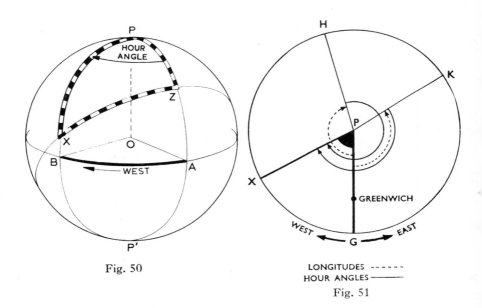

Fig. 50

LONGITUDES ------
HOUR ANGLES ———
Fig. 51

Effect of the Earth's rotation

In Chapter 4 it was explained that to an observer on the Earth, the Earth's steady rotation from west to east resulted in an apparent and equally steady rotation of the celestial sphere from east to west. During one rotation of the Earth, the hour angle of a body that is fixed in the celestial sphere will increase from 0°, when the heavenly body is on the observer's meridian, to 360° when it returns to this meridian. The hour angle of a heavenly body thus increases steadily throughout the day.

The Greenwich Hour Angle

When the observer is on the meridian of Greenwich, the hour angle of a heavenly body is known as the *Greenwich hour angle* or GHA. Thus, as Fig. 51 shows, the hour angle measured from an observer's meridian (or the 'local hour angle') is found by applying the longitude of that meridian to the Greenwich hour angle.

PX is the meridian of a heavenly body.

In the case of an observer east of the Greenwich meridian (at K):

Greenwich hour angle (GHA)	$= GX$	(measured clockwise)
Longitude	$= GK$	(measured anti-clockwise)
Local hour angle (LHA)	$= KGX$	(measured clockwise)
	$= GX + GK$	
	$=$ GHA + longitude.	

When the observer is west of Greenwich (at H):

GHA	$= GX$	(measured clockwise)
Longitude	$= GH$	(measured clockwise)
LHA	$= HX$	(measured clockwise)
	$= HG + GX$	
	$=$ GHA + (360° − longitude)	
	$=$ GHA − longitude	

(since the addition of 360° does not affect the actual angular distance).

Thus, to find the local hour angle of a heavenly body from its Greenwich hour angle, east longitude is always added, and 360° subtracted from the resulting sum when necessary; west longitude is always subtracted, 360° being added when necessary.

If, for example in Fig. 51, the Greenwich hour angle of a heavenly body is 62° 39', the longitude of the meridian through H is 164° 47'W, and that of the meridian through K is 121° 13'E, then:

At H		At K	
GHA	62° 39'	GHA	62° 39'
	360°	Long.	121° 13'E
	———		———
	422° 39'	Local hour angle	183° 52'
Long.	164° 47'W		———
	———		
Local hour angle	257° 52'		
	———		

Relation between Azimuth and Local Hour Angle

When the LHA of the heavenly body is less than 180°, the heavenly body itself must lie to the west of the observer's meridian; when the LHA is greater than 180°, it must lie to the east. Hence for LHAs between 0° and 180° the azimuth is west, and for LHAs between 180° and 360° the azimuth is east.

In Figs. 52a and 52b, which are drawn for an observer in north latitude, the azimuth of X is about N45°W and that of Y about N65°E, the LHAs of the two heavenly bodies being respectively 90° and 270°. Both X and Y therefore

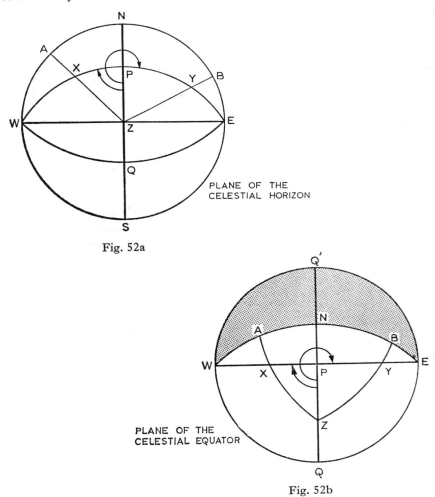

Fig. 52a

Fig. 52b

lie on the great circle passing through the pole and the east–west points. This particular circle is sometimes known as the 'six-hour circle,' and Fig. 52b is drawn on the plane of the celestial equator in order to emphasize it.

When the body is on the observer's meridian, it is neither east nor west; its declination and the observer's latitude combine to determine whether its bearing is 0° or 180°, that is, whether it lies north or south of the observer.

If the declination is greater than the latitude and of the same name (both are north or both are south), the heavenly body lies between the zenith and the elevated pole when the LHA is 0°. In these circumstances, the bearing of the heavenly body is north to an observer in north latitude, and south to one in south latitude.

Fig. 53 shows that if the declination is less than the latitude, both names being north, the bearing of the heavenly body is south when the LHA is 0°. The same heavenly body can also bear north, at X'. The LHA is then 180° and the heavenly body is said to *lie below the pole*, a position discussed in detail in Chapter 12.

Position in the celestial sphere

Although the position of a heavenly body is fixed in the celestial sphere by its sidereal hour angle (SHA)

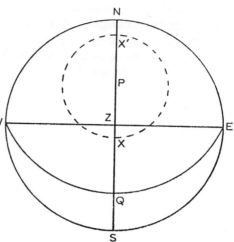

Fig. 53

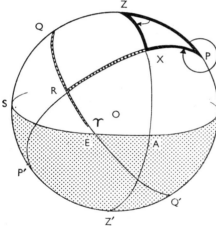

Fig. 54a

and declination, it can also be decided by its altitude and azimuth. Figs. 54a and 54b show the relation between the two methods. ΥR is the SHA and RX the declination, AX is the altitude and PZX the azimuth.

The position of X could also be defined by the hour angle (ZPX) and the declination (RX), but this method is not used in practice.

In actual measurement, the LHA of X is about 315°, the azimuth about N50°E, the altitude about 55°, the declination about 50°N, and the SHA about 30°.

Fig. 54a, it should be noted, is drawn for an observer in north latitude and with the east point showing. This is done to avoid having the heavenly body on the

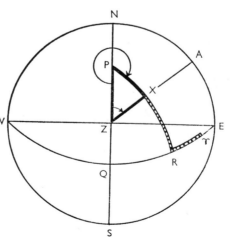

Fig. 54b

unseen hemisphere. The rules to be followed when a figure is to be drawn on the plane of the meridian therefore suggest themselves:

1. *If the LHA is less than* 180° (that is, if the heavenly body is west of the meridian) the north point, N, should be put on the left. A useful mnemonic is: LHA *less* than 180°, north point on *left*.

2. *If the LHA lies between* 180° *and* 360° (that is, if the heavenly body is east of the meridian), N should be put on the *right*.

3. *If the LHA is* 0° *or* 180° (that is, if the heavenly body lies on the meridian above or below the pole), N may be put on either the right or the left.

These rules still hold when the observer is in south latitude.

CHAPTER 7

Solar Time

The word 'time' suggests not only a duration but – as in the question 'What is the time?' – a particular instant in that duration. Particular instants can be related to the rhythmic repetitions of some recognizable patterns, and if those repetitions are numbered, then it becomes relatively easy to identify an instant in time. Duration of time can be expressed as a function of these same repetitions.

Definition of Time

The apparent motion of the Sun around the ecliptic may be said to form one main pattern. A 'year' is defined as the time taken for the Sun to complete this apparent revolution. The rotation of the Earth about its own axis reveals yet another pattern, one complete revolution defining a 'day'.

The year and the day are the principal divisions of time; they depend upon astronomical phenomena and the human race must accept them as they are. The lengths of shorter divisions of time – the hour, the minute and the second – are chosen to suit man's convenience and are quite arbitrary subdivisions of the day. Similarly, the week and the month are more or less arbitrary subdivisions of the year.

The Day

As explained in Chapter 4 the rotation of the Earth results in the apparent rotation of the celestial sphere, so that heavenly bodies are continually crossing and returning to an observer's meridian. *A day is the interval that elapses between two successive transits of a heavenly body across the same meridian.*

All heavenly bodies are thus timekeepers, but, for reasons which will be seen later, some are more convenient than others. The Sun is not a perfect timekeeper because its apparent speed along the ecliptic is not constant. The Sun, however, gives light and heat to the Earth and so governs life on the Earth. The human race is therefore compelled to accept the Sun as the heavenly body by which the day is decided in ordinary human affairs.

The Apparent Solar Day

The interval that elapses between two successive transits of the Sun across the same meridian is an *apparent solar day*. The apparent solar day is not an interval of fixed length, because the Earth does not move along its orbit round the Sun at a constant speed. Its speed is greatest when it is nearest the Sun, and least when it is farthest away. The distance it travels along its orbit in any fixed interval is therefore variable. The time taken for it to make one complete revolution of 360° on its axis gives such a fixed interval, but that interval will not be the length of a day as defined by the Sun.

If the Sun is on the observer's meridian when the Earth is at *A* (Fig. 55), it will not be on that same meridian when the Earth has completed one revolution of 360° because the Earth will have moved along its orbit to *B*. Before the Sun is again on the observer's meridian, the Earth must turn still more on its axis, and it will have moved along its orbit to *C* when the transit occurs. The interval between two successive transits of the Sun across the observer's meridian is therefore the interval that elapses while the Earth is travelling along its orbit from *A* to *C*, a distance that is neither constant in length nor described in a constant time. (A full explanation of this is to be found in Chapter IX of Volume III.)

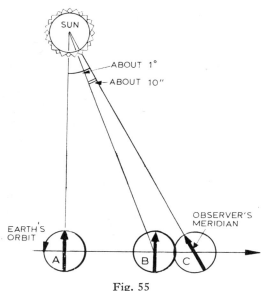

Fig. 55

Apparent Noon

When the Sun is on the observer's meridian, it is said to be *apparent noon* and, as Figs. 56a and 56b show, the Sun then reaches its greatest altitude, *SX*, above the observer's celestial horizon, the observer being assumed to be stationary.

SUN WEST OF MERIDIAN — ALTITUDE DECREASING

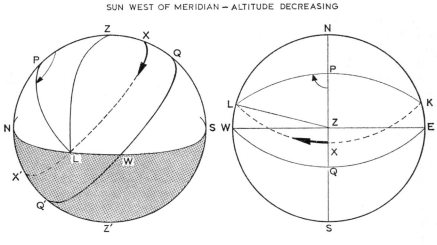

Fig. 56a   Fig. 56b

The path along which the Sun appears to travel during the day, moving westward in the direction shown by the arrow, is the parallel of declination of which XX' is a part. The moment it leaves the meridian, it therefore approaches the horizon and its altitude decreases.

When the Sun reaches L, the point where the parallel of declination cuts the horizon, the altitude is $0°$; the zenith distance has increased to $90°$, and the Sun is said to set.*

Apparent Solar Time

The local hour angle of the Sun at this moment is ZPL, the angle between the observer's meridian and the Sun's meridian, or the angle through which the Sun's meridian has appeared to move from its noon position, PZX.

Continuing westward along the parallel of declination, the Sun reaches K (Figs. 57a and 57b), at which point it is said to rise. Its local hour angle then is ZPK.

SUN EAST OF THE MERIDIAN — ALTITUDE INCREASING

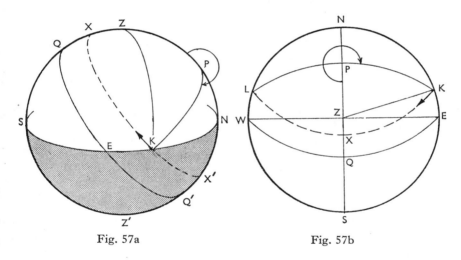

Fig. 57a   Fig. 57b

The value of the Sun's local hour angle, when expressed in conventional units of time (hours, minutes and seconds; 24 hours being equal to $360°$ in units of arc), would thus seem to provide a convenient measure of time. The day, however, would then begin at noon, while for practical purposes a day beginning and ending at midnight is more suitable. Apparent solar time is therefore measured from midnight. Hence the definition: *Apparent solar time is the local hour angle of the Sun ± 12 hours (or 180°).*

In Fig. 57b, the local hour angle of the Sun at sunrise, ZPK, is about 17^h ($255°$) but the apparent time of sunrise is 5^h; in Fig. 56b, the local hour angle of

---

* The obvious complications that arise because the observer, at what he calls sunset, watches the Sun's upper limb disappear below his visible horizon, whereas Figs. 56a and 56b, which are intended to represent the same instant of time, show the centre of the Sun on the celestial horizon, are fully explained in Chapter 16.

the Sun at sunset, *ZPL*, is about 7^h (105°) but the apparent time of sunset is about 19^h.

The local hour angle of the Sun is referred to as the LHATS. This is an abbreviation for 'local hour angle of the True Sun,' the Sun being so called when it may be confused with the Mean Sun (*see below*). When there is no possibility of confusion it is referred to as LHA Sun or LHA $\odot$.

The Mean Sun

It was stated at the beginning of this chapter that the apparent solar day is not a constant interval, because the Earth's orbital motion is not uniform. To an observer on the Earth, this irregular motion is revealed by corresponding variations in the apparent speed of the Sun along the ecliptic, and further variations are introduced when the Sun's motion is projected on to the celestial equator, where hour angles are measured. The hour angle of the True Sun does not, therefore, increase at a uniform rate, and it does not give a practical unit of measurement, which must be uniform.

To overcome this difficulty and yet maintain the connection with the True Sun, which is essential since the True Sun governs life on the Earth, *a Mean Sun* is introduced.

The Mean Sun is an imaginary body which is assumed to move in the celestial equator at a uniform speed round the Earth, and to complete one revolution in the time taken by the True Sun to complete one revolution in the ecliptic.

Mean Solar Time

This, by analogy with the definition of apparent solar time, is the local hour angle of the Mean Sun $\pm$ 12^h.

The local hour angle of the Mean Sun is always denoted by LHAMS.

The Mean Solar Day

The interval between two successive transits of the Mean Sun across the same meridian is called a *mean solar day*. In one mean solar day, the Mean Sun moves westwards from the meridian and completes one circuit of 360° in longitude in the 24 mean solar hours into which the day is divided. The rate of travel is thus 15° of longitude per mean solar hour.

The mean solar hour (called an hour for short) is further divided into 60 minutes, and these are in turn divided into 60 seconds. It must therefore be borne in mind that the units of time in everyday use are mean solar units.

The Civil Day

As the name suggests, the civil day is the day that suffices for human affairs. It begins at midnight when the Mean Sun makes its lower transit (that is when the LHAMS is 12^h) and it ends at the next midnight. It is divided into 24 mean solar hours, which are counted in two series of 12^h, the first denoted a.m. (*ante meridiem*) and the second p.m. (*post meridiem*). The first therefore extends from midnight to noon, a period during which the LHAMS lies between 12^h and 24^h, and the second from noon to midnight, when the LHAMS lies between 0^h and 12^h.

The Astronomical Day

For tabulation purposes, it is clearly more convenient to write 0915 and 2115, or 09^h 15^m and 21^h 15^m as in the *Nautical Almanac*, instead of 9.15 a.m. and 9.15 p.m. A day reckoned in one series of hours from 0 to 24 is therefore introduced and referred to as the *astronomical day*.

Local Mean Time (LMT)

This is the mean time kept at any place when the local hour angle of the Mean Sun is measured from the meridian of that place. Hence the definition:

LMT at any instant is the local hour angle of the Mean Sun at that instant, measured westward from the meridian of the place, $\pm 12^h$.

Greenwich Mean Time (GMT)

This is the local mean time on the meridian of Greenwich. Hence the definition:

GMT at any instant is the Greenwich hour angle of the Mean Sun at that instant, $\pm 12^h$.

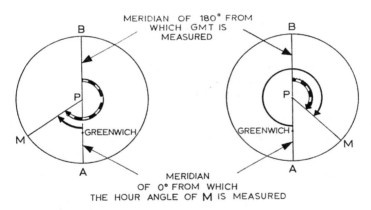

Fig. 58a   Fig. 58b

In Fig. 58a, the LMT at Greenwich is about 15^h, whereas the LHAMS is 3^h. GMT is thus (GHAMS + 12^h). In Fig. 58b the LMT at Greenwich is about $9\frac{1}{2}^h$, whereas the LHAMS is $21\frac{1}{2}^h$. GMT is thus (GHAMS − 12^h).

Longitude and Time

Since places on the Earth are identified by reference to the Greenwich meridian, longitude must provide the necessary connection between LMT at any place and LMT at Greenwich. This fact is revealed at once in the time-difference which exists between Greenwich and, for example, New York. The longitude of New York is roughly 75°W. The Mean Sun, travelling westward at 15° per hour, covers this angular distance in 5^h. New York is thus 5^h west of Greenwich.

When the Mean Sun reaches the New York meridian, its local hour angle with reference to that meridian is 0^h. But to an observer at Greenwich, who

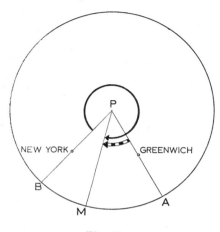

Fig. 59

measures the angle from the Greenwich meridian, its local hour angle is 5^h, because that is the period which has elapsed since the Mean Sun crossed the Greenwich meridian.

Similarly, when the Mean Sun is on the Greenwich meridian, its local hour angle there is 0^h, but to an observer at New York its local hour angle is $(24^h - 5^h)$ or 19^h, because 5^h must elapse before it reaches the New York meridian.

An intermediate time is considered in Fig. 59, with the Mean Sun at M; the Greenwich hour angle is APM and the New York local hour angle is BPM (measured westwards). In this figure, APM is about 3^h and the LMT at Greenwich would be 15^h; BPM however is about 22^h and the LMT at New York would thus be 10^h. The time of any event recorded by an observer at New York thus differs from the time recorded at Greenwich by the 5^h that form the time-equivalent of the d.long between the two places.

What has been said of New York in relation to Greenwich holds in principle if any other place is substituted for New York. To convert the LMT on one meridian into the LMT at Greenwich, it is therefore necessary to apply only the longitude expressed in time.

Rule for converting LMT to GMT

It is seen by comparing the time of the same event recorded by observers in New York and Greenwich, that LMT at New York, at a place 5^h west of Greenwich, is always 5^h behind or *slow* on LMT at Greenwich. It should be equally true to say that LMT at Greenwich, a place 5^h east of New York is 5^h ahead or *fast* on LMT at New York. Thus the fact that LMT on any meridian is fast or slow on the LMT on a second meridian depends entirely on whether the first meridian lies east or west of the second. When the second meridian passes through Greenwich, this relation between the two times is conveniently summarised thus:

Longitude west, Greenwich time best.
Longitude east, Greenwich time least.

If, for example, the GMT of an observation is 19^h 23^m 43^s the LMTs of the same observation at places in 48°W and $22\frac{1}{2}$°E are:

	In 48°W		In $22\frac{1}{2}$°E
	h m s		h m s
GMT	19 23 43	GMT	19 23 43
Long.	3 12 00 W	Long.	1 30 00 E
LMT	16 11 43	LMT	20 53 43

Standard Time

It is clearly impracticable for each place to keep the time of its own meridian. Nor is it practicable for places all over the world to keep the same time. A compromise is therefore effected, and places in the same locality, often including an entire country, elect to keep the same time. That time is usually based on a meridian running through the neighbourhood and differing in longitude from the Greenwich meridian by a convenient number of hours; it is known as the *standard time* of the neighbourhood. The standard times kept by various countries are listed in the *Nautical Almanac* and in the *Admiralty List of Radio Signals, Volume 5*.

Zone Time (ZT)

This, in effect, is an extension of standard time to the sea, where it is impossible for a ship to keep the time of her meridian because her meridian is always changing, unless she happens to be steaming north or south. The Earth is therefore divided into time zones, each bounded by meridians 15° or 1ʰ in time apart, and situated so that the central meridian of each zone is an exact number of hours distant from the Greenwich meridian. The time kept in each zone is the time of its central meridian. Zone time therefore differs from GMT by multiples of an hour, and is fast or slow according to the zone's position east or west of Greenwich. Fuller details of zone time may be found in Volume I.

Greenwich Date

It is shown in Volume I that zone time and GMT are connected by the number of the zone. The GMT, obtained from the zone time, is combined with the appropriate date to form what is called the *Greenwich Date* (GD).

For example:

ZT 1605 (+2), 1st April = GD 1805 1st April
ZT 0105 (−7), 2nd April = GD 1805 1st April
ZT 0510 (−5), 9th July = GD 0010 9th July
ZT 1610 (+8), 8th July = GD 0010 9th July

Use of GMT in tabulation

In the *Nautical Almanac*, and other publications used all over the world, it is clearly uneconomic to tabulate information relating to any given instant in each zone. This is because of the variety of headings necessary for anyone to find the given instant under the heading of the particular zone time which he happens to be keeping, e.g., 1605 (+2) 1st April, 0105 (−7) 2nd April, etc. Instead, that information is conveniently given under the appropriate GMT headings (1805 1st April) because any zone time can be referred to the Greenwich meridian. GMT is thus a 'standard' time for tabulation purposes.

Time-keeping in a ship

The ordinary clocks in a ship are adjusted as necessary for keeping zone time within a minute or two, and this is sufficiently accurate for the routine of the ship generally. Since all information, however, in the *Nautical Almanac* is given for GMT throughout the year, it is necessary to know the accurate GMT before the tables in the *Nautical Almanac* can be entered. Special clocks known as chronometers are therefore kept to give this accurate GMT.

Chronometers are never altered or disturbed, despite possible changes in zone time. They are checked daily by means of time signals, and their errors are tabulated as fast or slow on GMT. It is thus always possible to obtain the exact GMT of an event, such as the time of observation of a heavenly body. (For details of the method of checking these errors, *see* Volume I, Chapter XI; and for a description of the chronometer itself, *see* Volume III, Chapter XIX.)

Deck watches

In order to avoid moving the chronometer, the time of an observation is actually taken with an ordinary but reliable watch called a *deck watch*. This usually keeps approximate GMT, and its exact difference from GMT (known as its *error*) is found by means of radio time-signals or by comparison with the chrono-meter (*see* Volume I, Chapter XI).

Since deck watches (and chronometers) record a series of 12^h, they cannot distinguish between GMT 3^h, for example, and GMT 15^h, and it is not always obvious from the 'time of day' in a ship whether the time is forenoon or afternoon at Greenwich. It may be midnight on the ship's meridian but midday at Greenwich. Should there be any uncertainty, it can be removed by comparing the GMT obtained from the deck watch with the Greenwich date obtained from zone time.

EXAMPLE

Suppose that, at ZT 0530 (-11) in longitude 162° 30′ E on 20th September, the deck watch showed $6^h 28^m 43^s$ at the time of an observation, and that the deck watch was 31^s fast on GMT.

Then:

ZT 0530 20th Sept. (approx. time from ship's clocks)
Zone -11
GD 1830 19th Sept. (approximate GMT)

	h	m	s
DWT	6	28	43
DWE			31 fast
GMT	18	28	12 19th Sept. (*not* $6^h 28^m 12^s$)

The GMT must agree with the Greenwich date, which is, in effect, merely a term denoting 'approximate GMT'.

The Equation of Time

Although the assumption of an imaginary Mean Sun makes the ordinary clock possible, this same assumption also gives rise to a problem. The navigator, seeking to fix his position by observing the Sun, necessarily measures the altitude of the True Sun, and the True Sun keeps apparent solar time. He notes the instant of this observation, however, from a watch that keeps mean solar time. He must therefore be able to connect mean solar time with apparent solar time. The connection is known as the *equation of time*, which is defined as the excess of mean time over apparent time, that is:

$$LHAMS - LHATS$$

The steps by which the equation of time is found are explained in Volume III. For the present it is sufficient to realize that, since the True Sun moves with a varying speed in the ecliptic and the Mean Sun moves with a constant speed in the celestial equator, their hour angles will not keep in step. At certain times

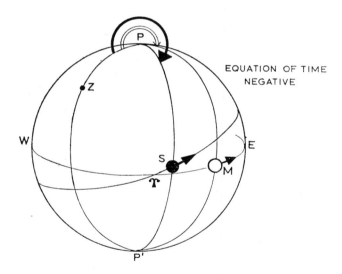

Fig. 60a

of the year LHATS will be greater than LHAMS, as shown in Fig. 60a. At other times it will be less, as shown in Fig. 60b. The equation of time may therefore be either positive or negative. About the 15th April, 14th June, 1st September, and 24th December, it becomes zero and changes sign. Its extreme values are $+14$ and -16 minutes. The value of the equation of time is tabulated in the *Nautical Almanac* for every 12 hours (at 0^h and 12^h) on the meridian of Greenwich.

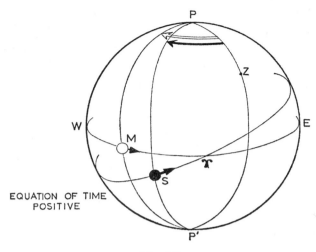

Fig. 60b

Local Hour Angle of the True Sun (LHATS)

The equation of time can also be defined as the excess of the Greenwich hour angle of the Mean Sun over the Greenwich hour angle of the True Sun.

Therefore:

$$GHATS = GHAMS - \text{equation of time.}$$
$$= GMT \pm 12 \text{ hours} - \text{equation of time.}$$

The local hour angle of the True Sun (LHATS) is found by simply applying the longitude to its Greenwich hour angle.

For the convenience of the navigator, who must work out his sight within a very few minutes, the Greenwich hour angle of the True Sun is tabulated against GMT in the *Nautical Almanac*. The method of determining it for a particular instant is explained in Chapter 9.

Conversion of Arc to Time and Time to Arc

Tables are provided in *Norie's Tables* for converting degrees, minutes and seconds of arc to hours, minutes and seconds of time, and vice versa. A conversion table is also included in the *Nautical Almanac*. If, however, these tables are not available, the conversion may be effected by remembering that, since the Sun completes its apparent revolution of 360° of longitude in 24^h:

$$15° \equiv 1^h$$
$$1° \equiv 4^m$$
$$15' \equiv 1^m$$
$$1' \equiv 4^s.$$

These simple facts explain the following methods:

Arc into Time

Method I. Multiply by 4 and divide by 60.

If, for example, the angle is 117° 34′, the calculation (which can be done in the head) would be:

$$4 \times 117° \div 60 = 468° \div 60 \equiv 7^h 48^m$$
$$4 \times 34′ \div 60 = 136′ \div 60 \equiv \quad 2^m 16^s$$
$$117° 34′ \equiv 7^h 50^m 16^s.$$

Method II. Divide by 15 and multiply the remainder by 4.

$$117° = (7 \times 15°) \text{ and } 12° \text{ over } \equiv 7^h 48^m$$
$$34′ = (2 \times 15′) \text{ and } \quad 4′ \text{ over } \equiv \quad 2^m 16^s$$
$$117° 34′ \equiv 7^h 50^m 16^s.$$

Time into Arc

Multiply the hours by 15 and divide the minutes and seconds by 4.

If, for example, the angle in time is $7^h 50^m 16^s$, the procedure would be:

$$7^h \equiv 7 \times 15° = 105°$$

$$50^m \equiv \frac{50°}{4} \quad = 12° 30′$$

$$16^s \equiv \frac{16′}{4} \quad = 4′$$

$$7^h 50^m 16^s \equiv 117° 34′.$$

CHAPTER 8

Sidereal Time

In the last chapter it was stated that a day is the interval between two successive transits of a heavenly body across an observer's meridian, and that all heavenly bodies are therefore timekeepers. If the heavenly body selected is a star, the interval is known as a *sidereal day*, to distinguish it from the solar day. For convenience, the First Point of Aries is taken instead of an actual star, and the sidereal day is therefore defined as the interval between two successive transits of the First Point of Aries across the same meridian.

The Sidereal Day

Figure 61 shows that the sidereal day is shorter than the solar day.

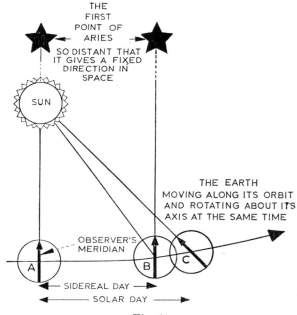

Fig. 61

When the Earth has turned through 360° and reached *B*, the First Point of Aries is again on the meridian. The Sun, however, will not be on the meridian again until the Earth has turned through about 361° with respect to the stars, and reached *C*. The sidereal day is thus shorter than a solar day by about 4 minutes, which is the time taken by the Earth to turn through this extra degree, and the difference between the arcs AC and AB affords a graphical representation of the difference between the two kinds of day. It must be remembered, however, that the arcs themselves do not form convenient standards of measurement, owing to the variations in the Earth's orbital velocity.

The sidereal day is not a practical unit in a world that is governed by the Sun, and, except in observatories, where some method of obtaining a uniform interval is essential, it can be ignored. Sidereal time, on the other hand, is important because it enters the problem of finding a star's hour angle, and, as such, it is of interest to the navigator.

Local Sidereal Time

This is defined as the local hour angle of the First Point of Aries. It is thus an expression of the angular distance of Aries from an observer's meridian, and the navigator is concerned with it only as that angular distance. He is not concerned with the duration of time which has elapsed since the First Point of Aries crossed his meridian, otherwise he would at once become involved with the sidereal hour and the sidereal minute – time units derived from the sidereal day and differing slightly from mean solar units – and the connection between the two sets of time units would have to be investigated more thoroughly. This labour, however, is avoided when he treats sidereal time as an angular distance, because the units of arc in which he expresses it are constant units suitable for expressing the angular distance of any heavenly body from his meridian.

Greenwich Hour Angle of Aries

On the meridian of Greenwich the local hour angle of the First Point of Aries is clearly the Greenwich hour angle, usually referred to as 'GHA Aries'. The fact that all bodies are related to the First Point of Aries by their sidereal hour angles enables a relation between GHA Aries and the GHA of any heavenly body to be established.

Fig. 62a shows that:
$$GX = G\Upsilon + \Upsilon X$$
or GHA body = GHA Aries + SHA body.

Fig. 62b shows that:
$$GX = G\Upsilon + \Upsilon X - 360°$$
or GHA body = GHA Aries + SHA body − 360°.

Since the subtraction of 360° does not affect the actual angular distance, then in all cases:

GHA body = GHA Aries + SHA body

Once the Greenwich hour angle of a body has been found, the local hour angle measured from any other meridian can easily be obtained by applying the longitude, as explained in Chapter 7.

Herein lies the importance of GHA Aries. Direct tabulation at short intervals of the Greenwich hour angles of all the stars likely to be observed by the

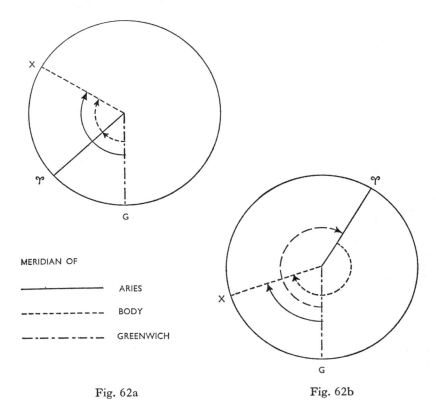

MERIDIAN OF

—————————— ARIES

— — — — — — — BODY

— · — · — · — · — GREENWICH

Fig. 62a   Fig. 62b

navigator would occupy far too much space; if space were cut down by increasing the intervals, elaborate interpolation tables would be necessary. This difficulty is avoided by tabulating the GHA Aries and a quantity which, for all practical purposes, remains constant for each particular star – its sidereal hour angle (SHA).

Relation between GMT and GHA Aries

The movement of the Mean Sun in the celestial equator enables a relation to be established between the GMT at which a star is observed and its Greenwich hour angle at that instant.

Substitute the Mean Sun for the True Sun in Figs. 27 and 28 (Chapter 4) and it will be seen that the Mean Sun's uniform movement in the celestial sphere, along which path sidereal hour angles are measured, implies an equally uniform decrease in its sidereal hour angle during the year.

The point X, which lies on the celestial equator in both Figs. 62a and 62b, may therefore be taken as the Mean Sun at the moment under consideration; it is at once apparent that the Mean Sun's hour angle and sidereal hour angle are related in the same way as a star's hour angle and sidereal hour angle, that is:

GHA Mean Sun = GHA Aries + SHA Mean Sun

or　　GHA Aries = GHA Mean Sun − SHA Mean Sun.

But GHA Mean Sun = GMT ± 12 hours, so that:

GHA Aries = GMT ± 12 hours − SHA Mean Sun.

The SHA Mean Sun decreases at a constant rate and can be predicted for any instant. It is possible, therefore, to calculate GHA Aries at any instant and, as a result of such calculations, GHA Aries is tabulated against GMT in the *Nautical Almanac*.

The Hour Angle of the Moon

If two successive transits of the Moon were observed across the same meridian, the interval between them would be one lunar day, and, since the Moon is itself describing an orbit about the Earth in the same direction as the Earth's spin, this interval would be longer than the mean solar day (Fig. 63).

AA' is a measure of the mean solar day, but while the Earth has moved from A to A', the Moon has reached C, and so the Earth will have to turn through a further angle approximately equal to $B'A'C$ before it is on the observer's meridian again. The average time taken to turn this extra angle is 50 minutes.

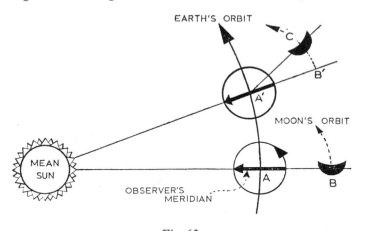

Fig. 63

The units derived from the lunar day are lunar units. It is not necessary, however, to work in lunar units to find the hour angle of the Moon. The formula for the hour angle of a heavenly body applies equally well to the Moon, and:

GHA Moon = GHA Aries + SHA Moon.

The sidereal hour angle of the Moon can be predicted. It is combined with the Greenwich hour angle of Aries in the *Nautical Almanac* to give the Greenwich hour angle of the Moon for every hour of GMT.

The Lunation, or Lunar Month

This is the interval between two successive new Moons, and it is important in tidal prediction.

The Moon makes one complete revolution about the Earth in $27\frac{1}{3}$ mean solar days, but if the Moon were new at the beginning of this period, when the

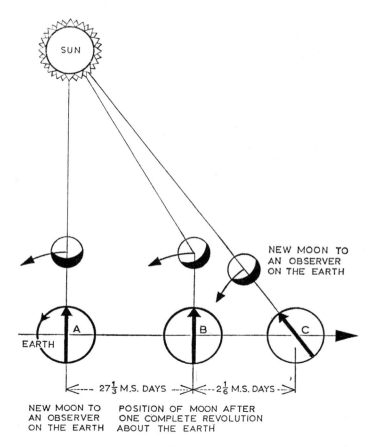

Fig. 64

Earth is at A in Fig. 64, it would not be new at the end of the period, because it would not lie in a straight line with the Sun and the Earth, which is now at B. To achieve this position it must move along its orbit round the Earth, and while this is happening the Earth continues along its own orbit round the Sun to a position C. A further $2\frac{1}{6}$ mean solar days approximately elapse before the Moon is again new, and a lunation or lunar month is therefore equivalent to $(27\frac{1}{3} + 2\frac{1}{6})$ or $29\frac{1}{2}$ mean solar days.

In this period the Moon must cross the meridian once fewer than the Sun, and this fact establishes the 50-minute difference between the mean solar day and the lunar day because:

$$28\tfrac{1}{2} \text{ lunar days} = 29\tfrac{1}{2} \text{ mean solar days}$$

$$\text{i.e.} \quad 1 \text{ lunar day} = \frac{29\tfrac{1}{2}}{28\tfrac{1}{2}} \text{ mean solar days}$$

$$\text{or } 1^{\text{d}} \, 0^{\text{h}} \, 50^{\text{m}}.$$

The Hour Angle of a Planet

The planets belong to the solar system, and their motion in the celestial sphere is therefore different from that of the stars. For the purpose of finding its hour angle, however, a planet can be treated in the same way as the Moon, that is:

GHA Planet = GHA Aries + SHA Planet.

The sidereal hour angles of the planets can be predicted. In the case of the four planets bright enough to be observed – Venus, Mars, Jupiter and Saturn – the sidereal hour angles are combined with the Greenwich hour angle of Aries in the *Nautical Almanac* to give their Greenwich hour angles for every hour of GMT.

CHAPTER 9

The Local Hour Angle from the
Greenwich Hour Angle

Before the navigator can attempt to draw a position line from an observation of a heavenly body, he requires to know the body's position relative to his own assumed meridian, that is, its LHA and declination. The determination of declination from the *Nautical Almanac* is explained in Chapter 4; it is the purpose of the present chapter to show how the LHA of a body may be obtained.

The general formula for the local hour angle of any heavenly body, derived from the two previous chapters, may be summarized as:

$$LHA = GMT \pm 12^h - SHA \text{ Mean Sun} + SHA \text{ body} \pm \text{ longitude.}$$

Here the sidereal hour angles of both the Mean Sun and the body vary with respect to time, and the navigator must obviously have an almanac which tabulates sufficient data to enable him to work out the LHA with minimum delay. In the ideal almanac the local hour angle of the particular body observed would be given for the GMT of observation and for the assumed longitude. Since there are more than 150 bodies bright enough to be observed, since GMT is read to the nearest second and since a wide range of longitudes is involved, an enormous number of tabulations would be required in order to be truly comprehensive, so that the ideal almanac is obviously a physical impossibility.

The Nautical Almanac

The methods adopted in the *Nautical Almanac* to overcome this difficulty, with minimum loss of precision and speed in use, will now be examined.

Firstly, this almanac tabulates Greenwich hour angle as opposed to local hour angle; it is thus independent of longitude. The navigator, however, will need to apply his longitude to the tabulated Greenwich hour angle in order to obtain the local hour angle – an additional step in the navigator's computation.

Secondly, the *Nautical Almanac* does not attempt to tabulate the Greenwich hour angles of all the stars. It tabulates, instead, that of the First Point of Aries. The Greenwich hour angle of a particular star is found by adding its sidereal hour angle (a quantity which is, for practical purposes, constant for that star) to the Greenwich hour angle of the First Point of Aries. In the case of stars, then, a further step in working must be accepted by the navigator.

This leaves only the Sun, the Moon and the four navigational planets – Venus, Mars, Jupiter and Saturn – to be considered. Their sidereal hour angles are varying continuously and at different rates. Instead of tabulating their sidereal hour angles it is just as easy to tabulate the sum of their sidereal hour angles and the Greenwich hour angle of Aries, that is their Greenwich hour angles, and this is what is done in the *Nautical Almanac*. The navigator is thereby saved the effort of one addition at no further expense of space.

The problem is now reduced to tabulating the Greenwich hour angles of seven bodies against GMT. To do this for every second of GMT would still make the almanac unwieldy. The interval is therefore increased and interpolation tables are provided.

The Greenwich hour angle of any body increases rapidly and the rate of increase is slightly different for each body. The larger the interval, the more elaborate become the interpolation tables, which means that some form of compromise is necessary. The interval adopted in the *Nautical Almanac* is one hour.

These interpolation tables, which give the increments to be added to the Greenwich hour angle for every minute and second within the hour, are most important and merit a closer examination.

Rate of change of Greenwich Hour Angle

It was shown in Chapter 8 that the Greenwich hour angle of the True Sun was equal to the difference between the Greenwich hour angle of the Mean Sun (adjusted by 180° or 12^h) and the equation of time. The Greenwich hour angle of the Mean Sun increases at exactly 15° per hour; the equation of time changes from about +14 minutes to −16 minutes and back again during a year, and its rate of change does not exceed about ± 0′·3 per hour. The hourly difference of the True Sun's Greenwich hour angle is therefore between 14° 59′·7 and 15° 00′·3.

Hourly difference

The Greenwich hour angle of the First Point of Aries is equal to the difference between the Greenwich hour angle of the Mean Sun and the sidereal hour angle of the Mean Sun. The latter quantity decreases uniformly from 360° to 0° during one year, that is, at 2′·5 per hour. The hourly difference of the sidereal hour angle of the Mean Sun is thus −2′·5.

The hourly difference of the Greenwich hour angle of the Mean Sun is exactly 15° 00′·0. The hourly difference of the Greenwich hour angle of Aries, being equal to the hourly difference of the Greenwich hour angle of the Mean Sun less the hourly difference of the sidereal hour angle of the Mean Sun, is thus approximately 15° 02′·5.

Owing to the Moon's movement along its orbit round the Earth, its sidereal hour angle decreases from 360° to 0° in one lunar month. Because the lunar orbit is inclined to the celestial equator at an angle of between 18½° and 28½°, the decrease in sidereal hour angle is not constant; it varies in fact between 25′ and 43½′ per hour, that is, its hourly difference lies between −25′ and −43½′.

Now:

$$\text{GHA Moon} = \text{GHA Aries} + \text{SHA Moon}$$

so that the limiting hourly differences of the Greenwich hour angle of the Moon are 15° 02′·5 − 43′·5, or 14° 19′·0, and 15° 02′·5 − 25′·0, or 14° 37′·5.

The planets revolve around the Sun. They will therefore have a movement relative to the First Point of Aries which can be expressed as a change of sidereal hour angle. The hourly differences in the SHA of the navigational planets lie between limits, as shown:

Venus $-3'\cdot5$ to $+2'\cdot5$
Mars $-2'\cdot5$ to $+1'\cdot5$
Jupiter $\Big\}$
Saturn $-0'\cdot5$ to $+0'\cdot9$

Consequently, the hourly differences of their Greenwich hour angles will vary thus:

Venus $14° 59'\cdot0$ to $15° 05'\cdot0$
Mars $15° 00'\cdot0$ to $15° 04'\cdot0$
Jupiter $\Big\}$
Saturn $15° 02'\cdot0$ to $15° 03'\cdot4$

The daily change in hourly difference for the Sun and planets is negligible. For the Moon it may be as much as $3'\cdot0$.

It is evident from what has been discussed that the construction of interpolation tables for an almanac giving Greenwich hour angles is a matter of some complexity. The rates of change of Greenwich hour angle of all the bodies considered (except the First Point of Aries) are varying continuously and in different ways.

In the *Nautical Almanac* fixed values for hourly differences are adopted.

These are:

Sun and planets $15° 00'\cdot0$
Moon $14° 19'\cdot0$
First Point of Aries $15° 02'\cdot46$

The interpolation tables give the increment to be added to the GHA at the tabulated hour, for every second of each minute for the Sun (and planets), Aries, and the Moon. They are based on the constant hourly differences given above. The tables for minutes 46 and 47 are shown in Appendix 2.

To allow for the discrepancy between the adopted value of hourly difference and its true value at the time, a quantity, denoted by v, is tabulated in the daily pages of the *Nautical Almanac*. This is equal to the excess or defect of the actual hourly difference over the adopted value. The adopted mean hourly differences have been chosen so that v is always positive (except in the case of Venus whose hourly difference may sometimes be less than $15° 00'\cdot0$). A further increment representing the proportion of v corresponding to the number of minutes after the whole hour (the seconds may be neglected) is extracted from the right-hand column of the interpolation table for the minute,

under the heading: $\dfrac{v}{d}$ or Corr^n.

Because the daily change of the Moon's hourly difference may be appreciable, it is necessary to tabulate the actual value of v for the Moon at each hour. The mean value of v (for the day) is sufficient for the planets because in their cases the change in hourly difference may be neglected.

The range of hourly difference for the Sun is very small; the tabulated values of its Greenwich hour angle have accordingly been adjusted to reduce the error caused by a constant difference of 15° 00'·0. Therefore, no v correction is given for the Sun and none must be applied.

The procedure for finding the local hour angle of the Sun, the Moon, a planet, or Aries may be summarized thus:

1. Find the GD.
2. Apply the error to the DWT and find the GMT.
3. Open the *Nautical Almanac* at the date; take out the GHA for the body at the nearest whole hour before the GMT (a), and take out v for the day (for the hour in the case of the Moon).
4. Open the *Almanac* at the interpolation table for the number of minutes of the GMT, copy the increment for the seconds of GMT (b), and the correction for v (c).
5. Add together (a), (b) and (c) to obtain the Greenwich hour angle.
6. Apply the longitude to obtain the local hour angle on the observer's meridian.

In the case of a star, its sidereal hour angle must be extracted from the star list in the *Nautical Almanac* and added to the hour angle of the First Point of Aries, obtained as described above, and the longitude applied to give the local hour angle of the star.

360° must be added or subtracted when necessary.

The following examples illustrate the procedure.*

Local Hour Angle of the Sun

At ZT 1548 (+11) on 9th December 1971 the deck watch showed 2ʰ 47ᵐ 30ˢ when an observation of the Sun was taken. The ship was assumed to be in longitude 158° 15'W, and the deck watch was 25ˢ slow on GMT.

ZT		1548	9th Dec.
Z		+11	
GD		0248	10th Dec.
DWT		02ʰ 47ᵐ 30ˢ	
DWE		25	slow +
GMT		02 47 55	10th Dec.

(a) GHA	(02ʰ)	211° 54'·2	*Note.*	No v correction
(b) Inc.	(47ᵐ 55ˢ)	11° 58'·8		for the Sun.
GHA	Sun	223° 53'·0		
Long.		158° 15'·0W		
LHA Sun		65° 38'·0		

---

* Extracts from the *Nautical Almanac*, 1971, relevant to these and subsequent examples, will be found in Appendix 2 to this volume.

Local Hour Angle of the Moon

At ZT 0848(0) *on* 10*th December* 1971 *the deck watch showed* 08^h 47^m 30^s *when an observation of the Moon was taken. The ship was assumed to be in longitude* 4° 25'E, *and the deck watch was* 3^s *slow on GMT.*

ZT	0848	10th Dec.
Z	0	
GD	0848	10th Dec.
DWT	08^h 47^m 30^s	
DWE	3	slow +
GMT	08 47 33	10th Dec.
(*a*) GHA (08^h)	24° 37'·1	$v = 16'·8$
(*b*) Inc. (47^m 33^s)	11° 20'·8	
(*c*) *v* Corr^n (16'·8)	13'·3	
GHA Moon	36° 11'·2	
Long.	4° 25'·0E	
LHA Moon	40° 36'·2	

Local Hour Angle of a Planet

If, instead of the Moon in the last example, Venus had been observed, its hour angle would have been:

ZT	0848	10th Dec.
Z	0	
GD	0848	10th Dec.
DWT	08^h 47^m 30^s	
DWE	3	slow +
GMT	08 47 33	10th Dec.
(*a*) GHA (08^h)	273° 04'·7	$v = -0'·9$
(*b*) Inc. (47^m 33^s)	11° 53'·3	
(*c*) *v* Corr^n (−0'·9)	−0'·7	
GHA Venus	284° 57'·3	
Long.	4° 25'·0E	
LHA Venus	289° 22'·3	

Note. Venus is the only body for which negative *v* is possible.

Local Hour Angle of a Star

In assumed longitude 120° 40′E *at ZT* 1747 (−8) *Mirfak was observed at DWT* 09ʰ 47ᵐ 04ˢ, *on* 10*th December* 1971. *DWE is* 12ˢ *slow.*

ZT	1747	10th Dec.
Z	−08	
GD	0947	10th Dec.
DWT	09ʰ 47ᵐ 04ˢ	
DWE	12	slow +
GMT	09 47 16	10th Dec.

(*a*) GHA   Aries (09ʰ)   213° 26′·4   *Note.* No *v* correction
(*b*) Inc. (47ᵐ 16ˢ)   11° 50′·9   for Aries.

GHA	Aries	225° 17′·3
SHA	Mirfak	309° 24′·7
GHA	Mirfak	534° 42′·0
Long.		120° 40′·0E
		655° 22′·0
		−360°
LHA Mirfak		295° 22′·0

CHAPTER 10

The Astronomical Position Line

The whole theory of position finding at sea depends on the ability to solve the triangle *PZX* when the necessary information is given, because this enables the navigator to relate the altitude he observes, which is theoretically exact, to his DR position, which is only approximate, and thus obtain a position line on the Earth's surface for the instant of observation.

The Position Circle

When the observed altitude of a heavenly body is corrected and then subtracted from 90°, the true zenith distance is obtained – *ZX* in Fig. 65. *Z*, however, may be any point on a small circle of radius *ZX* and centre *X*.

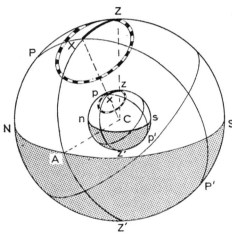

Fig. 65

On the Earth, the observer's position, *z*, lies on the circumference of a small circle, the centre of which is the heavenly body's geographical position. The radius of this circle is also the true zenith distance, *zx*, and since it is now measured on the surface of the Earth, it can be expressed in nautical miles. This circle is known as a *position circle*.

The astronomical position line is the small arc of this position circle on which the observer or navigator discovers his position to be. If *zx* is very small, some twenty miles or so, the geographical position can be plotted on the chart and the actual circle drawn without loss of accuracy; but in general *zx* will be large, of the order of 1,000 miles, and the geographical position will seldom be on the chart that the navigator is using for keeping his reckoning. The part of the position circle that concerns the navigator must therefore be found by methods which confine the necessary plotting to the neighbourhood of the ship's actual position. The method in common use is the 'Marcq St Hilaire', or 'Intercept', method.

MARCQ ST HILAIRE, OR INTERCEPT, METHOD

The navigator chooses any position in the neighbourhood of the position in which he thinks the ship is. His actual DR position or estimated position is in some ways the most convenient. In Fig. 66, *A* is the DR position and *Z* its zenith. The geographical position of the heavenly body *X* is *U*. *AU* is an

84

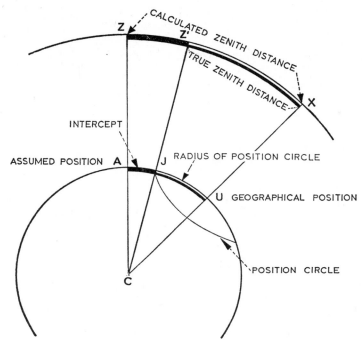

Fig. 66

arc of the great circle passing through A and U. The radius of the position circle found from an observed altitude of X is JU, and this will not, as a rule, be equal to AU. The difference AJ, is called the *intercept*.

Fig. 67 shows these positions, A, J and U, in relation to the pole, P, and it is at once clear that the distance AU (which is equal in angular measurement to ZX in the corresponding triangle on the celestial sphere) is simply the calculated zenith distance (CZD) found by solving the spherical triangle PAU or PZX. UJ is the true zenith distance (TZD), and the position of J is decided by the azimuth of the heavenly body, which is the angle PAU (in Fig. 67) or PZX (in Fig. 65).

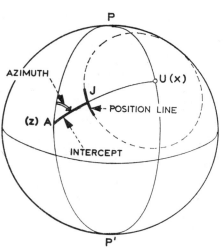

Fig. 67

If, for example, the CZD is 50°, the navigator knows that his DR position (or whatever position he chooses for working the sight) is 3,000′ from the geographical position.

E

If, at the same time, his true zenith distance is 49° 55', he also knows that his own position is 5' nearer the geographical position than the position from which he worked the sight. Also, his position lies on the circumference of the position circle. If, then, a line of bearing is drawn on the chart from the DR and a length equivalent to 5' marked off in the direction of the heavenly body, the point obtained will be the point *J* (Fig. 68), and the line of bearing will coincide with the radius of the position circle for a short distance.

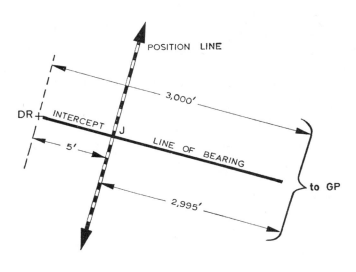

Fig. 68

J is therefore one point which is at the correct distance from the geographical position, but it is not necessarily the ship's position. That lies somewhere on the circumference of the position circle in the neighbourhood of *J*.

Since the circumference of a circle at any point is at right-angles to the radius at that point, the small arc which forms a position line is drawn in practice as a straight line through *J*, at right-angles to the line of bearing.

The Intercept

The essential feature of the intercept method is thus a comparison between the ship's known distance from the geographical position and the calculated distance of some arbitrary position from that same geographical position. The first distance is the TZD, and the second the CZD, the difference between them being the intercept.

If the TZD is greater than the CZD, the ship's actual position is farther away from the geographical position than the position arbitrarily chosen, and the intercept is therefore *away*. If the TZD is less than the CZD, the ship's actual position is nearer the geographical position, and the intercept is *towards*.

Assumptions made when the position line is drawn

There are three assumptions made when a position line is drawn as a straight line on a Mercator chart.

1. The bearing of the geographical position is the same at all points in the neighbourhood of J.

2. The intercept, which is laid off as a straight line and therefore represents a rhumb line, coincides with the great circle forming the actual line of bearing.

3. The position line itself, which is also laid off as a straight line and is, therefore, a rhumb line, coincides with the arc of the position circle over the small length shown on the chart.

All three assumptions are justified in normal circumstances because the error introduced is negligible. Only when the altitude is so large that the position circle can be drawn on the chart as a circle are these assumptions inadmissible. The procedure described in Volume III must then be followed. The first assumption is also discussed separately in that volume.

Solution of the third side of a spherical triangle

In Figs. 69a and 69b it is required to find ZX when:

$$PZ = 40°$$
$$PX = 110°$$
$$\angle ZPX = 37° 30'$$

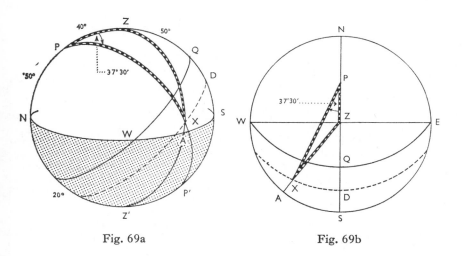

| Fig. 69a | Fig. 69b |

It is shown in Appendix 1 that if two sides of a spherical triangle and the angle included between them are known, the third side can be calculated. In the triangle PZX, then, if PZ, PX and $\angle ZPX$ are known, ZX can be calculated. These quantities are related most conveniently by the natural haversine formula which reads, for this triangle:

$$\text{hav } ZX = \text{hav } (PX \sim PZ) + \sin PX \sin PZ \text{ hav } \angle ZPX$$

$\angle ZPX$ 37° 30′	log hav 37° 30′	9·014 20
‘ PZ 40°	log sin 40°	9·808 07
PX 110°	(log sin 110° =) log sin 70°	9·972 99
$PX \sim PZ$ 70°	log hav	8·795 26
	hav	0·062 41
	hav 70°	0·328 99
	hav ZX	0·391 40

$\therefore ZX = 77° 27′·3$, and the three sides of the triangle are now all known.

The Azimuth

The angle $\angle PZX$ (or any other angle) can be calculated in a similar manner by using a different formula (described in Volume III).

This angle $\angle PZX$, in Fig. 69, is the azimuth and, if calculated, would be found to be in this case 144° 07′·5. If P is the north pole (the elevated pole), and as the local hour angle is (37° 30′) to the W of the meridian of Z, the azimuth is N144° 07′·5W, that is to say the true bearing of X from Z is (360° − 144° 07′·5) = 215° 52′·5, or approximately 215°·9.

TABLES OF COMPUTED ALTITUDE AND AZIMUTH

The solution of the PZX triangle by the natural haversine formula is lengthy and the number of calculations, entries to, and extracts from logarithmic tables gives considerable scope for arithmetical error, while special tables constructed to give directly the necessary solutions for all combinations of latitude, declination and local hour angle would be impossibly large. There are available, however, tables designed for use with the Marcq St Hilaire or intercept method of sight reduction, the navigator working his sight from a position, as explained later, in which the latitude is chosen as an integral degree and the local hour angle is made an integral degree by adjusting the DR longitude.

Two of the tables widely used at sea are NP 401, *Sight Reduction Tables for Marine Navigation*, and AP 3270, *Sight Reduction Tables for Air Navigation*.

Sight Reduction Tables for Marine Navigation (NP 401)

These tables provide computed values of altitude and azimuth for arguments of latitude, hour angle and declination tabulated at intervals of one degree. Precise interpolation of altitude only is required for intermediate values of declination.

The tables are arranged in six volumes according to latitude:

Volume	Latitude, North or South
1	0° to 15°
2	15° to 30°
3	30° to 45°
4	45° to 60°
5	60° to 75°
6	75° to 90°

Thus the first and last latitudes in each volume overlap those of the preceding and succeeding volumes. Each volume is arranged in two 8-degree sections or zones of latitude.

The Arguments

If tables were constructed for the actual sides of the PZX triangle (Fig. 70) it would be necessary to enter them with the co-latitude PZ, the polar distance PX ($90° \pm$ declination) and the local hour angle ZPX. It is simpler for the user to find the latitude ($90° - PZ$), the declination ($90° - PX$ for declination 'same' name as latitude, or $PX - 90°$ for declination 'contrary' name to latitude), and the local hour angle. The arguments, therefore, are for these values and not for the actual sides of the PZX triangle.

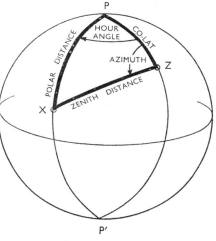

Fig. 70

Tabulated quantities

Solutions are tabulated on each opening of two facing pages of the tables. An example of an opening showing portions of the left- and right-hand page is given overleaf. The opening required for the working of a sight taken within a particular 8-degree zone of latitude, north or south, is found by the value of the LHA which is prominently displayed together with statements of Latitude and Declination 'SAME' or 'CONTRARY' name to indicate the appropriate page.

The LHAs on left-hand pages are always in the range of 0° to 90° and 360° to 270°, for latitude and declination of the SAME name. LHAs at the top of right-hand pages are always in the range of 0° to 90° and 360° to 270°, for latitude and declination of CONTRARY name. At the bottom of the right-hand pages the LHA values range from 180° to 90° and 180° to 270° for latitude and declination of SAME name.

The horizontal argument is latitude, each of the eight columns on a page being headed by an integral degree. The vertical argument is declination from 0° to 90°. The entry for declination should always be chosen as the integral degree less than or equal to the actual value; for example, if the actual declination is 68° 53', the declination entry is 68°. This is called the 'Tabulated Declination'.

Left-hand Page

Dec.	15° Hc	d	Z	16° Hc	d	Z	17° Hc	d	Z	18° Hc	d	Z	19° Hc	d	Z	20° Hc	d	Z	21° Hc	d	Z	22° Hc	d	Z	Dec.
0	30 47.3	+17.8	99.2	30 37.4	+18.9	99.8	30 26.9	+20.1	100.4	30 15.8	+21.2	100.9	30 04.2	+22.3	101.5	29 51.9	+23.4	102.1	29 39.1	+24.5	102.6	29 25.7	+25.6	103.2	0
1	31 05.1	17.2	98.1	30 56.3	18.4	98.7	30 47.0	19.5	99.3	30 37.0	20.7	99.8	30 26.5	21.8	100.4	30 15.3	22.9	101.0	30 03.6	24.0	101.6	29 51.3	25.0	102.1	1
2	31 22.3	16.6	97.0	31 14.7	17.8	97.6	31 06.5	19.0	98.2	30 57.7	20.1	98.8	30 48.3	21.2	99.3	30 38.2	22.4	99.9	30 27.6	23.4	100.5	30 16.3	24.6	101.1	2
3	31 38.9	16.0	95.8	31 32.5	17.2	96.4	31 25.5	18.3	97.0	31 17.8	19.5	97.7	31 09.5	20.7	98.3	31 00.6	21.8	98.8	31 14.0	23.0	99.4	30 40.9	24.0	100.0	3

Dec.	15° Hc	d	Z	16° Hc	d	Z	17° Hc	d	Z	18° Hc	d	Z	19° Hc	d	Z	20° Hc	d	Z	21° Hc	d	Z	22° Hc	d	Z	Dec.
87	16 05.5	31.1		17 34.4	31.3		19 05.2	31.2		19 34.2	31.1	2.7	20 34.2	31.1	2.7	21 34.1	31.1	2.7	22 34.0	31.0	2.8	23 34.0	31.0	2.8	87
88	16 34.4	31.2	2.7	17 34.4	31.4	2.7	18 34.3	31.2	2.7	19 03.1	31.4	1.8	20 03.1	31.3	1.8	21 03.0	31.4	1.8	22 03.0	31.4	1.8	23 03.0	31.4	1.8	88
89	16 03.2	31.5	1.8	17 03.1	31.4	1.8	18 03.1	31.7	0.9	19 31.7	31.7	0.9	20 03.1	31.7	0.9	21 31.6	31.6	0.9	22 31.6	31.6	0.9	22 31.6	31.6	0.9	89
90	15 00.0	-31.9	0.0	16 00.0	-31.9	0.0	17 00.0	-31.9	0.0	18 00.0	-31.9	0.0	19 00.0	-31.9	0.0	20 00.0	-31.9	0.0	21 00.0	-31.9	0.0	22 00.0	-31.9	0.0	90

Right-hand Page

Dec.	15° Hc	d	Z	16° Hc	d	Z	17° Hc	d	Z	18° Hc	d	Z	19° Hc	d	Z	20° Hc	d	Z	21° Hc	d	Z	22° Hc	d	Z	Dec.
0	30 47.3	+17.8	99.2	30 37.4	-19.5	99.8	30 26.9	-20.6	99.8	30 15.8	-21.7	100.0	30 04.2	-22.7	101.5	29 51.9	-23.9	102.1	29 39.1	-25.0	102.6	29 25.7	-26.1	103.2	0
1	30 28.9	18.9	100.3	30 17.9	20.0	100.9	30 06.3	21.2	101.4	29 54.1	22.3	102.0	29 41.3	23.8	102.6	29 28.0	24.4	103.1	29 14.1	25.5	103.7	28 59.6	26.5	104.2	1
2	30 10.0	19.5	101.4	29 57.9	20.6	102.0	29 45.1	21.6	102.5	29 31.8	22.7	103.1	29 18.0	23.8	103.6	29 03.6	24.9	104.2	28 48.6	25.9	104.7	28 33.1	26.9	105.2	2
3	29 50.5	20.0	102.5	29 37.3	21.1	103.0	29 23.5	22.2	103.6	29 09.1	23.3	104.1	28 54.2	24.4	104.7	28 38.7	25.4	105.2	28 22.7	26.4	105.7	28 06.2	27.5	106.2	3

Dec.	15° Hc	d	Z	16° Hc	d	Z	17° Hc	d	Z	18° Hc	d	Z	19° Hc	d	Z	20° Hc	d	Z	21° Hc	d	Z	22° Hc	d	Z	Dec.
87	12 51.3	32.4	3.5	13 51.4	32.5	3.5	14 51.1	32.5	3.5	16 23.6	32.6	3.5	16 56.9	32.7	3.5	17 23.5	32.7	2.7	19 23.4	32.5	2.7	20 23.3	32.5	2.7	87
88	13 23.7	32.3	2.6	14 23.7	32.3	2.6	15 23.6	32.4	2.6	16 23.6	32.3	2.6	17 23.5	32.4	2.7	18 23.4	32.5	2.7	19 23.4	32.4	2.7	20 23.3	32.5	2.7	88
89	13 56.0	32.1	1.7	14 56.0	32.1	1.8	15 56.0	32.1	1.8	16 55.9	32.2	1.8	17 55.9	32.2	1.8	18 55.9	32.2	1.8	19 55.8	32.3	1.8	20 55.8	32.3	1.8	89
90	14 28.1	31.9	0.9	15 28.1	31.9	0.9	16 28.1	31.9	0.9	17 28.1	31.9	0.9	18 28.1	31.9	0.9	19 28.1	31.9	0.9	20 28.1	31.9	0.9	21 28.1	31.9	0.9	90
90	15 00.0	+31.7	0.0	16 00.0	+31.7	0.0	17 00.0	+31.7	0.0	18 00.0	+31.7	0.0	19 00.0	+31.7	0.0	20 00.0	+31.7	0.0	21 00.0	+31.7	0.0	22 00.0	+31.6	0.0	90

For each combination of the arguments there are tabulated:

Altitude (Hc) to 0'·1,

Azimuth angle (Z) to 0°·1,

Difference (d) between the tabulated altitude for one declination entry and that for the next higher degree, to be used for interpolation as described later.

Azimuth is normally required only to the nearest half degree in sight work and is interpolated to the actual declination by inspection. The difference between successive tabulations of azimuth angle may be several degrees, and care is required in mental interpolation. The rules for converting tabulated azimuth (Z) to true bearing (Zn) differ according to the hemisphere, northern or southern, and the range of local hour angle; they are given on each opening at the top of the left-hand page and the bottom of the right.

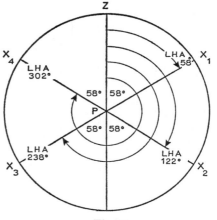

Fig. 71

It will be seen that there are four LHA values to an opening; these are the LHAs for bodies whose meridians make the same acute angle with the observer's meridian. This is demonstrated in Fig. 71, where the LHAs of four bodies, X_1 to X_4 are shown as 58°, 122°, 238°, and 302° (the values displayed in the example). The figure shows that for each body, the acute angle (ZPX) between its meridian and that of the observer is 58°. This quantity is used to compute all the solutions to the PZX triangles tabulated on that opening of the tables.

Each column of entries on right-hand pages contains a horizontal dividing line (not visible in the example) at which the tabulated altitude is zero. Above the line, the entries for latitude and declination of CONTRARY name, the altitude tabulations increasing in value up the column. Below the line, the tabulated altitudes increase downwards, the entries being for latitude and declination of SAME name. The dividing line appears as a series of steps across the columns of the right-hand page and indicates the degree of declination in which the horizon occurs. The entry for tabulated declination precludes ambiguity in extracting data above or below the dividing line. The data in the near vicinity of the dividing line need not concern the navigator, because the altitudes are too low for normal observation except in very high latitudes.

Use of Altitude instead of Zenith Distance

The intercept has been shown on page 86 to be the difference between the true and calculated zenith distances, and if it were convenient to calculate zenith distance this would be the best method of obtaining it. When making an observation by sextant the quantity obtained is the altitude, and a further subtraction is required to derive the zenith distance. It is convenient, therefore, to use altitude instead.

$$\text{Intercept} = \text{TZD} \sim \text{CZD}$$
$$= (90° - \text{True Alt.}) \sim (90° - \text{Calc.Alt.})$$
$$= \text{True Alt.} \sim \text{Calc.Alt.}$$

The intercept is thus also the difference between the true and calculated altitude (or tabulated when using tables). The sign of the intercept is now found to be:

> *away* if the true altitude is less,
> *towards* if the true altitude is greater.

The Chosen Positition

The altitude and azimuth can be found directly in the tables if they are entered with an integral degree of latitude, LHA and declination. If it could be arranged that this was possible, no interpolation would be necessary.

By working the sight from a position chosen so that the latitude is an integral degree and the longitude is such that the LHA of the body observed becomes an integral degree, interpolation, except that required for declination, is eliminated.

The possible errors arising from the use of a 'Chosen Position' of this nature will be discussed later, but they are almost always acceptable, because the simplicity of the method reduces the probability of errors arising through interpolation.

1. Choice of latitude. This offers no problem and should be the nearest whole degree to the DR. If the DR latitude is 46° 45′N, the sight is worked from latitude 47°N.

2. Choice of longitude. This can be quickly found, as the *Nautical Almanac* tabulates GHA in arc. If, for example, the DR longitude is 26° 38′W, and the GHA is 53° 18′·3, the longitude of the Chosen Position will be that nearest to 26° 38′W which makes the LHA a whole degree. Thus:

GHA	53° 18′·3
Chosen long.	26° 18′·3W −
LHA	27° 00′

Had the DR longitude been 26° 38′E:

GHA	53° 18′·3
Chosen long.	26° 41′·7E +
LHA	80° 00′

Had the DR longitude been 166° 38′E:

GHA	53° 18′·3
Chosen long.	166° 41′·7E +
LHA	220° 00′

If the DR longitude is 166° 38′W, i.e. greater than the GHA, 360° must be added to the GHA.

GHA	53° 18′·3
	+ 360°
	413° 18′·3
Chosen long.	166° 18′·3W−
LHA	247° 00′

If the DR longitude is East and the sum of the GHA and chosen longitude exceeds 360°, then 360° must be subtracted.

GHA	253° 18′·3
Chosen long.	166° 41′·7E+
	420° 00′·0
	− 360°
LHA	60° 00′

Interpolation Table

Computed values of altitude are tabulated in NP 401 for integral degrees of declination; therefore, as previously mentioned, interpolation is required for any excess minutes of declination.

The interpolation table, a portion of which is shown on page 95, has as its vertical argument the excess minutes of declination over the chosen tabulated declination. This is called the 'Declination Increase' (Dec.Inc.) and ranges from 0′·0 to 59′·9. The inside front cover of the tables and facing page provide for the range of Dec.Inc. 0′·0 to 31′·9, while the inside back cover and facing page provide for the range 28′·0 to 59′·9. The horizontal argument is the tabulated Altitude Difference, d, extracted from the body of the tables in minutes to 0′·1 with sign plus or minus. For convenience the d argument is divided into two parts: the first being multiples of 10 minutes of d from 10′ to 50′, the second, the remainder (units and decimals), in the range 0′·0 to 9′·9. The interpolation table for 'tens' of d comprises a column of values for each multiple of 10 minutes set against the vertical argument of Dec.Inc. For the 'remainder' the values are arranged in sub-tables against each range of one minute of Dec.Inc. (10 horizontal lines) with the decimal portion (·0 to ·9) as the vertical argument in each sub-table.

The interpolation correction for tens of d is extracted opposite the appropriate Dec.Inc. The correction for the remainder is found in the appropriate sub-table opposite the range of one minute in which the Dec.Inc. occurs. These corrections, known as first-difference corrections, are then applied to tabulated altitude in the same sense of the sign of d.

EXAMPLE

LHA of body	*302°*
Chosen latitude	*21°*N
Declination of body	*2° 28'·2*N
Chosen tabulated dec.	*2°* (same name)
Dec.Inc.	*28'·2*

The tables (page 90) are entered for latitude 21° and LHA 302°. For declination 2° (same name) the tabulated altitude (Hc) is found to be 30° 27'·6; d is $+23'·4$. Entering the interpolation table for Dec.Inc. 28'·2, the correction for tens of d (20') is 9'·4 (+). The correction for the remainder (3'·4) is 1'·6 (+).

Tab.Alt.	30° 27'·6	d	$+23'·4$
		Tens	20'
		Remainder	3'·4
First-diff corr^n (Tens)	$+9'·4$		
First-diff corr^n (Rem.)	$+1'·6$		
Corr. Tab. Alt.	30° 38'·6		

On occasions when the rate of change of altitude is large relative to one degree change in declination the quantity d will be changing rapidly and it may be necessary to make an additional interpolation correction known as the 'Double Second-Difference' (DSD) correction. This correction can be applied for special precision on any occasion, but to indicate when it is necessary to apply it in normal sight work the quantity d in the body of the tables is printed in italics followed by a dot.

Second differences are the differences between successive values of d, and these are not tabulated; thus the double second-difference has to be obtained mentally by determining the difference between the tabulated values for d immediately below and above the d for the chosen tabulated declination. Using the argument DSD in the column of the interpolation table headed 'Double Second Diff and Corr', the correction is taken from the critical table opposite the appropriate Dec.Inc. The DSD correction is always positive.

EXAMPLE

LHA of body	*29°*
Chosen latitude	*57°*N
Declination of body	*49° 35'·8N*
Chosen tabulated dec.	*49°* (*same name*)
Dec.Inc.	*35'·8*

Dec. Inc.	Tens 10'	20'	30'	40'	50'	Decimals	Units 0'	1'	2'	3'	4'	5'	6'	7'	8'	9'	Double Second Diff. and Corr.
28.0	4.6	9.3	14.0	18.6	23.3	.0	0.0	0.5	0.9	1.4	1.9	2.4	2.8	3.3	3.8	4.3	0.8
28.1	4.7	9.3	14.0	18.7	23.4	.1	0.0	0.5	1.0	1.5	1.9	2.4	2.9	3.4	3.8	4.3	2.4 0.1
28.2	4.7	9.4	14.1	18.8	23.5	.2	0.1	0.6	1.0	1.5	2.0	2.5	2.9	3.4	3.9	4.4	4.0 0.2
28.3	4.7	9.4	14.1	18.9	23.6	.3	0.1	0.6	1.1	1.6	2.0	2.5	3.0	3.5	3.9	4.4	5.6 0.3
28.4	4.7	9.5	14.2	18.9	23.7	.4	0.2	0.7	1.1	1.6	2.1	2.6	3.0	3.5	4.0	4.5	7.2 0.4
																	8.8 0.5
28.5	4.8	9.5	14.3	19.0	23.8	.5	0.2	0.7	1.2	1.7	2.1	2.6	3.1	3.6	4.0	4.5	10.4 0.6
28.6	4.8	9.5	14.3	19.1	23.8	.6	0.3	0.8	1.2	1.7	2.2	2.7	3.1	3.6	4.1	4.6	12.0 0.7
28.7	4.8	9.6	14.4	19.2	23.9	.7	0.3	0.8	1.3	1.8	2.2	2.7	3.2	3.7	4.1	4.6	13.6 0.8
28.8	4.8	9.6	14.4	19.2	24.0	.8	0.4	0.9	1.3	1.8	2.3	2.8	3.2	3.7	4.2	4.7	15.2 0.9
28.9	4.9	9.7	14.5	19.3	24.1	.9	0.4	0.9	1.4	1.9	2.3	2.8	3.3	3.8	4.2	4.7	14.8 1.0
34.0	5.6	11.3	17.0	22.6	28.3	.0	0.0	0.6	1.1	1.7	2.3	2.9	3.4	4.0	4.6	5.2	0.8
34.1	5.7	11.3	17.0	22.7	28.4	.1	0.1	0.6	1.2	1.8	2.4	2.9	3.5	4.1	4.7	5.2	2.5 0.1
34.2	5.7	11.4	17.1	22.8	28.5	.2	0.1	0.7	1.3	1.8	2.4	3.0	3.6	4.1	4.7	5.3	4.1 0.2
34.3	5.7	11.4	17.1	22.9	28.6	.3	0.2	0.7	1.3	1.9	2.5	3.0	3.6	4.2	4.8	5.3	5.8 0.3
34.4	5.7	11.5	17.2	22.9	28.7	.4	0.2	0.8	1.4	2.0	2.5	3.1	3.7	4.3	4.8	5.4	7.4 0.4
																	9.1 0.5
34.5	5.8	11.5	17.3	23.0	28.8	.5	0.3	0.9	1.4	2.0	2.6	3.2	3.7	4.3	4.9	5.5	10.7 0.6
34.6	5.8	11.5	17.3	23.1	28.8	.6	0.3	0.9	1.5	2.1	2.6	3.2	3.8	4.4	4.9	5.5	12.3 0.7
34.7	5.8	11.6	17.4	23.2	28.9	.7	0.4	1.0	1.6	2.1	2.7	3.3	3.9	4.4	5.0	5.6	14.0 0.8
34.8	5.8	11.6	17.4	23.2	29.0	.8	0.5	1.0	1.6	2.2	2.8	3.3	3.9	4.5	5.1	5.6	15.6 0.9
34.9	5.9	11.7	17.5	23.3	29.1	.9	0.5	1.1	1.7	2.2	2.8	3.4	4.0	4.5	5.1	5.7	17.3 1.0
																	18.9 1.1
35.0	5.8	11.6	17.5	23.3	29.1	.0	0.0	0.6	1.2	1.8	2.4	3.0	3.5	4.1	4.7	5.3	20.6 1.2
35.1	5.8	11.7	17.5	23.4	29.2	.1	0.1	0.7	1.2	1.8	2.4	3.0	3.6	4.2	4.8	5.4	22.2 1.3
35.2	5.8	11.7	17.6	23.4	29.3	.2	0.1	0.7	1.3	1.9	2.5	3.1	3.7	4.3	4.9	5.4	23.9 1.4
35.3	5.9	11.8	17.6	23.5	29.4	.3	0.2	0.8	1.4	2.0	2.5	3.1	3.7	4.3	4.9	5.5	25.5 1.5
35.4	5.9	11.8	17.7	23.6	29.5	.4	0.2	0.8	1.4	2.0	2.6	3.2	3.8	4.4	5.0	5.6	27.2 1.6
																	28.8 1.7
35.5	5.9	11.8	17.8	23.7	29.6	.5	0.3	0.9	1.5	2.1	2.7	3.3	3.8	4.4	5.0	5.6	30.4 1.8
35.6	5.9	11.9	17.8	23.7	29.7	.6	0.4	0.9	1.5	2.1	2.7	3.3	3.9	4.5	5.1	5.7	32.1 1.9
35.7	6.0	11.9	17.9	23.8	29.8	.7	0.4	1.0	1.6	2.2	2.8	3.4	4.0	4.6	5.1	5.7	33.7 2.0
35.8	6.0	12.0	17.9	23.9	29.9	.8	0.5	1.1	1.7	2.2	2.8	3.4	4.0	4.6	5.2	5.8	35.4 2.1
35.9	6.0	12.0	18.0	24.0	30.0	.9	0.5	1.1	1.7	2.3	2.9	3.5	4.1	4.7	5.3	5.9	
	10'	20'	30'	40'	50'		0'	1'	2'	3'	4'	5'	6'	7'	8'	9'	

The Double Second-Difference correction (Corr.) is always to be added to the tabulated altitude

From the body of the tables the tabulated altitude (Hc) is found to be 70° 59'·5; d is *34'·1·*, the italics and dot indicating that the DSD correction should be applied. Take the difference between the d on the line below that for the tabulated altitude (31'·9) and the d on the line above (36'·1) to obtain the DSD (31'·9 ∼ 36'·1 = 4'·2). From the interpolation table obtain the first-difference correction (tens and remainder) for Dec.Inc. 35'·8 and d + 34'·1, by the method previously described. Enter the critical table opposite Dec.Inc. 35'·8 with DSD 4'·2 to obtain the DSD correction 0'·3 (+).

Tab. Alt.	70° 59'·5	d	+34'·1	d (below) 31'·9
First-diff corr^n (Tens)	+17'·9	Tens	30'	d (above) 36'·1
First-diff corr^n (Rem.)	+ 2'·4	Rem.	4'·1	———
DSD corr^n	+ 0'·3			DSD 4'·2
Corr. Tab. Alt.	71° 20'·1			

EXAMPLE
of the use of the tables

An observer in DR 54° 45'N, 28° 45'W, obtains a true altitude of a heavenly body of 51° 08'·4. If the GHA of the body was 57° 38'·2 and the declination 22° 24'·6N, what is the intercept and true bearing and from what position are they plotted?

GHA	57° 38'·2
Chosen long.	28° 38'·2W
LHA to enter tables	29°
Chosen lat.	55°N
Declination	22° 24'·6N
Tabulated declination	22°
Dec.Inc.	24'·6

Tables are entered with:
   Latitude   55°
   LHA   29°   Latitude and Declination SAME name.
   Tab. Dec.   22°

The following is extracted:

Tabulated Altitude (Hc)	50° 32'·0	d	+53'·8
First-diff corrⁿ (Tens)	+20'·5	Tens	50'
First-diff. corrⁿ (Rem.)	+ 1'·6	Rem.	3'·8

Azimuth (Z)   135°·0
True Bearing (Z_n) = 360° − Z
                             (*Note* ii)

Corrected Tab.Alt.	50° 54'·1		
True Alt. (*Note* iii)	51° 08'·4	TB	= 225°

Intercept   14'·3 towards (*Note* iv) 225°

An intercept of 14'·3 is therefore plotted towards 225° from the chosen position 55°N, 28° 38'·2W.

Notes

(i) When actually working a sight the work should be laid out on a Sight Form, as shown in subsequent examples.

(ii) The appropriate rule for converting azimuth to true bearing is found on the page opening of the tables.

(iii) This is the sextant altitude corrected for IE, dip, refraction, semi-diameter and parallax from the *Nautical Almanac*.

(iv) 'Towards' is obtained as explained on page 92.

Summary of procedure for a sight worked from a Chosen Position using NP 401.

1. Choose a latitude nearest in whole degrees to the DR latitude.

2. Obtain the GHA of the observed body from the *Nautical Almanac*, and choose a longitude, nearest to the DR longitude, which will make the LHA a whole number of degrees.

3. Select the volume of the tables in which the chosen latitude is contained and the section covering the appropriate 8-degree zone of latitude.

4. Enter the section using the LHA to find the opening, and Latitude and Declination 'SAME' or 'CONTRARY' name to determine the right- or left-hand page.

5. Enter the column for chosen latitude opposite the tabulated declination and obtain tabulated altitude (Hc) and altitude difference (d). Obtain tabulated azimuth (Z) by interpolation to the actual declination. If d is printed in italics followed by a dot note that a DSD correction will be required (*see* 7).

6. From the rule printed at the top or bottom of the opening convert Z to true bearing (Zn).

7. Enter the interpolation table with the declination increase and tens and remainder of d to obtain the first-difference corrections. Obtain the DSD correction if required. Apply the corrections with the sign of d, except for the DSD correction which is always positive, to the tabulated altitude to obtain corrected tabulated altitude.

8. Compare the corrected tabulated altitude with the true altitude. The difference is the intercept, to be plotted from the Chosen Position (latitude as in 1, longitude as in 2), towards or away from the body whose true bearing is in 6.

EXAMPLE
of a Sun and Moon Sight

At 0947 (−4) on 10th December 1971, in DR 16° 50'N, 65° 42'E, the following observations were taken:

	Deck Watch Time	Sextant Altitude
Sun's Lower Limb	05ʰ 46ᵐ 16ˢ	42° 43'·8
Moon's Upper Limb	05ʰ 48ᵐ 13ˢ	29° 31'·0

Deck watch error 15ˢ fast on GMT. Index Error −2'·3. Height of eye 9·7 metres (32 feet).

Draw the position lines obtained.

For a reproduction of the Sight Form, showing the working of this example, see page 98.

The position lines are shown in Fig. 72, the Sun's intercept being plotted

	SUN – Lower limb	MOON – Upper limb
D.R. Position	16° 50′ N. 65° 42′ E	
Chosen Lat.	17′ N	
Body observed	SUN – Lower limb	MOON – Upper limb
Date and Z.T.	Dec. 1971 d 10 h 09 m 47	d h m
Zone	− 4	
Greenwich Date	10 05 47	
D.W.T.	h 05 m 46 s 16	h 05 m 48 s 13
D.W.E.	15 slow + fast −	15 slow + fast −
G.M.T.	05 46 01	05 47 58
Tabulated G.H.A.	256° 53.3′ v	340° 49.6′ v 16.8′ *
Increment	11° 30.3′	11° 26.7′
v corr? or S.H.A.	.	13.3
G.H.A.	268° 23.6′ ·	352° 29.6′
±360° if required		
Chosen Long.	65° 36.4′ W E. +	65° 30.4′ W E. +
L.H.A.	334° 00′ W.	418° 00′ W.
(360°−L.H.A. if req.)	E.	−360° E.
Tab. H.A.	334°	58°
Tabulated Dec.	22° 51.3′ S d 0.2	0° 49.3′ S d 13.4
d corr?	+ 0.2	+ 10.6
Dec.	22° 51.5′ S same	0° 59.9′ S same
Tab. Dec.	22° contrary	0° contrary
Dec. diff. / Dec. Inc.	51.5′	59.9′
Tab. Alt.	43° 25.5′ Δd d± −49.1	30° 26.9′ Δd d± −20.6
1st Alt. diff. ±	− 34.3′ 40′	− 20.0′ 20′
2nd Alt. diff. ±	− 7.8′ 9.1	− 0.6′ 0.6
Δd± / D.S. diff. +		
Corr. Tab. Alt.	42° 43.4′ Az. 146.7′ True Bg. 146½°	30° 06.3′ Az. 101.4′ True Bg. 258½°
Sextant Alt.	42° 43.8′ I.E. − 2.3′ Dip − 5.5′ *	29° 31.0′ I.E. − 2.3′ Dip − 5.5′ *
I.E. − Dip	− 7.8′ − 7.8′	− 7.8′ − 7.8′
Apparent Alt.	42° 36.0′	29° 23.2′
Corrections to } altitude	H.P. * + 15.2′	+ 59.2′ + 1.7′ H.P. 54.5 * − 30.0′
True Alt.	42° 51.2′	29° 54.1′
Corr. Tab. Alt.	42° 43.4′	30° 06.3′
Intercept	7.8′ to 146½° from	12.2′ to from 258½°

Example of Sun and Moon sight using NP 401

from *A*, 17°N, 65′ 36′·4E, and the Moon's from *B*, 17°N, 65° 30′·4E. These are the Chosen Positions in each case.

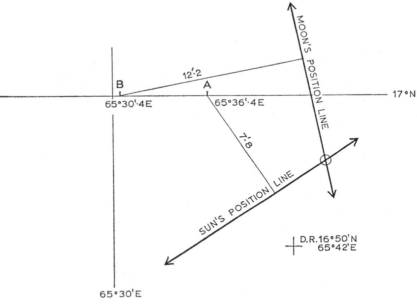

Fig. 72

Notes
  (i) No '*v* corrⁿ' is necessary for the Sun.
 (ii) For the Sun, Moon (and planets) the declination (called Tabulated Dec. on the form) and *d*, are copied from the *Nautical Almanac* at the same time as GHA and, for the Moon only, the horizontal parallax (HP) also.
(iii) The '*d* corrⁿ' should be extracted from the interpolation tables in the *Nautical Almanac* at the same time as the GHA increment and '*v* corrⁿ'.
 (iv) 'Tab. Dec.' is obtained as described on page 89 and is the vertical argument for entering NP 401.
  (v) '1st Alt.Diff. ±' and '2nd Alt.Diff. ±' refer to the 'Tens' and 'Rem.' first-difference corrections repectively, described on pages 93-95.

EXAMPLE
of Planet and Star Sight

At 1800 (+1) on 4th July, 1971, in DR 20° 55′S, 8° 48′W, the following observations were taken:

	Deck Watch Time	Sextant Altitude
Jupiter	06ʰ 58ᵐ 15ˢ	55° 05′·9
Arcturus	07ʰ 00ᵐ 37ˢ	47° 21′·9

Deck watch error 10ˢ slow on GMT. Index Error − 2′·3. Height of eye 9·7 metres (32 feet).
  Draw the position lines obtained.

	JUPITER	ARCTURUS
D.R. Position	20°55'S. 8°48'W	
Chosen Lat.	21'S	
Body observed	JUPITER	ARCTURUS
Date and Z.T.	July 1971 4ᵈ 18ʰ 00ᵐ	d h m
Zone	+ 1	
Greenwich Date	4 19 00	
D.W.T.	06ʰ 58ᵐ 15ˢ	07ʰ 00ᵐ 37ˢ
D.W.E.	10 slow + / fast	10 slow + / fast
G.M.T.	18 58 25	19 00 47
Tabulated G.H.A.	316° 57.8 v 2.6	207° 08.0 v *
Increment	14° 36.3	11.8
v corr. or S.H.A.	2.5	146° 24.3
G.H.A.	331° 36.6	353° 44.1
±360° if required		
Chosen Long.	8° 36.6 W.– / E.+	8° 44.1 W.– / E.+
L.H.A.	323° 00' W. / E.	345° 00' W. / E.
(360°—L.H.A. if req.)		
Tab. H.A.	323°	345°
Tabulated Dec.	18° 40.9 S d 0.0	19° 19.8 N d
d corr.	0.0	
Dec.	18° 40.9 S	19° 19.8 N
Tab. Dec.	18° same / contrary	19° same / contrary
Dec. diff. / Dec. Inc.	40.9	19.8
Tab. Alt.	55° 04.1 Δd d± +10.9	47° 23.3 Δd d± –56.1
1st Alt. diff.±	+ 6.9 10'	– 16.5 50'
2nd Alt. diff.±	+ 0.6 0.9	– 2.0 6.1
Δd± / D.S. diff.+		
Corr. Tab. Alt.	55° 11.6 Az. 87° / True Bg. 093°	47° 04.8 Az. 159.1 / True Bg. 021°
Sextant Alt.	55° 05.9 I.E. – 2.3 / Dip – 5.5 *	47° 21.9 I.E. – 2.3 / Dip – 5.5 *
I.E. – Dip	– 7.8 – 7.8	– 7.8 – 7.8
Apparent Alt.	54° 58.1	47° 14.1
Corrections to altitude	– 0.7 H.P.	– 0.9 H.P.
True Alt.	54° 57.4	47° 13.2
Corr. Tab. Alt.	55° 11.6	47° 04.8
Intercept	14.2 to from 093°	8.4 to from 021°

Example of a planet and star sight using NP 401

The worked example is shown on page 100. Fig. 73 shows the position lines, Jupiter's intercept being plotted from A, 21°S, 8° 36′·6W, and that of Arcturus from B, 21°S, 8° 44′·1W. These are the Chosen Positions.

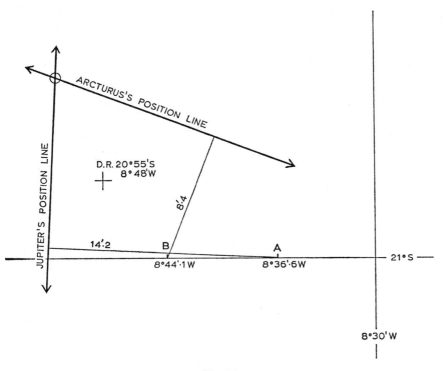

Fig. 73

Notes

(i) For the star, the 'Tabulated GHA' is the GHA Aries to which the star's SHA is added to give GHA.

(ii) The star's declination is copied from the *Nautical Almanac* at the same time as the SHA, and if the star is one of the selected 57 these quantities can be obtained directly from the daily pages; otherwise they must be obtained from the main star tables near the back of the book.

Sight Reduction Tables for Air Navigation (AP 3270)

These tables, designed for the rapid reduction of sights in air navigation, are also suitable for use at sea. They consist of three volumes of altitude and azimuth, Volume 1 being renewed about every five years, Volumes 2 and 3 being permanent. Volumes 2 (for latitudes 0°–39°) and 3 (for latitudes 40°–89°) provide for sights of the Sun, Moon and planets, using the same arguments (with a different layout) as NP 401. These volumes are described in Vol. III of the

Admiralty Manual of Navigation. AP 3270, Volume 1, contains tables, of which an extract is shown here, giving a selection of the seven best stars available for observation according to the observer's position and the time. Although NP 401 provides greater accuracy, much time and labour are saved by using AP 3270, Volume 1, provided stars can be observed that are among the selected seven.

LAT 42°S

LHA ♈	Hc Zn	Hc Zn	Hc Zn	Hc Zn	Hc · Zn	Hc Zn	Hc Zn
	*ARCTURUS	ANTARES	*RIGIL KENT.	ACHERNAR	CANOPUS	*Suhail	REGULUS
180	21 16 034	33 57 097	59 50 142	11 26 193	35 18 228	58 30 253	29 57 328
181	21 41 033	34 41 096	60 17 142	11 16 192	34 45 227	57 48 252	29 33 327
182	22 05 032	35 26 095	60 45 143	11 07 192	34 12 227	57 05 252	29 08 326
183	22 28 031	36 10 095	61 12 143	10 58 191	33 40 227	56 23 252	28 43 325
184	22 51 030	36 55 094	61 38 143	10 49 191	33 07 226	55 41 251	28 16 324
185	23 13 029	37 39 093	62 05 144	10 41 190	32 35 226	54 58 251	27 50 323
186	23 35 028	38 24 093	62 31 144	10 33 190	32 03 226	54 16 251	27 22 322
187	23 56 028	39 08 092	62 57 145	10 25 189	31 31 225	53 34 250	26 54 321
188	24 16 027	39 53 092	63 22 145	10 18 189	31 00 225	52 52 250	26 26 320
189	24 35 026	40 37 091	63 48 146	10 12 188	30 28 225	52 10 250	25 57 319
190	24 54 025	41 22 090	64 12 147	10 06 188	29 57 224	51 28 249	25 27 318
191	25 13 024	42 07 090	64 37 147	10 00 187	29 26 224	50 47 249	24 57 317
192	25 30 023	42 51 089	65 01 148	09 55 187	28 55 224	50 05 249	24 26 316
193	25 47 022	43 36 088	65 24 149	09 50 186	28 25 223	49 24 248	23 55 315
194	26 03 021	44 20 087	65 47 149	09 45 186	27 54 223	48 42 248	23 23 314
	*ARCTURUS	ANTARES	*Peacock	ACHERNAR	CANOPUS	*Suhail	REGULUS
195	26 18 020	45 05 087	24 33 146	09 41 185	27 24 222	48 01 248	22 51 313
196	26 33 019	45 49 086	24 59 145	09 37 184	26 54 222	47 20 247	22 18 312
197	26 47 018	46 34 085	25 24 145	09 34 184	26 25 222	46 39 247	21 45 312
198	27 00 017	47 18 085	25 50 145	09 31 183	25 55 221	45 58 247	21 12 311
199	27 12 015	48 03 084	26 16 144	09 29 183	25 26 221	45 17 246	20 38 310
200	27 23 014	48 47 083	26 42 144	09 27 182	24 57 220	44 36 246	20 03 309
201	27 34 013	49 31 082	27 08 144	09 25 182	24 28 220	43 55 246	19 28 308
202	27 44 012	50 15 081	27 35 143	09 24 181	23 59 220	43 15 245	18 53 307
203	27 53 011	50 59 081	28 02 143	09 24 181	22·· ·	·· 245	18 17 307
	·· ·· 010	51 43 080	28 29 142	··			·06

Extract from AP 3270 Volume 1

A reproduction of the Sight Form showing the working of an example is given on page 104. A more rapid method of sight reduction using AP 3270, Volume 1, is described in Chapter 23.

Arguments and tabulation

The entry arguments in Volume 1 are latitude and local hour angle of Aries, for which are tabulated the altitude (Hc) and true bearing (Zn) of the seven selected stars.

The pages are headed by integral degrees of latitude north or south. From 69° north to 69° south the tabulations for a single latitude occupy a complete opening of two facing pages. From 70° to 89°, north and south, tabulations for a single latitude occupy one page only.

The vertical argument is LHA Aries and ranges from 0° to 360° at intervals of 1°, except between latitudes 70° and 89°, where the entries are at intervals of 2°.

The seven selected stars for which latitude and true bearing are given remain the same over each 15° range of LHA Aries except on latitude-pages 70° to 89°, where the range is 30°. In both cases the seven selected stars remain the same for each group of 15 entries of LHA Aries. This can be seen in the extract, which also shows a typical change in the selection of stars from one group of entries to the next.

Each selection of seven stars is arranged from left to right in clockwise order of azimuths, and three stars in each selection are marked with an asterisk as being suitable for use in obtaining an observed position.

A total of forty-one stars is used in Volume 1, of which nineteen are first-magnitude (brighter than magnitude 1·5). The names of first-magnitude stars are given in capital letters.

Planning of observations

Latitude is chosen to the integral degree nearest the DR latitude of the proposed time of observation. GHA Aries is extracted from the *Nautical Almanac* and DR longitude applied to it to obtain LHA Aries. The tables are then entered with the chosen latitude to find the appropriate opening in which the entry for LHA Aries immediately gives the seven selected stars.

EXAMPLE

It is proposed to take stars at about 1715 (+2) on 4th July, 1971 in DR 42° 12'S, 29° 47'W. Find the stars available for working by AP 3270, Volume 1.

Chosen lat.	42°S
Tabulated GHA Aries (GMT 19^h)	207° 08'·0
Increment (15^m)	3° 45'·6
GHA Aries	210° 53'·6
Long.	29° 47'·0W
LHA Aries	181° 06'·6

Entering the tables for latitude 42°S, LHA Aries 181° (see extract) the selected stars are found to be: Arcturus, Antares, Rigil Kent, Achernar, Canopus, Suhail and Regulus.

Summary of procedure for a sight worked by AP 3270, Volume 1

1. Choose a latitude nearest in whole degrees to the DR latitude.
2. Obtain GHA Aries from the *Nautical Almanac* and choose a longitude, nearest to the DR longitude, which will make LHA Aries an integral degree.
3. Enter the tables with the chosen latitude, the value of LHA Aries found in 2 and the name of the star observed.
4. Extract the tabulated altitude (Hc) and the true bearing (Zn).
5. Compare the corrected sextant altitude with the tabulated altitude to obtain the intercept.

	ARCTURUS	RIGIL KENT
D.R. Position	42° 12′S 29° 47′W	
Chosen Lat.	42° S	
Body observed	ARCTURUS	RIGIL KENT
Date and Z.T.	July 1971 04^d 17^h 11^m	d h m
Zone	+2	
Greenwich Date	04 19 11	
D.W.T.	07^h 12^m 05^s	07^h 13^m 22^s
D.W.E.	10 slow + / fast −	10 slow + / fast −
G.M.T.	19 11 55	19 13 12
Tabulated G.H.A.	207° 08·0 v *	207° 08·0 v *
Increment	2° 59·2 *	3° 18·5 *
v corr. or S.H.A.	*	*
G.H.A.	210° 07·2	210° 26·5
±360° if required		
Chosen Long.	30° 07·2 W.− / E.+	29° 26·5 W.− / E.+
L.H.A.	180° 00′ W.	181° 00′ W.
(360°−L.H.A. if req.)	E.	E.
Tab. H.A.		
Tabulated Dec.	° ′ d *	° ′ d *
d corr.	*	*
Dec.		
Tab. Dec.	same / contrary	same / contrary
Dec. diff. / Dec. Inc.	° ′	° ′
Tab. Alt.	Δd d±	Δd d±
1st Alt. diff.±		
2nd Alt. diff.±		
Δd± / D.S. diff.+		
Corr. Tab. Alt.	21° 16′ Az. True Bg.− 034°	60° 17′ Az. True Bg.− 142°
Sextant Alt.	21° 24·9 I.E. +1·2 Dip − 5·8 *	60° 21·2 I.E. +1·2 Dip − 5·8
I.E. − Dip	− 4·6 − 4·6	− 4·6 − 4·6
Apparent Alt.	21° 20·3	60° 16·6
Corrections to altitude	− 2·5 H.P. *	− 0·6 H.P. *
True Alt.	21° 17·8	60° 16·0
Corr. Tab. Alt.	21° 16′	60° 17′
Intercept	1·8 to/from 034°	1·0 to/from 142°

Example of a star sight using AP 3270 Vol. 1

EXAMPLE

*At about 1715 (+2) on 4th July, 1971, in DR 42° 12'S, 29° 47'W, the
following observations were taken:*

	Deck Watch Time	Sextant Altitude
Arcturus	07ʰ 12ᵐ 05ˢ	21° 24'·9
Rigil Kent	07ʰ 13ᵐ 22ˢ	60° 21'·2

*Deck watch error 10ˢ fast on GMT. Index Error +1'·2. Height of eye 10·9 metres
(36 feet).*
Find the intercepts and true bearings.

The worked example is shown on page 104. The plotting of the sights to obtain
the position lines is done in the same way as shown in the previous examples.
A correction to allow for the effects of precession and nutation, terms explained
in Volume III, must be applied as a bearing and distance to a position line or
to an observed position (Chapter 14) for star sights worked by AP 3270. The
correction is obtained from the surface navigation version of the precession and
nutation correction tables supplied as a separate sheet with AP 3270. Towards
the end of the 5-yearly epoch for which Volume 1 of AP 3270 is produced the
correction may be as large as 5 miles, depending on the observer's latitude.

Accuracy of tables of computed altitude and azimuth

In NP 401 the tabular values for altitude have a maximum error of $\pm 0'·05$
and a probable (50%) error of $\pm 0'·025$. When second differences are completely
negligible, the maximum error of an interpolated altitude is $\pm 0'·19$ with a
probable error of $\pm 0'·04$. When the second differences are not negligible and
the DSD correction is included in the interpolation, the maximum error of the
calculated altitude will be $\pm 0'·31$, with a probable error of $\pm 0'·05$.

Although the errors arising from the use of the interpolation table are not
negligible in relation to the tabular accuracy of the tables, they can be generally
neglected in relation to the normal accuracy of sextant observations at sea.
The tabulated altitudes in AP 3270, Volume 1 are correct to 0'·5 and this is not
greatly in excess of observational errors that may arise. The absence of interpolation tables precludes further tabular errors.

In general, the probability of considerable error in altitude and azimuth
tables can be avoided by:

1. Restricting observations to altitudes below 65°.

2. Giving due caution to observations leading to long intercepts or large
   interpolating factors.

CHAPTER 11

Solution of Terrestrial Great-Circle Problems

The problems concerning great circles on the Earth's surface have been stated in Chapter 2. Their solution lies in the graphical methods given in Chapter 3, or in the logarithmic methods given in Volume III. It is, however, possible to solve these problems by applying a tabular method, using Tables of Computed Altitude and Azimuth, similar to that already employed for the celestial (*PZX*) triangle, to a sufficient degree of accuracy for practical purposes, thus avoiding laborious manipulation of logarithmic quantities.

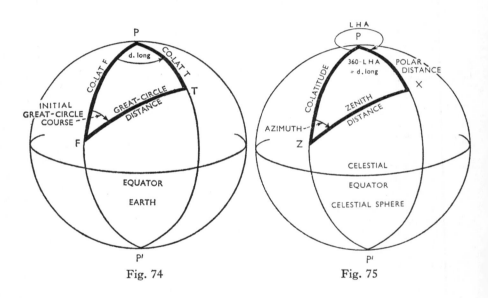

Fig. 74   Fig. 75

Figures 74 and 75 show that:

Earth		*Celestial Sphere*
Latitude of *F*	corresponds to	'Latitude' of observer's zenith (DR Lat.)
Latitude of *T*	corresponds to	Declination
d.long between *F* and *T*	corresponds to	Local hour angle/360° — LHA
Great-circle distance	corresponds to	Zenith distance (= 90° — Alt.)
Initial great-circle course	corresponds to	Azimuth

By entering NP401 with latitude of *F* for Latitude, d.long for LHA and the latitude of *T* for Declination, the great-circle distance can be obtained by sub-

106

tracting the tabulated altitude, Hc, from 90° (zenith distance on the celestial sphere) and converting the answer to minutes (=n.miles). The initial great-circle course is the tabulated azimuth angle, Z, converted to true bearing.

Note. Should the great-circle distance be greater than 90° it will be necessary to use 180° − d.long as LHA, adding 90° to Hc to obtain the distance and subtracting Z from 180° to obtain the course, as shown later.

If all the entering arguments are integral degrees, Hc and Z may be obtained directly from the tables without interpolation. If the latitude of T is in degrees and minutes, interpolation for minutes is done as in correcting Hc for any declination increment. Since all declinations appear on every page, the great-circle distance can always be found from that volume of the tables which covers the latitude belt containing the latitude of F.

If either the latitude of F or the d.long, or both, are non-integral, that is, in degrees and minutes, it will be necessary to interpolate graphically, using special diagrams provided in the tables. Instructions for using the diagrams are given in the Introduction to each volume.

Great-circle solutions belong in one of four categories or 'cases' as shown in the following table depending on whether the latitudes of F and T are of same or contrary name and on the great-circle distance being less or more than 5,400 n.miles (90°). It is always known if the latitudes of F and T are of same or contrary name, but whether the great-circle distance is less or greater than 90° may not be known. By testing Case 1 or Case 2 as appropriate, should no LHA entry be found for the Lat./Dec. argument then the distance must be greater than 90° and the solution will be by Case 3 or 4.

The initial great-circle course is obtained by naming Z (or 180° − Z) north or south according to the latitude of F, and east or west according to whether

	CASE 1	CASE 2	CASE 3	CASE 4
Name of Lat. F, T (N or S)	Same	Contrary	Same	Contrary
G–C Distance	< 90°	< 90°	> 90°	> 90°
ARGUMENT	TABULATED ARGUMENT			
Lat.F Lat.T	Lat. Dec. } Same	Lat. Dec. } Contrary	Lat. Dec. } Contrary	Lat. Dec. } Same
d.long	LHA	LHA	—	—
180° − d.long	—	—	LHA	LHA
SOLUTION	TABULATED SOLUTION			
G–C Distance	90° − Hc	90° − Hc	90° + Hc	90° + Hc
Initial G–C Course	Z	Z	180° − Z	180° − Z

the d.long is to the eastward or westward when moving from F to T. For example:
Case 1. Lat.F is North, d.long is East. Z is found to be 110°. Initial great-circle course is thus N110°E or 110°.
Case 4. Lat.F is South, d.long is West. Z is found to be 065°. Initial great-circle course is thus 180° − 065° = S115°W = 295°.

EXAMPLE 1

What is the great-circle distance between F, off Barentsburg (78° 04'N, 14° 14'E) and T, off Straumner (66° 25'N, 23° 08'W); and what is the initial great-circle course?

$$F \quad 78° 04'N \quad 14° 14'E$$
$$T \quad 66° 25'N \quad 23° 08'W$$

$$\text{d.long} \quad 37° 22'W$$

By inspection the great-circle distance is clearly less than 5,400 n.miles (90°) and as Lat.F and Lat.T are the same name the solution is Case 1.

The tables are entered for:

Lat. 78°	(Lat.F)	
LHA 37°	(d.long)	
Dec. 66° (same name)	(Lat.T)	
Dec.Inc. 25'		

	Hc	73° 58'·2	d (+) 53'·1	Z 117° (116°·8)
'Tens' Corr^n		20'·8	'Tens' 50'	
'Rem.' Corr^n		1'·3	'Rem.' 3'·1	

Hc interpolated for Dec.Inc. 74° 20'·3

Using the diagrams as described in the Introduction to the tables to interpolate for minutes of Lat.F (04') and minutes of d.long (22') the correction to Hc is found to be −6'·0, so that corrected Hc = 74° 14'·3. The great-circle distance is therefore 90° − Hc = 15° 45'·7 = 945·7 n.miles. The initial great-circle course is N117°W = 243°.

EXAMPLE 2

What is the great-circle distance between F, off Cape Bird (77° 08'S, 166° 30E') and T, off San Francisco (37° 49'N, 122° 25'W); and what is the initial great-circle course?

$$F \quad 77° 08'S \quad 166° 30'E$$
$$T \quad 37° 49'N \quad 122° 25'W$$

$$\text{d.long} \quad 71° 05'E$$

Lat.F and Lat.T are contrary name. It is not immediately evident that the great-circle distance is greater or less than 90°, therefore test in Case 2.

The tables are entered for:

Lat. 77°	(Lat.F)
LHA 71°	(d.long)
Dec. 37° (contrary name)	(Lat.T)
Dec.Inc. 49′	

It is found that these arguments are not available, therefore the great-circle distance must be greater than 90° and the solution is Case 4.

The tables are now entered for:

Lat. 77°	(Lat.F)
LHA 109°	(180° − d.long to nearest degree)
Dec. 37° (*same* name)	(Lat.T)
Dec.Inc. 49′	

Hc	31° 51′·8	d (+) 58′·1	Z 63° (62°·6)
'Tens' Corr^n	+40′·8	'Tens' 50′	
'Rem.' Corr^n	+6′·7	'Rem.' 8′·1	

Hc interpolated for Dec.Inc. 32° 39′·3

Using the diagrams to interpolate for minutes of Lat.F (08′) and d.long (in this case for 108° 55′) the correction to Hc is found to be +4′·8, hence the corrected Hc = 32° 44′·1. The great-circle distance is therefore 90° + 32° 44′·1 = 122° 44′·1 = 7,364 n.miles. The initial great-circle course is 180° − 63° = S117°E = 063°.

CHAPTER 12

Meridian Passage

In Chapter 6 it was seen that when the local hour angle of a heavenly body is 0° or 180°, the heavenly body is either due north or due south of the observer. Thus situated, it has a particular importance, because the position line obtained from it, being at right-angles to the bearing, lies along the parallel of latitude and gives the observer's latitude.

Upper Meridian Passage

This occurs when the body is on the observer's meridian, *PZP'* in Figs. 76a and 76b. The hour angle of the body is then 0°.

In the northern hemisphere the true bearing is 180° (Fig. 76a) or 000°, depending upon whether the latitude is greater or less than the declination (both with the same name). When the latitude and declination have opposite names, the bearing is 180° (Fig. 77a). In the southern hemisphere these bearings are reversed (Figs. 76b and 77b).

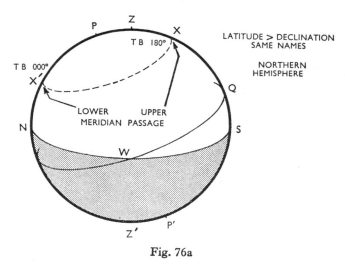

Fig. 76a

Lower Meridian Passage

This occurs when the body is on the meridian (*PZ'P'*) that differs in hour angle from the observer's meridian by 180°, and it is sometimes referred to as the 'meridian passage below the pole.' The hour angle of the body is then 180° and in the northern hemisphere, when the body is visible, the bearing is always 000°, no matter which is the larger, the declination or the latitude (Fig. 76a). In the southern hemisphere the bearing is always 180° (Fig. 76b).

When the latitude and declination have opposite names, lower meridian passage can never be observed, because the body is below the horizon.

110

Except in high latitudes, and even then for only part of the year, the Sun's lower meridian passage cannot be observed. The number of stars visible at lower meridian passage is, moreover, small. For these reasons the navigator is concerned chiefly with the upper passage, and unless otherwise stated the term 'meridian passage' always refers to the upper transit.

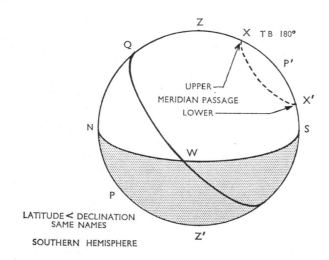

Fig. 76b

Maximum Altitude

In Figs. 76a and 76b, and in Fig. 77a, SX is the altitude of the heavenly body, and this is clearly the greatest altitude that the body can have, when measured by a stationary observer whose zenith is Z. To a stationary observer, the meridian

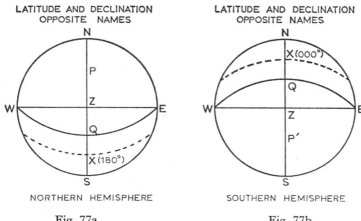

Fig. 77a

Fig. 77b

altitude is thus the maximum altitude, and in order to obtain it he has only to watch the heavenly body through the sextant telescope and note the altitude at the moment the heavenly body starts to dip. This, however, is difficult to do at any time, and moreover, the method would lead to 'appreciable error if it were employed by an observer in a ship moving in a direction other than east or west, because to an observer moving thus the Sun does not reach its greatest altitude at meridian passage.

Three factors govern the change in a heavenly body's altitude:

> the rotation of the Earth,
> the declination,
> the north–south component of the ship's movement.

The first of these factors ensures that, to an observer on the Earth, the body rises in the east, attains a maximum altitude, and then sets in the west.

The second factor does not, in practice, concern the navigator, because any change in declination, during the short period between meridian passage and the moment of greatest altitude, is too small to matter. Nevertheless, any change in declination means a change in the position of X relative to Z, and that is a change in altitude.

The third factor introduces a small but significant complication, because it is equivalent to a movement of Z. The Earth's rotation by itself would give the altitude its greatest value when the body reaches the meridian. If the ship is moving towards the body, however, the altitude will increase for a further period, until the rate at which the body is decreasing in altitude, due to the Earth's rotation, becomes equal to the rate at which the movement of the ship is increasing the altitude. The greatest altitude therefore occurs after meridian transit.

If the ship is moving away from the heavenly body, the greatest altitude occurs before meridian transit.

The time-difference between these two altitudes may lead to an error of 5′, if the ship's speed is high and her course approximately north or south. Only when the ship is steaming east or west will the greatest altitude occur at meridian passage.

Time of Meridian Passage

It is thus evident that a moving observer cannot as a rule take a meridian altitude by watching the heavenly body and noting when it starts to dip. Instead, he must work out the time when the heavenly body will be on his meridian, and take the altitude at that moment. This he can do by simple approximation, because the altitude changes slowly when the heavenly body is near the meridian, and an error of a few seconds in the calculated time of meridian passage makes no appreciable difference to the altitude. It is therefore customary to work out the time of meridian passage to the nearest minute.

The GMT at which the Sun crosses the meridian of Greenwich is tabulated for each day in the *Nautical Almanac*. The time of meridian passage of the four navigational planets is given for the middle day of the three days on the page, the times for intermediate days being determined by inspection. It is necessary, as will be shown later, to tabulate the time of the Moon's (upper and lower) meridian passage at the meridian of Greenwich for each day.

Meridian Passage of the Sun

No appreciable error is introduced if it is assumed that the Sun's apparent motion to the westward is exactly 15° of longitude per hour. The time of the Sun's transit at any meridian may therefore be found by applying the longitude (in units of time) to the GMT of transit at Greenwich, as tabulated in the *Nautical Almanac*, i.e., westerly longitude is added, easterly subtracted. For example:

What is the Zone time of the Sun's meridian passage on 3rd July 1971 in longitude 96° 04′W?

Meridian passage at Greenwich	1204 (from Almanac)
Longitude (96° 04′W)	0624 W
	———
GMT	1828 3rd July
Zone (+6)	−6
	———
Zone time	1228 (+6)
	———

It follows that the tabulation in the *Nautical Almanac* is also the local mean time of transit at any meridian, because:

$$GMT \pm Longitude = LMT$$

In a ship under way, however, the longitude of the ship at meridian passage will not be known exactly beforehand. It is necessary, nevertheless, to calculate the time of meridian passage before it occurs. A first approximation is obtained by using the ship's DR longitude. The ship's longitude at this approximate time of meridian passage can now be forecast and used to obtain a more accurate time of transit. This second approximation is normally accurate enough for navigational purposes, and it is not usually necessary to make a third approximation.

EXAMPLE

At ZT 0900 (+4) on 3rd July 1971 a ship was in position 30° 00′N, 62° 00′W, steaming on a course 300° at 15 knots. When will the Sun be on her meridian?

ZT	0900	3rd July
Zone	+4	
	———	
GD	1300	3rd July

First approximation

Meridian passage at Greenwich	1204 (from Almanac)
Longitude (62° 00′W)	0408 W
	——
GMT Meridian passage	1612 3rd July
Zone (+4)	−4
	——
Zone time	1212 (+4) 3rd July

The approximate run to meridian passage is therefore (12^h 12^m − 09^h 00^m) at 15 knots, that is 3^h 12^m at 15 knots, or 48 miles. This, on a chart, will be found to give a position of 30° 24′N, 62° 48′W. Alternatively, by traverse table for 48 miles, course 300°:

$$\text{d.lat} = 24'{\cdot}0\text{N} \quad \text{dep.} = 41'{\cdot}6\text{W}$$

$$\text{hence mean lat.} = 30°12'\text{N}$$

$$\therefore \quad \text{d.long} = 48'{\cdot}0\text{W}$$

The approximate longitude at meridian passage is therefore 62° 48′W. The time of meridian passage can now be calculated with this longitude.

Second approximation

Meridian passage at Greenwich	1204
Longitude (62° 48′W)	0411 W
	——
	1615 3rd July
Zone (+4)	−4
	——
Zone time	1215 (+4) 3rd July

The second approximation can be arrived at quickly by converting the difference of longitude (48′·0) into time (3^m) and applying directly to the Zone time. The change is westerly – in the direction of the Sun's apparent motion – and the 3^m must therefore be added. As before, the approximate time of meridian passage is 1215 (+4).

If extreme accuracy is required, a third approximation can be made, the run being taken for an interval of (12^h 15^m − 9^h 00^m) or 3^h 15^m instead of 3^h 12^m. The change of longitude in this three-minute difference is, however, of no importance to the navigator so far as it affects the calculated time of meridian passage. In practice he would avoid even a second approximation by taking his DR position from the chart and working from that to the nearest minute or half minute.

In the example just given the 1200 (+4) position is 30° 23′N, 62° 45′W, and the time of meridian passage found by using this longitude and working to the nearest minute is:

| Meridian passage at Greenwich | 1204 |
| Longitude | 0411 W |

| | 1615 3rd July |
| Zone (+4) | −4 |

| | |
| Zone time | 1215 (+4) 3rd July |

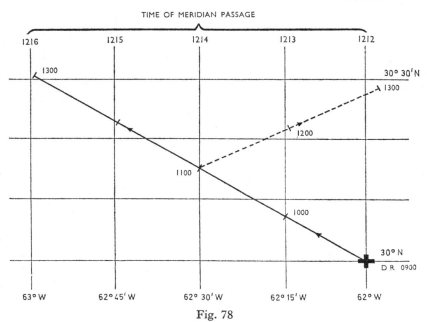

Fig. 78

Methods of successive approximation can be avoided altogether when the ship's track is being plotted on the chart. The Zone times of meridian passage for a few meridians in the vicinity of the ship's position are written against these meridians on the chart. The time when the Sun and ship are on the same meridian can then be obtained to the nearest half minute by inspection. Moreover, should unexpected alterations of course or speed be made before meridian passage, no fresh calculations are required; the new time is merely read off the chart.

Fig. 78 shows this method applied to the examples worked above.

Zone time of the Sun's meridian passage in longitude 62° 00′W is $12^h\ 04^m$ + $4^h\ 08^m$ − 4^h, or $12^h\ 12^m$.

The Sun is apparently moving westwards through 1° of longitude every four minutes, or through 15′ of longitude in one minute. The Sun will therefore cross the meridian 62° 15′W at 1213, the meridian 62° 30′W at 1214 and so on. These times are written against the corresponding meridians.

It is evident that if the ship maintains her present course and speed the Sun will be on her meridian at 1215 (+4).

Similarly, if the ship altered course to 065° at 1100, the Sun would be on her meridian at 1213 (+4).

Meridian Passage of the Moon

This is important for tidal prediction. The times of upper and lower meridian passage at Greenwich are given for each day of the year in the *Nautical Almanac*. In comparison with the Sun and stars, however, the rate of change of the Moon's sidereal hour angle is large and cannot be neglected. It cannot be assumed that its apparent motion to the westward is equal to 15° of longitude per hour, without introducing an appreciable error when its time of transit at meridians other than that of Greenwich is required.

It was shown on page 77 that the lunar day is longer than a mean solar day by an average of 50 minutes. This means that the Moon crosses an observer's meridian later each day by 50ᵐ on the average, and that once in a lunation it does not cross his meridian at all during the mean solar day. The exact difference in the times of transit at Greenwich is obtained by subtracting the time of transit on one day from the time of transit on the next. This difference varies between 39ᵐ and 64ᵐ.

The time of transit at Greenwich on 4th July 1971 is 20ʰ 51ᵐ. On 5th July it is 21ʰ 45ᵐ. The difference is 54ᵐ.

Fig. 79 shows the Moon and the Mean Sun on the Greenwich meridian at *A*. *B* is a place 75°W of *A*. When the rotation of the Earth has brought *B* to *A*, so that the Mean Sun is on the meridian of *B*, the Moon will have moved along its orbit to *C*.

While the whole 360° of longitude are passing under the Mean Sun, the Moon reaches *D*, and *AD* is a measure of the tabulated daily difference. *AC* will therefore be to *AD* in the

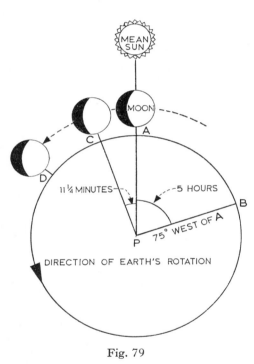

Fig. 79

ratio of the longitude of *B* to 360°. Thus:

$$\frac{AC}{AD} : \frac{75°}{360°}$$

i.e. $AC = \dfrac{75°}{360°} \times \text{(the daily difference)}$

If the daily difference is the 54^m already referred to, the Moon will cross the meridian of 75°W five hours after it crossed the Greenwich meridian plus an amount:

$$\frac{75}{360} \times 54^m$$

$$= 11\tfrac{1}{4}^m$$

The LMT of the transit at 75°W will therefore occur $11\tfrac{1}{4}^m$ after the LMT of the transit at Greenwich.

If B were 75°E of A the correction would have to be subtracted because meridian passage would occur at B before it occurred at A and the daily difference would have to be taken for the day in question and the previous day. The reason for this can be seen by considering the following table, which shows the local mean times of transits against the principal meridians.

DATE AND DAILY DIFFERENCE	MERIDIAN	CORRECTION	LMT OF TRANSIT
	Greenwich		2000
3rd July	90°W	$+12\tfrac{3}{4}^m$	$2012\tfrac{3}{4}$
(difference 51^m)	180°E (or W)	$+25\tfrac{1}{2}^m$	$2025\tfrac{1}{2}$
4th July	90°E	$-12\tfrac{3}{4}^m$	$2038\tfrac{1}{4}$
	Greenwich		2051
	90°W	$+13\tfrac{1}{4}^m$	$2104\tfrac{1}{4}$
(difference 54^m)	180°W	$+27^m$	2118
5th July	90°E	$-13\tfrac{1}{2}^m$	$2131\tfrac{1}{2}$
	Greenwich		2145

When transits are found with reference to the transit across the Greenwich meridian on 4th July, the daily difference involved is that between the 3rd and 4th for east longitudes, and the 4th and 5th for west longitudes. Hence the rules:

1. At a place in *West* longitude, meridian passage occurs *after* the transit at Greenwich, and a proportion of the difference between the times of the phenomenon on the day in question and the *next following* is *added* to the LMT at Greenwich to give the LMT on the observer's meridian.

2. At a place in *East* longitude, meridian passage occurs *before* the transit at Greenwich, and a proportion of the difference between the times of the

F

phenomenon on the day in question and the *preceding* day is *subtracted* from the LMT at Greenwich to give the LMT on the observer's meridian.

3. The proportion to be added or subtracted is always:

$$\frac{\text{longitude in degrees}}{360°} \times (\text{daily difference})$$

An interpolation table in the *Nautical Almanac*, when entered with longitude and daily difference, gives this proportion.

Zone Time of Moon's transit

The Zone time of the Moon's transit across any meridian can be found by converting the LMT of the phenomenon to GMT according to the ordinary rule: 'longitude west, Greenwich time best; longitude east, Greenwich time least.'

EXAMPLE 1

What is the Zone time of the Moon's meridian passage on 4th July, 1971, in 63° 30′ W?

LMT of transit at Greenwich	2051	4th July
Proportion of difference (from interpolation table, or 63½ × 54 ÷ 360)	+9½	
LMT of transit at 63° 30′W	2100½	4th July
Longitude	0414 W	
GMT of transit at 63° 30′W	0114½	5th July
Zone (+4)	−4	
ZT	2114½ (+4) 4th July	

EXAMPLE 2

What is the Zone time of the Moon's meridian passage on 4th July 1971, in 128° 15′ E?

LMT of transit at Greenwich	2051	4th July
Proportion of difference (from interpolation table, or 128¼ × 51 ÷ 360)	−18	
LMT of transit at 128° 15′E	2033	4th July
Longitude	0833 E	
GMT of transit at 128° 15′E	1200	4th July
Zone (−9)	+9	
ZT	2100 (−9) 4th July	

Meridian Passage of Aries

The time of meridian passage of the First Point of Aries over the Greenwich meridian is given in the daily pages of the *Nautical Almanac* for the middle day of the three days on the page. The interval between successive meridian passages is 23^h 56^m, so that times for intermediate days and other meridians can readily be derived.

The method of calculating the precise time of meridian passage on any day for any meridian is to find the GMT at which the LHA Aries is zero (or 360°).

Note that when converting the 'difference' (see examples) from arc to time, the interpolation table in the *Nautical Almanac* for increments to GHA Aries must be used.

EXAMPLES

What is the Zone time of meridian passage of Aries in longitude (a) 57° 51′W (b) 17° 02′E on 3rd July 1971?

| (a) LHA Aries | 000° 00′ |
| Longitude | 57° 51′W |

GHA Aries	057° 51′
Nearest GHA Aries for	
GMT whole hours (09)	055° 44′·2

| Difference | 2° 06′·8 = 08^m 26^s |

| GMT mer. passage | 09^h 08^m 26^s |
| Zone (+4) | −4 |

| ZT mer. passage Aries | 05   08   26 (+4) |

| (b) LHA Aries | 360° 00′ |
| Longitude | 17° 02′E |

GHA Aries	342° 58′
Nearest GHA Aries for	
GMT whole hours (04)	340° 31′·9

| Difference | 2° 26′·1 = 09^m 43^s |

| GMT mer. passage | 04^h 09^m 43^s |
| Zone (−1) | +1 |

| ZT mer. passage Aries | 05 ′09   43 (−1) |

In certain cases it may be doubtful which day should be be used for extracting the GHA Aries from the *Nautical Almanac*; this can easily be resolved by first finding the approximate GMT meridian passage of Aries at the required longitude.

EXAMPLE

What is the Zone time of meridian passage of Aries in longitude 154° 05′E on 4th July 1971?

Approx. LMT mer. passage Aries	0514	4th July
Longitude	1016E	
Approx. GMT mer. passage Aries	1858	3rd July

LHA Aries	360° 00′
Longitude	154° 05′E
GHA Aries	205° 55′
Nearest GHA Aries for	
GMT whole hours (19, July 3rd)	206° 08′·9

Difference	$13'·9 = 00^m 55^s$	
GMT mer. passage Aries	$18^h 59^m 05^s$	3rd July
Zone (−10)	+10	
ZT mer. passage Aries	04 59 05 (−10)	4th July

Meridian Passage of a Star

The method of calculating the precise time of meridian passage of a star on any day for any meridian is to find the GMT at which the sum of the LHA Aries and the SHA of the star is zero (i.e., LHA star = 0°).

EXAMPLES

What is the Zone time of meridian passage of Aldebaran in longitude 57° 51′W on 4th July 1971?

LHA Aries + SHA Aldebaran	= 360° 00′
SHA Aldebaran	291° 25′·9
LHA Aries	068° 34′·1
Longitude	057° 51′·0W
GHA Aries	126° 25′·1
Nearest GHA Aries for	
GMT whole hours (14)	131° 55′·7
Difference	$5° 30'·6 = 21^m 59^s$
GMT mer. passage Aldebaran	$13^h 38^m 01^s$
Zone (+4)	−4
ZT mer. passage Aldebaran	09 38 01 (+4) 4th July

What is the Zone time of meridian passage of Aldebaran in longitude 17° 02'E on 4th July 1971?

LHA Aries + SHA Aldebaran	= 360° 00'
SHA Aldebaran	291° 25'·9
LHA Aries	068° 34'·1
Longitude	017° 02'·0E
GHA Aries	051° 32'·1
Nearest GHA Aries for GMT whole hours (09)	056° 43'·3
Difference	5° 11'·2 = 20^m 41^s
GMT mer. passage Aldebaran	08^h 39^m 19^s
Zone (−1)	+1
ZT mer. passage Aldebaran	09 39 19 (−1) 4th July

In certain cases it may be doubtful which day should be used for extracting the GHA Aries from the *Nautical Almanac*. The time of meridian passage of the star occurs after that of Aries by an amount equal to 360° − SHA star. The approximate LMT of the meridian passage of the star can therefore be found and thence the approximate GMT at the required longitude.

What is the Zone time of meridian passage of Aldebaran in longitude 154° 05'E on 4th July 1971?

Approx. LMT mer. passage Aries	0514	4th July
360° − SHA Aldebaran = 068½°	= 0434	
Approx. LMT mer. passage Aldebaran	0948	4th July
Longitude	1016E	
Approx. GMT mer. passage Aldebaran in 154° 05'E	2332	3rd July
LHA Aries + SHA Aldebaran	= 360° 00'	
SHA Aldebaran	291° 25'·9	
LHA Aries	068° 34'·1	
	360° 00'	
	428° 34'·1	
Longitude	154° 05' E	
GHA Aries	274° 29'·1	

Nearest GHA Aries for GMT whole hours (00, July 4th)	$281° \; 21'\!\cdot\!2$
Difference	$6° \; 52'\!\cdot\!1 = 27^m \; 24^s$
GMT mer. passage Aldebaran	$23^h \; 32^m \; 36^s$ 3rd July
Zone (-10)	$+10$
ZT mer. passage Aldebaran	09 32 36 4th July

Lower Meridian Passage of a star

Should the time of a star's lower meridian passage be required, it can be calculated in the same way as the upper meridian passage except that the LHA of the star is 180° instead of 0° or 360°.

Meridian Passage of a planet

The times of meridian passages of the four navigational planets over the meridian of Greenwich are given in the daily pages of the *Nautical Almanac* for the middle day of the three days on the page. Times for intermediate days and meridians can readily be derived.

EXAMPLE

What is the approximate Zone time of meridian passage of Venus in longitude 76° 10'W on 4th July 1971?

LMT mer. passage	1100
Longitude	0505W
GMT	1605
Zone ($+5$)	-5
Approx. ZT mer. passage Venus	1105 ($+5$)

For normal navigational practice this approximation is sufficient, but it may be up to 3 minutes in error according to the daily differences in times of meridian passages. If a precise time of meridian passage is required, the same procedure should be followed as for Aries, i.e. finding the GMT at which the LHA of the planet is zero.

Practical application of Meridian Passages

The meridian passages of stars, planets and Moon have not the importance of that of the Sun, and in practice the navigator confines himself to stars and planets of convenient bearing and altitude at the time of morning and evening observations. If a planet or star happens to be on the meridian during the period of observation it is obviously advantageous to observe it at the time of meridian passage. The meridian passage of the two brighter planets Venus and Jupiter may well be observed during the day.

Altitude at Meridian Passage

Since the altitude at meridian passage is equal to 90° minus the zenith distance at meridian passage, the relations between latitude, declination and zenith distance must be examined.

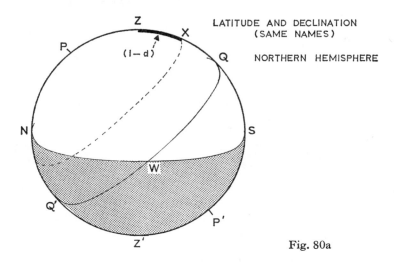

Fig. 80a

In Fig. 80a, where *the latitude is greater than the declination and of the same name*, PQ and ZS are each equal to 90°. Hence:

$$ZX = QZ - QX = \text{latitude} - \text{declination}.$$

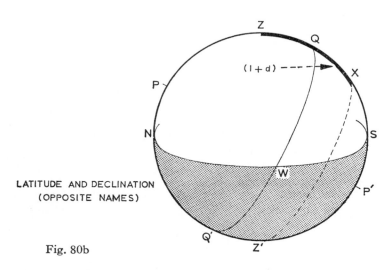

Fig. 80b

In Fig. 80b, where *the latitude and declination have opposite names:*

$$ZX = QZ + QX = \text{latitude} + \text{declination}.$$

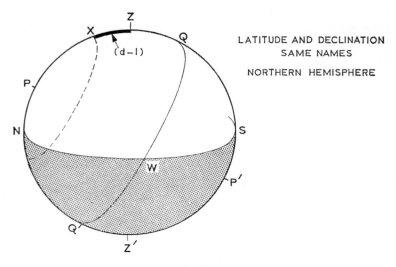

Fig. 81a

In Fig. 81a, where *the declination is greater than the latitude and of the same name*, the zenith distance is clearly given by:

$$ZX = \text{declination} - \text{latitude}.$$

That is, in combination:

$$\text{meridian zenith distance} = \text{latitude} \sim \text{declination}.$$

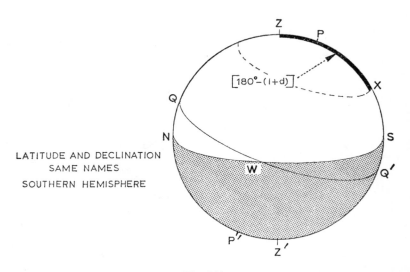

Fig. 81b

When the transit takes place below the pole (Fig. 81b):

$$ZX = 180° - (\text{latitude} + \text{declination}).$$

The altitude at upper transit is therefore:

$$90° - (l \sim d)$$

and at lower transit:

$$(l + d) - 90°.$$

Position Line from a Meridian Altitude

The actual position line is found from a meridian altitude in the same way as it is found from any other altitude. The advantage of the meridian altitude is that it avoids the labour of calculation. The latitude is found by application of the declination to the True Zenith Distance.

EXAMPLE

At ZT 1200 (+4) on 10th December 1971, in DR 30°N, 62° 00'W, the sextant meridian altitude of the Sun's lower limb was 37° 02'·6. The index error was − 0'·9 and the height of eye 14·6 m (48 ft). What was the latitude?

ZT	1200	10th Dec.
Zone	+4	
GD	1600	10th Dec.

This Greenwich date, which is approximately GMT, shows that the Sun's declination is 22° 53'·8S. Thus:

Sext.Alt.	37° 02'·6
IE	− 0'·9
Obs.Alt.	37° 01'·7
Dip	− 6'·7
App.Alt.	36° 55'·0
Corr^n	+ 15'·0
True Alt.	37° 10'·0
TZD	52° 50'·0
Dec.	22° 53'·8S
Latitude	29° 56'·2N

The latitude is therefore 29° 56'·2N, and the position line would appear on the plotting chart as shown in Fig. 82.

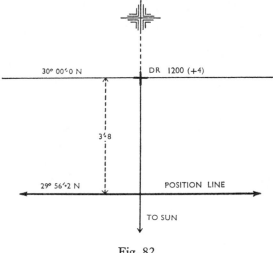

Fig. 82

Fig. 83 shows the relative positions of the principal points in the last example, and reference to it ensures that the declination is not applied the wrong way.

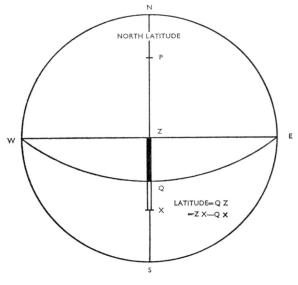

Fig. 83

The observer's latitude is given by:

$$QZ = ZX - QX$$
$$= \text{Zenith distance} - \text{declination.}$$

CHAPTER 13

Polaris, the Pole Star

Polaris (the Pole Star) is the name given to the second-magnitude star which lies close to the north celestial pole in the celestial sphere. If its position coincided with the north celestial pole, the problem of finding one's latitude in north latitudes would be easy, because the altitude of the pole is equal to latitude of the observer as shown on page 41. But the declination of Polaris, instead of being 90°N, as it would have to be for coincidence with the north celestial pole, is approximately 89°N. The polar distance is thus approximately 1°, and in the course of a day Polaris describes a small circle about the pole with that angular radius. The altitude of Polaris is thus not quite equal to the latitude of the observer.

Fig. 84 shows this small circle of angular radius p.

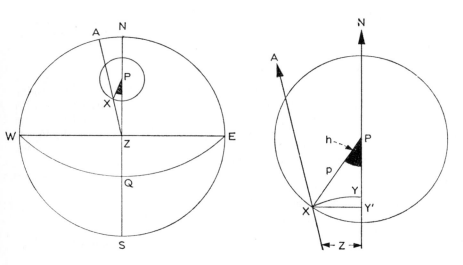

Fig. 84

Latitude by Polaris

When Polaris is at some position X, its altitude is AX, and the observer's latitude PN is given by:

$$PN = AX \pm PY$$

– where the position of Y is such that ZY is equal to ZX. For the situation depicted in Fig. 84, the minus sign must be taken.

The problem is therefore to find PY for any hour angle, because the length of PY clearly depends on the position of X, and the position of X depends on the hour angle.

The Polaris (Pole Star) Tables (*See extract opposite*)

Since the angular radius of the circle described about P is small, the arc XY approximates closely to the perpendicular XY', and the right-angled triangle PXY' is sufficiently small to be considered plane. Hence it follows that, as a first approximation:

$$PY = p \cos h$$

where h is the local hour angle of Polaris.

A first approximation to the observer's latitude is therefore given by:

$$PN = AX - p \cos h$$

where AX is the true altitude of Polaris.

$$\text{Now } h = \text{LHA Aries} + \text{SHA Polaris}$$
$$\text{or } h = \text{LHA Aries} + \text{constant.}$$

The *Nautical Almanac* tabulates three quantities, a_0, a_1 and a_2. Each of these quantities contains a constant to give it a positive value in all cases; the sum of these constants is $1°$. Hence:

$$\text{Latitude} = \text{True Altitude} + a_0 + a_1 + a_2 - 1°$$

Using the Polaris Tables, the table is entered with LHA Aries to determine the column to be used; each column refers to a range of $10°$. a_0 is taken, with interpolation if necessary, from the upper table with the unit of LHA Aries as argument. a_1 is taken from the second table with latitude as argument. a_2 is taken from the third table with month as argument. Interpolation for a_1 and a_2 is unnecessary because they are both small quantities.

Procedure for using Polaris Tables

This procedure may be set out in the following steps:

1. Correct the sextant altitude in the same way as the altitude of any other star is corrected.

2. From the deck watch time work out the local hour angle of Aries. Great accuracy is not required, since the maximum change of a_0 per degree is only $1'·0$. It is therefore sufficient to work to the nearest minute of time.

3. With this LHA Aries, take out a_0, interpolating as necessary.

4. Enter the second table in the same column with the latitude (to the nearest tabulated value), and take out a_1.

5. Enter the third table in the same column with the month, and take out a_2.

6. Add a_0, a_1 and a_2 to the true altitude and subtract $1°$. The result is the latitude.

POLARIS (POLE STAR) TABLES, 1971
FOR DETERMINING LATITUDE FROM SEXTANT ALTITUDE AND FOR AZIMUTH

L.H.A. ARIES	240°– 249°	250°– 259°	260°– 269°	270°– 279°	280°– 289°	290°– 299°	300°– 309°	310°– 319°	320°– 329°	330°– 339°	340°– 349°	350°– 359°
	a_0	a_0	a_0	a_0	a_0	a_0	a_0	a_0	a_0	a_0	a_0	a_0
0	1 44·3	1 39·3	1 33·1	1 25·9	1 17·8	1 09·2	1 00·2	0 51·2	0 42·4	0 34·1	0 26·5	0 20·0
1	43·8	38·7	32·4	25·1	17·0	08·3	0 59·3	50·3	41·6	33·3	25·8	19·4
2	43·4	38·1	31·7	24·3	16·2	07·4	58·4	49·4	40·7	32·5	25·1	18·8
3	42·9	37·6	31·0	23·5	15·3	06·5	57·5	48·5	39·9	31·7	24·5	18·2
4	42·4	37·0	30·3	22·8	14·4	05·6	56·6	47·7	39·0	31·0	23·8	17·6
5	1 41·9	1 36·3	1 29·6	1 22·0	1 13·6	1 04·7	0 55·7	0 46·8	0 38·2	0 30·2	0 23·1	0 17·1
6	41·4	35·7	28·9	21·1	12·7	03·9	54·8	45·9	37·4	29·5	22·5	16·6
7	40·9	35·1	28·1	20·3	11·8	03·0	53·9	45·0	36·5	28·7	21·8	16·0
8	40·4	34·4	27·4	19·5	11·0	02·1	53·0	44·2	35·7	28·0	21·2	15·5
9	39·8	33·8	26·6	18·7	10·1	01·1	52·1	43·3	34·9	27·3	20·6	15·0
10	1 39·3	1 33·1	1 25·9	1 17·8	1 09·2	1 00·2	0 51·2	0 42·4	0 34·1	0 26·5	0 20·0	0 14·6
Lat.	a_1	a_1	a_1	a_1	a_1	a_1	a_1	a_1	a_1	a_1	a_1	a_1
0	0·5	0·4	0·3	0·2	0·2	0·1	0·1	0·2	0·2	0·3	0·4	0·4
10	·5	·4	·3	·3	·2	·2	·2	·2	·3	·3	·4	·5
20	·5	·4	·4	·3	·3	·3	·3	·3	·3	·4	·4	·5
30	·5	·5	·4	·4	·4	·4	·4	·4	·4	·4	·5	·5
40	0·6	0·5	0·5	0·5	0·5	0·5	0·5	0·5	0·5	0·5	0·5	0·6
45	·6	·6	·6	·5	·5	·5	·5	·5	·5	·5	·6	·6
50	·6	·6	·6	·6	·6	·6	·6	·6	·6	·6	·6	·6
55	·6	·6	·7	·7	·7	·7	·7	·7	·7	·7	·6	·6
60	·7	·7	·7	·8	·8	·8	·8	·8	·8	·8	·7	·7
62	0·7	0·7	0·8	0·8	0·8	0·9	0·9	0·9	0·8	0·8	0·7	0·7
64	·7	·8	·8	·9	·9	0·9	0·9	0·9	0·9	·8	·8	·7
66	·7	·8	·9	0·9	1·0	1·0	1·0	1·0	0·9	·9	·8	·7
68	0·8	0·8	0·9	1·0	1·1	1·1	1·1	1·1	1·0	0·9	0·9	0·8
Month	a_2	a_2	a_2	a_2	a_2	a_2	a_2	a_2	a_2	a_2	a_2	a_2
Jan.	0·5	0·5	0·5	0·5	0·5	0·5	0·5	0·6	0·6	0·6	0·6	0·7
Feb.	·4	·4	·4	·4	·4	·4	·4	·4	·4	·5	·5	·6
Mar.	·4	·4	·3	·3	·3	·3	·3	·3	·3	·3	·4	·4
Apr.	0·5	0·4	0·4	0·3	0·3	0·2	0·2	0·2	0·2	0·2	0·2	0·3
May	·6	·6	·5	·4	·4	·3	·3	·2	·2	·2	·2	·2
June	·8	·7	·6	·6	·5	·4	·4	·3	·3	·2	·2	·2
July	0·9	0·8	0·8	0·7	0·7	0·6	0·5	0·5	0·4	0·3	0·3	0·3
Aug.	·9	·9	·9	·9	·8	·8	·7	·6	·6	·5	·5	·4
Sept.	·9	·9	·9	·9	·9	0·9	0·9	·8	·8	·7	·7	·6
Oct.	0·8	0·9	0·9	0·9	0·9	1·0	1·0	0·9	0·9	0·9	0·8	0·8
Nov.	·7	·7	·8	·9	·9	0·9	1·0	1·0	1·0	1·0	1·0	0·9
Dec.	0·5	0·6	0·7	0·7	0·8	0·9	0·9	1·0	1·0	1·0	1·0	1·0
Lat.	AZIMUTH											
0	0·5	0·6	0·7	0·8	0·8	0·9	0·9	0·8	0·8	0·7	0·6	0·5
20	0·5	0·6	0·7	0·8	0·9	0·9	0·9	0·9	0·8	0·8	0·7	0·5
40	0·6	0·8	0·9	1·0	1·1	1·1	1·1	1·1	1·0	0·9	0·8	0·7
50	0·7	0·9	1·1	1·2	1·3	1·3	1·3	1·3	1·2	1·1	1·0	0·8
55	0·8	1·0	1·2	1·3	1·4	1·5	1·5	1·5	1·4	1·3	1·1	0·9
62	0·9	1·2	1·4	1·5	1·6	1·7	1·7	1·7	1·6	1·5	1·3	1·0
65	1·1	1·4	1·6	1·8	1·9	2·0	2·0	2·0	1·9	1·7	1·5	1·2

Latitude = Apparent altitude (corrected for refraction) $-1° + a_0 + a_1 + a_2$

Extract from the *Nautical Almanac* (1971)

Because the azimuth of Polaris in latitudes suitable for observing the star itself (up to 70°N) does not exceed $2\frac{1}{2}$°, the position line may be taken as lying along the parallel of latitude.

EXAMPLE

At ZT 1548 (+2) on 9th December 1971, in DR 62° 11'N, 30° 47'W, the deck watch showed 05ʰ 47ᵐ 47ˢ when the sextant altitude of Polaris was 62° 22'·4. The index error was +2'·5, the height of eye 7·3 m (24 ft), and the deck watch was 12ˢ slow on GMT.

ZT	1548	
Z	+2	
GD	1748	9th Dec.

DWT	05ʰ	47ᵐ	47ˢ
DWE			12 slow +
GMT	17	47	59

GHA Aries	332° 47'·0
Inc.	12° 01'·7
	344° 48'·7
Longitude	30° 47'·0W
LHA Aries	314° 01'·7

Sext.Alt.	62° 22'·4
IE	+2'·5
Dip	−4'·8
Appt.Alt.	62° 20'·1
Corrⁿ	−0'·5
True Alt.	62° 19'·6
a_0	+47'·7
a_1	+ 0'·9
a_2	+ 1'·0
	63° 09'·2
	−1°
Latitude	62° 09'·2N

The position line is as shown
in Fig. 85.

Observation of
Polaris at Twilight

Since Polaris is not a particularly bright star (mag: 2·1), it
does not appear to the naked
eye until the horizon has become
indistinct in the gathering dusk.
An effective way of overcoming
this difficulty is to subtract a_0
from the DR latitude and
add 1°. If this approximate
altitude is set on the sextant,
the star will be visible in the
telescope long before the naked
eye can detect it, enabling an
observation to be taken while
the horizon is still good.

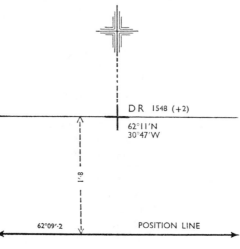

DR 1548 (+2)

62°11′N
30°47′W

62°09′·2

POSITION LINE

Fig. 85

Azimuth of Polaris

The *Nautical Almanac* gives a table of azimuth for latitudes from the equator
to 65°N, because these azimuths offer a ready means of checking the error of
the compass.

The azimuth of Polaris in the last example is N.1°·8E. That is, its bearing
is, for all practical purposes, 002°. If, at the moment the sight was taken,
Polaris bore 003° by compass, the compass would be reading 1° high.

CHAPTER 14

The Observed Position

In the explanation of the terrestrial position line given in Volume I it was stated that the use to which a position line can be put is independent of the source from which the line itself is obtained, because a position line does no more than tell the navigator that his position lies somewhere on it. A navigational fix requires at least two position lines.

The examples in this chapter are designed to show how the position of a moving ship can be found by observations of those heavenly bodies most familiar to navigators.

The reliance that can be placed upon the position obtained by a particular combination depends upon a number of factors; the method by which the sights are worked, the accuracy of the almanac from which the positions of the heavenly bodies are found, the precision with which the altitudes are measured, and the error involved in the estimation of any run between sights. Some of these factors have already been mentioned. All are discussed in Volume III. By taking 'simultaneous' sights during twilight the navigator clearly avoids the error that a long run between sights may introduce, and in addition he has the satisfaction of obtaining his position without delay. It should be remembered, however, that sights in practice may have to be taken singly whenever opportunity offers. A rapid method of reducing simultaneous star sights is described in Chapter 23.

DOUBLE SIGHTS

A double sight is one in which the position line obtained from the observation of a heavenly body is 'run on' and combined with a later observation of the same body (when its azimuth has changed through at least 45°) or with the observation of another body whose azimuth is suitable. A variety of double sights may be used:

1. Sun-run-Sun.

2. Sun-run-Sun's meridian altitude (or Sun's mer.alt.-run-Sun).

3. Sun-run-Moon (or Moon-run-Sun).

4. Venus or Jupiter-run-Sun (or Sun-run-Venus or Jupiter).
(Venus or Jupiter are frequently visible after sunrise and before sunset.)

The combination of an astronomical and a terrestrial position line may also be used under certain conditions to give an observed position.

The Sun-run-Sun's meridian altitude, type 2, is the most straightforward and common type of double sight; the following example shows the working.

EXAMPLE

*At 1047 (+3) 9th December 1971 in EP 00° 09′N, 51° 55′W, course 282°
and speed 26 knots, an observation of the Sun gave an intercept of 18′·2 away
from 137° using a Chosen Position on the equator in longitude 51° 48′·9. When
the Sun was on the meridian the true altitude was 66° 51′·4. Find the ship's position at the time of meridian altitude.*

1. To obtain the First Position Line

This is the normal procedure as already explained in Chapter 10, and the
position line is shown plotted in Fig. 86. The ship's position must be somewhere

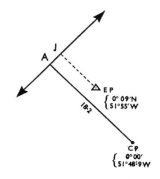

on the position line thus plotted. It is
clear however from the figure that the
Chosen Position (CP) from which the intercept is plotted is most unlikely to be the
best estimate of the ship's position, which
is of course the Estimated Position (EP) and
may in fact be many miles away.

Consider a ship in an EP 1° 23′N,
25° 30′W. An observation of, say, the
Sun worked from a chosen position of
1° 00′N, 25° 33′W gave an intercept of
30′·0 away from 130°. In Fig. 87, had
the ship's course been plotted on 280°
from position *J*, that point on the position line nearest to the EP, it would be
obvious that the ship was standing into

Fig. 86

danger. If, however, it had been plotted on from position *A*, the intersection of the intercept and position line, the navigator might well be
misled into believing that the ship would pass a safe distance from danger.

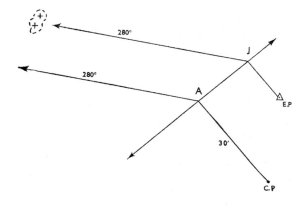

Fig. 87

It is recommended that the following procedure be adopted to avoid the above error. First plot the position line in the normal manner from the chosen position, then plot the EP and drop a perpendicular on to the position line from it to obtain the point *J*. The ship's position line is then run on from this point *J*.

It should be noted, however, that a better or safer position on this position line may be dictated by circumstances, and in this case that point would be used in preference to the point *J*.

The method of plotting point *J* presents no difficulty and it is recommended that this should be done rather than a difficult calculation by traverse table.

The result of this plotting is that the first intercept can be incorporated in the second EP, and the first position line can be transferred so as to pass through the second EP. Fig. 88 illustrates the general principle.

2. To find the Time of Meridian Passage

The time of meridian passage must be calculated before the run between sights can be found; this is done by the method explained in Chapter 12.

1st approximation

Meridian passage at Greenwich	1152
Longitude 52°W	0328W
GMT of meridian pass. in 52°W	1520
Zone (+3)	−3
ZT of meridian passage	1220 (+3)

The run to the time of meridian passage is $1^h 33^m$ (1047 to 1220) at 26 knots, or 40′·3, which, if plotted from point *J*, gives a longitude at 1220 of 52° 39′W.

2nd approximation

Meridian passage at Greenwich	1152
Longitude 52° 39′W	0331W
GMT of meridian pass. in 52° 39′W	1523
Zone (+3)	−3
ZT of meridian passage	1223 (+3)

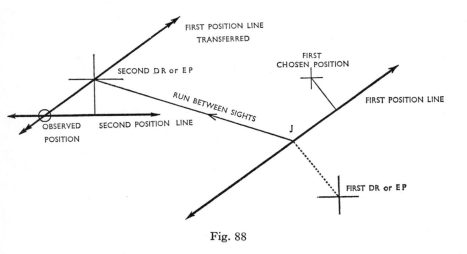

Fig. 88

3. To find the EP at 1223 (+3)

The run to the time of meridian passage should therefore have been 41′·6. Plotting this on a chart or mercatorial plotting sheet gives an EP at 1223 (+3) of 00° 24′N, 52° 40′·1W.

4. To find the Second Position Line (see Chapter 12)

ZT	1223	9th Dec.
Zone	+3	
GD	1523	9th Dec.
True Alt.	66° 51′·4	
TZD	23° 08′·6	
Dec.	22° 47′·9S	
Latitude	0° 20′·7N	

5. To combine the Two Position Lines

Fig. 89 shows the transferred position line *OB* and the second position line *JB*, cutting at *B*, the observed position. If using traverse table, the distances required are *OJ* (d.lat) and *BJ* (departure), both from the second EP, to give the observed position.

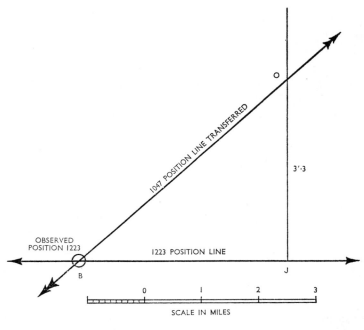

Fig. 89

From the chart, the observed position (*B*) will be found to be 0° 20′·7N 52° 43′·7W.

The Observed Position by Plotting Chart

Fig. 90 shows what the finished plot would look like on an ordinary chart, a mercatorial plotting sheet, or a plain plotting chart. The point *J* has been obtained as in (*1*) above. The only difference with a plotting chart is that as there is no longitude scale, the measurement of the final position must be obtained by converting the departure into d.long by use of the traverse tables (as explained in Chapter 1), or, if Chart 5004A is being used, by the latitude-longitude scale printed thereon, or any other convenient method.

The Observed Position by Traverse Table

In this case it is necessary to evaluate each run separately; from the chosen position to the point *A* in Fig. 87, and thence, allowing for the course and speed made good between observations, to a second position. It is emphasized that this second position is based on the chosen position used in calculating the first observation and is clearly not in itself a reliable estimate of the ship's position.

In practice a Mercator chart or mercatorial plotting sheet affords the quickest method of obtaining the observed position, because the longitude can be read

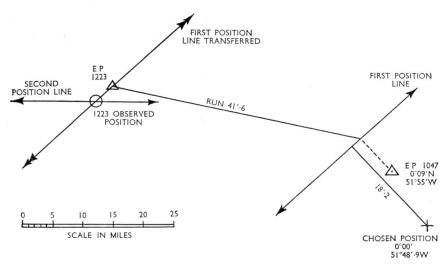

Fig. 90

directly without reference to departure. When plotting position lines on a Mercator chart, the accuracy is sufficient for most practical purposes in spite of the small scale.

SIMULTANEOUS SIGHTS

The word 'simultaneous' is commonly applied to sights which are taken at approximately the same time and which for that reason can be worked from the same DR. This does not mean that the interval which elapses between the observations of two separate stars can be ignored. If the ship is stopped or moving slowly, so that her run between the sights is negligible, then clearly no adjustment is necessary, but a fast-moving ship may cover an appreciable distance between sights, and the earlier position lines must be 'run on' accordingly, or all position lines adjusted to a particular time, in order to obtain an accurate observed position. The next example shows how this adjustment is made.

EXAMPLE

At 1650 (+2) DR 50° 07′N, 30° 47′W, course 070°, speed 25 knots, observations were found to give the following results:

Chosen Position	GMT	Body	Intercept
50°N, 30° 46′·3W	18^h 46^m 13^s	Moon	5′ away from 192°
„ 30° 18′·1W	18^h 47^m 55^s	Jupiter	11′ away from 162°
„ 30° 27′·8W	18^h 49^m 33^s	Aldebaran	11′ away from 090°

Find the position at 1650 (+2).

The use of sight reduction tables is in itself a source of small errors as previously explained; the position lines will not therefore necessarily meet in an exact point even if there are no other extraneous errors.

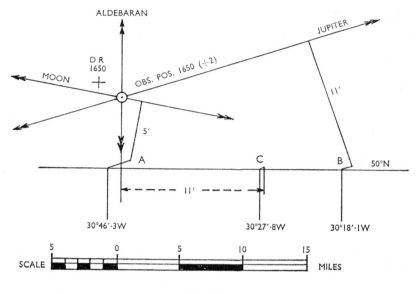

Fig. 91

Fig. 91 shows the plotting of the position lines obtained. From the GMTs of the observations it is seen that the Moon was actually observed at $1646\frac{1}{4}$ (+2).

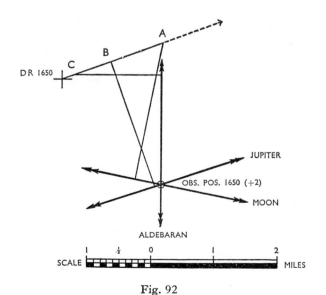

Fig. 92

The position is required at 1650 however, so that the position line must be run on for 3¾ minutes at 25 knots, or 1'·6; Jupiter's must be run on for 2 minutes, or 0'·8; and Aldebaran's for ½ minute or 0'·2.

In practice it is simplest to draw the Moon's intercept from a position A, 1'·6 on from the chosen position; that for Jupiter from a position B, 0'·8 on; and Aldebaran's from a position C, 0'·2 on.

From the figure, the observed position at 1650 (+2) is:

$$\begin{cases} 50° \ 05'·7N \\ 30° \ 44'·5W \end{cases}$$

Fig. 92 shows the process of plotting 'simultaneous' sights from the estimated position or DR position when the sights have been worked from that position using the haversine formula. Here the intercepts are plotted from the same position adjusted for the necessary run between the individual sights, and the points A, B and C referred to above are now all on the same line. This process slightly simplifies the plotting.

In this case the intercepts were:

Moon	2'·2	towards 191°
Jupiter	2'·1	towards 161°
Aldebaran	1'·4	towards 090°.

CHAPTER 15

Identification of Planets and Stars

THE SOLAR AND STELLAR SYSTEMS

The Sun, the Moon and the planets appear, to an observer on the Earth, to move against the fixed background of the stars. In addition to the Earth, the Sun is known to have eight large satellites. They are Mercury, Venus, Mars, Jupiter, Saturn, Uranus, Neptune and Pluto; but, as already stated, only four – Venus, Mars, Jupiter and Saturn – are sufficiently bright for navigational purposes. The number of small satellites and asteroids revolving about the Sun is known to be about 1,500.

The planets are relatively close to the Earth and shine with light reflected from the Sun. The stars transmit their own light from an immense distance. Of the 4,850 stars visible to the naked eye, only the brightest concern the navigator, and they amount to about 60.

Stellar magnitudes

It is customary to classify stars according to the amount of light received from them. Each star is given a magnitude, or measure of its relative brightness. This practice dates back to Hipparchus and Ptolemy, who arbitrarily graded the stars into six magnitudes. Stars of the sixth magnitude were those just visible to the naked eye. The discovery by Sir John Herschel in 1830 that a first-magnitude star is about one hundred times brighter than a sixth-magnitude star caused the Ptolemaic grading to be modified slightly, and now stars are graded according to the definition that a first-magnitude star is one from which the Earth receives one hundred times as much light as it receives from a sixth-magnitude star. By this definition a second-magnitude star is one hundred times brighter than a seventh-magnitude star; a third, one hundred times brighter than an eighth; and so on. Negative magnitudes are thus possible, because the star which is one hundred times brighter than a fifth-magnitude star must be of magnitude 0; and a star which is that amount brighter than a fourth-magnitude star must be of magnitude -1.

The Sun's magnitude is $-26 \cdot 7$, and the Moon's (at the full) is $-12 \cdot 5$.

The intervening magnitudes between 1 and 6 are found from a logarithmic scale, so that, if a is the numerical index of the quantity of light received:

$$a^6 : a : : 100 : 1$$
$$\text{i.e.} \quad a^5 = 100$$
$$\therefore \quad a = 2 \cdot 51$$

A first-magnitude star is therefore $2 \cdot 51$ times as bright as a second-magnitude star; $(2 \cdot 51)^2$ times as bright as one of third magnitude; $(2 \cdot 51)^3$ times as bright as one of fourth, and so on.

Vega, for example, with a magnitude of 0·1, is 2·51 times as bright as Aldebaran with a magnitude of 1·1; and Canopus, with a magnitude of −0·9, is two magnitudes brighter than Aldebaran. Sirius, the brightest star, has a magnitude of −1·6 and is 2·9 magnitudes brighter than Regulus (1·3). Sirius therefore gives $(2·51)^{2·9}$ or nearly 16 times the amount of light given by Regulus.

In practice, the first-magnitude stars are those brighter than magnitude 1. They are, in order of brightness, Sirius, Canopus, Rigil Kentaurus, Vega, Capella, Arcturus, Rigel, Procyon, Achernar, Hadar, Altair and Betelgeuse.

The few navigational planets and stars have magnitudes of about 2 and less. Stars brighter than magnitude 20 number about one thousand million.

THE NAVIGATIONAL PLANETS

The declinations of the four navigational planets rarely exceed the limits of 26°N and 26°S, and therefore an observer has a general idea about their positions in the sky. The mean distances of these planets and the Earth from the Sun are about:

Venus	—	67,000,000 miles
Earth	—	93,000,000 miles
Mars	—	142,000,000 miles
Jupiter	—	483,000,000 miles
Saturn	—	886,000,000 miles

Venus lies between the Earth and the Sun, and is therefore said to be an inferior planet. To an observer on the Earth it is never more than 47° removed from the Sun, for which reason it cannot be seen throughout the night in temperate latitudes. It is thus a 'morning or evening planet.' Its magnitude varies slightly, but is on the average −3·4. No other star or planet is so brilliant.

Mars, with an average magnitude of about −0·2, varies appreciably in brilliance, but is easily distinguished by its reddish light.

Jupiter has an average magnitude of −2·2 and ranks next to Venus in brilliance.

Saturn, with an average magnitude of 1·4, is not readily identified, and the methods of identification explained later in this chapter may have to be employed. Saturn's rings are not visible through the telescopes and binoculars normally used on the bridge.

THE CONSTELLATIONS

Of more general use to the navigator are the bright stars, because it is possible to identify them fairly quickly from the relative positions which they maintain. They appear mostly within certain well-defined constellations, and once the observer is able to pick out the key constellations he should have no difficulty in picking out the stars. At the same time, it should be remembered that these constellations still carry the fanciful names bestowed upon them by the earlier astronomers. These names give but little assistance to the student of the night sky, because the constellations seldom bear any resemblance to their classical descriptions.

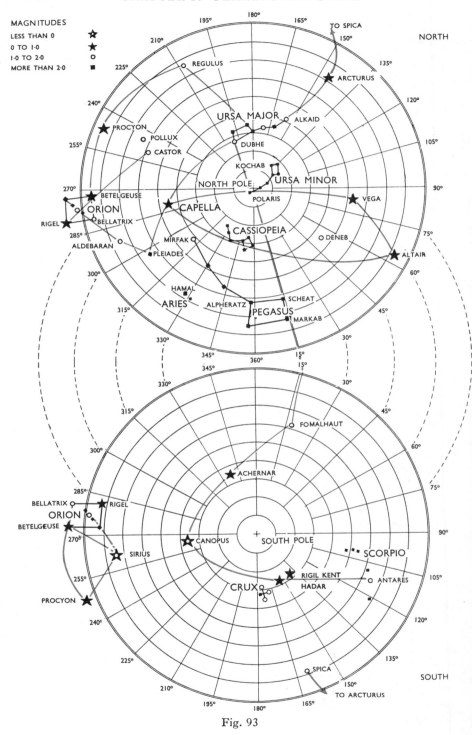

Fig. 93

The star charts in the *Nautical Almanac* show all the stars that are tabulated in the text and are likely to be used by the navigator.

Ursa Major or *The Great Bear*. This constellation is popularly known as *The Plough*, and it is important because a line drawn through its 'pointers' carries the eye to Polaris (the Pole Star). Fig. 93 shows the position of The Plough in relation to the other constellations, but it must be borne in mind that this position in the visible sky is not fixed. In the latitude of England the entire constellation is circumpolar, and below the pole it will appear as shown in Fig. 94a, whereas above the pole it will be as in Fig. 94b.

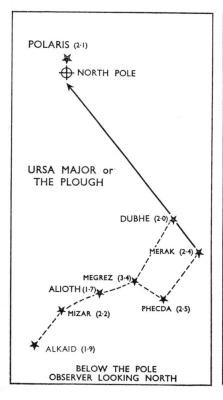

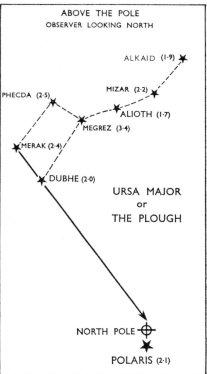

Fig. 94a   Fig. 94b

These charts also indicate why the two stars Dubhe and Merak are referred to as 'the pointers.'

Ursa Minor or *The Little Bear*. This is not unlike The Plough in shape, but to the navigator its sole claim to distinction lies in its possession of Polaris, which marks the tip of the handle of the 'plough.'

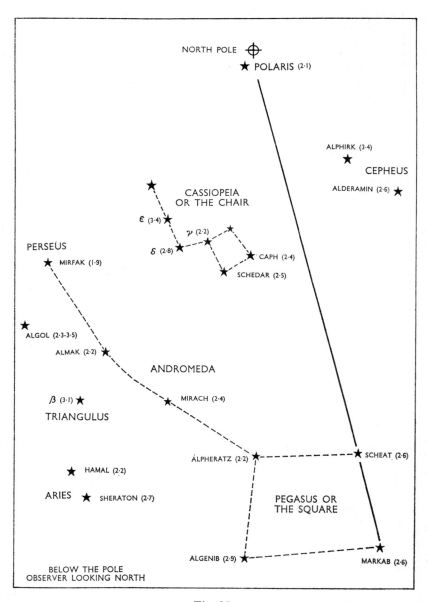

NORTH POLE

★ POLARIS (2·1)

ALPHIRK (3·4)
★

CEPHEUS

ALDERAMIN (2·6) ★

CASSIOPEIA
OR THE CHAIR

ε (3·4) ★

ν (2·2)

δ (2·8) ★

· CAPH (2·4)

PERSEUS

★ MIRFAK (1·9)

SCHEDAR (2·5)

ALGOL (2·3-3·5)
★

ALMAK (2·2) ★

ANDROMEDA

β (3·1) ★

MIRACH (2·4)

TRIANGULUS

ALPHERATZ (2·2) ★

SCHEAT (2·6)

HAMAL (2·2)

ARIES ★ SHERATON (2·7)

PEGASUS OR
THE SQUARE

ALGENIB (2·9) ★

MARKAB (2·6)

BELOW THE POLE
OBSERVER LOOKING NORTH

Fig. 95

Cassiopeia. This constellation – sometimes known as The Chair – is found on the side of the pole opposite to Ursa Major and about the same distance away. It does not contain any stars of first magnitude, but it is fairly prominent in the sky, and it is useful in helping to identify Pegasus as shown in Fig. 95.

Pegasus. This constellation (Fig. 95) – sometimes known as The Square (although the figure that is formed by joining the four principal stars would hardly have satisfied Euclid) – is useful to anybody wishing to obtain some idea of sidereal time, because the side formed by Alpheratz and Algenib lies almost on the meridian through the First Point of Aries.

Aries. The slowly accumulating result of the precession of the equinox described in Volume III is seen in the distance of the constellation Aries from the meridian through the First Point of Aries.

Orion. This important constellation, shown in Fig. 96, contains stars of north and south declination. It is supposed to resemble a 'giant,' and the three close

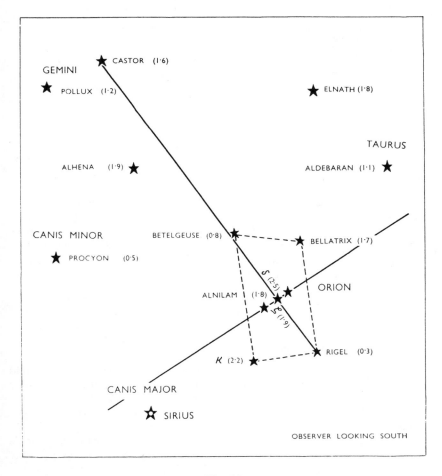

Fig. 96

stars in the centre of the constellation are referred to as Orion's Belt. The importance of this constellation lies in the signposts it affords the observer. The 'belt' points almost directly at Sirius, 'the dog star,' in the constellation of Canis Major or The Great Dog; and a line drawn through Rigel and its centre 'button' leads to Castor in the constellation of Gemini or The Twins.

The constellations of Canis Minor or The Little Dog (which contains Procyon) and Taurus or The Bull (which contains Aldebaran) lie close at hand, as shown in Fig. 96.

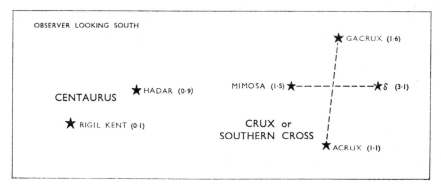

Fig. 97

Crux or *The Southern Cross*. This constellation (Fig. 97) only forms a cross if the observer imagines diagonal lines joining the four stars in it. Its significance is more poetic than navigational, and it is too far removed from the south celestial pole to be of any use in finding the observer's latitude directly, as may be done with Polaris in the northern hemisphere. Two bright stars in the constellation Centaurus help the observer to find it.

THE NAVIGATIONAL STARS

From his knowledge of the constellations just described, an observer should be able to pick out the navigational stars – if they are above the horizon – by referring them to imaginary lines in the celestial sphere.

Achernar (α *Eridani*, Mag. 0·6). This star lies midway between Canopus and Fomalhaut on the line joining them (Fig. 93).

Aldebaran (α *Tauri*, Mag. 1·1). This star can be fixed in relation to Orion's Belt, which points roughly at it in one direction and at Sirius in the other and lies almost midway between them (Fig. 96). Aldebaran is further distinguished by a reddish tint.

Altair (α *Aquilae*, Mag. 0·9). A line from Capella through Caph in Cassiopeia points to Altair, which also lies between two less bright but prominent stars in a line with Vega (Fig. 93).

Antares (α *Scorpii*, Mag. 1·2). This, another reddish star, lies at the centre of a small bow which points directly at another bow (Fig. 93).

Arcturus (α *Bootis*, Mag. 0·2). This is one of the brightest stars, and is found by continuing the curve of the Great Bear's 'tail' (Fig. 93).

Bellatrix (γ *Orionis*, Mag. 1·7). This is one of the three bright stars that mark corners of the quadrilateral in the constellation of Orion (Figs. 93 and 96).

Betelgeuse (α *Orionis*, Mag. 0·5–1·1). This is another of the three bright stars that mark corners of the quadrilateral in the constellation of Orion. It is easily identified by its reddish colour (Figs. 93 and 96).

Canopus (α *Carinae*, Mag. −0·9). Next to Sirius, Canopus is the brightest star. It lies about half-way between Sirius and the south celestial pole, and on the line joining Fomalhaut and Achernar (Fig. 93).

Capella (α *Aurigae*, Mag. 0·2). This bright star forms a rough equilateral triangle with Betelgeuse and Castor, about half-way between Orion and Polaris (Fig. 93).

Castor (α *Geminorum*, Mag. 1·6). A line from Rigel through the middle star of Orion's Belt points to Castor (Figs. 93 and 96).

Rigil Kent (α *Centauri*, Mag. 0·1), and Hadar (β *Centauri*, Mag. 0·9). These are two bright stars on the line joining Antares and Canopus (Fig. 93).

Fomalhaut (α *Piscis Australis*, Mag. 1·3). The line joining Scheat and Markab in Pegasus, produced away from Polaris, passes through Fomalhaut. (Fig. 93).

Polaris or *The Pole Star* (α *Ursae Minoris*, Mag. 2·1). A line through 'the pointers' of the Great Bear leads to this star, and the observer can easily verify that he has chosen the correct star by measuring its altitude, which is roughly his latitude (Figs. 93, 94a, 94b).

Pollux (β *Geminorum*, Mag. 1·2). This, as the name of the constellation suggests, will be seen close to Castor (Figs. 93 and 96).

Procyon (α *Canis Minoris*, Mag. 0·5). Procyon, Betelgeuse and Sirius form an equilateral triangle (Figs. 93 and 96).

Regulus (α *Leonis*, Mag. 1·3). A line from Bellatrix through Betelgeuse points to Regulus, which is about 60° from Betelgeuse (Fig. 93).

Rigel (β *Orionis*, Mag. 0·3). This is the third of the three bright stars that, together with κ *Orionis*, form the quadrilateral in the constellation of Orion (Figs. 93 and 96).

Sirius (α *Canis Majoris*, Mag. −1·6). Sirius is the brightest star. It lies to the south-east of Orion, approximately in a line with the 'belt' (Figs. 93 and 96).

Spica (α *Virginis*, Mag. 1·2). This bright star may be found by continuing the curve of the Great Bear's 'tail' through Arcturus, which lies about midway between the 'tail' and Spica (Fig. 93).

Vega (α *Lyrae*, Mag. 0·1). Vega is found by extending the line joining Capella to Polaris about an equal distance on the opposite side of the pole. Near Vega is a distinct 'W' of small stars (Fig. 93).

IDENTIFICATION OF STARS

In the practice of navigation, star sights are usually taken at morning and evening twilight when the horizon and only a few bright stars are visible at the same time. This means that there is usually no 'background' of constellations to assist the navigator in star identification. He must therefore find other methods.

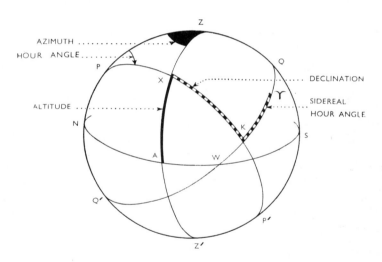

Fig. 98

The identity of a star is known when its sidereal hour angle (or right ascension) and declination are known, and the observer's task is to find these quantities from the star's bearing and altitude. In Fig. 98, for example, it is required to deduce ΥK (the sidereal hour angle) and KX (the declination) from AX (the altitude), the angle PZX (the azimuth) and the angle ZPX (which is the local hour angle found from the deck watch time).

Since $\Upsilon K = QK - Q\Upsilon = \text{LHA} - \text{LHA } \Upsilon$, the first step is to find the local hour angle of Aries.

The second step is to solve the triangle PZX in which PZ (the co-latitude), ZX ($90° -$ altitude) and the angle PZX (the azimuth) are known. This gives PZ and therefore KX, the declination.

The Star Globe (Fig. 99)

This instrument gives a mechanical solution of the problem. It is easy to use and offers by far the best method of identifying a star in the given circumstances. It is also most useful for choosing stars and planets suitable for observation as described in Chapter 18. It consists, principally, of a globe on which stars are shown in the places they occupy in the celestial sphere. Parallels of declination, the celestial equator, the ecliptic, and the celestial meridians at 15° intervals are also shown. The equator carries two scales: on the north side the scale of local hour angle of Aries in units of arc, on the south side the scale of right ascension in units of time.

The globe revolves about its polar axis in a vertical brass ring which is graduated in degrees and represents the observer's meridian. The meridian

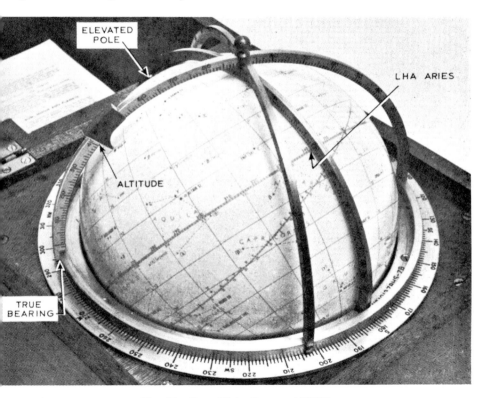

Fig. 99 Star Globe Pattern 160133

ring is supported in a grooved base-block in the bottom of the box which allows approximately one hemisphere of the globe to be seen. The meridian ring is held vertical by two slots cut in a horizontal ring (the azimuth ring) which is mounted on the box. The meridian ring and globe can be turned in the slots for setting the latitude. The outer edge of the azimuth ring is graduated in degrees. Over the globe is then fitted a hemispherical cage which rests on the azimuth ring and consists of four quadrants graduated in degrees and corresponding to circles of altitude; the observer's zenith lies at their point of intersection.

There are two patterns of star globe in service, Patt. 760 and Patt. 160133, both patterns giving the positions of stars for Epoch 1975. All new star globe outfits are Patt. 160133, as shown in Fig. 99, but Patt. 760 star globes will continue to be repaired and reissued by the makers, and navigators may be issued with either pattern from naval stores. The difference between the two patterns is in the circle on the globe represented by the inner edge of the azimuth ring. In Patt. 760 the inner edge of the ring represents the celestial horizon circle, 90° from the observer's zenith. In Patt. 160133 the globe is raised on its base-block by 6° of altitude, the inner edge of the azimuth ring representing a circle 6° below the horizon. As the limit of civil twilight is when the sun is 6° below the horizon and since the position of the sun on the globe is marked on the ecliptic for each day of the year, the Patt. 160133 globe can be set for morning or evening twilight without recourse to the *Nautical Almanac*. The procedure is clearly described in the instructions in the lid of the box. A similar procedure can be used with the Patt. 760 star globe, but the setting-up is more complicated and is not recommended.

To use the star globe:

1. Set the elevated pole to the latitude. The best method is to align an altitude quadrant with the meridian ring and set the elevated pole to the altitude on the quadrant corresponding to the latitude. Another method when using Patt. 760 is to elevate the pole until the meridian ring reads latitude against the inner edge of the azimuth ring; it should be noted that this method will give an incorrect setting when using Patt. 160133.

2. Revolve the globe until the computed local hour angle of Aries appears under the meridian ring. This quantity is the same as right ascension.

3. Turn the brass cage until one of the altitude quadrants lies along the observed true bearing of the body on the azimuth ring, and then move the small cursor along the quadrant to the required altitude.

The cursor will now indicate the star which has been observed, or, if no star is indicated, the position of the planet. The planet is identified by noting its right ascension (in degrees) on the scale at the equator, and its declination. By subtracting the RA from 360° the SHA is obtained. Inspection of planets' SHAs and declinations in the daily pages of the *Nautical Almanac* will show which one has been observed.

The following examples illustrate the use of the star globe. Fig. 99 shows the star globe set for Example 1.

EXAMPLE 1

At ZT 0400 (+1) on 4th July 1971, in DR 35°N, 15°W, the altitude of a bright body bearing 294° is 41°. What is it?

ZT	0400	4th July
Z	+1	
GD	0500	4th July
GHA Aries	356° 33'·5	
Longitude	15° 00'·0W	
LHA Aries	342° (to nearest whole degree)	

1. Elevate the north pole on the globe to correspond to latitude 35°.
2. Revolve the globe in the ring until the meridian marked 342° appears under the meridian ring.
3. Turn the brass cage until one of the altitude quadrants lies along true bearing 294° and then move the cursor along this quadrant to 41°. Vega lies under the cursor.

EXAMPLE 2

At ZT 1700 (−1) on 4th July 1971, in 45°S, 29°E, the altitude of a bright body bearing 068° is 46°. What is it?

ZT	1700	4th July
Z	−1	
GD	1600	4th July
GHA Aries	162°	
Longitude	29°E	
LHA Aries	191°	

1. Elevate the south pole on the globe to correspond to latitude 45°.
2. Revolve the globe in the ring until the meridian 191° appears under the meridian ring.
3. Adjust the brass cage to bearing 068° and the cursor to altitude 46°.

No bright star appears in the position indicated, and the body must therefore be a planet.

From the scale along the equator, its right ascension is seen to be 236°. The SHA is therefore 124°. Its declination is about 19°S. The *Nautical Almanac* shows that only Jupiter has a SHA and declination approximating to these values on that day.

G

In practice, the positions of the planets are plotted on the globe with a chinagraph pencil and their identities at once become obvious. By subtracting the tabulated SHA of a planet (given in the *Nautical Almanac*) from 360°, its RA can be quickly found. It will only be necessary to alter their positions at the following intervals:

> Jupiter and Saturn—every month
> Mars—every 2 weeks
> Venus—every week.

The Star Identifier

This affords both a visual and mechanical means of identifying stars and planets. It consists of a star chart, over which is superimposed a set of transparent grids, varying in latitude. On the chart are printed the navigational stars (and others for markers), and on the grid are rings of latitude and curves of azimuth. The edge of the chart is marked in LHA Aries for alignment with the meridian of the grids. When set up with the bearing and altitude of a star that has been observed, its name will be found printed on the star chart. If the positions of navigational planets are plotted on the star chart, they can be identified in the same way.

The Planet Diagram

The *Nautical Almanac* Planet Diagram shows in graphical form the local mean time of meridian passage of the Sun and the five planets Mercury, Venus, Mars, Jupiter and Saturn, together with lines showing the LMT of meridian passage of even-hour circles of right ascension (every 30° of SHA). The horizontal argument on the page is date, and the vertical argument local mean time.

A band on either side of the time of transit of the Sun is shaded to indicate the bodies within this area on a particular date which are too close to the Sun for observation. The lines joining the times of transit of the five planets are each drawn in a distinctive manner to avoid confusion.

The diagram is mainly intended for planning purposes when a star globe is not available, and gives, by simple entering with the date, the following information:

1. Whether a planet is observable on that day or whether it is too close to the Sun (within the shaded area).

2. The local mean time of meridian passage (when a meridian altitude sight will be available).

3. Whether it is a morning or evening star. A body in the bottom half of the diagram is a morning star, and one in the top half an evening star.

4. Whether or not it will be at a low altitude during twilight. When meridian passage is between 0^h and 2^h, the planet is observable low in the west during morning twilight. When meridian passage falls just below the shaded area, it is visible low in the east during morning twilight. When

meridian passage falls just above the shaded area, it is visible low in the west during evening twilight. When meridian passage is between 22^h and 24^h, the planet is observable low in the east during evening twilight.

5. Whether other planets are in the immediate vicinity, when care must be taken to avoid confusion.

6. The time of meridian passage of a star by inspection, if its SHA is known.

Navigators can, if they desire, plot in lines corresponding to particular stars and so determine the meridian passages of those stars immediately.

CHAPTER 16

The Rising and Setting of Heavenly Bodies

A knowledge of the rising and setting of heavenly bodies is essential to the navigator because, for one reason, the times at which he can take his star sights are governed by the times of sunrise and sunset. Also, certain naval operations require to be undertaken in total darkness: the navigator must therefore be able to find the times of beginning and end of twilight and of moonrise and moonset.

Theoretical rising and setting

Theoretical rising or setting occurs when the centre of the heavenly body is on the observer's celestial horizon, east or west of his meridian. At these times the true zenith distance is 90°.

Visible rising and setting

These phenomena occur when the upper limb of the heavenly body is just appearing above or disappearing below the observer's visible horizon. It will be shown later in this chapter that the Moon's centre lies practically on the celestial horizon at these moments; but when the Sun's centre lies there, the Sun itself appears appreciably above the visible horizon.

SUNRISE AND SUNSET

Visible sunrise and sunset

Visible sunrise or sunset occurs when the Sun's upper limb appears on the visible horizon. At this moment the observed altitude of the Sun's upper limb is 0° 00′.

True Altitude at Visible Sunrise and Sunset

By correcting this zero altitude, the true altitude and therefore the true zenith distance of the Sun's centre can be found. Thus, if the observer is assumed to have no height of eye, and the Sun's semi-diameter on the day is question is 16′·0:

Obs. Alt.	0° 00′·0	
Refraction	− 34′·0	
	− 0° 34′·0	
Semi-diameter	− 16′·0	
True altitude	− 0° 50′·0	

The true zenith distance is therefore taken as 90° 50'·0, and the Sun's centre is about 1° below the celestial horizon when its upper limb is just visible. For this reason visible sunrise occurs *before* theoretical sunrise, and visible sunset *after* theoretical sunset.

Times of Theoretical Sunrise and Sunset

These times are not usually required in the practice of navigation; but, if they should be, they can be found by solving the spherical triangle for the angle at the pole when the zenith distance is 90°. This angle is the LHA Sun at sunrise or sunset. Some of the earlier patterns of altitude–azimuth tables also give, at the foot of each column, the apparent times of rising and setting.

Times of Visible Sunrise and Sunset

The *Nautical Almanac* gives, on the right-hand pages, the times of sunrise and sunset for a range of latitudes from 60°S to 72°N. These times, which are given to the nearest minute, are strictly the GMT of the phenomena on the Greenwich meridian for the middle day of the three on each page. They are approximately the LMT of the corresponding phenomena on any other meridian and may be used for any of the three days on the page. Interpolation for latitude is done with the aid of Table 1 at the back of the *Nautical Almanac* using the nearest tabular latitude that is *less* than the true latitude.

EXAMPLE

What are the Zone times of sunrise and sunset in 61° 12'N, 33°W, on 10th December 1971?

	Sunrise	Sunset
LMT in 60°N, 33°W	0850	1455
Corr^n to 61° 12'N (Table 1)	+12	−12
LMT in 61° 12'N, 33°W	0902	1443
Longitude	0212W	0212W
GMT	1114	1655
Zone (+2)	−2	−2
Zone time	0914 (+2)	1455 (+2) 10th Dec.

To find precise times, interpolation is necessary. A proportion of the daily difference, depending on the longitude (expressed as a fraction of a day), is added/subtracted for W/E longitudes. Also, if the day is other than the middle day of the page, one-third of the tri-daily difference must be added or subtracted as appropriate. In high latitudes the tri-daily difference may exceed 15 minutes; therefore the effect of corrections for longitude and date may be considerable.

EXAMPLE

What is the Zone time of sunrise in 61° 12'N, 155°W, on 9th December 1971?

LMT for 60°N	0850	10th Dec.
LMT for 60°N	0845	7th Dec.
	————	
Tri-daily difference	5	earlier
	————	
LMT in 60°N, 0°E/W	0850	10th Dec.
Corr^n to 61° 12'N (Table 1)	+12	
Corr^n for long. $\frac{155}{360} \times \frac{1}{3} \times 5^m$	$+\frac{1}{2}$ (+ for long. W)	
Corr^n for date $\frac{1}{3} \times 5^m$	$-1\frac{1}{2}$	
	————	
LMT in 61° 12'N, 155°W	0901	9th Dec.
Longitude	1020W	
	————	
GMT	1921	9th Dec.
Zone (+10)	−10	
	————	
Zone time	0921 (+10)	9th Dec.

TWILIGHT

Twilight is that period of the day when, although the Sun is below the horizon, the observer is still receiving light reflected and scattered by the upper atmosphere. For convenience, this period is divided into three stages:

1. *Civil twilight.* This is said to end or begin when the Sun's centre is 6° below the celestial horizon, and it is roughly the time when the horizon begins to grow indistinct or become clear.

2. *Nautical twilight.* This is said to end or begin when the Sun's centre is 12° below the celestial horizon.

3. *Astronomical twilight.* This is said to end or begin when the Sun's centre is 18° below the celestial horizon, at which moment absolute darkness is assumed to begin or end so far as the Sun is concerned.

Tables of nautical twilight are given in the *Nautical Almanac.* They are used in exactly the same way as those for sunrise and sunset.

Duration of twilight

Morning twilight, whether civil, nautical or astronomical, begins when the Sun's centre is at the appropriate depression below the celestial horizon, and lasts until visible sunrise.

Evening twilight begins at visible sunset and lasts until these depressions are reached.

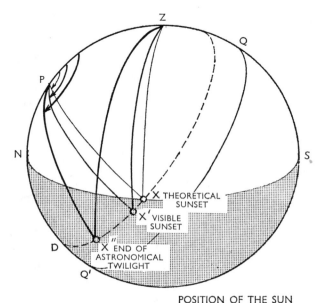

POSITION OF THE SUN

Fig. 100

Fig. 100 shows the relative positions of the Sun at theoretical and visible sunset, and at the end of astronomical twilight – X, X' and X'' being the positions; ZPX, ZPX' and ZPX'' the corresponding hour angles; and ZX (90°), ZX' (90° 50′) and ZX'' (108°) the zenith distances.

If the circle of declination does not fall 18° below the horizon, astronomical twilight does not end until sunrise the following morning. This occurs when the latitude and declination have the same name and their sum is not less than 72°.

In Fig. 100, PN is the latitude, DQ' the declination; and PQ' is 90°. Therefore, if $(PN + DQ')$ is greater than 72°, DN must be less than 18°.

Similar limits for civil and nautical twilights are obtained by writing 6° and 12° respectively, instead of 18°.

Since astronomical twilight lasts until the Sun's centre is 18° below the horizon, the actual duration of twilight depends on the angle which the Sun's path makes with the horizon. If that angle is small, as it must be in high latitudes

(Fig. 101a), twilight lasts considerably longer than it does in low latitudes where the angle is large (Fig. 101b). Thus twilight in the tropics usually lasts about an hour, but in the south of England at midsummer, for example, it lasts all night.

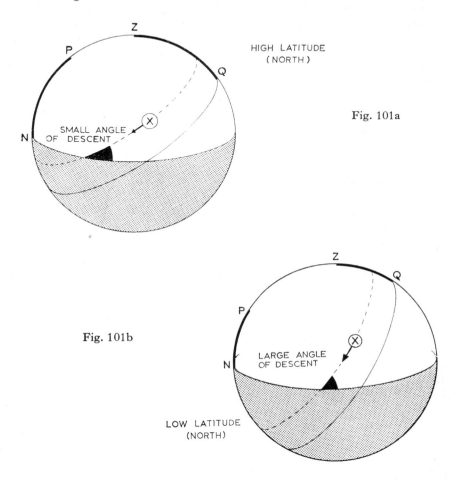

Fig. 101a

Fig. 101b

Artificial light becomes necessary for most purposes when the Sun is about 6° below the horizon.

The duration of twilight can be obtained from the tables, the difference being taken between the time of visible sunset and the end of twilight, or the beginning of twilight and sunrise; but it can be calculated, if necessary, because it is simply the angle $X'PX''$ (in Fig. 100), and that is the difference between the hour angles in the two triangles PZX' and PZX''.

'The Midnight Sun'

If the circle of declination does not reach the horizon the Sun can never set. In the northern hemisphere, the limiting latitude for this to occur is, from

Fig. 102, 90° minus the Sun's greatest northerly declination $(90° - 23\frac{1}{2}°)$N, that is, in $66\frac{1}{2}°$N, though in that latitude the Sun will remain above the horizon all night on one occasion only during the year.

For a similar reason, astronomical twilight will last all night on one night of the year in $(90° - 23\frac{1}{2}° - 18°)$N; that is, in $48\frac{1}{2}°$N.

These limits, with their names altered to south, also apply in southern latitudes.

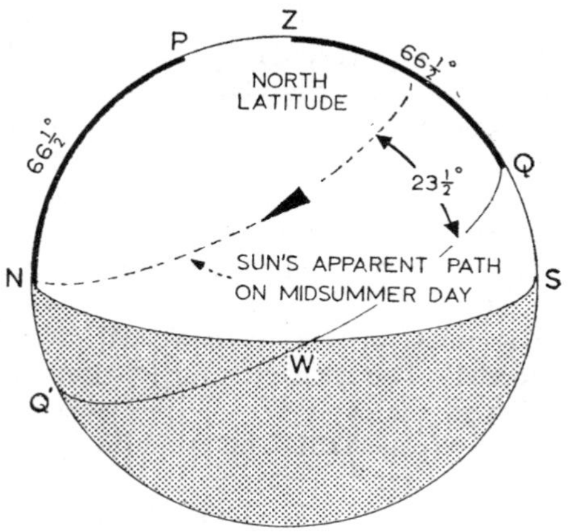

Fig. 102

Circumpolar bodies

Although every heavenly body is circumpolar in that, to an observer on the Earth, it describes a circle about the pole, the term 'circumpolar', when prefixed to a heavenly body, denotes that the heavenly body never sets and is always above the observer's horizon.

MOONRISE AND MOONSET

The times of moonrise and moonset may be found by solving the triangle *PZX* for the local hour angle in the same way as it can be solved for the Sun, but the calculation is even more laborious, the Moon's declination and sidereal hour angle are both changing so rapidly that a method of successive approximation must be employed in order to obtain the proper declination and Greenwich hour angle at the instant of moonrise or moonset. To avoid this, tables are incorporated in the *Nautical Almanac* giving the times, to an observer on the Greenwich meridian with no height of eye, when the Moon's upper limb is just touching the visible horizon.

At this instant the true altitude of the Moon's centre is approximately

Obs. Alt.	0° 00′
Refraction	− 34′
	− 0° 34′
Semi-diameter	− 16′
	− 0° 50′
Parallax (average)	+ 57′
True altitude	0° 07′

Therefore, when the Moon's upper limb is touching the visible horizon, the Moon's centre is roughly on the celestial horizon.

The exact LMT of moonrise and moonset on the Greenwich meridian is given for every day on the right-hand page of the *Nautical Almanac* and, in addition, the first day of the next page to help interpolation, for a range of latitudes between 72°N and 60°S.

Where no phenomenon occurs during a particular day (as happens once a month) the time of the phenomenon on the following day, increased by 24 hours, is given. For example, there is no moonrise in latitude 40°N on 9th December 1971. The time 2408 refers to the rising at 0008 on 10th December.

The LMT of moonrise and moonset cannot be considered constant for all longitudes – it must be corrected for the daily difference (at the latitude considered). The correction for longitude must be applied to the LMT at Greenwich in the same way as the correction is applied to the Moon's meridian passage (page 116). The proportion applied is:

$$\frac{\text{longitude in degrees}}{360°} \times (\text{daily difference})$$

When the observer is in *west* longitude, this proportion is *added* to the LMT of the phenomenon at Greenwich in order to give the LMT on the observer's meridian, and the difference is taken between the day in question and the next following. When the observer is in *east* longitude, this proportion is *subtracted* from the LMT of the phenomenon at Greenwich in order to give the LMT on the observer's meridian, and the difference is taken between the day in question and the preceding day.

Table II (interpolation of moonrise and moonset for longitude) at the back of the *Nautical Almanac* gives this proportion for arguments of longitude and daily difference.

EXAMPLE

What are the Zone times of moonrise and moonset on 11th December 1971, in 33° 27′ S, 125° 00′ E, and 76° 31′ W?

	Long. 125° 00′E		Long. 76° 31′W	
	Moonrise	*Moonset*	*Moonrise*	*Moonset*
LMT in 30°S	0037	1327	0037	1327
Lat. Corrⁿ	− 2	+ 3	− 2	+ 3
Long. Corrⁿ	− 9	− 19	+ 6	+ 12
Correct LMT	0026	1311	0041	1342
Long.	0820E	0820E	0506W	0506W
GMT	1606 (10th Dec.)	0451	0547	1848
Zone	+ 8	+ 8	− 5	−5
Zone time (11th Dec.)	0006 (−8)	1251 (−8)	0047 (+5)	1348(+5)

HIGH LATITUDES

Rising and Setting Diagrams for High Northern Latitudes (NP 90) are available for finding the LMT of sunrise, sunset, all the twilights, moonrise and moonset in latitudes above 70°N, with an accuracy of about 10 minutes.

CHAPTER 17

The Marine Sextant

The sextant is so called because the length of its graduated arc is about one-sixth of a circle. The principle on which the sextant is built is that if a ray of light is reflected twice in the same plane by two plane mirrors, the angle between the first and the last directions of the ray is twice the angle between the mirrors. For this reason the arc of the sextant is graduated up to 120°. The proof of this principle is given in Volume III.

DESCRIPTION

The two types of sextant in use are the 'micrometer' sextant and the now obsolescent 'vernier' sextant. The difference between the two types consists mainly in the method of measuring and reading the scales, as later described. The great advantage of the micrometer sextant lies in its clearness and in the speed and ease with which it can be read without a microscope under poor light. On the other hand the vernier sextant is no less accurate, and, having fewer moving and wearing parts, it may be expected to remain in adjustment for a longer period.

Fig. 103 illustrates a micrometer sextant; the instrument consists of:

The *main frame*, one edge of which is the *arc*.

An arm called the *index bar*, which can rotate about the centre of the arc.

A small frame mounted on the index bar over the centre of the arc; it carries a mirror called the *index glass*.

A small frame, mounted perpendicular to the main frame, in which is fitted a mirror called the *horizon glass*, the left half of which is unsilvered.

The arc is graduated in degrees, and so arranged that when the index glass is parallel to the horizon glass, the *index mark* on the index bar should point to the zero on the scale. The graduations are continued over a small arc on the other side of the zero; this is called the 'arc of excess' and angles read on this part are said to be 'off' the arc.

The index bar can be set to any position on the arc by means of the *clamp*; this releases or engages a worm thread in the teeth of a rack that extends along the entire periphery of the arc. When clamped, the index bar can be given a slow motion along the arc in either direction by turning the *micrometer drum* which rotates the worm in the rack. With this arrangement it is the worm and rack that govern the accuracy of the setting. One rotation of the drum moves the index bar one degree along the arc. When reading the sextant, the engravings on the arc are read against the index mark to the nearest whole degree, while the drum provides the intermediate reading for minutes. In Fig. 103 the setting may be seen to read $48° 04' \cdot 2$.

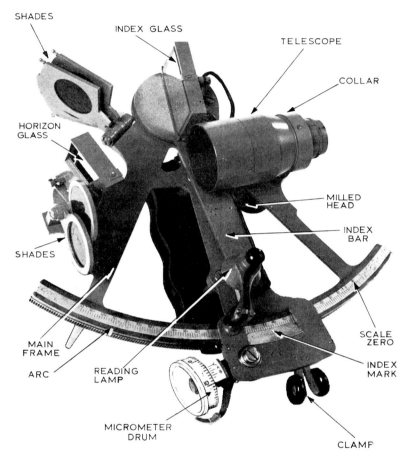

SHADES

INDEX GLASS

TELESCOPE

COLLAR

HORIZON
GLASS

MILLED
HEAD

INDEX
BAR

SHADES

SCALE
ZERO

MAIN
FRAME

INDEX
MARK

ARC

READING
LAMP

MICROMETER
DRUM

CLAMP

Fig. 103

Measurements on the vernier sextant (Fig. 104) are made on the engraved arc, the endless worm of the *tangent screw* providing only slow motion for fine adjustment of the *vernier*, which will be mentioned later.

The *telescope* is carried in a *collar*, which can be raised or lowered by means of a *milled head* beneath the frame. In the normal position of the telescope, equal parts of the silvered and unsilvered halves of the horizon glass should be visible. The action of raising or lowering the telescope regulates the brilliance of the reflected image, which will be greatest when the telescope is screwed hard down. As the telescope is raised, less of the silvered part of the horizon appears in the field and the reflected image is less bright. This action is most useful when it is necessary to regulate the relative brilliance of the horizon and the reflected heavenly body. The telescope is so arranged that its axis makes the same angle with the plane of the horizon glass as the latter makes with the line joining the centres of the index and horizon glasses.

A set of neutral *shades* of increasing density is mounted in front of both the index glass and the horizon glass for use when observations of bright objects are taken. On the opposite side of the frame to that shown in Fig. 103 are three legs and a handle. The handle contains a battery and a button switch for operating the *reading lamp*, which is mounted on the index bar on a swivel.

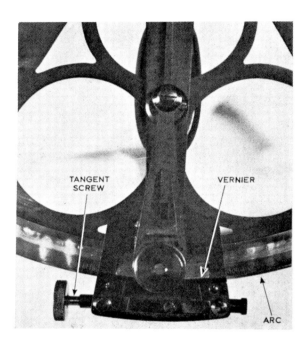

Fig. 104

The sextant telescopes

A sextant is generally provided with two telescopes. The principal telescope is called the 'inverting telescope,' because, on account of the arrangement of the lenses, objects seen through it appear to be inverted. It has two eyepieces, one of which is of higher magnifying power than the other; and each is fitted with cross-wires at its focus to define the line of collimation, which is the line joining the focus to the centre of the object-glass. The eyepiece of higher power generally has two cross-wires and the lower-power eyepiece has four. The high-power eyepiece should be used when the horizon is bright and the ship is steady.

In addition to the inverting telescope, there is usually a 'star telescope,' which is bell-shaped and has a large object-glass. It is an erecting telescope, and since it is intended for taking observations of stars, its magnifying power is not high.

The purpose of the large object-glass is to overcome the restriction of the field of view which results from the erecting eyepiece, and to give increased illumination. The star telescope is also of considerable value when angles between two terrestrial objects are measured, and it should always be used when such observations are made.

Note

The various additional refinements and attachments which can be supplied are outside the scope of this chapter.

The vernier

The principle of the vernier is described in Volume III. The vernier itself consists of a scale which slides along the sextant arc and permits the sextant arc to be read with an accuracy greater than that obtained by a direct reading.

On the arc of the sextant each degree is divided into six divisions of 10'. The arc of the vernier is divided usually into ten major divisions, each representing one minute of arc, and each of these major divisions is subdivided into five smaller divisions, each therefore representing 12 seconds of arc. Thus the vernier enables the arc to be read to the nearest 0·2 of a minute.

When angles *off the arc* are read, the 1' and 0'·2 intervals *must* be counted from the *left-hand* end of the vernier.

ERRORS OF THE SEXTANT

There are two types of errors of the sextant:

1. Adjustable errors which can be detected and eliminated by the observer. These errors are listed below in the order in which they should be corrected.

2. Certain other errors which can be corrected only in the workshop.

1. Adjustable errors

Perpendicularity. *The index glass must be perpendicular to the plane of the instrument.*

Set the index bar near the middle of the arc. Hold the instrument horizontally, and look obliquely into the index glass from that end of the instrument. The reflected image of the arc should now be seen in line with the arc itself. Should the two not appear in line, they can be made to do so by rotating a small screw in the centre of the frame of the index glass.

This error must always be corrected first.

Side error. *The horizon glass must be perpendicular to the plane of the instrument.*

Ship the inverting telescope and, with the sextant vertical, look at some well-defined object, preferably a star, and move the index across the zero of the arc. The reflected image should pass over the direct image of the star. If it does not do so, the error can be taken out by a screw in the centre of the frame of the horizon glass.

H

Collimation error. *The axis of the telescope when shipped should be parallel to the plane of the instrument.*

First take out perpendicularity error and side error, then ship the inverting telescope with the wires parallel to the plane of the instrument. Choose two heavenly bodies not less than 90° apart, and bring them into accurate contact on one wire of the telescope. Move the sextant until the bodies are on the other wire. They should still be in contact. If not, there is collimation error. This can be corrected in some sextants by two screws on the collar.

Index error

By a suitable arrangement of mirrors, the sextant enables an observer to look directly at the horizon and, by moving the arm of the sextant to which one of the mirrors is attached to reflect the image of body so that it appears to rest on the horizon. The position of the arm on the sextant arc indicates the altitude of the body – the angle *SOH* in Fig. 105.

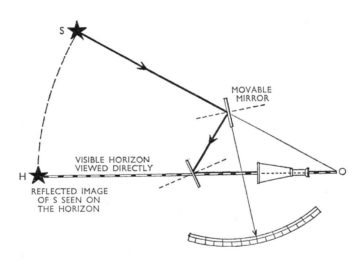

Fig. 105

When a heavenly (and therefore distant) body is viewed directly, the angle between it and its image as reflected in a sextant is zero, and the reading on the arc of the sextant should be zero. This, however, seldom occurs in practice because the mirrors are rarely in exact adjustment. Thus the zero of the sextant scale is not usually the true zero of the instrument. For example, if the sextant reading of the angle between the direct and reflected rays from the same distant object is 3′·0 *on the arc*, the instrument is reading 3′·0 too high and 3′·0 must be subtracted from all angles measured with the instrument. If, instead of reading 3′·0 too high, another sextant reads 2′·0 too low, 2′·0 must be added. These errors, denoted by −3′·0 and +2′·0 respectively, are known as the 'index errors' of the sextants.

When in correct adjustment, the horizon glass should be parallel to the index glass when the index is at zero. With a vernier sextant this is when the index arrow is set to read 0° 00′·0 on the arc. With a micrometer sextant it is immaterial if the arrow reads, by estimation, a few minutes off the zero, but the micrometer drum must be set to read 0° 00′·0 ± correction for back-lash if present in an appreciable amount. The method of determining the amount of back-lash of a micrometer sextant is described later.

Index error can be determined in several ways:

A. By observing the diameter of the Sun 'on' and 'off' the arc.

Set the sextant approximately at zero and work the micrometer drum to make the two images of the Sun just touch each other. Note the reading 'on' the arc.

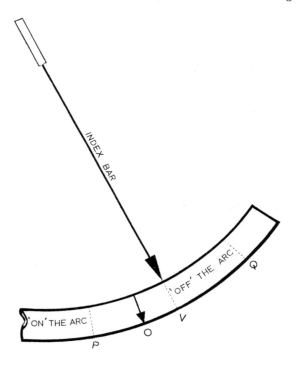

Fig. 106

Then reverse the images and note the reading 'off' the arc. Half the difference of these readings is the index error, which is positive (+) if the greater reading is 'off' the arc, and negative (−) if the greater reading is 'on' the arc. This can be seen in Fig. 106 where:

O is the zero graduated on the arc,

P is the position of the index when the Suns are touching 'on' the arc,

Q is the position of the index when the Suns are touching 'off' the arc,

V is the point at which the arc should therefore be graduated zero.

H*

When the index is at *P* 'on' the arc, the reflected Sun, which is shaded, is below the direct Sun, which is not shaded. When the index is at *Q*, 'off' the arc, the positions are reversed, as shown in Fig. 107. In each of these observations the angle measured is that subtended by the Sun's diameter, since the upper limb of one image is made to touch the lower limb of the other.

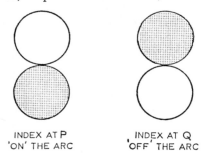

INDEX AT P
'ON' THE ARC

INDEX AT Q
'OFF' THE ARC

Fig. 107

OP and *OQ* are the sextant readings when the observations are made, and clearly they differ by twice *OV*, the index error. The index error is thus half the difference between two sextant readings of the Sun's diameter. The sextant readings, 'on' and 'off' the arc, added together and divided by four, should be the semi-diameter of the Sun given in the *Nautical Almanac* for the day, and this affords a check upon the accuracy of the observations.

B. *By observing a star*

Set the index bar a few minutes one side or other of zero; then observe a star and bring the two images together so that one is indistinguishable from the other. The reading is the index error, minus (−) if 'on' the arc, and plus (+) if 'off' the arc.

It can be seen in Fig. 106 that if the index is at *V* when the images coincide, *OV* is the index error 'off' the arc and therefore plus (+).

C. *By observing the horizon*

Index error can be found by observing the horizon in a similar way to finding the error by observing a star. This method should only be used when there is no heavenly body available.

Notes on Index Error

(i) With a vernier sextant it is not a good policy to correct small index errors (under 3′), since there is always a danger of straining the horizon glass and making the adjusting screw slack. A small index error should be allowed for arithmetically in the working of the sight.

(ii) If the index error becomes large and unwieldy (over 3′) it should be corrected by the small screw at the side of the base of the horizon glass. If this adjustment is made, side error should also be checked.

(iii) When the index error is corrected, it is a good plan to ensure that any index error remaining is negative (−), because this simplifies the working of sights since the index error is combined with dip, which is always negative.

(iv) With a micrometer sextant, the index setting may be further adjusted by releasing the friction clutch of the micrometer drum, resetting lightly, then, by trial and error, reducing the index setting (as read on zero) to a negligible quantity. The clutch should then be retightened carefully but firmly.

(v) *Back-lash of a micrometer sextant.* In conjunction with operation *B* above, the amount of back-lash may be determined by making coincidence on a star, first by clockwise rotation of the micrometer drum, reading the result, and then by anti-clockwise rotation, noting the difference, if any, between the two readings. Should the back-lash show an amount large enough to justify a correction, it may be applied by either (a) 'bringing up' the drum in opposite directions and adopting the mean of the readings (back-lash will thus be cancelled), or (b) 'bringing-up' the drum in one direction and applying the total back-lash as a correction to the observed altitude (+ or −, according to the direction in which the drum has been revolved). With new instruments back-lash should be negligible.

2. Errors which cannot be corrected by the observer

Centring error

This exists when the pivot of the index glass is not at the centre of the arc. The resultant error varies in amount and sign over different parts of the arc.

Worm and rack errors

These errors are peculiar to micrometer sextants. They vary in amount and sign. Until a sextant has been 'run in' it is liable to small and progressive changes and, for this reason, it is advisable to have a micrometer sextant recalibrated periodically according to the amount of use it has received.

Optical errors

These include prismatic errors of the mirrors and the shade glasses; also aberrations of the telescope lenses. With a sextant that has received a National Physical Laboratory Class 'A' certificate, the sum of these errors is relatively small, but in the event of any replacements to original glassware it is advisable to have the instrument recalibrated.

CERTIFICATES

All new sextants issued to HM Service have been optically and mechanically tested at the National Physical Laboratory; the residual errors* are tabulated on the N.P.L. certificate attached to the lid of the box.

A later certificate, Form C.D.7, for cleaned and recalibrated sextants for Service use, is issued by the Admiralty Compass Observatory.

---

* *Note:* On the certificates, the signs of these residual errors are reversed so that they can be applied as corrections. A Class 'A' certificate denotes that these corrections do not exceed 0′·8 on any part of the arc.

THE CARE OF A SEXTANT

1. Always handle a sextant with great care. A slight blow is liable to derange the adjustments.

2. When lifting, always hold the instrument by the frame or handle and never by the arc or by the index bar.

3. With the micrometer sextants additional care is necessary to prevent damage to the worm and rack. When disengaging the worm from the rack, the clamp in Fig. 103 must be pressed until the worm is fully disengaged. Grinding the gears is fatal to future accuracy of a micrometer sextant. The rack should be kept free from dirt and corrosion and the worm should run smoothly. For this purpose the periodical application of a little light oil, well brushed off afterwards, will assist in keeping the worm and rack in serviceable condition.

4. When screwing a telescope into the collar, take care not to burr the threads.

5. Never leave the sextant exposed to the Sun's rays when not in use.

6. After using the sextant in damp weather or when there is spray, wipe away all traces of moisture, using a chamois leather or a clean handkerchief and paying particular attention to the arc and mirrors.

7. Always stow the sextant in a place where it is not liable to be moved. If possible the stowage should be free from vibration and damp.

8. On a vernier sextant the fine graduations may, if they become difficult to read, be made clearer by a coating of lamp-black and fine oil. The surplus coating should then be lightly wiped off in a direction across the graduations. The arc should never be polished.

9. If the sextant is being stowed away for a long period, a thin coat of Vaseline on the arc and on the worm preserves the instrument.

10. As far as possible, avoid allowing a sextant to travel in hands other than those of its owner or some equally responsible person.

11. When replacing a sextant in its case, see that the shades are closed, index bar is set as requisite, and securing clamp firm; then lower lid gently. The sextant should not be allowed to rattle in its case.

Notes on sextants

(i) Always test the sextant for perpendicularity, side error and index error before taking sights. The first two should be removed. If the index error is under 3', it is advisable to leave it in and allow for it arithmetically.

(ii) Following any adjustments to the index or horizon glasses, see that the glass concerned is firm in its mount and that none of the adjusting screws is loose. After adjusting, it is a good plan to flick the glass with the finger-nail, and then note if any change in adjustment ensues.

(iii) The inverting telescope should always be used for sun sights, since it gives greater accuracy than the star telescope.

(iv) It is convenient to mark the various telescopes at infinity for the personal focus of the observer.

(v) When angles are measured with a sextant, it is important that the objects should be observed in the centre of the field of the telescope in order that the ray from each of the objects may be parallel to the plane of the instrument.

(vi) When measuring very small angles such as vertical danger angles, or the angles measured when the index error is checked by the sun, read both 'on' and 'off' the arc.

(vii) When reading a vernier sextant, avoid holding it sideways to the light, but let the light come straight along the index-bar to the vernier.

(viii) It is preferable to use a dark glass at the eye end of the telescope instead of using the shades.

(ix) The glasses are apt to get coated with moisture, especially after sunset.

CHAPTER 18

Notes on Sights

A single observation of a heavenly body or a terrestrial object gives a position line. Although it is not possible to obtain the ship's position from a single position line, the line itself can be of great use when the ship is near land.

The use of a single position line

Suppose that, in Fig. 108, a ship wishes to pass 10 miles from the lighthouse and proceed up a channel in thick weather, and that an astronomical observation (before the weather became thick) gave the position line shown.

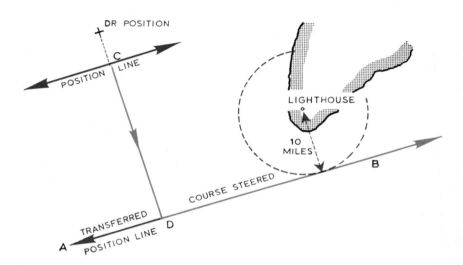

Fig. 108

If the line *AB* is drawn tangential to the 10-mile circle, parallel to the position line, and the ship steams the distance *CD* and then alters course along *AB*, she should, if there is no unknown tidal stream or current, pass 10 miles clear of the lighthouse.

The Fix and the Observed Position

One position line combined with another gives the ship's position. If the two position lines are obtained from shore objects, her position is called a 'fix.' If they are obtained from heavenly bodies, it is called an 'observed position.'

The distinction is made because a position obtained from astronomical observations is not so reliable as one obtained from terrestrial bearings. (*See also* Volume I, Chapter III.)

The transferred position line

If two position lines are obtained at approximately the same moment, the ship's position is decided by their point of intersection. If there is an appreciable interval between the times at which they are obtained, the first position line must be 'run on' to allow for the distance that the ship covers in that interval. The ship's position at the time of the second position line is then decided by the intersection of the second position line and the first position line transferred.

Too much reliance must not be placed upon a position found by the transference of a position line if:

1. there is a long interval between sights, because the run is never accurately known, especially in tidal waters;

2. the angle of cut between the two position lines is less than 30°, because even small errors in the altitude will then considerably affect the position found. (*See also* Volume I, Chapter IV.)

Heavenly bodies suitable for observation

In daylight it is sometimes possible to obtain simultaneous observations of the Sun and the Moon, or the Sun and Venus, or Venus and the Moon, and so avoid a long run between sights. The best observations, however, are obtained of the Moon, planets, and stars at *morning and evening twilight*.

The most reliable observed position is obtained if the bearings of the two heavenly bodies differ by about 90°.

Visibility of heavenly bodies

Stars can be observed with a marine sextant when the Sun is at a depression of 3° or more below the horizon; the horizon, however, becomes invisible when the Sun is depressed more than 9° below the horizon. The altitudes of stars may therefore be measured when the Sun's depression is between 3° and 9°, and the middle of this observing period is the time of the beginning or end of civil twilight. The time of civil twilight is tabulated in the *Nautical Almanac* and plans for taking star sights should be based on this time.

Abnormal refraction

Positions obtained from sights taken during the day can be dangerously misleading owing to abnormal refraction. Mirage effects are an indication that the refraction *is* abnormal, while any unusual difference between the sea-surface and air temperatures indicates that it *may be*. In the Red Sea, for example, abnormal refraction is a common experience, because the wind which blows off the land has been heated to a temperature considerably higher than that of the sea.

If abnormal refraction is suspected, sights should be treated with the utmost caution.

Star sights at morning and evening twilight are more likely to give accurate results than observations taken at other times.

Procedure for morning and evening observations of stars and planets

1. Set up the star globe beforehand for the time of beginning or end of civil twilight.

2. Choose three or more stars and planets to give the best cuts. Two should be about 90° apart. The best combination is, if possible, four stars 90° apart in azimuth, because any abnormal refraction error will be eliminated by using opposite horizons. Stars should be selected with altitudes between 30° and 60° and, where possible, with approximately the same altitude. At least four additional stars should also be selected as standbys, in case the sky is partly clouded and the originally chosen stars are obscured.

3. When choosing stars, note the weather and the direction in which the horizon is likely to be clearest.

4. Make a list of the approximate altitudes and bearings of the chosen stars and a rough sketch showing the bearings relative to the course of the ship; this will make identification easier. It is a good plan to set on the sextant the altitude of the brightest star chosen. Then, knowing the approximate bearing relative to the ship's head, look through the star telescope and sweep the horizon at this point. The star will frequently be found before it is visible to the naked eye, when the horizon is still good.

   Familiarity with this method is invaluable if there is broken cloud, for then a star may be visible only for a few moments. It is possible to take sights in this way without seeing the stars with the naked eye.

Note
This is the best method of finding Polaris.

Taking observations

1. *In clear weather.* Take observations from the highest convenient position.

2. *In fog, haze or mist.* Take observations from the lowest convenient position.

3. *With an indistinct, cloudy or hazy Sun,* the perimeter of the Sun's disc is uncertain and it is more accurate to bisect the disc on the horizon than to make the lower limb touch the horizon. If this is done, the altitude corrections, less that for semi-diameter, must be applied separately.

4. When possible, check the sextant for side error before taking sights.

5. When possible, take the index error *before* and *after* sights.

6. When observing the Sun, use sufficiently strong shades to avoid any possibility of dazzle.

7. When possible, take observations of a heavenly body in sets of three or five at approximately equal time-intervals.

8. Having brought the heavenly body to the horizon, always swing the sextant a few degrees each side of the vertical plane to make the body appear to describe the arc of a circle. This arc should then be raised or lowered by means of the micrometer drum, until it just touches the horizon. If the

observed altitude is measured at this point, there will be no doubt that the vertical angle is obtained.

An alternative method is to bring the heavenly body down to the horizon and then note whether it is rising or setting. (If the body is west of the meridian it will be setting, if east of the meridian it will be rising.) If it is setting, move the micrometer drum until the object is slightly above the horizon; then, leaving the sextant set, swing it gently from side to side until the star or limb just touches the horizon. If it is rising, move the micrometer drum until the object is slightly below the horizon, and carry out this same procedure.

9. *When the horizon is poor*, it is essential to take several altitudes of each body and to set the sextant to a given increase or decrease of altitude between each observation. If the time intervals are not approximately equal, the sights should be either discarded or used with extreme caution.

10. Having taken a set of observations of a star or planet, the identity of which is uncertain, take a compass bearing of it.

11. Make sure that the minute and second hands of the deck watch are 'lined up,' so that there can be no possibility of an error in the reading of the minute hand. If times are being taken by an assistant it is advisable to check the minute hand yourself.

Times should be read to the nearest second. It is useful to be able to count in seconds so that, if there is no one available to take times, you can walk to the chart table counting the seconds and there read the deck watch.

12. Sometimes difficulty is found in bringing a faint star down to the horizon. When this happens, a good plan is to reverse the sextant in the hand and look direct at the star with the index bar at zero. Bring the horizon *up to the star;* then reverse the sextant and proceed in the normal manner.

13. *When the ship is rolling heavily*, errors due to rapidly changing dip may be reduced, and more accurate observations obtained, by observing from a position close to the centre line of the ship.

14. Observe stars as early as possible at evening twilight and as late as possible at morning twilight. The horizon will then be clearest.

15. On a clear night within about two days of Full Moon, star sights can be taken with a horizon illuminated by moonlight. This should only be attempted when the Moon is high. The horizon on the bearing of the Moon appears to dip and is therefore suspect. The Moon itself and stars near it should not be used.

CHAPTER 19

Elementary Meteorology

Navigation has been defined as the science of fixing a ship's position and the art of conducting her from place to place in safety. The ease with which the passage is made will depend to a great extent upon the weather conditions encountered; high seas or bad visibility, for example, will add to the difficulties of making the passage. The navigator therefore requires forewarning of weather likely to endanger the ship or impede the voyage.

The navigator, in order to make the best use of the weather forecast supplied to him and to appreciate the limitations of the forecast, must understand the causes of weather, and he must have some knowledge of the technique of weather forecasting. He should also be able to make use of the Fleet Weather Messages and construct weather maps from them so that he will have a background knowledge of the general weather situation. This will enable him to interpret better the forecasts which he will be receiving by signal from meteorological authorities. In addition, he should be able to log and report in standard form, for transmission to the shore, the weather he is experiencing, so that other operational authorities may in turn be supplied with the most up-to-date weather appreciation possible.

The following chapters outline the subjects of meteorology and weather forecasting. More comprehensive information is contained in *Meteorology for Mariners* (NP407).

In accordance with international practice temperature is given in degrees Celsius (formerly Centigrade). Where height or distance is quoted in metres the approximate equivalent in feet is also given.

Historical introduction

The fact that Aristotle wrote the first treatise on meteorology in about 350 B.C. shows that a great deal was known even then about the relations of wind and weather. The weather signs he described are similar to those spoken of today but for a period of about 2,000 years no appreciable progress was made in formulating a theory which explained these signs.

Torricelli, an Italian, invented the barometer in 1643, and this led to the 'weatherglass' with its inscriptions, 'storm', 'much rain', rain', 'change', 'fair', 'set fair' and 'very dry'. Scientists realised the inaccuracy of these barometrical forecasts, but little progress was made until 1820, when the relation between wind and pressure distribution was first defined. Later, in 1857, the value of simultaneous observations of pressure, wind, temperature, and weather conditions at a number of places was fully appreciated, and the Dutchman Buys Ballot produced the law (described later in this chapter) which holds good to the present day.

In 1860, Admiral Fitzroy, then head of the Meteorological Office in London, which had then been established only a few years, began to collect, by telegraph from various stations, daily reports describing the local weather at certain fixed times. As a result of these reports the first weather forecasts were issued to the Press.

International co-operation was established in 1872, and with the advent of wireless telegraphy an ever-increasing amount of meteorological information became available.

At an early date it was recognized that a knowledge of the conditions in the upper air would be of assistance in weather forecasting, but it was not until the First World War (1914–1918) that aircraft were used for observing upper-air temperatures, and the balloon tracked by theodolite became the standard method for observing the upper winds.

During the Second World War, the development of the 'radiosonde' and the introduction of a technique for tracking balloons by radar led to a great increase in the amount of information about winds and temperatures in the upper air, particularly over the continents. In 1947, Ocean Weather Ships began to operate; these are also equipped to make routine upper-air soundings and, in consequence, knowledge of conditions over the oceans is now being rapidly accumulated.

THE ATMOSPHERE

The air, which is referred to as the 'atmosphere', covers the whole surface of the Earth in the form of a thin film. Half of the total weight of this air is within about $3\frac{1}{2}$ miles of the surface of the Earth; above this is a further layer of 6 miles containing about one quarter of the weight of the total mass, and the remaining quarter is spread up to a height of at least 130 miles. At the height of the summit of Mount Everest, 9000 metres (29,000 ft), the density of the air is about two-fifths of the density at sea-level, and is so rarefied that great difficulty in breathing is experienced.

The air is a mixture of gases of which 99 per cent is oxygen and nitrogen, and there is always present an appreciable quantity of water vapour. The amount of this water vapour, which is increased by evaporation and decreased by rain and dew, is always a variable quantity, and this fact accounts, to some extent, for the wide variations of weather experienced at any place.

Were it not for this water vapour in the atmosphere, the Earth would be subjected to extremes of temperature that would render life impossible.

PRESSURE

Consider the column of air resting on one square inch of the Earth's surface. This column has a cross-section of one square inch and height equal to that of the atmosphere. Its weight is about $14\frac{1}{2}$ pounds, and this weight, which is called the atmospheric pressure, is measured by the barometer (*see* Chapter 21).

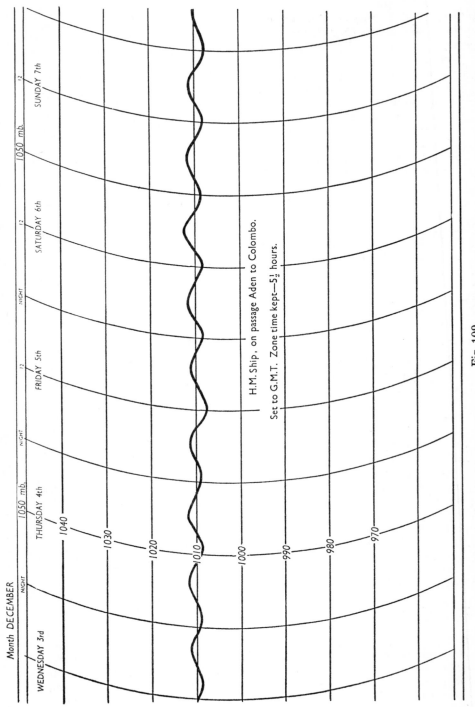

Fig. 109

The Bar

Barometric pressure used to be measured in inches of mercury, but in modern meteorology the unit used is the 'bar', which is the pressure due to a vertical column of mercury 750·062 mm (29·53 in.) high under the standard conditions of temperature 0°C and acceleration of gravity 980·665 cm/sec².

The bar is derived from the metric system in which a pressure of 1,000 dynes per square centimetre is equal to one millibar, a dyne being the force that acting on a mass of one gramme produces an acceleration of one centimetre per second per second.

The average atmospheric pressure at sea-level is 1013 mb.

Because pressure at any point is due to the weight of air above that point, pressure must decrease with increasing height. The rate at which this occurs is about 34 mb for each 300 m (1,000 ft) of ascent.

The diurnal range of the barometer

This results from atmospheric pressure waves, with a period of nearly 12 hours, which sweep regularly round the Earth from east to west. They are at a maximum in the tropics where they are clearly indicated by the rise and fall of the barometer, as shown in Fig. 109. The barometer rises from 0400 to 1000 h., then falls until 1600. After that it rises again till 2200, when it once more falls until 0400. These times, which are approximate, are in the Local Mean Time of the place.

The diurnal variation has a range in the tropics of about 3 mb. In latitude 51° the range is about 0·8 mb and is usually masked by other pressure variations. In higher latitudes it is inappreciable.

Isobars

In order to illustrate the pressure distribution over the Earth's surface at any given time, simultaneous barometer readings can be plotted. Lines called *isobars* are then drawn connecting places of equal pressure (reduced usually to sea-level).

WIND

Wind is the flow of air over the surface of the earth. The primary cause of this air flow is the temperature variation in columns of air over different places. This in turn creates areas of different atmospheric pressure. In trying to achieve a uniform pressure distribution the air flows from a region of high pressure to a region of low pressure.

The effect of the Earth's rotation on the wind direction

On account of the Earth's rotation, air which is drawn towards a centre of *low pressure* is deflected to the *right* in the *northern hemisphere*, and a circulation is set up in an *anti-clockwise* direction about the centre. Around a centre of *high pressure* a *clockwise* circulation is set up in the *northern hemisphere*.

In the *southern hemisphere* these directions are reversed.

Buys Ballot's Law

These rotating movements explain the law which takes its name from a Dutch professor.

Stand facing the true wind, and the centre of low pressure will be about 90° to 130° on your right hand in the northern hemisphere and on your left hand in the southern hemisphere.

The practical value of this law to the seaman is described further on in the present chapter, under the discussion of tropical revolving storms.

Backing and veering

When the wind changes in a clockwise direction, that is, N–E–S–W, it is said to *veer*; when it changes in the reverse direction it is said to *back*. These terms are used in both northern and southern hemispheres.

Surface wind

It is necessary to consider the effect of friction on wind passing over the Earth's surface. At heights of 450 m (1,500 ft) or more above the sea, surface friction is almost negligible and the wind blows along the isobars. Near the Earth's

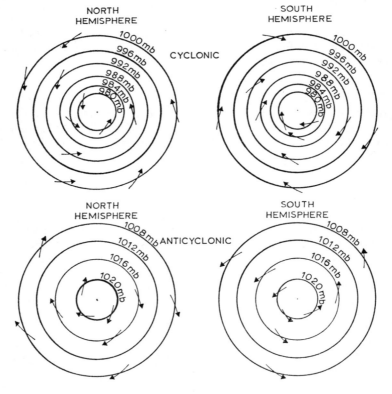

Fig. 110

surface, however, the observed wind-speed is considerably reduced, more so over the land than over the sea. This reduction in speed of the surface wind causes the wind to leave the isobars and flow either towards a centre of low pressure or away from a centre of high pressure.

Cyclonic winds

A wind circulation about an area of low pressure is said to be *cyclonic*. For ease of illustration, the isobars in Fig. 110 are circular and are shown evenly distributed about the centres of high and low pressure. Actually they are seldom found in this form. In cyclonic depressions the shape of the isobars is usually oval.

In a cyclonic circulation the inward inclination of the wind direction from that of the isobars in the latitude of the British Isles is about 10° to 15° over the sea, and about 30° over the land. In the tropics the angle of inward inclination is greater. The outward inclination for an anticyclonic system is similar.

Anticyclonic winds

A wind circulation about an area of high pressure is *anticyclonic*, as shown in Fig. 110.

SEA AND SWELL

Waves that are set up by wind blowing at the place and time of observations are termed 'sea'. Waves caused either by wind at a distance from the place of observation, or by winds in the locality previous to the time of observation, are termed 'swell'.

Ocean waves result from the action of the wind on the surface of the water. When first formed they are short and steep, but if the wind continues to blow in the same direction for a considerable time, their 'length' and their 'height' increase. At the same time, the 'period' of the waves increases until a balance of forces is reached. When waves have been formed, the wind has its greatest effect on their crests, which it tends to drive faster than the main body of the waves. It thus causes the waves to break. In deep water, waves have no motion of translation, but on reaching shallow water their troughs are retarded, with the result that the waves themselves rush forward and break with considerable violence. From this action they are known as 'breakers'.

The following are definitions of terms frequently used in connection with waves.

The *length* of a wave is the horizontal distance (usually expressed in metres or feet) from crest to crest or trough to trough.

The *height* of a wave is the vertical distance (usually expressed in metres or feet) from trough to crest.

The *period* of a wave is the time, in seconds, between the passage of two successive wave crests or troughs past a fixed point.

The *velocity* of a wave is the rate at which its crest appears to travel. It is obtained by dividing the length by the period, the result being the velocity in metres (or feet) per second.

Dimensions of waves

The dimensions of waves vary in different localities and with different velocities and directions of the wind. The longest waves are encountered in the South Pacific, where their lengths vary from 180 to 300 m (600 to 1,000 ft) and their periods from 11 to 14 seconds. Waves of from 150 to 180 m (500 to 600 ft) in length are occasionally encountered in the Atlantic, but more commonly the lengths are from 48 to 97 m (160 to 320 ft) and the periods from 6 to 8 seconds. The longest wave recorded is 830 m (2,720 ft), with a period of 25 seconds. The relation between the length of a wave and the velocity and direction of the wind is not yet fully understood.

TEMPERATURE

The interchange of heat between one body and another occurs in one or more of three different ways:

Conduction is the transference of heat from one particle of a body to the next particle. Different substances vary in their degree of conductivity. Solids are usually better conductors than liquids, which in turn are better than gases.

Convection is the interchange of heat by means of warm currents of gas or liquid. The gas or liquid when heated expands, decreases in density, and rises. Colder gas or liquid flows in to take its place, and convection currents are created.

Radiation is the transmission of heat in the form of electromagnetic energy such as that which enables the Earth to receive heat from the Sun.

Measurement of temperature

Temperatures can be measured by thermometers according to various scales, those most frequently used being Celsius, Fahrenheit, and Absolute.

Some idea of the relative values of the scales can be obtained from the following table.

	Water freezes	*Water boils*
Celsius	0°	100°
Fahrenheit	32°	212°
Absolute	273°	373°

Absolute temperature thus equals Celsius temperature increased by 273°.

The temperature of the atmosphere

The atmosphere derives its heat indirectly from the Sun. Its temperature depends not so much upon the direct rays of the Sun as upon the conduction and radiation from the surface of the Earth heated by the Sun's rays.

The Sun's rays have their greatest effect when they are perpendicular to the Earth's surface, and this effect diminishes as their obliquity increases. The land absorbs heat and loses it a great deal more readily than water. These two circumstances will be considered separately.

Temperature decreases with height at an average rate of about 0·5°C per 100 m (330 ft), so that, for example, if the surface temperature is about 10°C the temperature at 2000 m (6,600 ft) is likely to be about 0°C, i.e. the freezing level is then at about 2000 m. Sometimes the 'lapse rate', as it is often called, of temperature with height is greater than this, and at times it is less. On clear calm nights the air near the ground is cooled well below the temperature of the air thirty metres or so above the surface, thus giving an increase of temperature with height in place of the normal decrease. At times there is a noticeable increase of temperature spread over a layer of perhaps 600 m (2,000 ft) or so at some height well above the ground. An increase of temperature with height is known as an 'inversion', and, if confined to a hundred metres or so from the surface, is called a 'surface inversion.'

Over the land

The surface of the Earth, to a depth of a few centimetres, is heated daily while the Sun shines, but the surface does not become cumulatively hotter day by day because the heat is radiated back into the atmosphere and is also transferred by conduction and convection. By conduction some of the heat which the surface receives during the day is transferred to the layer of the atmosphere in contact with the surface, but the effect of this transference is confined to a very shallow layer unless there is also convection, and in general the effect is small compared with that of radiation.

The effect of radiation is most marked at night when the sky is clear, since surface cooling is then most rapid. Clouds reduce the fall in temperature that results from the loss of heat by radiation at night, because they intercept and largely radiate back this heat. By day they check the rise in temperature by reflecting away much of the incoming solar radiation.

The temperature of the atmosphere over the land normally rises rapidly at the surface, and at a progressively smaller rate up to a height of about 450 m (1,500 ft), from sunrise until about 1400 LMT.

Over the sea

The diurnal variation of sea surface temperature and hence that of the air at sea level is practically zero. This is due to the fact that in the sea the solar radiation penetrates to a considerable depth, so that the increase in surface temperature is only slight, and is also because the turbulence due to waves causes the heat acquired at the surface to be spread downwards.

The temperature of the air over the sea changes mainly as a result of changes in the place of origin of the wind, and owing to ocean currents. The influence of clouds upon the air temperature over the open sea is negligible.

The effect of local heating

The surface of the Earth consists of different formations in different localities, and the heating effects of the Sun's rays vary accordingly. For instance, a tarmac road is heated to a much greater extent than a plantation of trees growing nearby. The air thus becomes heated to a different extent even in immediately adjacent localities.

Stable and unstable conditions

Warm air is lighter than cold air, and when surrounded by air which is appreciably colder it will rise like a balloon filled with hydrogen (or even with hot air). This 'bubble' of warmer air, which, in practice, may be anything from a few yards to a few miles across, will continue to rise until it is surrounded by air of its own temperature, that is, until it is no longer lighter than its surroundings. A hot, sunny day over land has the same effect as a gas jet beneath a kettle of water: the bottom layer expands and rapidly becomes lighter than the layer overhead, so that there is a tendency for the upper layers to fall to the bottom while those at the bottom rise to the top. This tendency to overturn is known as *instability*.

As in a kettle, the bottom layer does not rise to the top in one mass, but in columns of successions of 'bubbles'. This process is known as *convection* and is similar to that which takes place over a land surface when the Sun is heating it. An aircraft flying at, say, 300 m (1,000 ft) will pass through alternate columns of rising (warm) and falling (cold) air – conditions that the pilot describes as 'bumpy'.

Because pressure decreases with increasing height, bubbles of rising air undergo a progressive reduction in pressure and expand as they rise, in accordance with Boyle's Law. Expansion results in loss of temperature at the rate of about 0·9°C per 100 m (330 ft) rise.*

Since the lapse rate does not usually exceed 0·5°C per 100 m it follows that these 'bubbles' will not normally be able to rise far before they have been cooled by expansion (consequent upon reduction of pressure) to the same temperature as their surroundings. Sometimes the lapse rate is appreciably greater than 0·5°C per 100 m and conditions in the upper air are said to be *unstable;* thunderstorms may then occur due to the transport of relatively warm air from the surface upwards, and of the cold air aloft down to the surface in exchange.

The air is said to be *stable* if the lapse rate is less than 0·5°C per 100 m, which precludes the possibility of convection. The extreme case of stability is a surface inversion with the coldest (and therefore heaviest) air underneath, when no vertical exchange can possibly take place.

---

* Actually the 'bubble' loses temperature at this rate only until it is cooled to its 'condensation', or dew, point. Any further ascent, and consequent cooling, results in the condensation of surplus water vapour in the form of cloud. The latent heat released as condensation takes place results in a net loss of nearly 0·5°C per 100 m on the part of the bubble instead of about 0·9° as hitherto. It will be evident then that when the lapse rate of the surrounding (still) air is 0·5° or more, and some of the bubbles are able to reach their condensation level before being cooled to the same temperature as their surroundings, they will then be able to rise to great heights, hence the towering clouds known as *cumulonimbus*.

Types of stability conditions (Fig. 111)

(a) represents the normal lapse rate of about 0·5°C per 100 m.

(b) represents conditions that are definitely unstable near the surface, where the curve is more nearly horizontal. If the air near the sea level is moist, conditions are also unstable in higher levels, because the lapse rate exceeds the normal of 0·5°C per 100 m. This curve is similar to that which obtains when a cold air mass flows over relatively warm water.

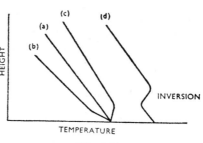

Fig. 111

(c) represents stable conditions, i.e. the rate at which temperature falls off with height is less than the normal. A surface inversion is shown similar to that which will be experienced in a warm air mass travelling over relatively cold water, or on a calm night with clear skies over land.

(d) represents another case of stable conditions such as may occur near the centre of an anticyclone and – less marked, perhaps – ahead of a warm front.

The Troposphere and Stratosphere

The atmosphere can be regarded as being divided into two separate parts so far as temperature is concerned, as shown in Fig. 112 overleaf.

The lower part extends to a height of about ten miles above the equator and five miles above the poles, and in it there is a fairly regular and considerable lapse of temperature with height. This region is known as the *troposphere*.

The upper part extends for about twenty miles above the troposphere. Here there is little material change of temperature with height. This region is called the *stratosphere*.

The level dividing the troposphere and the stratosphere is known as the *tropopause*. Because the tropopause is considerably higher over the equator than it is over the poles, the lowest temperatures in the atmosphere occur in the stratosphere of equatorial regions, despite the high surface temperatures.

HUMIDITY

Between the particles of the air there are particles of water vapour which evaporation has released into the atmosphere. The amount of water vapour in a unit mass of air at any moment is known as the *humidity*.

Saturation

Warm air can hold more water vapour than cold air, and when the air contains the largest possible quantity of water vapour that it can hold without increase of temperature, it is said to be *saturated*.

Relative humidity

The proportion of moisture present in the air at any time to the total amount of moisture necessary for saturation is known as the *relative humidity* and is

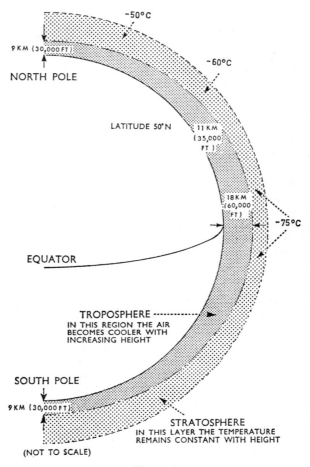

Fig. 112

expressed as a percentage. For any given amount of moisture in the air, the relative humidity therefore increases with a decrease in temperature.

Relative humidity is measured by means of a psychrometer (originally called a hygrometer). Details are given in Chapter 21.

Dew and hoar frost

The temperature at which a mass of air reaches saturation at constant pressure is called the *dew point*. The dew point is also measured by a psychrometer; its determination from the wet and dry bulb temperatures is explained in Chapter 21. When, through any cause, the mass of air is chilled below the dew-point temperature, the water vapour which can no longer be held in suspension condenses. When it is condensed on blades of grass, the deck of a ship, etc., the deposit is known as *dew*.

If the dew point is below freezing point, the moisture is deposited in the form of *hoar frost*.

FOG

Fog is formed by the condensation of water vapour on small hygroscopic particles or nuclei which are always present in the air. Over the land, some of these nuclei are dust or smoke particles, while over the sea they mostly consist of salt crystals. The latter have such an affinity for water that they start to pick up moisture when the relative humidity is about 75 per cent.

The formation of fog therefore depends upon the number of nuclei in the air, and upon the relative humidity. The colder the air, the less moisture can it hold in an invisible state. If, therefore, air of high relative humidity is progressively cooled, it will sooner or later become saturated; any further cooling will result in the condensation of some of the water vapour into visible drops of water. Such condensation, when it occurs in the surface layers of the atmosphere, constitutes *fog*. The cooling of damp air is thus the primary cause of fog, and upon the method of cooling depends the type of fog actually formed.

The 'lid' effect of a ground inversion, by which the lowest layer of air is prevented from rising, greatly facilitates the formation of fog because it keeps the same patch of air in contact with the cold earth or sea.

When dust, smoke, or sand particles obscure vision in the surface layers, the reduction in visibility is known as *haze*.

Types of fog

Advection or sea fog. This is associated with relatively warm, moist air flowing over a colder sea surface. The lower layers of the air are cooled, and a surface inversion is created beneath which the fog forms. Taking the world as a whole, about 85–90 per cent of fogs experienced in the open sea are formed in this manner. In general, this type of fog is most frequent in the late spring and early summer, at which seasons the sea surface temperature is most likely to be below that of the air blowing over it. It is particularly frequent in the vicinity of cold ocean currents (e.g. the Labrador Current), or along coasts where the prevailing wind is such as to cause the surface water to be deflected away from the coast, with consequent upwelling of colder water from below (e.g. along the coasts of SW Africa). (*See* Chapter 22.)

Radiation fog forms over land on quiet nights with clear or nearly clear skies. In such circumstances the Earth rapidly radiates its heat into space and becomes cool, thus chilling the air in contact with it to its dew point and forming a surface inversion. In flat calm conditions the resulting condensation is likely to be in the form of dew or hoar frost (*see above*), but with a gentle breeze the cooling will be spread through a greater depth of air, and fog will form. Such fogs may drift to seaward and interfere with coastal navigation.

The necessary clear skies and light winds occur most frequently in anti-cyclones, but sometimes also in ridges in the rear of depressions.

Radiation fog is most frequent and persistent in temperate and high latitudes in winter, when the long nights permit the maximum degree of nocturnal cooling. It is especially common in the vicinity of large industrial areas, and is generally thickest during the latter part of the night or early part of the day.

Arctic sea smoke, frost smoke or steam fog. This is caused by the passage of very cold air over much warmer water. In these circumstances two processes occur. First, the cold air absorbs moisture by direct evaporation from the warm water, and secondly, the lowest layers of the cold air are heated by contact with the warm sea and so tend to rise. This rising air immediately meets air colder than itself, is rapidly chilled to its dew point, and fog is formed. The sea has the appearance of steaming, and in fact the steam over a hot bath or cup of tea is an example of this type of fog. It is unlikely to reach any great height before the surplus moisture is absorbed by the colder and drier air above. This form of fog is therefore usually low-lying, and a lookout placed aloft will often be able to see over it.

In order that fogs of this type may form, it is necessary for the temperature of the air to be very much lower than that of the sea surface. Such fogs are therefore rare in temperate latitudes. In Arctic regions, however, they are common, and are experienced when off-shore winds bring very cold air from over ice or snow-covered land masses; or close to the ice-edge when the wind is blowing off the ice.

Dissipation of fog

Fog can be dissipated in the following ways:

By heat. Over land, the heat of the Sun warms the surface of the Earth, a process known as *insolation*. In turn the Earth heats the air in contact with it and thus increases its capacity to hold water vapour. The fog thus starts to disappear. In the latitude of the British Isles in winter, however, the insolation is sometimes too weak to cause dissipation of the fog, which may thus persist throughout the day.

It is important to bear in mind that insolation is only effective in dispersing land fog, and has little or no effect over the sea, the surface temperature of which remains virtually unchanged from day to night. A similar effect, however, occurs when a sea fog drifts over a patch of warm water, or over a warm current.

By a considerable increase in the strength of the wind. In these circumstances the various layers become mixed, the inversion is destroyed, and eventually the temperature of the mixed air is raised above dew point.

By a change in direction or new source of the wind. This probably means the passage of a front. The properties (temperature and humidity) of the new air mass are likely to be widely different from those of the old.

Locality of fog

Full details are given in the various *Sailing Directions*. The following table shows the open sea areas in which a high frequency of fog occurs, and the season in which it is most common.

LOCALITY	SEASON OF GREATEST FREQUENCY
Newfoundland Banks, Nova Scotia and New England coasts	Late spring and summer
Coast of SW Africa	January to June
West Coast of S America (south of about lat. 35°S) ...	Summer and autumn
China Coast (South)	Spring
,, ,, (North)	Summer
Japan–Aleutians area	Summer
Coasts of British Columbia, Washington, Oregon and northern California	Summer and autumn
Polar Regions	Summer

Outside the areas mentioned in the above table, fog over the open sea scarcely ever occurs within 30° of the equator. In temperate latitudes it is most likely to be encountered in late spring and early summer.

In harbour or coastal waters in temperate and high latitudes, winter is generally the season of greatest frequency.

CLOUD

Cloud is formed by the condensation of the water vapour in the atmosphere at a height above the Earth's surface. Condensation is caused by cooling, the cooling in its turn being caused by the ascent of air for some reason.

There are two main types of cloud: *stratiform* or layer cloud, that is, cloud formed in horizontal sheets; and *cumuliform* ('woolpack' or 'cauliflower') cloud, with much greater vertical development than horizontal extent.

Cumuliform clouds are formed when moist air is caused to rise quickly – for example, during periods of vigorous convection or when warm air is forced rapidly above cold air, as at cold fronts (*see* Chapter 20). Stratiform clouds are formed when the moist air rises at a more moderate speed – at warm fronts, for example, or when stable air is forced to rise over mountain ranges or elevated coasts. They are also formed when surface friction causes turbulence sufficient to produce saturation and condensation in the upper part of the turbulent layer.

The height at which condensation takes place depends upon the relative humidity. Cloud types are further classified by the heights at which they form.

High clouds are fleecy and usually more or less transparent. They are known as *cirrus* and are composed of ice crystals formed by the condensation of water vapour at a very low temperature. There are various forms of cirrus cloud found between heights of 6000 m (20,000 ft) and 12 000 m (40,000 ft). They may be either cumuliform or stratiform (*cirrocumulus, cirrostratus*). Continuous sheets of cirrostratus often cause a 'halo' to be seen round the Sun and at night round the Moon.

Low clouds, below 2400 m (8,000 ft) include *cumulus* (or 'woolpack' cloud) and *stratus* (or sheet cloud).

Medium clouds lie between 2000 m (6,500 ft) and 6000 m (20,000 ft) and consist of the high cumulus and high stratus types (*altocumulus* and *altostratus*).

TABLE OF CLOUDS

FORM OF CLOUD	USUAL HEIGHT OF BASE		REMARKS
	FEET	METRES	
Cirrus (Ci) Cirrocumulus (Cc) Cirrostratus (Cs)	Between 20,000 and 40,000	Between 6 and 12 km	In the tropics the upper level may be 15 km (50,000 ft) or more.
Altostratus (As) Altocumulus (Ac)	Between 6,500 and 20,000	Between 2 and 6 km	
Cumulonimbus (Cb)	2,000 to 5,000	600 to 1500	Sometimes as low as 300 m (1,000 ft) or as high as 2400 m (8,000 ft). Tops may reach 9 km (30,000 ft) in middle latitudes and 15 km (50,000 ft) in the tropics.
Cumulus (Cu)	1,000 to 5,000	300 to 1500	
Stratus (St)	Surface to 2,000	Surface to 600	Sometimes as high as 1200 m (4,000 ft).
Stratocumulus (Sc)	1,000 to 4,500	300 to 1400	Sometimes as low as 150 m (500 ft) or as high as 2400 m (8,000 ft).
Nimbostratus (Ns)	500 to 2,000	150 to 600	Sometimes practically down to the surface; sometimes as high as 1200 m (4,000 ft).
Fractostratus (Fs)	300 to 2,000	100 to 600	Known as 'scud'. Found below nimbostratus.
Fractocumulus (Fc)	2,000 to 5,000	600 to 1500	Ragged cumulus in which the different parts show constant change.

Diurnal variation of cloud

When cumulus or cumulonimbus clouds are being formed in convective currents set up by heated land surfaces there is maximum activity in the late afternoon and early evening, when the land reaches its highest temperature, but the clouds tend to dissipate at night, when the land is cooled by radiation. This effect is particularly noticeable in the tropics.

Over the sea, showers have maximum frequency during the night and minimum frequency during the afternoon. This is because instability increases at night over the sea as the air temperature decreases and the sea temperature remains more or less steady.

Over land, layers of stratiform cloud are warmed by terrestrial radiation during the day and may be dissipated; such layers therefore decrease in vertical extent during the day (thin layers may disappear altogether) and thicken during the night, when cooling, caused by radiation from the top surface, takes place.

Prognostic significance of clouds

The distribution of clouds in a depression is explained in the next chapter and illustrated by Figs. 127 to 130.

Operational importance of clouds

Clouds are of importance in air operations, because they provide cover for aircraft in both offence and defence. Altostratus is the most useful cloud, as the visibility inside is usually good enough to permit formation flying. Stratocumulus is also useful, although there is a risk of aircraft icing. Cumulus and cumulonimbus do not give continuous cover; dangerous bumpiness may be experienced, and there is a liability to icing. Nimbostratus and stratus have very low bases so that the tops of even the lowest hills may be obscured; severe bumpiness is also common in nimbostratus.

PRECIPITATION

Rain is the result of further condensation of the water vapour within a cloud. When the temperature of the air in the cloud is further lowered by ascent the minute spherical drops of water of which cloud is composed are increased in size and weight by a further condensation of water vapour, and also by the union of several drops. Finally they become too heavy to be supported in the air and start to fall as rain.

Continuous rain or drizzle usually falls from stratiform clouds (altostratus and nimbostratus), while showers fall from cumuliform clouds – mainly cumulonimbus.

Hail is formed by the freezing of raindrops held in suspension. This occurs when strong convectional currents carry the raindrops to great heights, where they freeze, eventually falling as balls of ice.

Snow is formed by the condensation of water vapour at a temperature below freezing point in the form of ice crystals.

Sleet is the name given to falling snow which has been almost melted by passage through the warmer surface layers.

Glazed frost is formed when rain falls from warmer air aloft (for example, ahead of a warm front) onto a frozen surface; the rain freezes as it alights, forming a sheet of ice. This is a fairly rare occurrence at sea, but ice similarly forms on the superstructure of a ship when spray strikes the ship in air temperatures below about $-2°C$. This can be a serious hazard, particularly in small ships, and action to reduce the hazard should be taken early.

Thunder and lightning

When the raindrops in a cloud are swept upwards by a rising current of air, they increase in size. This increase, however, is not indefinite. When they attain a diameter of 5 mm, the raindrops disintegrate. This action liberates an electrical charge which in time creates a difference of potential between the top and bottom of the cloud large enough to cause a discharge. The discharge may take place between the cloud and the Earth, or between two clouds, and if it is visible it is known as 'forked lightning'. If the reflection only can be seen it is known as 'sheet lightning'. The noise of the expansion and subsequent contraction of the air due to this discharge is called 'thunder'.

GENERAL PRESSURE AND WIND DISTRIBUTION

The distribution of pressure, and the winds which would result over a uniform rotating Earth, are shown in Fig. 113, together with the terms long used by seamen to describe the various regions. This idealized distribution is known as

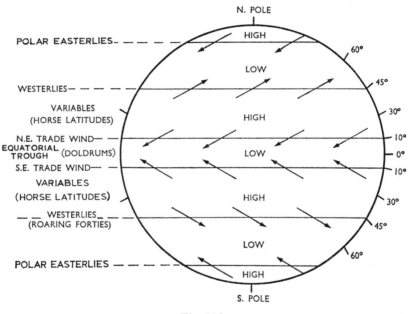

Fig. 113

the 'planetary system' of pressure and wind. It should be noted that the Doldrums area is generally referred to nowadays as the 'Equatorial Trough'.

The Earth, however, does not have a uniform surface; there are continental areas and oceanic areas. Furthermore, the amount of heat received from the Sun in any zone varies with the season.

The effect of the above factors is discussed on page 213.

(See Chapter 19, and A.I.R.S., Vol. 3)

Photo by G. A. Clarke

Photo by G. A. Clarke

C$_L$1   **Fair-weather cumulus.** The clouds look rather like cauliflowers. The bases tend to be flat and to be at a uniform level. They are scattered and have a flat and deflated appearance, even when convection is greatest (in the early afternoon). Their horizontal extension is greater than the vertical. The words 'fair weather' are not to be interpreted as a forecast; they refer to the weather at the time, and imply that there is no evidence in the sky of precipitation in the neighbourhood. (C=8)

Photo by Commander E. R. Trendall, R.N.

$C_L 2$ **Towering cumulus.** The difference between towering and fair-weather cumulus is that the tops of the former, instead of remaining rounded (and apparently quiescent), begin to bulge upwards and 'rising heads' appear. Their edges are still well defined and are not softening at the top into cirrus cloud.

Crown Copyright

$C_L 3$ **Cumulonimbus without anvil.** Distinguished from $C_L 2$ by the fact that the tops are beginning to acquire a fibrous appearance and by showers falling from the base. The tops are, however, definitely not cirriform or anvil-shaped, and the type is therefore $C_L 3$, not $C_L 9$. $(C = 9)$

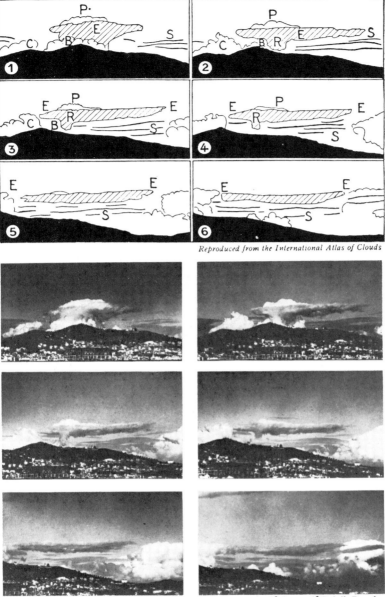

Reproduced from the International Atlas of Clouds

Photo by the Fundació Concepció Rabell, Barcelona

C_L4   **Stratocumulus** formed by the spreading-out of cumulus. This cloud is formed in two ways: (*a*) during the day, when there is a stable layer or an inversion which the convective cumulus clouds reach and cannot penetrate; (*b*) in the evening, when convection weakens, with or without an inversion above the cumulus. It is most common in the evening. (C = 6)

The time from the beginning to the end of the series shown is 20 minutes. 1. It is clear that the top of the cloud that is growing out is of the rounded cumulus type (B) without any cirriform parts. The spreading out has been at (E) and the head of the cumulus has penetrated the extension at (P). 2. (P) has developed a little, but (B) is decreasing and (E), which is increasing in extent, is beginning to separate off, so that the extreme base of the cloud (R) is now seen. 3. (P) grows smaller, (B) has completely settled down and is detached at (R), while (E) is still developing in extent. 4. (P) has completely settled down, (R) is melting away, (E) is completely independent. 5 and 6. There is no longer any trace of (P) or (R), while (E) is fully formed: notice the pendent shreds of cloud on the lower surface. In all the photographs other bands of stratocumulus may be seen in the distance which are being drawn out into stratus; they probably originated in the same way.

Photo by W. J. Day

Photo by C. J. P. Cave

C$_L$5   **Stratocumulus** not formed by the spreading-out of cumulus. The individual cloud masses may be detached and more or less lenticular in shape or close together in a continuous, or nearly continuous layer,. Stratocumulus is often a dark cloud, particularly in winter, but it may be fairly light – usually when it is at a fairly high level. The lower picture shows the stratocumulus layer below a layer of altocumulus. (C=6)

Photo by G. H. D. Evans

C_L6 **Stratus.** The illustration shows the typical structureless low stratus frequently seen in hilly country. (C=7)

Photo by G. A. Clarke

Photo by F. W. Baker

C$_L$7   Ragged, low clouds of bad weather. These low clouds, collectively known as **fractostratus,** often show up very dark against the relatively lighter background of altostratus or nimbostratus. The lower picture shows typical scud (fractostratus) below a background of nimbostratus; the upper picture shows an example that is, perhaps, less typical, but is, nevertheless, one in which the ragged, low clouds are the predominant features. (C=7)

Photo by G. A. Clarke

C_L8 **Cumulus** and **stratocumulus.** The base of the cumulus is lower than that of the stratocumulus, distinguishing C_L8 from C_L2 or C_L4. (C=8 and C=6)

Photo by Royal Air Force

Photo by G. A. Clarke

C$_L$9   **Cumulonimbus with anvil.** Ragged, low clouds of bad weather are often present, as in the lower example. The anvil-shaped mass of cirriform cloud, which is exceptionally well seen in the upper photograph, may be hidden from a near-by observer by lower parts of the cloud mass. It is important, therefore, to keep a close watch on the sky in order to ensure accurate differentiation between C$_L$3 and C$_L$9. (C=9)

Photo by G. A. Clarke

C_M1 Typical **altostratus (thin)**. This is a darkish veil usually covering the whole sky, though not always. It looks rather like a thinly fogged photographic plate. The Sun or Moon appears as though shining through ground glass and does not cast a shadow. Halo phenomena are not seen in altostratus. A sheet of this cloud resembles thick cirrostratus (*see* C_H7) from which it is often derived. (C=4)

Photo by G. A. Clarke

C_M2 Typical **altostratus (thick)** (C=4; Sun and Moon invisible), or **nimbostratus** (C=5). The Sun and Moon are generally hidden or are indicated only by the lighter colour of one part of the cloud. Typical thick altostratus can be formed either by a thickening of thin altostratus or by the fusing together of the cloudlets in a sheet of altocumulus. The picture illustrates an example rather on the thin side; in many cases the lightness will be less evident or will not appear at all.

Photo by G. A. Clarke

C_M3 Single layer of **altocumulus** or **high stratocumulus.** Altocumulus often resembles a woolly fleece. This type generally forms a single layer; it is fairly regular and of uniform thickness, the cloudlets always being separated by clear spaces or lighter gaps; the cloudlets are neither very large nor very dark. This layer is generally fairly persistent, and does not change or disappear quickly. Occurrences of altocumulus which are so dense that the waves do not show lighter parts should be reported as C_M7. (C=3)

Photo by G. A. Clarke

C_M4 **Altocumulus** in isolated patches – often lenticular. The cloudlets may be as small as in cirrocumulus, but lenticular altocumulus shows delicate colouring ' irisation '. Where this is so, the clouds are often scattered over the sky quite irregularly and may be at different levels. Though individually they may be changing, the amount of cloud over the whole sky generally remains about the same. (C=3)

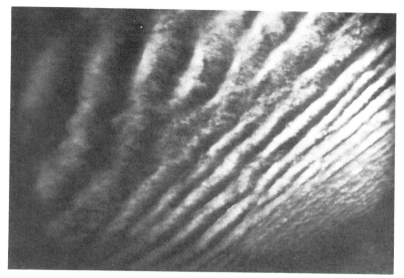

Photo by G. A. Clarke

C_M5 **Altocumulus** in bands (increasing). In this type, either the bands are great elongated masses, sometimes appearing rather dark and often of a roughly lenticular shape; or the ordinary altocumulus waves are crossed by blue lanes, so that they appear like bands (with the waves across the bands). An essential feature of this type is that the sky becomes more and more covered. Often the layer thickens up, as in the photograph; or another layer of cloud, lower and darker, forms beneath it. $(C=3)$

Photo by G. A. Clarke

C_M6 **Altocumulus** formed from the spreading-out of cumulus. Cumulus clouds of sufficiently great vertical development may undergo an extension of their summits, while their bases may gradually melt away. The process is similar to that of C_L4 but at a higher level. The apparently anvil-shaped cloud must not be confused with C_L9. $(C=3)$

Photo by Royal Air Force

C$_M$7 **Altocumulus** associated with **altostratus.** There may be two definite layers of altostratus and altocumulus; or the altocumulus may be thickening into altostratus by the cloudlets fusing together as in this photograph; or altostratus may break up into altocumulus.   (C=3 and C=4)

Photo by Bristol Evening Post

C$_M$8 **Altocumulus floccus.** The cloudlets are of ragged appearance without definite shadows and with the rounded parts slightly domed. There are often pronounced trails (*virga*) of cirriform appearance, as in the above example. (C=3)

Photo by C. J. P. Cave

$C_M 8$ **Altocumulus castellanus.** The character common to the types of altocumulus $C_M 8$ is vertical development – a turret or a dome shape. These clouds are often the precursors of thunderstorms. Altocumulus castellanus is composed of small cumuliform masses with more or less vertical development, either detached, as in the above example, or forming a band. ($C = 3$)

Photo by G. A. Clarke

C_M9 **Altocumulus** in several layers, generally associated with fibrous veils and a chaotic appearance of the sky. The sky has a disordered, heavy and stagnant appearance. It is very complex, with patches of medium cloud – more or less fragmentary – superposed; often it is badly defined, giving all the transitional forms between low altocumulus and the fibrous veil. (C=3)

Photo by C. J. P. Cave

C_H1 **Fine cirrus,** not increasing. Wisps of cloud at a very high level; they may be scattered over a large part of the sky, but the amount does not increase noticeably, either in time or in any particular direction. The clouds do not collect into sheets and bands, and there is no tendency for the elements to fuse together into masses of cirrostratus. Cirrus cloud the strands of which end in an upturned hook or tuft must not be included in this class, but in C_H4. (C=0)

Photo by C. J. P. Cave

C$_H$2 **Dense cirrus** in patches or twisted sheaves. Cirrus of this type is more 'woolly' in appearance than C$_H$1 and is possibly, but not certainly, the debris of the upper part of cumulonimbus. (C=0)

Photo by C. J. P. Cave

C_H3 **Cirrus,** often **anvil-shaped,** usually dense, which is known to be either the remains of the upper part of a disintegrated cumulonimbus or part of a distant cumulonimbus the rest of which is not visible at the time of observation. (C=0)

Photo by C. J. P. Cave

C_H4 **Hooked cirrus.** This type of cirrus, which is in the form of streaks ending in a little upturned hook or in a small tuft, increases in amount both in time and in a certain direction. In this direction it reaches to the horizon, where there is a tendency for the cloud elements to fuse together, but the clouds do not pass into cirrostratus. (C=0)

Photo by G. A. Clarke

C_H5 **Cirrus** or **cirrostratus** increasing; still below 45° altitude; often in polar bands. Sheet of fibrous cirrus partly uniting into cirrostratus, especially towards the horizon in the direction where the cirrus strands tend to fuse together. The cirrus is often in a herring-bone formation or in great bands converging more or less to a point on the horizon. In this class is also included a sheet of cirrostratus which does not cover the sky and is below 45° altitude. (C=2, or = 0 if cirrus predominates)

Photo by G. A. Clarke

C_H6 **Cirrus** or **cirrostratus** increasing and reaching above 45° altitude; often in polar bands. The definition of this type is the same as that of the previous one, with the exception that the cloud reaches more than 45° above the horizon. (*Note.* Altitudes, if not measured instrumentally, are deceptive; it is common to over-estimate a point in the sky. A point at 30° altitude will appear to be at about 45° altitude.) (C=2, or =0 if cirrus predominates)

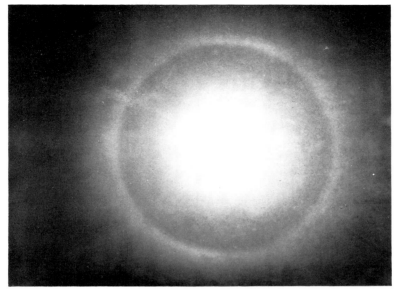

Photo by C. J. P. Cave

C_H7 **Veil of cirrostratus** covering the whole sky, either (*a*) a thin, uniform nebulous veil, sometimes hardly visible, sometimes relatively dense, always without definite detail, but producing halo phenomena round the Sun and Moon; or (*b*) a white fibrous sheet, with more or less clearly defined fibres, often like a sheet of fibrous cirrus from which, indeed, it may be derived. (C=2)

Photo by G. A. Clarke

C_H8 **Cirrostratus** not increasing and not covering the whole sky. This is a case of veil or sheet cirrostratus reaching the horizon in one direction, but leaving a segment of blue sky in the other direction. This segment of blue sky does not grow smaller; otherwise it would be reported as C_H5 or C_H6. Generally the edge of the sheet is clear-cut and does not tail off into scattered cirrus. (C=2)

Photo by G. A. Clarke

C$_H$9   **Cirrocumulus** predominating, and a little cirrus. Cirrocumulus is a wavy type of 'mackerel' sky with a delicate, fine structure. Cirrocumulus is not to be confused with small altocumulus. There must be either evident connexion with cirrus or cirrostratus, or the cloud observed must result from a change in cirrus or cirrostratus. Cirrocumulus may occur with any of the types C$_H$1 to C$_H$8. (C=1)

Effect of variations in the Sun's declination

The effect of the seasonal change of declination is to cause the belts of pressure and their associated winds to move towards the north in the northern summer, and towards the south in the southern summer. The amount of this oscillation is much smaller than that of the Sun itself and, in general, amounts only to some 4 degrees of latitude. Furthermore this movement lags some 6 to 8 weeks behind that of the Sun, so that the zones shown in Fig. 113 reach their most northerly position in July–August and their most southerly position in January–February.

Effect of the distribution of land and sea

The effect of large land masses is to modify greatly the 'planetary' distribution of pressure and wind. The belts of high pressure in about latitude 30° north and south are split into separate cells of high pressure (anticyclones) situated over the eastern part of each of the oceans; the belt of low pressure in about latitude 60°N is likewise modified into separate areas of low pressure situated in the vicinity of Iceland and the Aleutian Islands. In the southern hemisphere, there is little or no land in the zone covered by this low-pressure belt, and consequently it extends almost without interruption around the Earth.

Superimposed upon the above modifications of the general planetary system, temperature over large land masses becomes high in summer and low in winter, while over the oceans the seasonal variation is much less. As a result, pressure becomes relatively high over land masses in winter and low in summer. This seasonal change in pressure distribution causes corresponding modifications to the oceanic winds in the vicinity, and in certain areas results in the establishment of seasonal winds or monsoons.

GENERAL DESCRIPTION OF OCEANIC WINDS AND WEATHER

The Climates of the Oceans

The general distribution of oceanic winds in winter and summer is shown in Figs. 114 and 115. Mean barometric pressure in January and July is shown in Figs. 116 and 117.

More detailed information regarding oceanic winds and weather can be found in the *Atlases of Meteorological Charts*, while detailed information relating to specific localities is given in the *Admiralty Sailing Directions*.

The Equatorial Trough (Doldrums)

This is the name given to that part of the ocean lying in the equatorial trough of low pressure situated between the Trade winds of the two hemispheres.

K

The normal positions of the Equatorial Trough (Doldrums) in February and August are shown in Figs. 114 and 115. The characteristic features of this zone are calms and light variable winds alternating with squalls, heavy rains and thunderstorms. The width of the zone averages about 200 miles, but there are very considerable seasonal and day-to-day variations. The severity of the weather also varies greatly; at times a ship may cross the belt and experience fine weather, while on other occasions severe squalls, violent thunderstorms and much heavy rain may be encountered. It has been found that weather in the Equatorial Trough is generally worst when the strength of the Trade winds is greater than the normal, and best when the Trades are abnormally light.

The Trade winds

Between the Equatorial Trough and the oceanic high-pressure areas in each hemisphere blow the Trade winds, north-easterly in the northern hemisphere and south-easterly in the southern hemisphere. These winds blow permanently and with great steadiness and persistence throughout the year. Trade winds, however, do not blow in all the oceans; the South-west Monsoon winds (*see below*) in the East Atlantic, North Indian Ocean and in the western part of the North Pacific Ocean show this.

The average strength of the Trades is about force 3–4, though variations occur between different oceans and at different seasons.

Weather in this zone is generally fair or fine,* with small detached cumulus clouds. On the eastern sides of the oceans cloud amounts and rainfall are small, while on the western sides cloud amounts are larger and rain is comparatively frequent, being a maximum in the summer months. Both cloud and the frequency and intensity of rain increase towards the Equatorial Trough.

Poor visibility occurs fairly frequently in the eastern parts of the Trade wind belts, due in part to mist or fog forming at times over the cold currents and in part to sand and dust being carried out to sea by the prevailing offshore winds. On the western sides of the oceans visibility is good – except when reduced by heavy rain – and fog is rare.

The Variables

In the areas covered by the oceanic anticyclones, and situated between the Trade winds and the Westerlies farther polewards, there exist zones of light and variable winds. In the North Atlantic this region is known as the Horse Latitudes. The weather in these zones is generally fair or fine; cloud amounts are small and rainfall scanty.

The Westerlies

On the polar sides of the oceanic anticyclones the wind direction becomes prevailingly westerly. These winds are not, however, permanent winds in the same way as are the Trade winds on the equatorial side of the 'highs'. The constant passage of depressions from a westerly to an easterly point across this zone causes the winds to vary greatly in direction and strength.

---

* *Caution.* The generally fair weather of the Trades is liable, at certain seasons and in certain localities, to be interrupted by the dangerous tropical storms which are described in detail on pages 222–232.

Gales are frequent, especially in winter; the weather is subject to rapid changes, and fine weather is seldom prolonged. In the Southern Ocean the frequency of gales in the belt encircling the Earth south of about latitude 40°S has earned for it the name of the Roaring Forties.

In the northern hemisphere fog is common in the western parts of this zone during the summer. It also occurs fairly frequently in the Southern Ocean in the summer of that hemisphere.

Ice may be encountered in certain parts of this zone at certain seasons (*see* Volume I, Chapter XIII).

The Polar Regions

The greater part of the region lying on the polar sides of the Westerlies is unnavigable on account of ice. The prevailing wind is generally from some easterly point and gales are common in the winter months, though less so than in the zones of the Westerlies. Weather is usually very cloudy and fog is frequent in the summer months.

Seasonal winds and Monsoons

As mentioned above, the alternate heating and cooling of large land masses results in the formation there of areas of low pressure in the summer and of high pressure in winter, and consequently in a seasonal change in the prevailing winds over the adjacent oceans.

The most important areas subject to these seasonal winds are the Indian Ocean and western Pacific and the regions adjacent to the coasts of West Africa and North America.

Monsoons of the North Indian Ocean and Western Pacific*

The South-west Monsoon. In the northern summer the vast land mass of southern Asia becomes greatly heated, which results in the establishment of a large area of low pressure centred approximately over north-west India (*see* Fig. 117). The SE Trade winds of the South Indian Ocean and western South Pacific are drawn across the equator, are deflected to the right by the effect of the Earth's rotation, and join in the cyclonic wind circulation set up around this area of low pressure. The resulting south-westerly wind which is felt in the Arabian Sea, Bay of Bengal, China Sea, and western North Pacific is known as the South-west Monsoon. The season of the SW Monsoon is from about May to September. It is only a light wind in the western Pacific and China Sea and is moderate to fresh elsewhere, except in the western part of the Arabian Sea, where it blows fresh or strong and frequently attains gale force at the height of the season.

---

* The numerous islands lying in the SW Pacific, many of them of considerable size and height, cause marked differences in the winds and weather experienced in different localities; it is not possible therefore to give here more than a general picture of the situation. Detailed information of the several localities will be found in the meteorological section of the appropriate volume of the *Admiralty Sailing Directions*.

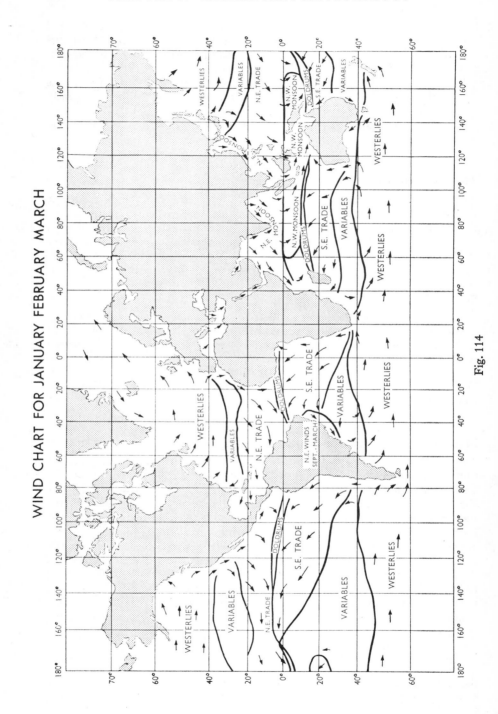

WIND CHART FOR JANUARY FEBRUARY MARCH

Fig. 114

Weather in the Arabian Sea and Bay of Bengal is generally cloudy and rather unsettled at this season, being worst when the monsoon is blowing strongest. Both cloud and rainfall increase greatly to windward of high ground, and rainfall on the west coasts of India and Burma is very heavy. In the open ocean of the western Pacific north of the equator conditions are generally fair, but with an increase in cloud and showers during the night and early morning. In the Timor and Arafura Seas, where the SE Trades prevail at this season, cloud amounts are small and rainfall is scanty, especially in the former area.

Visibility is good in the open ocean except when reduced by rain. In the Timor and Arafura Seas, however, extensive haze prevails to leeward of Australia – especially in the Timor Sea towards the end of the season. Fog is prevalent on the China coast in the spring and summer, reaching its maximum frequency in April off Hong Kong, in June off the Yangtse, and in July off Shantung.

The NE and NW Monsoons. In the northern winter the great land mass of Asia becomes very cold, and an intense area of high pressure becomes established over Mongolia (*see* Fig. 116). The anticyclonic circulation thus set up results in the establishment in the western North Pacific, Bay of Bengal and Arabian Sea of north-easterly winds known as the NE Monsoon. In the South Indian Ocean between the equator and the Equatorial Trough, the NE Monsoon is deflected to the left on crossing the equator and is felt here as a north-westerly wind. The limits of this north-westerly wind – or 'cross monsoon' as it is sometimes called – are indicated in Fig. 114. In a similar manner, in the western Pacific south of the equator the north-easterly winds, being deflected to the left, are felt as far as about latitude 12°S to 15°S as westerly or north-westerly winds known as the NW Monsoon.

The season of the NE Monsoon is from about October to March and that of the NW Monsoon from about November to March. Winds are light in the North Indian Ocean, but fresh and sometimes strong in the China Sea and in the North Pacific east of T'ai-wan and the Philippines. Elsewhere they are generally moderate or light.

Weather in the Arabian Sea and Bay of Bengal is generally fine, cloud amounts are small, and rain is rare except in the extreme south-west of the Bay of Bengal, where it is cloudy with considerable rain to windward of the coasts of Southern India and Sri Lanka. In the open ocean of the western Pacific weather is generally fair, with an increase of cloud and showers by night and in the early morning. In the China Sea north of latitude 20°N cloudy or overcast skies are common and there are frequent periods of light rain and drizzle. Among the islands to the south and south-east of the Philippines weather is generally cloudy and unsettled, with considerable rainfall.

Seasonal winds in other oceanic areas

In no other oceanic areas are the adjacent land masses of sufficient size to cause so radical a change in the oceanic winds as are experienced in the North Indian Ocean and western Pacific. Nevertheless fairly well-marked seasonal changes in the prevailing winds occur over the oceans adjacent to other large land masses.

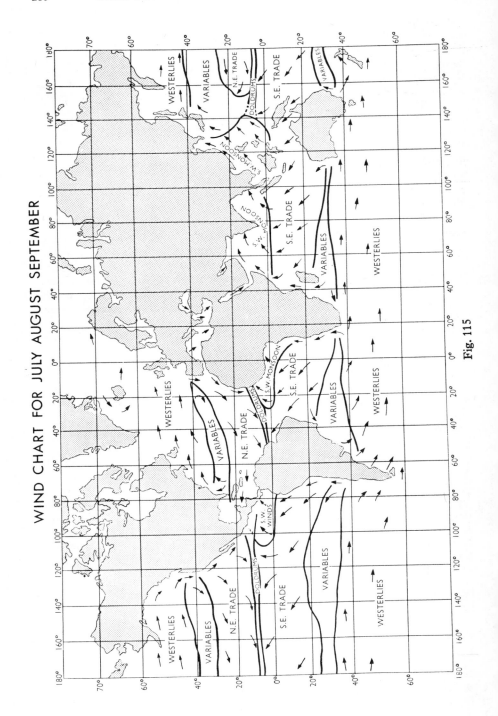

WIND CHART FOR JULY AUGUST SEPTEMBER

Fig. 115

The most important areas thus affected are as follows:

West Africa. In the northern summer pressure is low over northern Africa and the Equatorial Trough is distorted towards the north. The SE Trades on crossing the equator are deflected to the right, and are felt as south-westerly winds between about latitude 0° and 10°N, and east of about longitude 30°W. The season of these south-westerly winds is at its height in August (*see* Fig. 115). They bring cloudy and very wet weather to these coasts, in marked contrast to the fine, hot weather experienced in the winter months.

Eastern Pacific. The establishment of relatively low pressure over the North American continent during the summer, and the consequent bending of the Equatorial Trough towards the north, results in the SE Trades being deflected to the right on crossing the equator and in the prevalence of south-westerly winds at this season between the equator and about latitude 10°–15°N and east of about longitude 120°W (*see* Fig. 115). These south-westerly winds replace the normal NE Trade wind which prevails in this area during the northern winter and bring wet, cloudy weather to the west coasts of Central America.

LOCAL WINDS

Land and sea breezes

The regular alternation of land and sea breezes is a conspicuous feature of most tropical and subtropical coasts and islands (other than very small ones). Land and sea breezes also occur at times in temperate latitudes in fine, settled weather in the summer, though they are here much weaker and less well marked than in lower latitudes.

The cause of these breezes is the unequal heating and cooling of the land and the sea by the Sun's radiation. By day the surface of the Earth rapidly acquires heat under the influence of the Sun's rays, whereas the sea temperature remains virtually unaffected. The heat of the land is communicated to the air in contact with it, which expands and rises. Air from over the sea flows in to take its place, producing an onshore wind known as the 'sea breeze'. By night the land rapidly loses heat by radiation, and becomes much colder than the adjacent sea. The air over the land is chilled, becomes denser and heavier, and flows out to sea under the influence of gravity. This constitutes the 'land breeze'.

The sea breeze usually sets in at about 1000–1100 h local time, attains its maximum strength (usually about Beaufort force 3–4) at about 1400, and dies away about sunset. It extends normally about 20 miles to seaward, though under favourable conditions it has been detected at as much as 100 miles from the coast. The land breeze is usually less well marked and weaker than the sea breeze – often being inappreciable. It starts during the first watch and blows until shortly after sunrise. The effect of these breezes may be to deviate the prevailing wind, to reinforce it, to neutralize it, or even to reverse it.

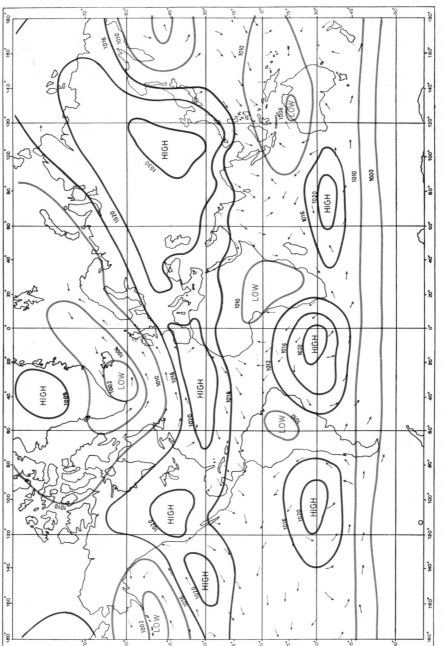

Fig. 116   Average pressure at mean sea-level and prevailing winds at the surface in January

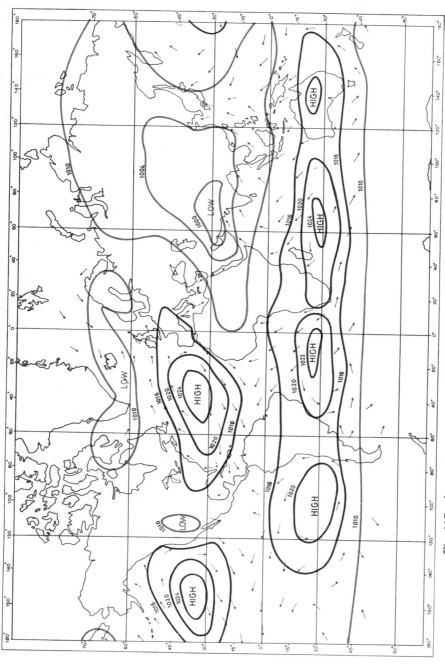

Fig. 117 Average pressure at mean sea-level and prevailing winds at the surface in July

The following factors are favourable to the formation of well-marked land and sea breezes:

1. A dry desert coast, as opposed to forests and swamps.
2. High ground near the coast.
3. A weak prevailing wind.

A cold current along the coast also has the effect of favouring the establishment of a well-marked sea breeze.

The breeze produced by two adjacent land masses is the resultant of the two effects. Small islands less than 10 miles in diameter will not usually produce land and sea breezes.

Katabatic winds

On clear nights there is often a downward flow of air on mountain and hill slopes, and particularly along valley bottoms, known as *katabatic wind*. It is caused by the gravitational flow of air cooled by contact with a land surface which is losing its heat by radiation. In temperate and high latitudes where the coast is backed by snow-covered mountains, such winds may occur by day as well as by night. In these circumstances, radiation from the snow-covered high grounds is intense, and a mass of cold air accumulates among the mountains. A light general offshore wind then suffices to impel this cold air towards the seaward-facing slopes, down which it flows with gathering momentum, being felt off the coast as a strong or gale-force wind. The usually sudden onset of these winds coupled with their strength often makes them a menace to small craft and to ships at anchor.

Among areas where these winds are common are the coasts of Greenland, Norway, the northern Adriatic, and the eastern part of the Black Sea.

Föhn winds

A föhn is a warm, dry wind experienced to leeward of high ground. The air is forced to rise up the windward side of the mountains and during its ascent it is cooled and condensation takes place in the form of cloud and rain. The temperature of the air first decreases at a rate of 0·9°C per 100 m (330 ft) of ascent, but after it becomes saturated and condensation occurs, its temperature falls off at only about 0·5°C per 100 m. Having attained the summit, the air descends the lee side of the range. Having precipitated much of its moisture on the windward slopes, and being heated by compression consequent upon its descent, it soon ceases to be saturated. Its temperature therefore increases at a rate of 0·9°C per 100 m, and it arrives at the bottom of the slope both warmer and drier than at its starting point on the windward side of the range.

TROPICAL REVOLVING STORMS

In December 1944, vessels of the United States Pacific Fleet, operating to the east of the Philippines, were caught near the centre of a typhoon of extreme violence. Three destroyers capsized and went down with practically all hands. Serious damage was sustained by a light cruiser, three small carriers, three escort carriers and three destroyers. Lesser damage was sustained by at least 19 other vessels, from heavy cruisers down to escort vessels. Fires occurred in three aircraft carriers when planes were smashed in their hangars; some 146 aircraft were damaged beyond repair by fires, by being smashed up, or by being washed overboard. About 790 officers and men were lost or killed. Several surviving destroyers reported rolling 70° or more.

The following reports were typical during this storm:

1. Visibility zero to one thousand yards.

2. Ships not merely rolling but heeled over continually by the force of the wind, thus leaving them very little margin for further rolling to leeward.

3. Water being shipped in quantity through ventilators, blower intakes and every upper-deck opening.

4. Switchboards and electrical machinery of all kinds short-circuited and flooded; fires resulting from short-circuits.

5. Loss of steering control, failure of power and lighting and stopping of main engines; loss of radar and all communications facilities.

6. Free water up to two or three feet over engines or engine-room deck-plates and in many other compartments.

7. Wind speeds and seas which carried away masts, funnels, boats, davits and deck structures generally and made it impossible for men to secure gear which had gone adrift, or to jettison or strike below topside weights, when the necessity had become paramount.

8. Ships lost took a long roll to leeward, varying from 50° to 80°, hung there for a little while and then capsized, floating for only a short time before sinking.

All these are major hazards to seamen and may be experienced in a fully developed tropical revolving storm. These storms therefore merit a special study.

Tropical revolving storms are so named because they originate in certain tropical oceanic areas and because the wind blows round an area of low pressure situated at the centre. The direction of rotation is anti-clockwise in the northern hemisphere, and clockwise in the southern hemisphere. The wind does not revolve round the centre of the low pressure in concentric circles, but has a spiral movement inwards towards the centre.

A tropical storm is not so extensive as the depression of higher latitudes (*see* next chapter), but within 75 miles or so of the centre the wind is often far more violent, and the high and confused seas near the centre may cause considerable damage even to large and well-found ships. The danger is even greater when ships are caught in restricted waters without adequate room to manoeuvre. Within 5 to 10 miles of the centre the wind is light or moderate and variable, the sky is clear or partially so, and there is a heavy, sometimes mountainous, confused swell; this area is known as the 'eye' of the storm. Owing to torrential rain and sheets of almost continuous spray, visibility near the storm-centre (but outside the 'eye') is almost nil.

Every ship navigating in an area subject to tropical storms during the season of their occurrence should be constantly on the alert for any sign of their approach, so that steps can be taken to avoid the danger zone while there is still time and sea-room.

Locality

Tropical storms occur for the most part on the western and equatorial sides of the subtropical anticyclones, although they are also experienced in the Arabian Sea and Bay of Bengal, the south-east Indian Ocean, off the north-west coast of Australia and off the west coast of Central America. They are unknown in the South Atlantic. They are given various names according to the region in which they occur:

Western North Atlantic ⎫	
Eastern North Pacific ⎬	Hurricanes
South Pacific ⎭	
Western North Pacific	Typhoons
Indian Ocean ⎫	
Bay of Bengal ⎬	Cyclones
Arabian Sea ⎭	
North-west Australia	Willy-willies

Season

They are most frequent during the late summer and early autumn of their hemisphere; they are comparatively rare in the southern hemisphere from mid-May to November, and in the northern hemisphere from mid-November to mid-June. In the Arabian Sea, however, storms are most likely to occur at the change of the monsoon, i.e. October–November and May–June, though they average only one or two a year. Out-of-season storms occur from time to time, particularly in the western North Pacific, where no month is entirely safe, and in the Indian Ocean, where one is reported south of the equator perhaps once in two years outside the usual season.

Frequency

The following table shows the average number of severe tropical storms per year for various areas:

West Indies and North Atlantic	4·7
China Sea and western North Pacific	22
Western South Pacific	2·3
South Indian Ocean (west of 80°E)	5·8
South Indian Ocean (east of 80°E)	2·0
Bay of Bengal	4·7
Arabian Sea	1·2
Eastern North Pacific	3·1
West coast of Australia	1

It should be noted that variations in any one year amounting to 50 per cent above or below the average are not unusual.

Life history

Storms originate as a general rule between the parallels of 7° and 15°, though some may originate nearer the equator. Those which affect the western parts of the Pacific, South Indian, and North Atlantic Oceans are first reported in the western parts of those oceans, though there are exceptions such as in the North Atlantic during August and September when an occasional storm originates near the Cape Verde Islands.

In the northern hemisphere they move off in a direction between 275° and 350°, though most often within 30° of due west. When in a latitude of 25° or so, they usually recurve away from the Equator, and by the time they have reached the 30th parallel they will be moving along a north-easterly course. In the southern hemisphere they move off from the area of origin in a WSW to SSW direction (usually the former), recurve in latitude 15°S to 20°S (approximately), and thereafter adopt a south-easterly path. Some storms, however, do not recurve but continue in a west-north-westerly (or west-south-westerly) direction until they reach the mainland, where they fairly quickly fill.

The speed of these storms is usually about 10 knots in their early stages, increasing a little with latitude; it seldom exceeds 15 knots before recurving, but thereafter 20 to 25 knots is usual, though speeds of 40 knots or even more have been known.

Occasionally storms move erratically, the path turning towards the Equator, or adopting an easterly component in a low latitude, or even making a complete loop; but on such occasions their speed is low, generally less than 10 knots while the unusual path is being followed.

The extent of the storm area varies considerably with individual storms, but generally speaking winds of force 7 or more are improbable at more than 200 miles from the centre (especially on the equatorial side of the storm area); while winds of force 8 are unlikely to be exceeded at more than 100 miles from the centre in latitudes lower than 20°. Hurricane-force winds are likely within 75 miles of the centre, and gusts of over 150 knots have occasionally been reported within 50 miles (except in the eye of the storm). Thereafter the radius increases with latitude, so that these distances are nearly doubled in latitude 35°, but the intensity near the centre diminishes. Subsequently the storms usually acquire the characteristics of deep temperate-latitude depressions (*see* next chapter) and continue to move north-eastwards (or south-eastwards), eventually filling up and disappearing.

Nomenclature

The *Point of Recurvature* is the most westerly point reached by the centre of the storm before it recurves.

The *Navigable Semicircle* is that semicircle which lies on the side of the path farthest from the normal direction in which the storm recurves (that is, on the equatorial side of the path). A low-powered or sailing ship situated within this semicircle will tend to be blown away from the storm centre, and the recurvature of the storm will increase her distance from the centre (*see* Fig. 118).

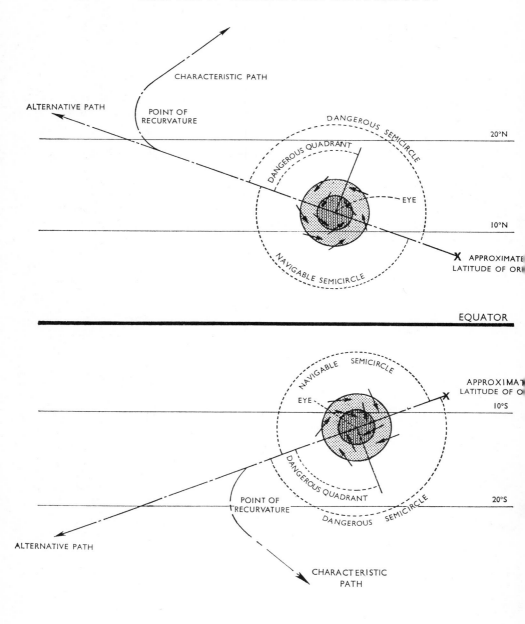

WINDS OF FORCE 7 OR LESS   WINDS OF FORCE 8 OR HIGHER

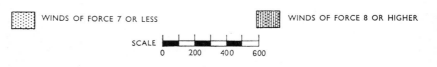

Fig. 118

After the storm has recurved the navigable semicircle is on the polar side of the path.

The *Dangerous Semicircle* lies on the side of the path towards the usual direction of recurvature, i.e. the right-hand semicircle (looking along the path) in the northern hemisphere, and the left-hand semicircle in the southern hemisphere. A low-powered or sailing ship caught in the dangerous semicircle may be blown towards the path along which the storm will pass, or the storm may recurve and the centre pass over her.

The *Dangerous Quadrant* is the leading quadrant of the dangerous semi-circle. When warning of a storm has been received, course and speed should normally be adjusted so that the ship keeps out of this quadrant.

Warning signs

In most cases warning of the position, intensity and probable movement of a storm is given by radio at frequent intervals. *Admiralty List of Radio Signals, Volume 3* contains up-to-date information for all areas of the times at which warnings are broadcast. They are usually repeated on operational circuits with high signal priority.

Sometimes, however, there is insufficient evidence available for an accurate warning or even a general warning to be given, and ships must be guided by their own observations, always bearing in mind that very little warning may be expected of an intense storm of unusually small diameter.

Barometer. At sea in the tropics, the barometric pressure varies very little except for diurnal variation (*see* page 179). When the barometer reads 3 millibars or more below the mean for the time of the year, as shown in a climatic atlas or in the *Sailing Directions* for that area, it may mean that a storm is approaching or forming, and action, such as preparing to use extra power, should be taken to meet any development. It should be noted that the barometer must be corrected not only for height and temperature, but also for diurnal variation, the amount of which is given in the climatic atlases and in the *Sailing Directions* for the area. If the reading, thus corrected, is 5 mb or more below normal, there can be little doubt that there is a tropical storm in the vicinity, and it is time to take avoiding action. According to an analysis of observations in the western Pacific, the centre of the storm is probably by this time not more than 200 miles away. At this distance, at any rate in the China Sea vicinity, the wind has usually increased to about force 6.

Of all the indications of the proximity of a tropical storm, the fall of barometric pressure is by far the most reliable within 20° of the Equator. When proceeding through an area liable to be visited by these storms it is advisable to take hourly readings of the barometer.

In normal circumstances, and on occasions when a storm is going to pass uncomfortably close to the observer, there are usually three fairly definite phases in the fall of the barometer:

1. A slow fall during which the diurnal variation is still apparent on the barograph trace. This usually occurs between 500 and 120 miles from the centre of the storm.

2. A distinct fall during which the diurnal variation is almost completely masked. This usually occurs between 120 and 60 miles from the centre. Throughout this phase the barometer is sometimes very unsteady.

3. A rapid fall. This usually occurs between 60 and 10 miles from the centre.

In the rear of the storm, the barometer rises as rapidly as it fell in advance of the storm.

It is not uncommon for the barometer at the centre of a storm to stand 60 to 70 mb lower than in the region just outside the storm field. The steepest barometric gradient normally encountered is 11 mb in 15 miles.

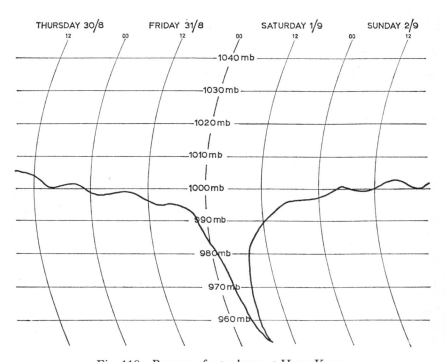

Fig. 119   Passage of a typhoon at Hong Kong

Fig. 119 is a reproduction of the barograph trace at Hong Kong when the centre of a typhoon passed very near to the island.

Swell. In the open sea, if there is no intervening land between the ship and the centre, the swell may give the first indication of a tropical revolving storm. The swell may extend to a distance of over 1,000 miles from the actual storm, and in a fully developed storm can usually be relied on to make itself felt 400 miles from the centre. The swell moves out from the centre of the storm, and its direction thus gives a good idea of the bearing of the centre.

When the storm is at a distance greater than 200 miles from a ship the direction of the swell is the most reliable of all indications of the direction in which the centre lies.

Although the swell increases as a storm approaches, its state does not give any reliable indication of the *distance* of the centre.

Wind. An appreciable change in the direction and/or an appreciable change in wind force may indicate the presence or formation of a tropical storm.

Sky. Extensive cirrus cloud generally precedes a storm, followed, as the storm centre becomes closer, by much altostratus cloud and subsequently nimbostratus and 'scud'.

Radar. See page 266.

Although the precursory signs of the approach of a storm have been dealt with independently, it is important to realise that factors of wind, sea, cloud, weather and barometer must be taken into consideration together. The recorded paths of storms in different months (included in the weather handbooks for the different stations, and in the more recently revised *Sailing Directions*) should be studied, since the place of origin and the path often vary with the season. By so doing, the most likely course of the storm may be estimated. It is only by using all the information available that the fullest measure of success in prediction can be obtained.

Reports by ships

In accordance with regulations drawn up by the International Convention for Safety of Life at Sea, it is the duty of every ship which suspects the presence or formation of a tropical revolving storm immediately to inform other vessels and shore authorities with all the means at her disposal. Weather reports should be made by radio at frequent intervals, giving as much information as possible, especially barometer readings. Such readings should be corrected in the normal way, but *not* for diurnal variation.

Practical rules for avoiding tropical storms

To decide on the best course of action when a storm is suspected to be in the vicinity, a seaman requires to know:

1. the bearing of the centre of the storm,
2. the path of the storm,
3. whether the ship is in the dangerous or navigable semicircle.

The bearing of the storm's centre can be found by applying Buys Ballot's Law, modified slightly, as follows:

Stand facing the true wind, and the centre of the storm will be from 100° to 120° on your right hand in the northern hemisphere and on your left hand in the southern hemisphere.

This is true when the centre of the storm is about 200 miles away; the barometer will by then be about 5 mb below the mean, and the wind will have increased to force 6 or thereabouts. As a rule the nearer one is to the centre the more closely does the angular displacement approach 90°.

The path of the storm may be approximately determined by taking two such bearings with an interval of from two to three hours between observations and allowing for the ship's movement. It can, however, be assumed that the storm is not travelling towards the equator; while in latitudes lower than 20° its path is most unlikely to have an easterly component. On the rare occasions when neither of these statements applies, the storm is moving very slowly.

It is a matter of vital importance to avoid passing within 50 miles or so of the centre of the storm. It is preferable to keep outside a radius of 200 miles or more, because at this distance the wind does not exceed force 7 (and is generally not more than force 6) and freedom to manoeuvre is maintained. If a ship has at least 20 knots at her disposal and shapes a course that will take her most rapidly away from the storm, it is unlikely that the wind will increase sufficiently to restrict her movement, and risk of damage is remote.

Sometimes a tropical storm moves so slowly that a vessel, if ahead of it, can easily outpace it; or, if astern of it, can overtake it. Since, however, she is unlikely to feel seriously the effects of a storm so long as the barometer does not fall more than 5 mb (corrected for diurnal variation) below the normal, it is recommended that frequent readings should be made if the presence of a storm in the vicinity is suspected or known, and that the vessel should continue on her course until the barometer has fallen 5 mb or until the wind has increased to force 6 and the barometer has fallen at least 3 mb. If and when either of those events occurs, she should alter course in accordance with the following paragraphs until the barometer has risen again above the limits just given and the wind has decreased below force 6. If it is certain that the ship is behind the storm, or in the navigable semicircle, it will evidently be sufficient to alter course away from the centre.

In the Northern Hemisphere

If the wind is veering, the ship must be in the dangerous semicircle. A power-driven vessel should proceed with all available speed with the wind 10° to 45° (depending upon her speed and that of the storm) on the starboard bow. A sailing vessel should heave to on the starboard tack. Either type of ship should haul round to starboard as the wind veers, thereby tracing a course relative to the storm centre, as shown by track (1) in Fig. 120a.

If the wind remains steady in direction, or if it backs, so that the ship seems to be nearly in the path of the storm, or in the navigable semicircle respectively, a power-driven vessel should bring the wind well on the starboard quarter and proceed with all available speed.* A sailing vessel should run with the wind on the starboard quarter. Either type of ship should alter course to port as the wind backs, thus tracing a course relative to the storm as shown by track (2) in Fig. 120a.

If there is insufficient room to run when in the navigable semicircle, and it is not practicable to seek shelter, a vessel should heave to with the wind on the starboard bow.

---

* It is sometimes difficult to determine satisfactorily if the ship *is* nearly in the path because the wind does not always behave according to rule.

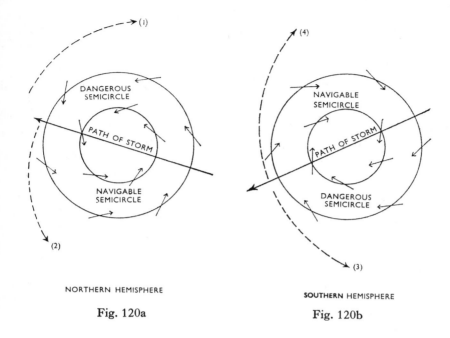

NORTHERN HEMISPHERE

Fig. 120a

SOUTHERN HEMISPHERE

Fig. 120b

In the Southern Hemisphere

If the wind is backing, the ship must be in the dangerous semicircle. A power-driven vessel should proceed with all available speed with the wind 10° to 45° (depending upon her speed and that of the storm) on the port bow. A sailing vessel should heave to on the port tack. Each type of ship should haul round to port as the wind backs, thereby tracing a course relative to the storm similar to track (3) in Fig. 120b.

If the wind remains steady in direction or if it veers, so that the ship is in the path of the storm or in the navigable semicircle respectively, a power-driven vessel should bring the wind well on the port quarter and proceed with all available speed. A sailing vessel should run with the wind broad on the port quarter. Either type of ship should alter course to starboard as the wind veers; track (4) in Fig. 120b shows the relative track of a ship under these conditions.

If there is insufficient room to run when in the navigable semicircle and it is not practicable to seek shelter, a vessel should heave to with the wind on the port bow.

Precautions in harbour

When in harbour, as much care must be taken as at sea in watching the shifting of the wind and estimating the relative movement of the storm. By so doing berth can be shifted with advantage or other steps taken according to circumstances. For instance, if the centre of the storm passes over the ship, it may be possible to point the ship in the direction of the violent squall which follows the lull. It is much preferable, however, to put to sea, if this can be done in sufficient time to avoid the worst of the storm. Riding out a tropical storm in an anchorage or harbour when the centre passes within 50 miles or so, even if some shelter is afforded, is an extremely uncomfortable and hazardous experience, especially if there are other ships in company.

Discretion must of course be used. For instance, in the case of a low-powered or small vessel with insufficient warning to enable her to gain adequate distance from the storm by putting to sea, it will be preferable to remain in a reasonably sheltered harbour. Conversely, if at sea and warning of an approaching storm is given, and if there is considered to be insufficient time or sea-room to avoid the dangerous part of the storm area, it may be advisable for ships of this type to seek shelter.

Storm tides

When a tropical storm approaches a coast, serious flooding often occurs. At sea the winds in the storm field create waves which travel out ahead of it and eventually reach the shore, where they cause a rise in the water beginning when the storm is 300 to 500 miles away and continuing until the storm crosses the coast. The height of the flood level reached at the shore near the centre of the storm is sometimes as much as 4·5 m (15 ft) above the predicted tide level.

CHAPTER 20

Weather Forecasting

It was seen in the previous chapter that the climate of an oceanic locality depends very approximately upon its latitude and varies to a greater or lesser extent with the season. The weather experienced does not vary much from day to day in the Equatorial Trough, the Trades or the Horse Latitudes; fog is practically unknown except in certain areas mentioned in Chapter 19; and dangerously strong winds are associated only with tropical storms or short-lived squalls. In the Westerlies and Roaring Forties, on the other hand, the weather is subject to large variations over periods of hours only, and gales and fog are experienced much more frequently.

It will be shown that in temperate latitudes disturbed weather is associated with the interaction of two streams of air of different physical properties such as temperature and humidity. Inspection of the Planetary System (page 192) shows that, over the oceans at any rate, the temperate latitudes lie between belts of high pressure (the Horse Latitudes and the polar high-pressure caps). Air flows outwards from these high-pressure areas, and cold air from polar areas is thus constantly meeting warm air from the sub-tropics in the temperate latitudes. Weather forecasting in these latitudes is therefore largely the study of air streams meeting there and their effect upon each other.

The following paragraphs refer to the eastern North Atlantic, with particular reference to the British Isles and adjacent areas. The principles apply in all temperate latitudes, but with modifications due to geography.

AIR MASSES

Air which comes from the subtropical high-pressure belt is known as 'tropical air', that from the polar high-pressure cap as 'polar air'. Both tropical and polar air-streams arrive at the British Isles, but their properties when they arrive will depend upon the path they have taken, that is, whether they have travelled over the sea or over the land and whether they have come directly from the areas of origin or by a roundabout track.

Air which originates over an ocean is classified as 'maritime'; that which originates over a land mass as 'continental'. Fig. 121 shows how both polar and tropical air can arrive in the British Isles by either maritime or continental routes.

Thus there are four main types of air mass affecting the British Isles: maritime polar, maritime tropical, continental tropical and continental polar. The first two are those most frequently experienced in the British Isles.

As long as an observer remains in a stream of a particular kind of air, he will experience the weather characteristic of that type of air. The problem in forecasting is to decide when the type of air-stream will change and what will

233

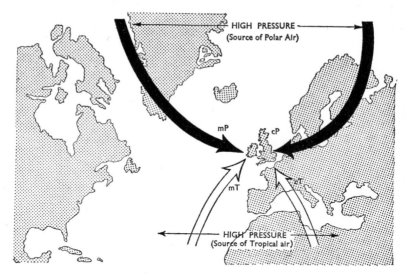

Fig. 121

happen during the change from one type of air-stream to the other. The properties and weather associated with different air-streams are as follows.

Maritime Tropical (mT)

Maritime tropical air originates in the oceanic area between the Azores and the West Indies. It travels north-eastwards over sea which is getting steadily colder as the latitude increases. The lower layers will therefore cool down by contact with the sea surface, and the relative humidity near the surface will increase. The fall of temperature with height (lapse rate) will be slow, and the air will be stable; inversions of temperature may occur near the surface.

The weather to be expected in a stream of maritime tropical air will therefore be as follows:

(*a*) Wind will usually be from the south-west quadrant.

(*b*) Clouds will be of stratiform type.

(*c*) Precipitation, if any, will be in the form of drizzle.

(*d*) Visibility will be poor and there will be a tendency for sea fog to form.

(*e*) Temperature of the air will usually be a little higher than that of the sea.

(*f*) Relative humidity will be high.

Maritime Polar (mP)

This type originates in the polar regions and arrives at the British Isles over the Atlantic Ocean. It travels over sea which is getting warmer as the latitude decreases. The lower layers are therefore being warmed up and the lapse rate will be increasing so that instability may develop. Although containing

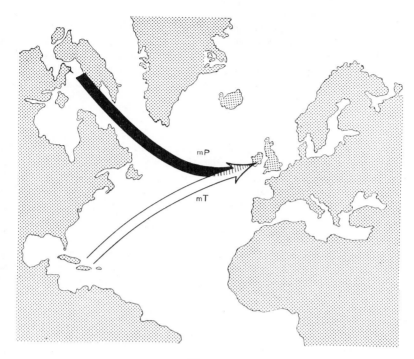

Fig. 122

only small amounts of water vapour when it leaves the polar regions, it picks up a certain amount from the warmer sea over which it is passing, though it is not likely to become saturated.

The weather associated with a stream of maritime polar air will therefore be:

(a) Wind will usually be gusty and from a direction between south-west and north.

(b) Clouds will usually be of cumuliform type.

(c) Rain, when it falls, will be in the form of showers.

(d) Visibility will be good except in rain.

(e) Temperature of the air will usually be slightly lower than that of the sea.

(f) Relative humidity will be somewhat lower than that of maritime tropical air.

The longer the track of the air over the sea, the warmer and more humid does maritime polar air become. In Fig. 122, for example, the air originates north of the Davis Strait and has a very long trajectory over the ocean, eventually arriving over the British Isles as a south-westerly wind. Its temperature and humidity will also be high and it is not always easy to differentiate between streams of maritime polar and maritime tropical air under these conditions.

Continental Tropical (cT)

The source region of this air is North Africa and (in summer) South Russia. It leaves its source with a high temperature. Its properties when it arrives over the British Isles depend upon its track. If, for example, it crosses the Alps, the moisture which it picks up over the Mediterranean will be deposited on the Alps and it will arrive as a warm, dry wind, causing heat waves during summer.

Continental Polar (cP)

This type originates over North Russia and Scandinavia in winter. It usually brings very cold weather to the British Isles, and generally overcast skies due to the moisture picked up during its passage across the North Sea. If, however, the air reaches the British Isles from a south-easterly direction after only a short passage over the sea it brings fine, frosty weather.

The Polar Front

Polar and tropical air masses do not mix; there is usually a definite boundary between them across which there are discontinuities of temperature, humidity and wind. The boundary between the two air-streams is known as the Polar

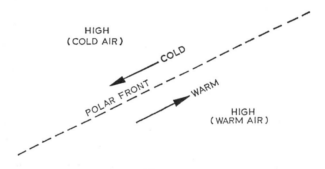

Fig. 123

Front. Fig. 123 shows how the two air-streams and the Polar Front may well be arranged; in this case there is no wind component at right angles to the front and it will be stationary.

Owing to the difference in density between the two air masses and to the rotation of the Earth, the Polar Front is not vertical but inclined at a slope varying between 1 in 50 and 1 in 200 towards the cold air.

DEPRESSIONS

Occasionally a surge of tropical air northwards, or of polar air southwards, causes a wave to form on the Polar Front. This wave then usually begins to move along the front in a north-easterly direction. In Fig. 124 a wave has formed with its apex at *A* and it is moving off to the north-east. At the same time there is a general fall of pressure in the area, because dense, cold air is

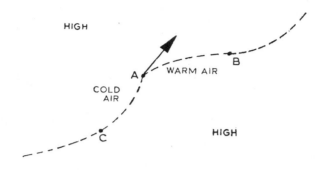

Fig. 124

being replaced by lighter, warm air. This continues until a definite cyclonic air circulation is established around the area of low pressure.

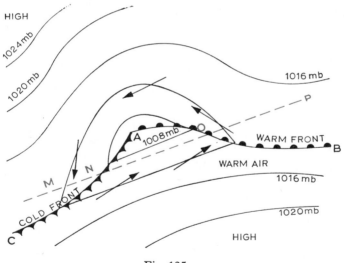

Fig. 125

The section *AB* of the Polar Front (Fig. 125) is now moving in an east-north-east direction; as it passes over a place, polar air is replaced by tropical air at that place. It is therefore called a 'warm front'. Warm fronts are denoted by red lines on working charts and by the symbol ●▬●▬● on printed charts.

The section *AC* of the Polar Front has begun to move south-eastward. When it passes a place, tropical air is replaced by polar air and it is therefore called a 'cold front'. Cold fronts are indicated by blue lines on working charts and by the symbol ▲▲▲ on printed charts.

The warm front assumes a slope of about 1 in 100; the slope of the cold front, however, is found to be of the order of 1 in 50. A vertical section through

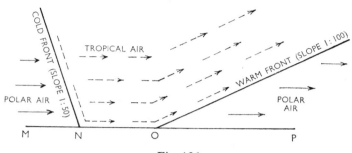

Fig. 126

the fronts (along a line *MNOP*, say) would appear as shown in Fig. 126. The cold front usually moves at a somewhat higher speed than the warm front. The warm air is therefore made to rise over the cold air at both the warm front and the cold front.

The warm air is normally of maritime tropical origin and is consequently moist. Above the warm and cold fronts, therefore, the water vapour in the warm air is condensing and there are wedges of stratiform or layer cloud. At the cold front, the warm air is rising more rapidly and there are also cumulonimbus clouds and short periods of heavier rain. As the depression develops, condensation continues and rain falls from the stratiform cloud ahead of the warm front

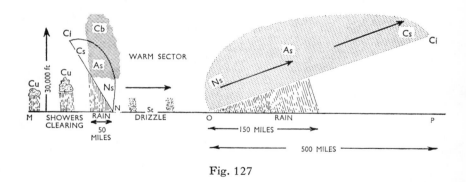

Fig. 127

and astern of the cold front. Fig. 127 shows a vertical cross-section of the cloud and weather in a typical depression.

As the depression deepens, that is to say as the barometric pressure at the centre falls, the air is made to circulate more rapidly. In most depressions an increase of wind strength is experienced; in deep depressions the wind usually rises to gale force.

The cold front is travelling faster than the warm front. The time comes when the cold front overtakes the warm front, and all the air in the original warm sector is lifted up and 'occluded', as shown in Fig. 128. When this occurs, the source of energy is removed and the depression slowly dies. It is then said to have filled up (Fig. 129). 'Occlusions', as occluded fronts are called, are denoted by adjacent red and blue lines on working charts, and by the symbol ▲●▲●▲ on printed charts.

Fig. 130 shows in plan the cloud, weather and wind direction associated with typical

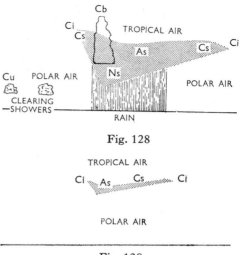

Fig. 128

Fig. 129

'warm sector' and occluded depressions. The changes in weather experienced by an observer stationed south of the centre of the depression are shown in the table on page 240.

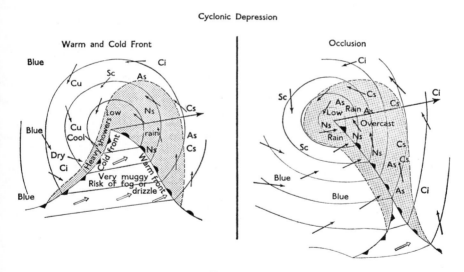

Fig. 130

The changes when a front passes can be summarized as:

1. a veer in wind direction and possibly a change of strength,
2. a rain belt,
3. an alteration in the sky,

CHANGE IN WEATHER DURING THE PASSAGE OF FRONTS

(This table assumes the front to be travelling in an easterly direction)

	1 IN ADVANCE OF WARM FRONT	2 AT PASSAGE OF WARM FRONT	3 IN WARM SECTOR	4 AT PASSAGE OF COLD FRONT	5 IN REAR OF COLD FRONT
Wind	Backs to S or SE and increases	Veers to SW and may continue to freshen	Little change in direction, but may continue to freshen	Veers to W or NW with squalls	Continues to veer, for a time, and moderates
Barometer	Falls rapidly	Fall is checked	Steady or slow fall	Rises sharply	Continues to rise but progressively more slowly
Temperature ...	May rise gradually	Rises slowly	Steady	Falls sharply	Usually continues to fall slowly
Relative humidity ...	Increases slowly	Increases rapidly	Little change	Begins to increase	Decreases rapidly
Visibility	Deteriorates slowly	Poor	Poor	Poor	Improves rapidly
Sky	Becomes overcast in the order Ci, Cs, As, Ns	Overcast with As and Ns	Clouds thinner but much St and Sc	Overcast with As, Ns, Sc, and Cb	Clears. Cu and blue sky only
Rain	Becoming continuous	Ceases and gives way to intermittent or continuous drizzle	Continuous or intermittent drizzle	Continuous heavier rain and possibly thunder	Occasional showers

4. a change of temperature,
5. a change of relative humidity,
6. an alteration in the rate of change of the barometer.

When an occluded depression passes to the north of an observer the sequence of events is that of columns 1, 4 and 5 of the table, omitting columns 2 and 3.

When the centre passes to the south of an observer, no front will be experienced. The wind backs from the south-east quadrant to the north-east quadrant, the barometer falls steadily and then begins to rise steadily again (there is no abrupt change), and there will be a period (probably prolonged) of stratiform cloud and rain.

It is important to note that, in practice, frontal systems are often not as simple as implied in the preceding paragraphs; a lack of clearance behind a cold front, for example, usually means that a second cold front is approaching.

The formation of secondaries

When a depression is occluded, its speed of advance is reduced and it may even stop. When this occurs secondary disturbances or waves are liable to form on the trailing cold front. They will rotate anti-clockwise round the parent depression, bringing with them similar changes of weather, usually on a smaller scale. Sometimes the only effect is that the barometer ceases to rise and there is a temporary reversion to an overcast sky with little or no rain.

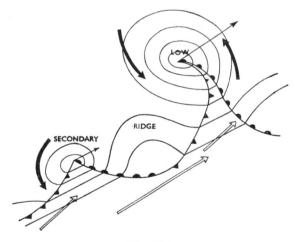

Fig. 131

A secondary depression may, however, develop to a considerable extent and become as deep as its parent and cause much rain and wind.

Fig. 131 shows a secondary depression following its parent depression.

The movement and development of depressions

On a weather chart, a depression appears as a system of closed isobars with the lowest pressure in the centre.

Various points should be noted when the movements and development of depressions are considered.

1. They usually move from south of west to north of east in the eastern North Atlantic and Western Europe.

2. Over the sea a depression that has been moving in a certain direction for a period of twelve hours will probably continue to move in approximately the same direction for the following twelve hours, unless it meets land during this time.

3. The track is usually parallel to the isobars in the warm sector.

4. The probable movement will be:

   (a) towards the place where the barometer is falling most rapidly;
   (b) away from the place where the barometer is rising most rapidly.

5. If the barometer is rising behind a depression more rapidly than it is falling in front of the same depression, the probability is that the depression is filling up and slowing down.

6. If the barometer is falling in front of a depression more rapidly than it is rising behind the same depression, the probability is that the depression is deepening and increasing its speed of advance.

7. If two depressions of similar intensity are adjacent in the northern hemissphere, they will rotate anti-clockwise round each other, eventually combining into one single depression.

8. When meeting land, depressions are frequently slowed down and eventually fill up because there is no longer a plentiful supply of warm, moist air. They often alter course to avoid passing over land.

OTHER PRESSURE SYSTEMS

Ridges

A ridge, as shown in Fig. 131, is the area of relatively high pressure between two depressions, which usually brings a brief spell of fine clear weather. An elongation of an anticyclone also constitutes a ridge.

Anticyclones

On a weather chart an anticyclone, like a depression, appears as a system of closed isobars, but with the highest pressure in the centre, as shown in Fig.135. The isobars are normally farther apart than in a depression, an anticyclone being a region of light winds. The movement of anticyclones is usually slow and irregular; they sometimes remain without any appreciable change of position for several days. The weather is usually fine, but in winter, particularly in the northern half of the anticyclone, the sky may be overcast when the wind has travelled over the sea.

The absence of strong winds and the stable condition of the atmosphere are very favourable for the formation of fog over the land, and most of the fogs in autumn and winter occur during anticyclones.

Cols

A col, as shown in Fig. 132, is a saddle-backed region between two lows and two highs. Since there will often be two air-streams of different origins adjacent to each other in this area, the weather may be unsettled. Calms or very light

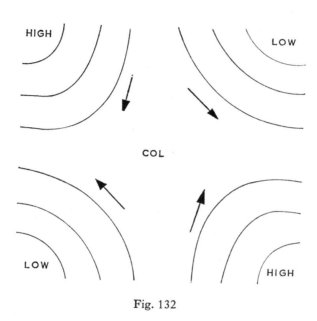

Fig. 132

winds are always experienced in cols; in winter fog and mist can be expected, and in summer sultry weather with risk of thunder.

Line squalls

A 'line squall' is the name given to the phenomenon which occurs with the sudden and complete change of air-stream at an unusually well-marked cold front. With a rapidly rising barometer, violent squalls of cold wind, and probably heavy showers, are experienced.

The phenomenon occurs along a line usually running in a north–south direction, and is sometimes shown by a long, low roll-cloud which appears like a black arch when low down over the horizon. It is in, or under, this roll-cloud that the violent whirlwinds called 'waterspouts' (over the sea) or 'tornadoes' (over the land) may occur.

Fig. 133 overleaf shows the detailed structure of a line squall.

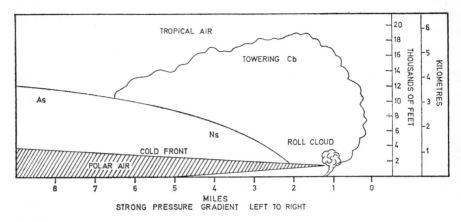

Fig. 133

THE WEATHER FORECAST

A weather forecast is a statement of the weather expected in a certain area during a specified period, usually in the immediate future. Reliable forecasts can usually be made for periods of at most one day.

When an area lies in an air mass of a particular type (*mP*, *cP*, *mT*, *cT*) the weather will be characteristic of that air mass. As long as there is no fundamental change in the type of air mass there is not likely to be any important change in the weather. The forecaster's problem is to decide when the air-stream will give way to one of a different type and what will happen during the changeover. He knows that when the change has taken place the weather will be characteristic of the new air-stream.

Air masses do not mix, but are separated by boundaries called 'fronts' as already described in this chapter. The change from one air-stream to another, therefore, is marked by the passage of a front. For example, when maritime tropical air replaces maritime polar air a warm front passes; and when polar air replaces tropical air a cold front passes.

The boundaries of the air masses have first to be located. This is done with the aid of a weather map, or 'synoptic chart', of the area. A weather map is drawn for a definite instant of time; at that time a number of stations in the area report by radio or land-line the weather they are experiencing. These stations comprise airfields, lighthouses, lightships, sea-going vessels (including weather ships) and aircraft. The international grouping of these stations, the information sent out, and the method of plotting synoptic charts are fully dealt with in *Meteorology for Mariners;* only a brief description can be given in this chapter.

The reports sent in by these stations are plotted on an outline chart; inspection of the chart enables the fronts to be drawn in, the centres of high and low pressure to be fixed, and isobars drawn so that the pressure systems can also be determined. The time at which a front will pass through the area can thus be estimated.

The weather associated with the passage of warm fronts, cold fronts and occlusions has already been described. These phenomena vary considerably for different fronts, but the individual weather reports from areas through which a front is passing indicate the severity to be expected.

Theoretically the wind flows along the isobars at a speed varying inversely with the distance between the isobars: the closer the isobars are together the higher the wind speed. Moreover, the higher the latitude the greater the

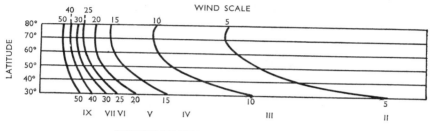

The approx. spacing of 4 mb isobars to produce surface wind OVER THE SEA of speed in knots given by the figures 5 to 50 is indicated by the curves to which these numerals are added. The corresponding figures according to Beaufort scale are shown in Roman numerals. The spacing is measured horizontally from the vertical line at the left edge of the scale along the appropriate latitude.

Fig. 134

'geostrophic wind', as this theoretical wind is called. A wind scale (Fig. 134) is printed on all meteorological working charts to enable the geostrophic wind speed to be calculated for any latitude. The geostrophic wind speed is approximately the wind which is being experienced at 600 m (2,000 ft). The geostrophic wind is sufficiently accurate for most practical purposes, but it makes no allowance for the curvature of the isobars. The geostrophic wind can be corrected by *Curves and Tables for Determination of Gradient Wind* (NP 484) to give the more accurate 'gradient wind'.

The wind speed at the surface is reduced by friction; over the sea it is roughly equal to two-thirds of the geostrophic wind speed, and to one-third of it over the land.

The surface wind direction is also altered from that of the geostrophic wind by friction; it is made to blow across the isobars, inwards, towards the low pressure side, by an amount rarely greater than 20° over the sea and a little more over land. By applying these rules it is possible to determine the wind speed and direction for any place or area for which the isobaric pattern can be drawn.

L

The speed of movement of fronts is related to the geostrophic wind speed. A cold front advances at about the instantaneous speed of the geostrophic wind in its rear; the speed of advance of a warm front is less than this by an average amount of 10 knots. When the air behind an occlusion is colder than the air ahead of it the rule for cold fronts applies; an occlusion having warmer air behind it follows the warm-front rule.

It must be borne in mind that when a homogeneous air-stream is being experienced – that is, no fronts are expected to affect the area – the weather will be generally characteristic of that type of air-stream, but the degree to which the characteristics are being experienced may alter with time. For instance, a shift in the position of the controlling pressure system will alter the trajectory of the air, thus increasing or decreasing its humidity and stability. Diurnal heating and cooling must also be considered, as this will influence the formation of land and sea breezes, convective showers, radiation fog, etc.

It will be seen that few general rules for forecasting can be laid down; every case has to be considered against its own background.

Meteorological broadcasts

In order to obtain a detailed picture of the meteorological situation and to forecast the weather for general or special (e.g. aviation) purposes, a large number of weather reports covering a wide area is required. To facilitate the rapid exchange of reports received at national collecting centres by land-line and/or radio, various types of collective meteorological broadcasts have been established. These broadcasts contain surface and upper-air reports from land stations and ships; reports from transport and special meteorological recon-naissance aircraft; a wide variety of surface and upper-air analysis messages; and miscellaneous data, such as reports of thunderstorm activity (Sferics) and mean monthly values of meteorological elements (wind, pressure, etc.) for climato-logical purposes.

In the European Region, Bracknell (Berkshire) is the centre responsible for the broadcast of European and eastern North Atlantic data. Other centres in Europe are Paris, Rome and Moscow.

Similar arrangements have been made in the other regions, viz.: Africa, Asia, North and Central America, South America, and the SW Pacific.

In addition there are:

1. *Weather bulletins for shipping*—broadcast by selected (usually coastal) stations. They contain plain-language forecasts and storm warnings for specified sea areas, and, occasionally, selected reports from ships and coastal stations, e.g. the Atlantic Weather Bulletin broadcasts from Portishead.

2. *Special broadcasts for aviation*—the rules co-ordinating collective broad-casts for the protection of civil aviation are established regionally by the International Civil Aviation Organization. These broadcasts contain aviation forecasts for specified areas, landing forecasts, and reports from selected airfields.

3. *Miscellaneous radio broadcasts*—e.g. storm warnings, and forecasts issued by the BBC for farmers and the general public.

Certain ships in the Fleet are equipped to receive radio facsimile transmissions which are a valuable supplement to the data carried on broadcasts already mentioned. Details of facsimile transmissions are contained in *Admiralty List of Radio Signals, Volume 3*.

Fleet Weather Messages

Although the broadcasts listed above contain most of the data required by HM ships, it is usually inconvenient and uneconomical from a watch-keeping point of view for ships without full-time meteorological organizations to read these broadcasts. In order to ensure that the meteorological information required by these ships is readily available, Fleet Synoptic, Fleet Analysis, and Fleet Forecast Messages (known collectively as Fleet Weather Messages), specially designed to meet the requirements of these ships, are broadcast on naval routine broadcasts.

Fleet Synoptic Messages. These messages contain a representative selection of surface and upper-air reports from land stations, ships, and aircraft; they are intended to provide qualified meteorological officers with basic data which, together with the Fleet Analysis Messages, will enable them to forecast the weather in areas in which they are interested. Fleet Synoptic Messages may also contain special data for Aircraft Direction purposes, and they are a useful stand-by for ships with full-time meteorological organizations if for any reason the broadcasts required by these ships have not been read.

Fleet Analysis Messages. These messages give the positions and probable movements of pressure systems and fronts, and the positions of 'key' isobars and areas of significant weather at specified times. Special upper-air analyses for Aircraft Direction purposes may also be included.

By plotting only the analysis message (this takes half-an-hour or so), the recipient is able to prepare a reasonably accurate forecast of wind and weather, without going through the technical and somewhat difficult, though otherwise essential, procedure for analysing synoptic data. With a certain amount of training and with practice, a fair degree of success can be achieved by the use of this message. It has the great advantage over a forecast message that not only can it be seen at a glance what the weather situation is over a fairly large area, but it can easily and quickly be determined, to within two hours or so as a rule, at what time a change of weather will take place in the recipient's locality. The use of analysis messages is further described below.

Forecast Messages. These are simple plain-language statements of expected conditions in a given area over a period of several hours. Their interpretation requires practically no specialized knowledge. Such a forecast has the unavoidable disadvantage, in comparison with the deductions that can be made from an analysis message, that it applies to a relatively large area as opposed to a particular locality, and can only indicate in broad terms the times at which changes will take place.

Full details of all Fleet Weather Messages are contained in the *Admiralty List of Radio Signals, Volume 3 – Meteorological Services, Codes, etc.*

THE INTERNATIONAL ANALYSIS CODE (FLEET)

If the positions, courses, speeds and intensities of all the centres of high and low pressure, cols, warm and cold fronts, occlusions and other phenomena affecting an area had to be broadcast in plain language, a very long, unwieldy message would result. A code has been devised, therefore, which presents this information as a series of five-figure groups – a form eminently suitable for transmission by radio.

The code used is known as the 'International Analysis Code (Fleet)', usually abbreviated to 'IAC (Fleet)'. It has been adopted internationally for marine use and is supplied to most HM ships on a printed sheet (NP 455), which gives the meaning of the groups and symbols of the code, and the specification tables for the individual elements. The same information may be extracted from the *Admiralty List of Radio Signals, Volume 3.*

Plotting the analysis

Specially designed outline charts for plotting Fleet Forecast and Analysis Messages are published for use on most naval stations. Available charts are listed in the *Hydrographic Supplies Handbook* (NP 133) and the *Meteorological Supplies Handbook* (NP 452).

The position of a pressure system is marked on the chart with a small **x**; the type (High or *H*, Low or *L*, etc.) is written just below the position, the barometric pressure in millibars just above. The intensity of the system should be written on the left-hand side of this. An arrow from the **x** indicates the direction in which the pressure system is moving, and its speed in knots is written close to the arrow. In the case of an elongated system, such as a ridge or trough, the axis should be denoted by a long arrow pointing towards the vertex. This procedure is not, of course, obligatory, but has been shown by experience to be the most convenient.

Fronts should be shown as smoothed curves through the points given; a kink or sharp angle between the two fronts only at or near the centre of a low, that is, at the tip or inner end of a warm sector. Fronts are usually bellied out with the wind, like a sail. The direction of movement and speed of a front usually refer to its central portion. The direction is indicated by an arrow drawn at approximately the mid-point of the front, and the speed in knots is written close to this arrow. The intensity of the front is usually written along the front.

The analysis message gives positions for the key isobars of each pressure system at 4-mb, 8-mb or 12-mb intervals. The isobars are drawn as smooth curves through the positions given, and the chart is completed by interposing isobars at 4-mb intervals between those given at greater intervals.

In a warm sector, the isobars are parallel straight lines running in approximately the same direction as that of the movement of the centre. Elsewhere, except where forming a trough or ridge, the direction of an isobar is approximately at right angles to the bearing of the centre of the nearest anticyclone or depression.

The wind invariably veers at a front in the northern hemisphere and backs in the southern; hence when an isobar crosses a front it must have a V shape, with the point of the V on the front, pointing to the higher pressure. If no fronts are given, the isobars should be spread so as to conform with the general pressure differences of the chart, remembering that within about 300 miles of the centre of an anticyclone the distance between isobars is usually that which will cause a surface wind of not more than about force 3–4.

The following example shows the procedure for constructing a weather map from a Fleet Analysis Message. The message was received during the evening of 26th May from C-in-C Fleet Weather and Oceanographic Centre, Northwood.

FM   CINCFLEETWOC
TO   ALL SHIPS AND AUTHORITIES READING THIS BROADCAST
FLEET ANALYSIS MESSAGE

10001	33300	02612	99900	81278	59336	00320	81316	39057	10000
80206	64092	62170	00615	85332	42485	00415	85234	48118	00405
85224	39021	10000	88014	66086	88023	42010	88023	45297	99911
66417	30397	35385	38378	42345	45305	00910	66451	45305	49258
57235	62285	00630	66650	62285	61345	59377	00120	66253	62285
62205	59097	56068	00320	66457	56068	55017	58072	59140	62240
01120	66620	62240	70290	00615	66222	62240	55200	50170	01010
99922	44980	60338	59358	58356	59335	60338	44988	62285	61356
59395	57385	57328	62285	44004	65315	63407	57466	53365	57235
62205	65315	44012	53486	51355	53238	61155	66215	67328	68455
70505	44020	50505	48428	49355	49258	59097	60088	58035	55011
54101	50160	46101	43051	40070	37022	35056	36065	38018	43077
40115	35145	30258	35345	42345	41375	36415	30445	44028	47505
46457	47345	45357	40448	35506	44028	54098	52015	49043	45007
45078	42156	39208	45227	51167	54098	44032	51105	49055	46096
45156	48165	51105	44016	31006	31058	32098	30147	44020	70065
68086	70165	44012	70072	68081	63016	57061	58160	57212	65301
44008	66123	63043	60082	60180	62223	66123	19191		

The message can be decoded and plotted at the same time. When decoded it reads as follows:

10001 33300	Indicator groups meaning analysis message in IAC (Fleet) follows.
02612	Date-time group meaning that the observations on which the analysis was based were made at 1200Z on the 26th.
99900	Indicates Pressure Systems follow.

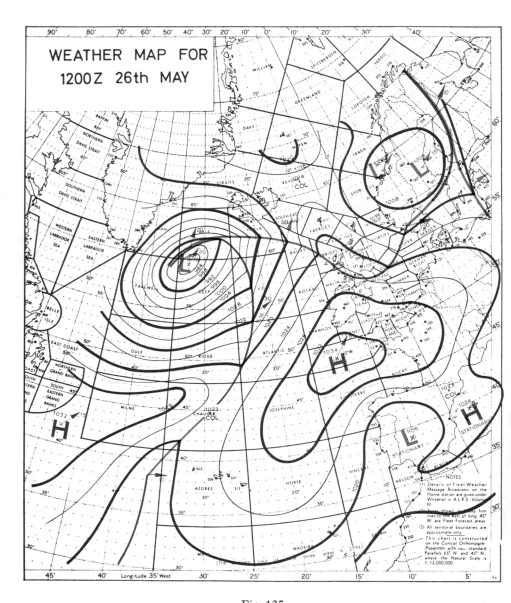

Fig. 135

Note

The last digit in each position group is used to specify where necessary a ½° increment to latitude and/or longitude as explained in the code sheet (NP 455).

81278	59336	00320		Low, little change, pressure at centre 978 mb, in position 59°·5 N, 33°W, moving on course 030° at 20 knots.
81316	39057	10000		Low, deepening, pressure at centre, 1016 mb, in position 39°N, 5°·5 W, stationary.
80206	64092	62170	00615	Complex Low system, little change, pressure at centres 1006 mb, in positions 64°N, 9°·5 E and 62°N, 17°E, moving on course 060° at 15 knots.
85332	42485	00415		High, intensifying, pressure at centre 1032 mb, in position 42°N, 48°W, moving on course 040° at 15 knots.
85234	48118	00405		High, little change, pressure at centre 1034 mb in position 48°·5 N, 11°·5 W, moving on course 040° at 5 knots.
85224	39021	10000		High, little change, pressure at centre 1024 mb, in position 39°·5 N, 2°E, stationary.
88014	66086			Col, pressure 1014 mb, in position 66°·5 N, 8°W.
88023	42010			Col, pressure 1023 mb, in position 42°N, 1°E.
88023	45297			Col, pressure 1023 mb, in position 45°N, 29°·5 W.
99911				Indicates Frontal systems follow.
66417 to 00910				Cold front, weak intensity, decreasing, with waves – passing through positions indicated, mid-point of front moving 090° at 10 knots.
66451 to 00630				Cold front, moderate intensity, no change, frontal activity decreasing, passing through positions indicated, mid-point of front moving 060° at 30 knots.
66650 to 00120				Occlusion, moderate intensity, no change, no specification for the character of front, passing through positions indicated, mid-point of front moving 010° at 20 knots.
66253 to 00320				Warm front, moderate intensity, no change, frontal activity increasing, passing through positions indicated, mid-point of front moving 030° at 20 knots.
66457 to 01120				Cold front, moderate intensity, no change, with waves – passing through positions indicated, mid-point of front moving 110° at 20 knots.
66620 to 00615				Occlusion, weak intensity, little change, no specification for the character of front, passing through positions indicated, mid-point of front moving 060° at 15 knots.

66222 to 01010	Warm front, weak intensity, little change, little change in frontal activity, passing through positions indicated, mid-point of front moving 100° at 10 knots.
99922	Indicates isobars follow.

Positions are then given for the isobars of 980, 988, 1004, 1012, 1020, 1028, 1028, 1032, 1016, 1020, 1012 and 1008 millibars.

19191	Message ends.

In the North Atlantic it will be most convenient to draw the weather map on a copy of meteorological working chart B 487; this chart also shows the areas referred to in Fleet Forecast Messages and gale warnings. Fig. 135 shows the completed weather map; isobars whose positions are given in the message are shown as heavy lines, other isobars (at 4-mb interval) by thinner lines. This arrangement is adopted only to illustrate this example; in practice, there is no differentiation between the thickness of isobars.

Making the forecast

The navigator will usually be able to tell from his own observations of wind, cloud, weather and visibility what type of air-stream is being experienced. Unless there is a fundamental change of air mass, such as is experienced when the ship passes through a front or close to a depression, the weather can be expected to continue more or less unchanged for the next few hours.

By plotting his own track during the next few hours on the weather map, the navigator will be able to determine if and when he will pass through a front or fronts. He must then decide what will happen during any change of air mass; the characteristics of pressure systems and fronts included in the analysis message assist him to do this. He must also decide what weather to expect in the new air-stream; his knowledge of the characteristics of the various types of airstream, in conjunction with the isobaric pattern of the weather map, enable him to make this decision. Allowance must also be made for the movement of systems between the time for which the chart was drawn and the time for which the forecast is required.

The following points should be borne in mind when interpreting the weather map (with particular reference to the North Atlantic):

1. An oceanic anticyclone is usually oval or egg-shaped, lying in a WSW–ENE direction. This is particularly so in the case of the 'Azores anticyclone'. It is rarely thin or cigar-shaped.

2. The weather near the centre of a high, where the winds are light and variable, is usually fair, the sky being only partly covered with fair-weather cumulus. The farther from the centre, the more strongly does the wind usually blow and the cloudier is the sky. On the west and north sides, the sky becomes nearly or quite overcast, while on the other sides it is about half-covered.

3. Depressions usually travel with the wind along the polar side of an oceanic anticyclone. It follows that their most common course in the North Atlantic is between east and north-east.

4. When a depression becomes occluded, with little or no recognizable warm sector, its speed is much reduced and its direction of movement may become erratic. The wind circulating round the centre, however, does not necessarily decrease at the same time, so that the occlusion moves faster than the centre and gets ahead of it.

5. In a warm sector, the air is of tropical origin, and the sky is nearly always overcast with very low cloud (base at 300 m (1,000 ft) or less). The more southerly the wind, the lower is the cloud likely to be, and the worse the visibility. If the isobars in the warm sector are more or less west to east, that is, more or less parallel to the sea isotherms, visibility will be about 10 miles and cloud base 300 m (1,000 ft). If the isobars are about SSW–NNE, visibility may be less than 4 miles and the cloud base below 200 m (600 ft).

6. In any type of air, visibility is seldom much more than 7 miles or so when the wind is blowing with gale force. This is partly due to the effect of spray. In winds of force 10 or higher the visibility is likely to be reduced to a mile or less.

7. Sea fog is unlikely to form in strong winds, because the air is so disturbed that any given particle of air is never in contact with the water long enough to be cooled appreciably. In a warm sector, the visibility is very unlikely to be less than 2 to 3 miles in winds of force 7–8, except over one of the cold-water currents (Great Bank of Newfoundland, for example).

8. The sky in true polar air is usually about 4/8ths covered with cumulus cloud, some of which may be sufficiently developed (3000 m (10,000 ft) or more from top to base) to produce a shower of rain (or snow). Except when rain or snow is falling, the height of the base of the cloud averages nearly 1000 m (3,000 ft).

9. A polar air mass having a long sea passage in a west–east direction, i.e. experiencing a smaller rate of increase of sea surface temperature, will have a more overcast sky and a lower cloud base, averaging about 600 m (2,000 ft) if the wind is westerly. If it is returning polar air, i.e. proceeding in a direction north of east so that the sea temperature is actually falling, the cloud base will average about 300–450 m (1,000–1,500 ft).

10. If the barometer fails to rise after passage of a cold front, and the sky is mostly overcast with low cloud below 600 m (2,000 ft) there is probably another front coming – either a second cold front or an occlusion – and the weather will not improve until this second front has passed.

11. The largest rain area is nearest the line of advance of the 'low'. The amount of rain depends on:

(*a*) the recent history of warm air; for example, if it is southerly from the coast of North Africa, there will be no rain and only a little cloud, because the air is necessarily very dry;

(*b*) the extent of the wind shift at the warm front, a big shift being associated with much rain and a small veer with little rain.

12. The intensity of a cold front, i.e. the squalliness and amount of rain as the front passes, depends largely on the veer of wind and the difference in temperature between warm and cold air masses. If the veer is only 5 to 10 degrees, there will be little rain as a rule and not a very noticeable squall.

Cold fronts are usually more marked in the western half of the North Atlantic and near the east coast of Greenland than elsewhere, because the cold air coming from off-shore has not had time to be warmed up over the sea, much of which is at a particularly low temperature in these localities.

If a cold front is followed by a ridge of high pressure there will be a rapid clearance, with little or no rain behind the front. If on the other hand the front is followed by a polar outbreak, i.e. by winds that continue to veer slowly (because the isobars continue to bend towards the north, as opposed to curving back round a ridge), showery conditions will persist for 6 to 12 hours after passage. (This statement is, in effect, similar to that in the preceding paragraph.)

The following was the forecast issued by the Fleet Weather and Oceanographic Centre based on the 1200Z chart on 26th May (Fig. 135) and broadcast to All Ships and Authorities at 1800Z. Wind force is given on the Beaufort Scale (Chapter 21).

FROM:CINCFLEETWOC

FLEET FORECAST MESSAGE

Gale Warnings in Operation
Bailey, Hebrides, Rockall, Malin.

Inference from 1200Z chart 26th May.
Large anticyclone centred 200 miles west of Ushant drifting north-east, maintaining ridge south-east to Azores. Slowly filling vigorous depression 300 miles east of Cape Farewell moving slowly north-east.
Associated warm frontal belt moving north-east over Scotland and northern sea areas.
Pressure remaining low over Spain and the Baltic.

Forecast Period 262000Z to 270800Z, Outlook to 272000Z May

Fair Isle	North-westerly 4 to 5 backing south-westerly, increasing in the
Cromarty	north. Occasional light rain or drizzle spreading from the west
Forth	with fog patches in Fair Isle.
Tyne	Visibility: good becoming moderate to poor.
Dogger	Outlook: little further change.

German Bight   North-westerly 4 to 6. Occasional rain clearing to scattered showers.
Visibility: moderate to good.
Outlook: moderate north-westerly. Fair.

Humber
Thames   North-westerly 3 to 4, locally 5 in the east. Occasional light rain at first, becoming fair.
Visibility: moderate to good.
Outlook: no further change.

Dover
Wight
Portland
Plymouth   North-west to north 2 to 3, locally 4 at first in the east. Fair at first, but local coast fog patches later in period.
Visibility: otherwise moderate to good.
Outlook: light northerly. Fair.

Sole   Variable 1 to 3. Fair.
Visibility: moderate to good.
Outlook: becoming light easterly.

Fastnet
Lundy
Irish Sea   South-westerly or variable 1 to 3. Coast fog patches.
Visibility: otherwise moderate.
Outlook: increasing south-westerly moderate in North Irish Sea, otherwise no change.

Shannon   South-westerly 3 to 4, locally 5 in the north and west. Patches of drizzle and fog especially near coast.
Visibility: otherwise moderate.
Outlook: moderate to fresh south-westerly.

Rockall
Malin
Hebrides   South-westerly 4 to 5, locally 6 at first increasing locally to gale 8 in the north late in period. Occasional rain or drizzle and fog patches.
Visibility: moderate locally poor.
Outlook: fresh to strong south-westerly.

Finisterre
Vincent   North-easterly locally 7 to gale 8 near Cape Finisterre at first, otherwise 4 to 6. Fair.
Visibility: good.
Outlook: wind decreasing slowly.

Sarah
Nelson   North-easterly 2 to 4. Fair.
Visibility: moderate near coast, otherwise good.
Outlook: moderate north-easterly.

Note

Extra areas *Dogger* and *German Bight* were included for the following reasons:

(i) ACS *St Margarets* requested sea area *Dogger*.

(ii) HMS *Soberton* was known to be on passage to Sonderberg, ETA 27th May via the Kiel Canal.

Local modification of weather near the coast

When preparing a weather forecast for a coastal area, the effect of the topography of the coast upon the weather deduced from climatic or air mass considerations must always be borne in mind. Fairly detailed information on local meteorology is given in Chapter I of the *Sailing Directions* for the area, but this cannot attempt to deal with the local effects on the weather of each separate headland, bay or creek. The following notes, however, should prove helpful in showing how the weather near the coast is likely to be modified by the shape of the land.

1. If the coastline is steep-to, onshore winds that approach it at an angle are usually deflected along the shore and increase somewhat in speed.

2. When the wind approaches a strait (or estuary) whose direction is somewhat similar to that of the wind, the wind tends to blow along the strait and increases in speed as the strait narrows. This effect is most marked in the afternoon, and there is often no such tendency during night and early morning.

3. When a strong wind blows directly towards a very steep coast, there is usually a narrow belt of contrary, gusty winds close to the coast.

4. An offshore wind is often squally on the lee side of hilly coasts, especially when the air is much colder than the sea – as, for example, when it blows off snow-covered land and when the wind over the open sea is force 5 or more.

5. Near headlands or islands with steep cliffs there may be large changes in direction (up to about 90°) and speed of the wind, in addition to those mentioned above.

6. The wind deduced from the isobaric pattern may be modified by the onshore sea breeze on fine, warm days, and by the offshore land breeze on clear nights.

7. In true sea fog, visibility is better close to leeward of a hilly island or promontory than to windward. This effect is most marked during the afternoon in summer when the land is warmest, and it then applies to low-lying land as well.

8. Radiation fog which has spread out from the land over adjacent sea is least thick during the afternoon and is often worst during the first hour or two after sunrise.

9. Visibility is often reduced to leeward of an industrial area.

10. Drizzle and very poor visibility are often experienced along coasts towards which a warm, moist air-stream is flowing.

11. In polar air, cloud amount and shower activity over the land are greatest in the afternoon; with offshore winds this also applies to adjacent sea areas.

FORECASTING IN THE TROPICS

'Tropics' is understood to refer to the area covered by the Trade winds, whose climatic characteristics were briefly dealt with in Chapter 19, and to the equatorial region between them.

In general, over the open sea, the weather in these regions changes little from day to day, and can be inferred by reference to the appropriate climatic charts. There is, however, a pronounced diurnal variation in almost all weather elements. Thus, cloud amount is usually greatest in the early morning and least in the afternoon, and rainfall is most frequent in the early hours of the day. Over and in the immediate vicinity of land, on the other hand, cloudiness and rainfall are generally greatest in the afternoon or early evening. The diurnal variation of the barometer has already been dealt with, and tends to overshadow other variations in pressure; hence the barometer is of limited value for forecasting in these regions. (*But see remarks under* 'Tropical Revolving Storms' – Chapter 19.)

Over the coasts, land and sea breezes predominate and may affect winds and weather over large areas. The monsoons of the equatorial Atlantic (West African coast), Indian Ocean and western Pacific may be regarded as examples of large-scale seasonal land and sea breezes.

Except at night over land, the temperature decreases sharply with height in the lower troposphere and thus the lower atmosphere in the tropics is always in a state verging on instability. Very slight local disturbances are sufficient to 'trigger' large-scale convection which results in towering cumulonimbus clouds, downpours of rain, and sometimes lightning and thunder.

Intertropical Convergence Zone

The regions of worst weather generally occur near the equator, where the Trade winds of the two hemispheres converge. This region is often one of light, variable winds and is known variously as the Doldrum belt, the Intertropical Convergence Zone (ITCZ), the Intertropical Front (ITF), the Equatorial Front, the Equatorial Trough or the Shear Line. The severity of the weather depends upon the amount of convergence of the near-surface winds. When convergence is absent this region may be crossed without sight of cloud, but more often it appears as a broken line of shower clouds with more extensive upper cloud and sometimes as a zone of severe thundery showers accompanied at times by sudden squalls. The line of this region is usually east–west and varies in width from a few miles to many tens of miles, but the wind direction on one side of it is invariably different from that on the other and it is for this reason that it is referred to as a 'shear line'. The worst conditions are usually encountered at daybreak over the open ocean and the weather improves in daylight hours; overland it is worst in the afternoon.

Generally speaking, the only hazards which the weather of the tropics presents to surface craft arise from tropical revolving storms and the sudden squalls accompanying the thunderstorms. The large-scale operation of aircraft in recent years, however, has necessitated intensive study of tropical weather systems, which has led to the recognition of some characteristic features of the circulation. These features are sometimes referred to in broadcast weather bulletins and therefore two of them are appended below for completeness, but it is emphasized that their significance from the surface weather point of view may be very slight.

Trough in Westerlies

This originates in the middle-latitude Westerlies as a trough of low pressure in the upper air. It extends southwards, bringing polar air into the region of low-latitude easterlies, and where these are shallow, i.e. fairly low-level, the trough may affect the surface weather. The trough usually moves eastwards and is principally a feature of the western sides of the oceans.

Trough in Easterlies

This is a wave-like pressure trough accompanied by an increase in the depth (vertical extent) of the easterlies (i.e. the Trades). Weather is usually fine ahead of the trough, but there may be an extensive unsettled area in the rear. The trough line moves towards the west.

Tropical Revolving Storm (*See* Chapter 19).

STORM SIGNALS

Visual storm warnings and radio broadcasts of storm warnings for shipping are primarily domestic matters, and details of such warnings are established by individual State Meteorological Services; but in order to obtain the maximum possible degree of uniformity the following definitions have been widely adopted.

Type of Warning	*Corresponding Wind (Beaufort)*
Gale warning	Force 8–9
Storm warning	Force 10–11
Hurricane warning*	Force 12

* or local synonym, e.g. cyclone, typhoon, etc.

Note
These three types of warning are referred to collectively as Storm Warnings.

Most countries transmit warnings by radio in plain language, and in addition display visual warnings at coast stations. Details of broadcasts will be found in the *Admiralty List of Radio Signals, Volume 3*, and visual signals are described in the appropriate volume of the *Sailing Directions*.

Warnings for HM ships are broadcast on naval routine broadcasts.

Storm warnings may be broadcast in two languages, i.e. the language of the issuing country and English, and usually contain the following information:

International Call (TTT).

Type of warning (Gale, Storm or Hurricane).

Time of reference (GMT).

Type of disturbance causing the warning (e.g. a deep depression) and the pressure at the centre of this disturbance in millibars.

Lat. and long. of the disturbance at Time of reference.

Direction of movement and speed of the disturbance at Time of reference.

Extent of the area(s) affected.

Force and direction of the wind in various parts of the area(s) affected.

Further indications, e.g. probable duration of the gale.

EXAMPLE

'*TTT. Storm Warning. At 0600 GMT, 4th August, a deep depression, central pressure 980 millibars, in position 45°N, 27°W, was moving NE at 30 knots; accompanied by winds of force 8 over an area extending 400 miles from the centre, and force 10–11 in the NE quadrant for a distance of 200 miles from the centre. The depression is expected to slow down and turn northward with little decrease in wind during the next 24 hours.*'

British Storm Warnings

For the specified sea areas around the United Kingdom storm warnings are issued jointly in plain language by the Fleet Weather and Oceanographic Centre, Northwood, and the Meteorological Office, Bracknell, when winds of Beaufort force 8 or over are expected over the open sea or on exposed coasts. The following is a summary of the arrangements for promulgating these warnings to shipping:

1. HM ships and Naval Authorities afloat are warned by radio on naval routine broadcasts.

2. Post Office Coastal Radio Stations broadcast warnings affecting the sea areas served by the transmitters at Wick, Stonehaven, Cullercoats, Niton, Land's End, Portpatrick, Valentia and Malin Head. These warnings are broadcast on receipt, and if a warning is received outside the watchkeeping hours of single-operator ships it is repeated immediately after the first silent period in the next single-operator watchkeeping period.

   The expected time of onset of a gale, for example, is indicated in the following terms:

   Imminent—within six hours of the time of origin of the warning.

   Soon—between six and twelve hours (approx.) after the time of origin.

   Later—after twelve hours (approx.).

3. Warnings of storms (i.e. Beaufort force 10 or above) expected to affect the North Atlantic east of long. 40°W are broadcast from Portishead in the Atlantic Weather Bulletin. These warnings include the terms *imminent*, *soon*, and *later*.

4. The BBC broadcasts warnings on 1500 m (200 kHz) as soon as they are received from the Meteorological Office, the programme being interrupted if necessary for this purpose. Summaries of gale warnings in operation are given at the beginning of weather bulletins.

Full details of the frequencies and call signs of these broadcasts, and limits of areas likely to be mentioned, are given in the *Admiralty List of Radio Signals, Volume 3*.

British Visual Storm Signals

Orders to hoist or lower storm cones are issued by the Meteorological Office by telegram to selected coastguard stations, lighthouses, light-vessels, harbour masters, and other coastal authorities.

A gale-warning signal indicates that a gale is expected within a distance of 50 to 100 miles of the place where the signal is hoisted. The gale will usually develop within 12 hours of the time of hoisting the signal. Occasionally, however, it develops more slowly, and the period may be 20 or even 30 hours. The signal will be lowered when the gale has passed and it is expected that there will be a period of not less than 6 hours free from gales and high winds, but it is kept hoisted during a temporary abatement of the wind if a renewal of the gale is expected. The warning signals are as follows:

By day: a black or a white cone, 3 ft high and 3 ft wide at the base.

At night: three lights in the form of a triangle, 4 ft wide at the base; this signal is exhibited at a few stations only.

The *north cone* (point upwards) is hoisted for gales starting from a northerly point. For gales starting from east or west, the north cone is hoisted if the gale is expected to change to a northerly direction.

The *south cone* (point downwards) is hoisted for gales starting from a southerly point; such gales often veer, sometimes as far as north-west. For gales starting from east or west, the south cone is hoisted if the gale is expected to change to a southerly direction.

Gales sometimes follow each other in quick succession.

Full information concerning the distribution of gale warnings and other meteorological information by radio is given in the *Admiralty List of Radio Signals, Volume 3.*

RADAR STORM-DETECTION

Meteorological echoes

The way in which meteorological factors can modify nearly-horizontal propagation paths of radar frequency radiation and produce super-refraction is described in the *Radar Manual*. The weather, however, plays yet another important role in centimetric radar operations in that it is itself a creator of echoes on radar displays. Bad-weather phenomena produce echoes very different from those produced by other targets, and the radar display may be regarded as presenting an actual picture of storms within range of the radar set. Very severe storms may show up on the display at ranges of a hundred miles or more, and an experienced observer can accurately determine their movement, area and development, enabling warning to be issued several hours before their arrival.

(*See page* 265.)

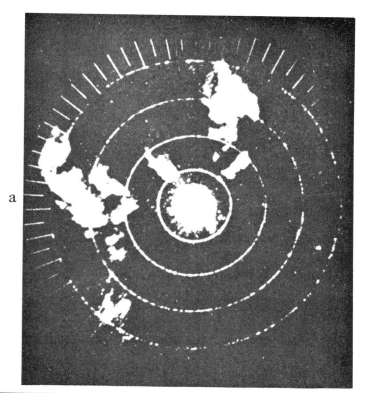

a

b

Figure 136
(a) Typical shower echo
(b) Actual cloud formation depicted by radar in (a)

L*

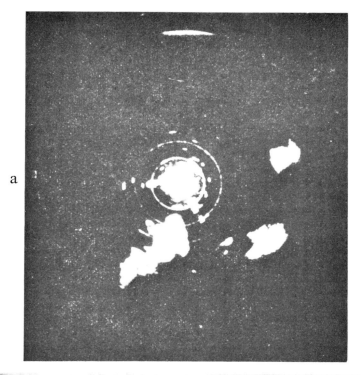

Figure 137

(a) Typical thunderstorm radar-echo

(b) Actual cloud formation depicted by radar in (a)

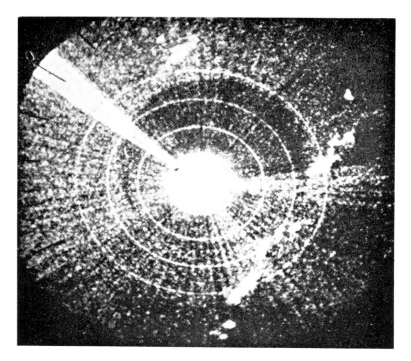

Figure 138. Typical cold-front radar-echo

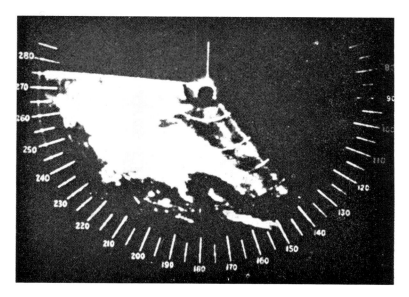

Figure 139. Typical warm front radar-echo

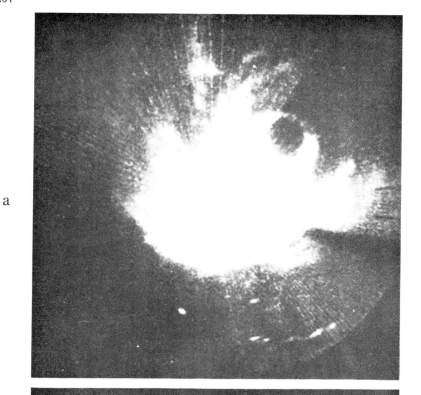

a

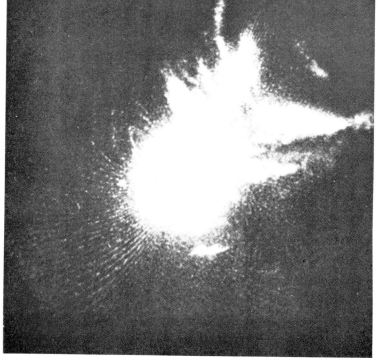

b

Figure 140.   Typical revolving-storm echoes

Intensity of weather echoes

A radar meteorological echo is produced by moisture droplets in the weather phenomenon scattering part of the incident radar energy back along a parallel path to the receiver. The intensity of the echo depends upon the amount of water per unit volume and upon the size of the individual water droplets. Consequently, the more moisture-laden the phenomenon, the greater the echo. This fact enables a qualitative assessment to be made of the severity of a storm; the brighter and more distinct the echo, the more active the storm.

The echo intensity also depends upon the power output and frequency of the radar used. The larger the power output the greater the radar energy that can be returned to the receiver and the brighter the echo. Also, as the wavelength is shortened, the radar waves are less able to penetrate a mass of moisture, and will detect weak storms more easily than will a radar of longer wavelength. Thus it would appear that for general-purpose storm-detection, 10-cm radar is preferable to 3-cm, because it can 'see' farther through storms.

Characteristics of weather echoes

Meteorological echoes differ from fixed echoes in that they are constantly changing in size, shape and intensity. Groups of echoes may break up into smaller echoes and then combine again as they travel across the display. In general, storm echoes move in the direction and with the speed of the winds aloft.

Owing to their vertical extent and size, storms are detectable at great distances – far in excess of normal echo returns from fixed targets. The maximum range at which a storm can be detected depends upon its height, and with surface radar, for example, ranges out to the maximum range of the display may be expected for storms with considerable vertical development.

Sources of weather echoes

The exact physical processes that cause weather echoes are not yet completely understood. It can be stated, however, that cloud from which precipitation in the form of light, moderate or heavy rain, hail, sleet or snow is falling will give radar echoes. Echoes are not usually produced by fair-weather cumulus clouds, or by clouds from which only drizzle or very light rain is falling. Low stratus clouds and fog patches do not generally give rise to echoes.

Showers, thunderstorms, active fronts, and tropical revolving storms are all capable of detection by radar.

Shower echoes (Fig. 136a) are located at random on the display, and exhibit a hazy, indistinct character with ill-defined edges. The echoes usually travel with the direction and speed of the wind aloft.

Thunderstorms (Fig. 137a) of great vertical extent show up as bright echoes with clearly defined edges. If the thunderstorms are of frontal origin, the echoes will be organized in a band or zone.

Cold Fronts (Fig. 138) are usually characterized as a line of individual, well-defined echoes. The more active the cold front the higher and more distinct the individual echoes. The echoes may join, break up and re-form as they move across the display.

Warm Fronts (Fig. 139) give indistinct echoes which usually cover a wide and irregular area of the display. The echoes are of variable brightness, owing to the changing character of the precipitation associated with warm fronts, i.e. light drizzle followed by light and then moderate rain.

Occlusions show echoes which may resemble either cold or warm fronts, depending upon their character and intensity.

Tropical Revolving Storms (Fig. 140) are easily recognized by their large, solid, circular shape and whorls on the display. The echoes cover a vastly greater area than echoes from any other type of weather phenomenon, as well as being far more intense. The 'eye' or centre of the storm may also be a prominent feature, and even if the centre is off the display, it is often possible to estimate its position from the curvature of the whirling cloud echoes.

BIBLIOGRAPHY

The following is a summary of other sources of information which are available; these should always be consulted when detailed meteorological or climatic data are required for specific areas:

Admiralty Sailing Directions and Supplements (*Pilots*). Each of these contains, in Chapter I of the text, notes on the local meteorology of the area concerned. Climatological tables, giving statistical information for various places, are also included. It is emphasized that the information given in the *Climatic Tables* applies to the place of observation, and may not be representative of conditions over the open sea or in the approaches to ports in the vicinity. The more recently revised *Pilots* contain notes on the manner in which such tables may be misleading.

Admiralty List of Radio Signals, Volume 3 (*Meteorological Services*). This book gives full details of the codes used by ships when making weather reports; it enumerates weather messages available to ships (forecasts, map analysis, gale warnings, etc.) together with the times at which they are broadcast and the frequencies and call signs of the stations.

Atlas of Meteorological Charts. These are available for the Western Pacific Ocean, Greenland and Barents Sea, Eastern Pacific Ocean, Atlantic Ocean and Indian Ocean. They contain the frequencies of various phenomena (temperature, wind force and direction, cloud height and amount, precipitation of different kinds, swell, visibility, etc.) at different times of the year for the localities for which sufficient observations are available. HM ships holding chart folios for any of the above areas will also be issued with the appropriate meteorological atlas.

World Climatic Charts – Sheet I (January) and Sheet II (July). These charts show the mean isobars, isotherms, prevailing winds, areas in which gales and fog are frequent, ice limits, the mean position of the Equatorial Trough (Doldrum belt) and rainfall over land areas.

International Analysis Code (IAC Fleet NP 455). This is a sheet containing the details of the International Analysis Code (*see* p. 248 *et seq.*), which enables the navigator to construct weather maps from broadcast map-analysis messages.

Station Weather Handbooks. These books contain information for the various stations, additional to that included in the *Sailing Directions.* Each handbook presents detailed general and local information and, in certain cases, aids to forecasting.

Ice Charts. See Volume I, Chapter XIII.

Meteorology for Mariners (NP 407) and the *Meteorological Glossary* (NP 443) are textbooks issued to the majority of HM ships.

The Mariner's Handbook (NP 100) contains a chapter on general meteorology.

A complete list of these publications and of meteorological working charts, together with details of distribution, are contained in *Hydrographic Supplies Handbook* (NP 133) and *Meteorological Supplies Handbook* (NP 452.)

CHAPTER 21

Meteorological Observations

Observations of the weather are made by HM ships at sea, and are signalled to shore meteorological authorities so that they can be used in the analysis of the current weather map, thus facilitating the issue of forecasts. These reports are usually the greatest value to the shore forecaster, because there is always a scarcity of reports from sea areas. The seaman who sends in regular and accurate reports of the weather he is experiencing is performing a service which will benefit all seamen (including himself), because the meteorological officer ashore will have more comprehensive information and will be able to issue more reliable forecasts.

These observations are doubly useful in that certain of them have to be recorded in the ship's log; they will be used eventually to improve our knowledge of climatology, lack of which makes any type of operation difficult to plan.

Some meteorological elements, such as pressure and temperature, are quantitative and require for their observation specially adapted scientific instruments. Other elements, such as cloud-form and weather, do not require instrumental aid for their observation. Observations are therefore of two types, 'instrumental' and 'non-instrumental'.

INSTRUMENTAL OBSERVATIONS

(*Pressure, Air Temperature, Sea Temperature and Humidity*)

There are three types of barometer in use in HM ships:

The aneroid barometer.
The precision aneroid barometer.
The barograph.

The mercurial barometer is no longer supplied to HM ships. Port meteorological stations (Captain of the Port's office at HM naval bases) normally carry a mercurial barometer for checking purposes.

The Aneroid Barometer

This instrument consists of a thin cylindrical metal chamber, partly exhausted of air and hermetically sealed. It is thus susceptible to the slightest changes in external pressure. The top of the chamber is connected to a pointer by an arrangement of springs and levers, and this has the effect of greatly magnifying its movement.

The advantages of the aneroid are:

1. It is simple to read.

2. It is easily transported and may be placed or hung in any convenient position.

3. By adjusting the fixed or shorter pointer by means of the metal thumb-screw at the centre of the glass face, it is readily apparent whether the barometer is rising or falling.

The moving pointer can be adjusted by means of a screw at the back of the instrument. Since the metal of which the aneroid chamber is made cannot be relied on to maintain its form indefinitely, the zero will vary slightly. The reading of the instrument should therefore be compared frequently with that of a precision aneroid or a mercurial barometer, as described later. Before the instrument is read the glass face should be tapped gently.

HM ships are supplied with Pattern 0552/461–9298, which is graduated in millibars as shown in Fig. 141.

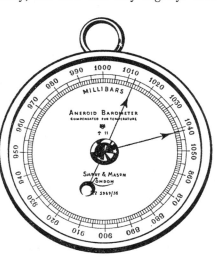

Fig. 141

To check an aneroid barometer with a precision aneroid or a mercurial barometer

Set up the aneroid in the place where it is to be used. Read the precision aneroid or mercurial barometer in the usual way and make the barometric correction (page 272), thus obtaining the corrected barometric pressure at sea level; return to the aneroid and set it to this reading by means of the adjusting screw at the back. As long as it remains at the same height, the aneroid should now continue to read the corrected barometric pressure at sea level.

Adjustment by means of the screw should be limited to a correction not exceeding 5 millibars. For larger adjustments, the glass should be removed by pushing off the bevelled ring. The pointer, which is a push-on fit, should then be removed and reset near the correct reading. The final adjustment can then be made with the screw at the back.

On all occasions of checking the aneroid barometer, details should be entered on the check card attached to the instrument. This card, which is constructed and renewed as may be necessary by ship's staff, should be similar in layout to that shown on page 270.

If the aneroid is moved to a higher position the reading must be increased by the adjusting screw by 0·3 mb for every 10 feet (3·05 m) that it is raised. If it is moved to a lower position, the reading must be decreased in a similar way.

To log aneroid barometer readings

Barometric observations in all HM ships which are supplied only with an aneroid barometer should be made and recorded in millibars. In the ship's log

CHECK CARD
(Actual size: 8″ x 5½″)

ANEROID BAROMETER Nº _____

The pressure reading of this instrument should be checked against that of a standard barometer ashore as frequently as possible, adjusting the Aneroid, if necessary, to agree with the standard barometer. (See Admiralty Manual of Navigation Vol II)

Details of all checks carried out should be entered on this card which must be kept attached to the instrument concerned.

BAROMETER CHECKS

1	2	3	4	5	6	7
DATE	LOCATION OF BAROMETER USED AS CHECK	AIR TEMP ° C	PRESSURE READING OF BAROMETER CORRECTED TO SEA-LEVEL	PRESSURE READING OF ANEROID BAROMETER	ERROR OF ANEROID − OR +	ANEROID ADJUSTMENT MADE BY

(Layout of front of card)

1	2	3	4	5	6	7
DATE	LOCATION OF BAROMETER USED AS CHECK	AIR TEMP ° C	PRESSURE READING OF BAROMETER CORRECTED TO SEA-LEVEL	PRESSURE READING OF ANEROID BAROMETER	ERROR OF ANEROID − OR +	ANEROID ADJUSTMENT MADE BY

When card is full, the earliest entry on it should be erased to make room for particulars of subsequent checks. Erase <u>one</u> entry at a time.

(Layout of back of card)

the actual pressure at sea level should be recorded; this is given directly by the instrument when adjusted in accordance with the preceding paragraph.

Precision Aneroid Barometer

This is the more accurate form of the aneroid barometer (see Fig. 142). The sensing element consists of a stack of three-disc aneroid capsules fixed to the inside of a metal box. The movement of the capsule with changes in pressure is magnified by means of a lever pivoted on jewelled bearings. One end of the lever is kept in contact with the capsule by means of a light hairspring. A micrometer screw, which extends through the case of the instrument, is brought into contact with the other end of the lever by the observer. Movement of the micrometer is measured by a digital counter. Contact is indicated by a small cathode-

Fig. 142

ray tube. A continuous line indicates that contact is made, whilst a broken line indicates that contact is broken.

Procedure for reading

Press the black switch button and observe the cathode-ray indicator. If the thread of light is broken turn the knurled knob so that the pressure reading decreases until the thread just becomes continuous. When the thread is continuous turn the knurled knob so that the pressure increases until the thread of light just breaks. The process should be repeated to avoid errors due to 'over-shooting' the correct setting. The pressure may then be read in the window. If parts of two figures show equally in the tenth-of-a-millibar position the odd number should be taken. Since corrected sea-level pressures are reported the precision aneriod barometer reading needs to be corrected by means of the following table.

TABLE FOR CORRECTION OF MILLIBAR BAROMETERS TO MEAN SEA LEVEL
(*These corrections are to be added to the barometer readings*)

HEIGHT IN FEET	AIR TEMPERATURE (DRY BULB IN SCREEN), °C										HEIGHT IN METRES
	−15°	−10°	− 5°	0°	5°	10°	15°	20°	25°	30°	
5	0·2	0·2	0·2	0·2	0·2	0·2	0·2	0·2	0·2	0·2	1·5
10	0·4	0·4	0·4	0·4	0·4	0·4	0·4	0·4	0·3	0·3	3
15	0·6	0·6	0·6	0·6	0·6	0·5	0·5	0·5	0·5	0·5	4·5
20	0·8	0·8	0·8	0·8	0·7	0·7	0·7	0·7	0·7	0·7	6
25	1·0	1·0	1·0	0·9	0·9	0·9	0·9	0·9	0·9	0·9	7·6
30	1·2	1·2	1·2	1·1	1·1	1·1	1·1	1·1	1·0	1·0	9
35	1·4	1·4	1·4	1·3	1·3	1·3	1·3	1·3	1·2	1·2	10·7
40	1·6	1·6	1·6	1·5	1·5	1·5	1·4	1·4	1·4	1·4	12
45	1·8	1·8	1·8	1·7	1·7	1·6	1·6	1·6	1·5	1·5	13·7
50	2·0	2·0	1·9	1·9	1·9	1·8	1·8	1·8	1·7	1·7	15·2
55	2·2	2·2	2·1	2·1	2·1	2·0	2·0	1·9	1·9	1·9	16·7
60	2·4	2·4	2·3	2·3	2·2	2·2	2·2	2·1	2·1	2·1	18·3
65	2·6	2·6	2·5	2·5	2·4	2·4	2·4	2·3	2·3	2·2	19·8
70	2·8	2·8	2·7	2·7	2·6	2·6	2·5	2·5	2·4	2·4	21·3
75	3·0	3·0	2·9	2·9	2·8	2·8	2·7	2·7	2·6	2·6	23
80	3·2	3·2	3·1	3·1	3·0	2·9	2·9	2·8	2·8	2·7	24·4
85	3·4	3·4	3·3	3·2	3·2	3·1	3·1	3·0	2·9	2·9	26
90	3·6	3·6	3·5	3·4	3·4	3·3	3·3	3·2	3·1	3·1	27·4
95	3·8	3·8	3·7	3·6	3·6	3·5	3·4	3·4	3·3	3·3	29
100	4·0	4·0	3·9	3·8	3·7	3·7	3·6	3·6	3·5	3·4	30·5

Checking the barometer

The regular checking, at least every three months, of the accuracy of the precision aneroid barometer should be made against a reliable barometer ashore. If a series of comparisons over a range of pressure consistently shows a difference, no adjustment should be made to the precision aneroid barometer, but the appropriate correction should be applied when reading the instrument. If the mean difference between the instrument and the standard barometer is found to be greater than 1·0 mb it should be returned immediately for recalibration.

The Barograph

This instrument is an aneroid barometer provided with a lever and pen which records variations of pressure on a chart attached to a revolving drum (*see* **Fig. 143**). The drum is driven by clockwork and makes one revolution in seven **days**. The paper form fitted on the drum is graduated to show the day and time of day, as well as the height of the barometer in millibars. Means are provided for adjusting the pen point so that it corresponds with the reading of the barometer, and a lever enables the pen to be withdrawn from the paper while the instrument is being moved or guns are being fired. If possible, the barograph should be secured in an athwartship position, so that the pen is less likely to leave the paper when the ship is rolling.

The barograph is useful not only because it enables an observer to detect casual errors in the reading of the barometer, but also because it gives a continuous record of barometric pressure for reference. Moreover, the barograph registers minor fluctuations of atmospheric pressure which are seldom noticeable in the action of the precision aneroid or the mercurial barometer. The instrument should therefore be secured or suspended in a position where it is least likely to be affected by concussion, vibration, or the movement of the ship.

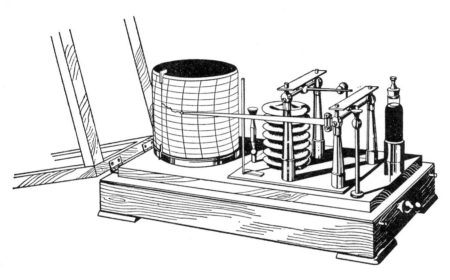

Fig. 143

The barograph ordinarily supplied to HM ships is the Pattern 0552/461-9299 (Fig. 143). The 'open-scale' barograph (Pattern 0552/461-9303) is similar to the ordinary barograph, but the pressure scale is expanded so that more detailed observation is possible; this type is normally supplied to ships carrying meteorological officers. The paper forms are as follows:

Metform No. 4237, for Pattern 0552/461-9299.
Metform No. 5823, for Pattern 0552/461-9303.

The Thermometer

Temperature is measured with the thermometer. HM ships are supplied with ordinary thermometers graduated from $-30°C$ to $45°C$.

Thermometers are normally used for measuring the 'dry bulb' and 'wet bulb' temperatures of the air, and for measuring the temperature of the sea.

Thermometers used for measuring air temperatures have to be screened; otherwise they are affected by radiation of heat to and from surrounding objects.

The usual form of screen is a wooden box, painted white; the sides are louvered so that air can circulate freely round the bulbs of the thermometers. The type used on board HM ships, the Modified Shipboard Screen (similar to a Stevenson

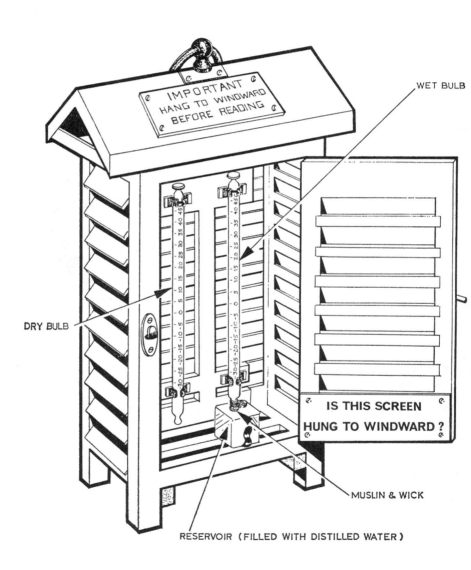

Fig. 144

Screen), is illustrated in Fig. 144, where the left-hand thermometer is used to measure the air temperature, while that on the right, the 'wet bulb' thermometer, is used to obtain the humidity. The wet bulb thermometer is an ordinary thermometer with its bulb covered with muslin, which is kept continually moist by means of a strand of cotton wick, one end of which is immersed in a reservoir of distilled water. Evaporation from the wet muslin causes cooling of the air immediately surrounding the bulb so that the thermometer indicates a reduced temperature. The evaporation is brisker as the dryness of the air increases; the difference between the dry and wet bulb thermometer readings is therefore in inverse relation to the humidity. When the air is saturated there can be no evaporation and the wet bulb temperature is the same as the air temperature. This arrangement of dry and wet bulb thermometers in a shipboard screen is a form of psychrometer.

To make an observation, the screen should be mounted in a position about 5 feet above the upper deck in the open air, as free as possible from radiation and warm draughts from galleys, engine rooms, boiler rooms and funnels. Since it is important that the temperature and humidity of the free air is obtained, the weather side is usually the best side for exposure. Wick, water, and muslin should be scrupulously clean, and should therefore be frequently changed.

At least 15 minutes should elapse between mounting and reading, but if the clean water is not at the temperature of the air a much longer time is required.

In very cold weather evaporation will take place from the thin layer of ice formed on the surface of the wet bulb, but at a different rate of evaporation off the surface of the water.

It sometimes happens that the wet bulb reads above the dry when the temperature is falling. The dry bulb follows the change of temperature with only a small time-lag, but the wet bulb, being coated with muslin, has a greater lag; if the temperature is falling sufficiently quickly, this may produce the result mentioned, which should not be logged (*see Note* iii).

The readings should be taken to 0·1°C by estimation and the index errors of the thermometers should be applied. These errors are tabulated on a form supplied with each thermometer.

The relative humidity and dew point (which is also a measure of the humidity) for the observed dry bulb temperature and the depression of the wet bulb temperature below that of the dry bulb may be extracted from the *Hygrometric Tables (Stevenson Screen Readings)* (NP 474A).

Notes

(i) If the two readings are the same, and the weather is not foggy, it is probable that the cistern is empty or that the dry bulb is coated with salt or dirt.

(ii) The instrument should be frequently examined to ensure that the cistern is full of distilled water and that the bulbs, muslin and wick are clean.

(iii) The wet bulb temperature should never be logged as reading higher than the dry bulb temperature.

(iv) Sometimes a broken mercury column may cause the wet bulb to read higher than the dry bulb. When this is apparent, the thermometer must be taken out and shaken until the mercury reunites.

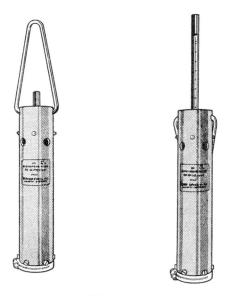

Fig. 145

Sea-Surface-Temperature Bucket

Sea surface temperature is measured by means of a rubber bucket (*see* Fig. 145) fitted with a brass sheath containing a thermometer. To measure sea surface temperature the bucket is trailed submerged in the sea on a length of heaving line for about a minute. It is important that it be immersed well forward of all discharges on the lee side of the ship. The bucket is then hauled in and the brass sheath withdrawn as far as possible to enable the thermometer to be read.

Temperatures obtained from the thermometer in the engine-room circulator intake should not be used, unless it is impossible in rough weather conditions to obtain a reading in the manner described above.

NON-INSTRUMENTAL OBSERVATIONS

Wind

When a ship is not fitted with an anemometer, the direction and force of the wind must be estimated.

Wind direction is specified as that point of the true compass from which the wind blows, and should be observed to the nearest ten degrees. Since the wind direction is seldom constant, and may at times fluctuate through 45° to 90° in a few seconds, it is necessary to estimate the mean direction. The appearance of the sea and the general run of the waves are good guides. Unless the ship is stationary, it is almost invariably misleading to base the estimate of wind on an observation of funnel smoke.

Wind force is expressed by means of the Beaufort Scale, a numerical scale devised by Admiral Sir Francis Beaufort in 1808, which has since been revised from time to time. This scale (*see* pages 278 and 279) is used in plain-language weather broadcasts. (In ship's weather reports to shore meteorological authorities and in the ship's log the wind speed is recorded in knots.) The scale numbers are attributed to the wind force at the time of observation, according to the observer's judgment. For the purpose of the meteorologist, only winds of force 8 and higher are 'gales'. The gale warning signal in the British Isles is hoisted for winds which may reach force 8 or above; a wind of force 7 is not considered a gale.

Weather

In HM ships at sea the weather is recorded every six hours, at 0000, 0600, 1200 and 1800 GMT, in the ship's log. The code form used is given in the back of the log and is the form used by the World Meteorological Organization.

Sea and swell

It is necessary to note carefully the distinction between 'sea' and 'swell'. 'Sea' is defined as the waves caused by the wind at a place, whereas 'swell' is caused by waves formed by past wind, or wind at a distance. The heights of sea waves and swell are entered in the ship's log, and also the direction of the swell. The latter is specified as the point of the compass from which the swell travels. The direction of sea waves is not logged, because this is always the same as the wind direction.

It is sometimes required to report the period of the swell, that is, the time interval in seconds between the passage of two successive crests.

On board a moving ship it is very difficult to measure dimensions of waves accurately. In a confused sea it is almost impossible to attempt any measurements of the sea or swell; only in seas caused by well-defined wave-motion of some uniformity is it possible to take observations, or even to estimate successfully. Any estimate of wave height is complicated by the fact that it must be made from a ship which partakes, to a certain degree, of the motion of the water surface and also has motions (pitching and rolling) of its own. The most reliable estimates of wave height are obtained by observation of another ship in company. The height from trough to crest of a wave against her side can be estimated as a fraction of some known vertical dimension, the distance from deck to boot-topping, for example. Failing this assistance, the observer must make observations on his own ship in such a way that the possible errors due to her motion are reduced to a minimum. Observations should be made from amidships, where the pitching motion is least, and preferably with the ship heading into the waves, when the rolling is least. If this latter condition is impossible to fulfil, there will usually be occasional short intervals when the rolling is only slight. During such a period, the difference between water level at trough and crest must be estimated

BEAUFORT WIND SCALE AND CORRELATIVE SEA DISTURBANCE TABLE

BEAUFORT NUMBER	LIMITS OF VELOCITY IN KNOTS*	MEAN EQUIVALENT PRESSURE IN POUNDS UPON A CIRCULAR DISC OF ONE SQUARE FOOT*	DESCRIPTIVE TERMS	COASTAL CRITERION	SEA CRITERION	PROBABLE MEAN HEIGHT OF WAVES† (FEET)	PROBABLE MEAN HEIGHT OF WAVES† (METRES)
0	Less than 1	0·0	Calm ...	—	Sea like a mirror	—	—
1	1–3	0·01	Light air ...	Sufficient to give good steerage to fishing smacks with the 'wind free'.	Ripples with the appearance of scales are formed, but without foam crests...	– (¼)	0·1 (0·1)
2	4–6	0·08	Light breeze ...	Fishing smacks with topsails and light canvas, 'full and by' make up to 2 knots.	Small wavelets, still short but more pronounced; crests have a glassy appearance and do not break ...	½ (1)	0·2 (0·3)
3	7–10	0·28	Gentle breeze...	Smacks begin to heel over slightly under topsails and light canvas, make up to 3 knots 'full and by'.	Large wavelets. Crests begin to break. Foam of glassy appearance. Perhaps scattered white horses	2 (3)	0·6 (1)
4	11–16	0·67	Moderate breeze	Good working breeze. Smacks heel over considerably on a wind under all sail.	Small waves, becoming longer; fairly frequent white horses	3½ (5)	1 (1·5)
5	17–21	1·31	Fresh breeze ...	Smacks shorten sail.	Moderate waves, taking a more pronounced long form; many white horses are formed. (Chance of some spray.)...	6 (8½)	2 (2·5)
6	22–27	2·3	Strong breeze...	Smacks double-reef gaff mainsails.	Large waves begin to form; the white foam crests are more extensive everywhere. (Probably some spray.) ...	9½ (13)	3 (4)
7	28–33	3·6	Near gale ...	Smacks remain in harbour and those at sea lie to.	Sea heaps up, and white foam from breaking waves begins to be blown in		

8	5·4	34–40	Gale ...	Smacks take shelter if possible.	Moderately high waves of greater length; edges of crests break into spindrift. The foam is blown in well marked streaks along the direction of wind	18 (25)	5·5 (7·5)
9	7·7	41–47	Strong gale ...	—	High waves. Dense streaks of foam along the direction of the wind. Crests of waves begin to topple, tumble and roll over. Spray may affect visibility	23 (32)	7 (10)
10	10·5	48–55	Storm ...	—	Very high waves with long overhanging crests. The resulting foam in great patches is blown in dense white streaks along the direction of the wind. On the whole the surface of the sea takes a white appearance. The tumbling of the sea becomes heavy and shock-like. Visibility affected	29 (41)	9 (12·5)
11	14·0	56–63	Violent storm...	—	Exceptionally high waves. (Small and medium-sized ships might for a long time be lost to view behind the waves.) The sea is completely covered with long white patches of foam lying along the direction of the wind. Everywhere the edges of the wave crests are blown into froth. Visibility affected ...	37 (52)	11·5 (16)
12	Above 17·0	64 and over	Hurricane ...	—	The air is filled with foam and spray. Sea completely white with driving spray; visibility very seriously affected	Over 45	Over 14

* Determined at coast stations for a height of 10 m (33 ft) above sea level. The Gale Warning Signal is hoisted in the British Isles for winds which may reach Force 8 or more.

† Note.—(i) This table is only intended as a guide to show roughly what may be expected in the open sea, remote from land. **It should never be used in the reverse way, i.e., for logging or reporting the state of the sea**

(ii) In enclosed waters, or when near land with an off-shore wind, wave-lengths and heights will be smaller, especially the latter.

(iii) Figures in brackets indicate the probable approximate maximum height reached by about one wave in ten.

by looking over the side, using as a yard-stick the relative heights of known points on the side.

The preceding method works when the waves are fairly small compared with the ship; if they are large the ship as a whole rises and falls with the water. Under these circumstances the best results are obtained by moving up and down in the ship until, when the ship is in the wave trough and is vertical, the oncoming

Fig. 146

waves are just level with the horizon (*see* Fig. 146). The wave height is then equal to the height of eye of the observer above the level of the water beneath him. The position of the waterline on the ship's side abreast the observer at the moment of taking the observation must be noted by a second observer. The difference between the two levels can be found from the ship's drawings.

To measure the period, observe the rise of a piece of spent foam, and when it reaches the crest of a wave start a stopwatch; then observe the descent of the foam to the trough, and stop the watch when the foam reaches the top of the next crest.

Clouds

Cloud amount only is recorded in the ship's log, but when making weather reports, it is necessary to consider the amount of cloud and the cloud formation at various levels.

Cloud formation

The various forms of cloud and the code numbers used to report them are illustrated by the cloud photographs in Chapter 19. Cloud forms are shown in more detail in the *International Cloud Atlas* (NP 476).

The amount of cloud is denoted by a figure on a scale from 0 to 8. Figure 0 signifies a sky free from cloud. An overcast sky in which no patches of blue sky are visible is denoted by 8. The code numbers refer solely to the amount of sky covered, in 'oktas' (eighths of the sky), and not to the density, height or other features of the cloud.

The amount of low cloud should be separately estimated, imagining that every other visible form of cloud is replaced by blue sky.

Times of observations

Ships making weather reports should, in all parts of the world, use Greenwich Mean Time. The four principal hours of observation for ships are 0000, 0600, 1200 and 1800 GMT. Observations should be made, recorded and signalled at as many of these times as possible. It is most important to be punctual in taking the observations and despatching the messages. Normally, observations should be completed at the exact hour, and the observation of the element which is varying the most rapidly should if possible be made last, that is, at the exact hour.

Coding and transmitting the ship's weather reports

Weather reports from ships are made in the International Code forms as drawn up by the World Meteorological Organization. Full details of these codes are given in *Admiralty List of Radio Signals, Volume 3*. The necessary code tables for ship reports are also set out on a code card (NP 453) supplied to all ships that are required to make weather reports. A specimen ship report is given on the back of the code card.

Details of authorities to whom weather reports are made by HM ships are included in current *Defence Council Instructions* and the *Naval Weather Service Handbook* (NP 510). Other ships wishing to make weather reports can find details of the appropriate addresses and methods of communication in *Admiralty List of Radio Signals, Volume 3*.

Sea State Code

This is Code 3700 in *Radio Weather Messages for use in the Naval Weather Service* (NP 464). It is used extensively on occasions other than weather reporting, and it has become necessary for HM ships to use it during joint exercises.

STATE OF SEA *Code figure*	DESCRIPTIVE TERMS	HEIGHT* *Metres*	*Feet* *(approx.)*
0	Calm (glassy)	0	0
1	Calm (rippled)	0–0·1	0–$\frac{1}{3}$
2	Smooth (wavelets)	0·1–0·5	$\frac{1}{3}$–$1\frac{2}{3}$
3	Slight	0·5–1·25	$1\frac{2}{3}$–4
4	Moderate	1·25–2·5	4–8
5	Rough	2·5–4	8–13
6	Very rough	4–6	13–20
7	High	6–9	20–30
8	Very high	9–14	30–45
9	Phenomenal	Over 14	Over 45

* The average wave height as obtained from the larger well-formed waves of the wave system being observed.

M

CHAPTER 22

Ocean Currents

An ocean current is a general movement of the water of the ocean, which may be permanent or semi-permanent. The term should not be used to include tidal streams which are subject to regular reversal within a period of 24 hours or less. Currents flow at all depths in the oceans and may have both horizontal and vertical components. The navigator is interested only in the near-surface current flow, which may be defined as the flow at a depth of about half the ship's draught.

Drift currents

The main cause of most surface currents in the open sea is the direct action of the wind on the sea surface. A current formed in this way is known as a *drift current*, and a close correlation exists between the directions of the prevailing drift currents and the prevailing winds.

General circulation of drift currents

Among the major wind belts of the world the Trade winds are those which blow with the greatest constancy. These, in fact, correspond to the two broad belts of westward-setting currents in the tropics (the North and South Equatorial currents) which may be regarded as the mainsprings of the surface current circulation of the two hemispheres. In the Atlantic and Pacific Oceans the North-east and South-east Trade winds drive an immense body of water westwards over a width of some 50° of latitude, broken only by the narrow belt of east-going Equatorial Counter-current which is found a few degrees north of the Equator in both these oceans. A similar westward surge of water occurs in the South Indian Ocean, resulting from the action of the South-east Trade wind.

In the temperate latitudes of both hemispheres there are wide belts of predominantly east-going currents. In each hemisphere these two contrasting easterly and westerly flows form the northern and southern flanks of vast closed circulations roughly centred on the areas of permanent high pressure, with which the wind circulations are also associated, in approximately 30°N and 30°S. There are also regions of drift circulation due to various causes, outside the main eddies but associated with them or dependent upon them. As an example, part of the North Atlantic Current branches from the main system and flows past the north of Scotland and northward along the coast of Norway. It branches again, a part of it flowing past Spitsbergen into the Arctic Ocean, while a part enters the Barents Sea.

In the main monsoon regions – the north part of the Indian Ocean and the extreme west of the North Pacific Ocean (China Seas and Eastern Archipelago) – the current reverses seasonally, flowing in accordance with the monsoon blowing at the time.

The South Atlantic, South Indian, and South Pacific Oceans are all open to the Southern Ocean; and the Southern Ocean Current, encircling the globe in an easterly direction (south of latitude 40°S approximately), completes the southern part of the main circulation of each of these three oceans.

The general surface circulation of the world is shown in Fig. 147. Apart from the major changes of direction in the monsoon areas, there are some minor seasonal changes of position of currents which cannot be shown on a single general chart (for example, the Equatorial Counter-current of the North Atlantic Ocean originates much farther eastward from February to April, in about longitude 25°W). For details of seasonal changes, reference should be made to the *Sailing Directions* and *Current Atlases*.

Effect of the Earth's rotation on the direction of drift currents

The direction of a drift current does not depend entirely on the wind direction. It is also affected by the Earth's rotation. Theoretically, in the deep ocean, the current should be diverted 45° to the right of the wind direction in the northern hemisphere and to the left in the southern hemisphere. Recent tests suggest that in practice the diversion may be somewhat less, somewhere between 30° and 45°.

Gradient currents

Currents are also produced when there is a gradient of pressure in the water, and are known as *gradient currents*. Such a gradient may result in two ways:

(*a*) if the sea level is actually sloping,

(*b*) if masses of water of different density lie adjacent to one another.

Such density differences arise from differences of temperature or salinity or, more usually, of both; the level of the warmer or less saline water will be a little higher than that of colder or saltier water when two such masses of water are adjacent on the surface. Owing to the Earth's rotation, the movement of water will be deflected to the right of the downward slope or increasing density gradient in the northern hemisphere, and to the left in the southern hemisphere.

Effect of wind blowing over a coastline

For example, in the region of the Benguela Current (southern hemisphere), the SE Trade winds tends to drive water away from the coast so that the sea level the sea level slopes down to the coast. When the wind blows from the sea to the land, the slope of the sea level is upwards to the coast. The resulting current is deflected to right or left of the direction of the downward slope, depending upon the hemisphere.

For example, in the region of the Benguela Current (southern hemisphere), the SE Trade wind tends to drive water away from the coast so that the sea level slopes down to the coast. The current is deflected to the left of the slope, so the current flows north-north-westwards. The direct effect of the wind stresses exerted by the SE Trade is to produce a north-westward flow, which is deflected

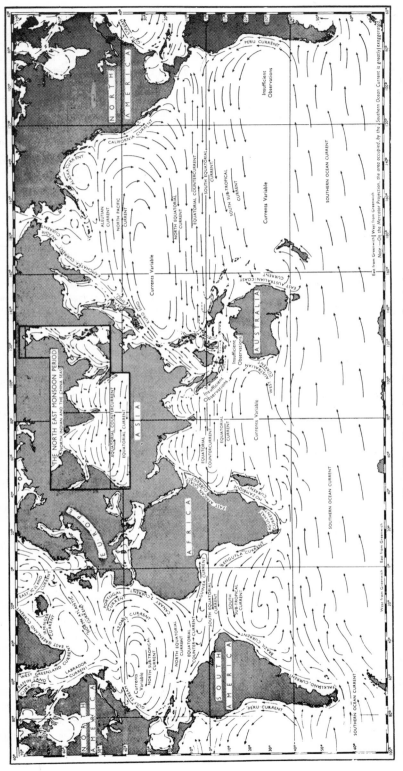

Fig. 147.   General surface-current circulation

to a more nearly westerly flow by the earth's rotation. The result of these gradient and drift currents is thus approximately north-westerly.

Variability of currents

Currents, like winds, are variable; and, like winds, the degree of variability differs considerably from one place to another and in some cases from one season to another. In parts of the Equatorial currents, for example, more than 75 per cent of the currents set in directions within the quadrant centred upon the predominant direction, and there is an almost complete absence of observations in the opposite direction. In other regions the current observations are spread almost uniformly around the compass, so that no direction can be described as predominant. In most regions the variability is between these two extremes, with sets in one quadrant significantly more frequent than those in the other quadrants, yet with an appreciable frequency of sets in the opposite direction.

Warm and cold currents

Currents may be classified as follows:

1. Currents, the temperature of which corresponds to the latitude in which they flow. They are warm, cold or intermediate.

2. Currents, the temperature of which does not correspond to the latitude in which they flow. They are warmer or colder than currents of class (1) flowing in the same latitudes.

Charts showing sea surface isotherms indicate the nature of currents. In currents of class (1) the isotherms run approximately east and west, while in class (2) their trend is more or less markedly north and south.

Examples of class (1) are the warm west-going Equatorial currents of all oceans and the cold east-going Southern Ocean Current encircling the globe. Examples of class (2) are the warm Gulf Stream and the warm Kuro Shio, which transport the warm water of the Equatorial currents to higher latitudes; and the cold East Greenland Current, transporting cold water from the Arctic basin to lower latitudes.

Cold currents of class (2) may be subdivided further, depending on the origin of the cold water:

(a) Currents which bring the cold water of polar regions to lower latitudes (East Greenland, Labrador, Falkland, and Oya Shio Currents).

(b) When the current is away from an extended coastline, the surface water moving away from the coast has to be replaced by water 'upwelling' from sub-surface depths. The upwelling water is colder than surface water should be in that latitude (but not so cold as water of polar origin arriving in the same latitude). These currents form the eastern parts of the main circulations, except in the Indian Ocean, where there is no extended coastline to the east.

The warm currents, transporting warm water to higher latitudes, are found on the western sides of the main closed circulations in both hemispheres. These currents, and the colder ones on the eastern sides, can be tabulated as follows:

	Warm current on Western side of Ocean	Cold current and area of upwelling on Eastern side of Ocean
North Atlantic Ocean ..	Gulf Stream	Canary Current
South Atlantic Ocean ..	Brazil Current	Benguela Current
North Pacific Ocean ..	Kuro Shio	California Current
South Pacific Ocean	East Australian Coast Current	Peru Current
Southern Indian Ocean ..	Mozambique and Agulhas Currents	—

Cold currents from high latitudes have a special significance for navigators because they transport ice to lower latitudes. They are also responsible for the high frequency of fog and poor visibility in certain areas (*see* page 188).

CURRENTS OF THE OCEANS

A brief account of the main currents of the oceans now follows. Unless otherwise stated, it can be assumed that the currents described rarely exceed a speed of 2 knots. Further details of currents in specific areas may be found in the appropriate chapters of *Ocean Passages of the World* and in the *Sailing Directions* for these areas. More detailed information is available in the *Current Atlases* which are listed in *Hydrographic Supplies Handbook* (NP 133).

Atlantic Ocean Currents

The *South Equatorial Current* and the *South Subtropical Current* set to the west across the Atlantic roughly between the parallels of 2°N and 20°S. When about 300 miles east of Recife the flow divides, each part following the coast. One part runs south and forms the Brazil Current, and the other runs north-west along the north coast of South America towards the Caribbean Sea, where it joins the North Equatorial Current.

West of longitude 30°W, this current may exceed 3 knots.

The *Brazil Current* runs southwards along the coast of Brazil as far as the River Plate, where it turns eastwards and merges with the Southern Ocean Current. Inshore of the Brazil Current, the currents run in the same direction as the prevailing wind. During the winter, the Brazil Counter-current sets to the north.

The *Falkland Current* runs northwards up the east coast of South America as far as the River Plate. In winter it is extended to the north by the Brazil Counter-current and may exceed 2 knots.

The *Benguela Current*. Off the Cape of Good Hope the part of the Agulhas Current which has entered the South Atlantic is joined by an offshoot of the Southern Ocean Current, forming the Benguela Current. This current sets to the north along the west coast of Africa to the equator, where it turns westwards and feeds the South Equatorial Current.

The *Equatorial Counter-current*. The area of the Equatorial Trough (Doldrums), where there is insufficient wind to set up a drift current, affords a suitable area for the return passage of surface water displaced by the North and South Equatorial Currents. This current starts in about latitude 8°N and longitude 50°W, except from February to April, when it originates much farther eastwards, in about longitude 25°W and latitude 5°N.

The *Guinea Current* is an easterly extension of the Equatorial Counter-current into the Gulf of Guinea. It may reach speeds of 2–3 knots when augmented by the drift current due to the West African monsoon.

The *North Equatorial Current* and the *North Subtropical Current* sweep westwards across the Atlantic between latitudes 10°N and 30°N, approximately.

The *Gulf Stream*. Owing to the shape of the South American continent which diverts the South Equatorial Current towards the Caribbean, much of the flow of both the South Equatorial and North Equatorial Currents is diverted into this sea and flows through the Yucatan Channel into the Gulf of Mexico. The latter constitutes a *cul-de-sac* in which the water piles up to a measurable extent. Since the Gulf is shallow and the climate extremely hot, the water is further heated before it escapes through the only exit open to it – the narrow Florida Strait between Florida and Cuba. Turning through north-east to north, following the Florida coast, the Florida Current, as it is here called, flows northwards through the narrows between Florida and the Bahama Banks. It reaches the open sea as a belt of excessively salt warm water some 50 miles wide whose mean speed on the axis of maximum flow is 3–4 knots. It is intensely blue, and its boundaries with the ordinary ocean water are well marked. But for the coral banks round the Bahamas it would go far out to sea. These banks, however, deflect it northward along the coast of S Carolina. Here it becomes broader and shallower; between Bermuda and New York it is about 250 miles wide.
The term 'Gulf Stream' is commonly applied to the whole extent of the warm and rapid current between the Bahamas and the Tail of the Great Bank of Newfoundland. As it approaches latitude 40°N the Gulf Stream becomes more easterly and continues in this direction past the Tail of the Great Bank.

The *North Atlantic Current*. After passing the longitude of the easternmost part of North America, the Gulf Stream, as such, ceases to exist, but the prevailing westerly winds continue the easterly set as the North Atlantic Current. On approaching Europe the current divides: one branch continues northeastwards to the Arctic, while the other branch, the *Portugal Current*, runs to the south and east in the direction of the African Coast.

The *Canary Current*. The southern end of the Portugal Current is now under the influence of the North-east Trade wind and extends as the Canary Current through the Canary Isles to Cape Verde, where it turns westerly again and merges with the North Equatorial Current.

The *Labrador Current* is a cold current which flows south-eastwards along the coast of Labrador in response to the prevailing north-westerly winds.

Off south-east Newfoundland the current fans out, part of the flow turning eastwards to flow parallel with the North Atlantic Current, and part turning west-south-westwards to form a cold counter-current between the Gulf Stream and the American coast. The boundary between the Gulf Stream and the Labrador Current is most marked, by both the colour of the water and the change of temperature. The Labrador Current, being mostly composed of fresher water from melted glacier ice, is green, but the Gulf Stream, being very salt, is blue. The temperature difference at the surface may be as much as 15°C.

In the late spring and summer, when the Davis Strait is no longer frozen over, the Labrador Current brings with it large quantities of ice and icebergs.

Pacific Ocean Currents

It will be seen from Fig. 147 that the currents of the Pacific bear a strong resemblance to those of the Atlantic. The principal difference is the periodic change of drift current in the China Sea resulting from the change of direction of the monsoons.

The *South Equatorial Current* and the *South Subtropical Current* flow west-wards between the parallels of about 3°N and 20°S. On the eastern side of the ocean the South Equatorial Current averages about 1 knot and at times reaches 2–3 knots. When these currents reach the numerous islands between the meridians of 160°E and 170°E, they divide into two branches. One branch, the *East Australian Coast Current*, sets south along the east coast of Australia with a speed which averages about 1½ knots, and which may reach over 3 knots at times during the southern summer and autumn, until it meets the Southern Ocean Current, when it is deflected eastward towards New Zealand.

The other branch passes among the islands to the north of Australia. During the period of the South-west Monsoon this branch penetrates westwards to Sumatra and is then deflected north-eastwards into the China Sea. During the North-east Monsoon, however, it is not felt to the west of New Guinea; the southerly monsoon drift passes through the China Sea and is diverted to the east along the north coast of Java, reaching as far east as the western coasts of New Guinea.

The *Peru Current*, also known as the *Humboldt Current*, sets to the north along the west coast of South America, and finally merges into the South Equatorial Current.

The *Equatorial Counter-current* runs eastwards between the parallels of about 4°N and 9°N, until it strikes the coast of Central America.

The *North Equatorial Current* flows westwards between the parallels of 8°N and 20°N, until it reaches the Philippines, where it is deflected to the north-east and becomes the Kuro Shio. West of longitude 152°E it may exceed 2 knots.

The *Kuro Shio* is a warm, dark current. It corresponds to the Gulf Stream of the Atlantic, but is less clearly defined on account of the various islands which it encounters, and it is considerably influenced by the prevailing monsoon. It flows along the east coasts of the Philippines and Japan; it then curves east and merges into the North Pacific Current. Its speed, west of longitude 150°E, averages about 1½ knots in the region of maximum flow and, on occasion, may rise to as high as 4 knots.

The *Kamchatka Current* corresponds to the Labrador Current of the North Atlantic and flows southwards from the Bering Sea along the coast of Kamchatka to the Kuril Islands.

The *Oya Shio* is the extension of the Kamchatka Current southwards from the Kurils towards the northern islands of Japan. Here it meets the Kuro Shio and some of it is deflected eastwards across the Pacific as the *Aleutian Current* parallel with the North Pacific Current which represents the broadened and weakened extension of the Kuro Shio; the rest sinks below the lighter and warmer water from the south.

The *California Current* is a cold current corresponding to the Peru Current of the South Pacific. It sets down the coast of North America and Mexico, finally turning west and merging with the North Equatorial Current.

The *Davidson Current* sets northwards along the west coast of the United States inside the California Current during the winter and is caused by the prevailing southerly winds along this coast during that season.

Indian Ocean Currents

The currents of this ocean are greatly dependent on the monsoons.

The *Equatorial Current* flows westwards between the parallels of 0° and 5°S, according to the monsoon, and 20°S. This current is liable to exceed 2 knots near Madagascar. On reaching Mauritius it divides, one part flowing north and one south of Madagascar.

The *Somali Current*. The branch of the Equatorial Current which goes north of Madagascar again divides when it meets the African coast. One part turns north and, during the south-west monsoon, flows along the coast of Somalia to join the north-easterly drift in the Arabian Sea. This northerly current often exceeds 3 knots.

During the north-east monsoon the northgoing coastal current does not extend beyond about latitude 2°S, but turns eastwards to feed the Equatorial Counter-current. In this season the Somali Current flows southwards along the coast of East Africa as far south as about latitude 2°S, where it also turns eastwards to join the Equatorial Counter-current. The southgoing Somali Current occasionally exceeds 3 knots.

The *Mozambique Current*. The part of the Equatorial Current which passes north of Madagascar and is then deflected to the south by the African coast is known as the Mozambique Current.

The *Agulhas Current* flows southwards along the east coast of Africa, south of Delagoa Bay. It is formed by the junction of the Mozambique Current and that branch of the Equatorial Current which passes south of Madagascar.

Both the Mozambique and Agulhas Currents may exceed 3 knots, more particularly the latter.

The *West Australian Current* runs northwards along the west coast of Australia, eventually turning west and merging with the Equatorial Current.

The *Equatorial Counter-current* flows eastwards just south of the equator during the North-east Monsoon (which blows from north-west after it crosses the equator). During the northern hemisphere summer the northern boundary of the Equatorial (westerly) Current is in about latitude 5°S, and easterly sets extend far into the northern hemisphere as the summer monsoon drift. These South-west Monsoon currents have average speeds of 1–1½ knots and on occasions are well in excess of 2 knots to the south of Sri Lanka.

Currents in the Red Sea. The general set is to the south except during the North-east Monsoon. The North-east Monsoon drift is then forced into the Gulf of Aden and causes a northerly set in the southern part of the Red Sea.

Mediterranean Sea Currents

The rate of evaporation from this sea is high, and the inflow of water from the rivers entering it is not sufficient to maintain the level of the sea. Water therefore flows in from the Atlantic through the Strait of Gibraltar. The effect of the Earth's rotation is to deflect this water to the right, so the inflow current is forced to run along the whole length of the African coast, and a counter-clockwise circulation is thus maintained.

The currents in this sea are generally weak and variable, but the easterly current in the western basin may attain a speed of between 2 and 3 knots.

CHAPTER 23

The Rapid Sight Reduction Method and the Astroplot

The Rapid Method was introduced to reduce the time that elapses between taking observations of heavenly bodies and obtaining the observed position. Whereas the Standard Method (NP 401) takes fifteen to twenty minutes for a four-star observation, the Rapid Method can take about two minutes, but precomputation must be used to its fullest extent. The plotting of the observations can be done on a 'Diagram to facilitate plotting a ship's position from star sights by Rapid Reduction Method' (Diagram 5035), which is supplied to all HM ships, or on the Astroplot, which is supplied to frigates and larger ships. In favourable conditions, using an Astroplot, it is possible to plot an observed position from seven heavenly bodies in eight minutes to an accuracy of two miles without parallel ruler or dividers.

To obtain a fix so quickly may be important operationally, but it must be remembered that the Rapid Method is not so accurate as the Standard Method. Rapid methods are being taught as a supplementary method to the Standard Method and they provide an excellent check for training junior officers to become proficient in taking accurate sextant observations.

The precomputation required for planets, Sun and Moon is complicated and involves too much work for practical purposes.

THEORY

In the Standard Method the sextant altitude is compared with a computed altitude obtained from *Tables of Altitude and Azimuth* with arguments of latitude, declination and hour angle. In the Rapid Method the sextant altitude is compared at the time of sight with a tabulated altitude (precomputed), for which the declination and hour angle, which vary with time, must be known.

It will be obvious that an altitude could be precomputed for a particular instant of time, but it may not be possible to take the sight precisely at that time. So it is necessary to precompute a number of altitudes for a particular heavenly body for the period of observation.

Owing to the Earth's motion about its axis, the geographical positions of stars move westwards over the surface of the Earth with an angular velocity of 15° per sidereal hour or 1° per sidereal 4 minutes. Hence a computed altitude can be obtained for the beginning of the observation period, using the LHA at that time, and subsequently at intervals of 4 sidereal minutes or every 1° increase of LHA. An observer taking a sight would then note the stop-watch time since the beginning of the observation period to obtain the relevant tabulated altitude with which to compare his sextant altitude and obtain the intercept.

The stop-watch, which records sidereal time, is started when a whole degree of LHA Aries crosses the 'selected meridian', and continues to run throughout the twilight period, each 4-minute interval corresponding to one particular LHA and hence to one particular tabulated altitude. For example, if the sidereal stop-watch is started at the beginning of the observation period (Fig. 148)

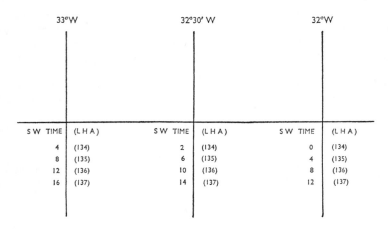

33°W			32°30′ W			32°W	
S W TIME	(L H A)		S W TIME	(L H A)		S W TIME	(L H A)
4	(134)		2	(134)		0	(134)
8	(135)		6	(135)		4	(135)
12	(136)		10	(136)		8	(136)
16	(137)		14	(137)		12	(137)

Fig. 148

when the LHA Aries on a meridian of 32°W (near the DR position) is 134°, after 4 sidereal minutes this LHA has moved 1° farther west and is crossing the meridian of 33°W, while the next LHA (135°) has arrived at the meridian 32°W. Thus an observer somewhere between 32°W and 33°W would compare his sextant reading, made at stop-watch time between 0 and 4 minutes, with a tabulated altitude obtained for a LHA of 134°; for an observation made between 4 and 8 minutes for a LHA of 135°; and so on. The intercept is obtained in the usual way by comparing the sextant altitude with the tabulated altitude corresponding to the appropriate LHA. As the position of this whole degree of LHA moves westward 1° longitude in 4 sidereal minutes, the intercept must be drawn from the longitudinal position of this LHA at the instant of the sight. In other words there is a moving 'chosen position' which varies with time. A time scale is constructed on the plotting sheet or chart with the DR longitude as the central meridian (corresponding to stop-watch times 2, 6, 10, 14 minutes etc.) and extending 30′ of longitude east and west of it. The zero of the time scale is 30′ east of the DR longitude and corresponds to stop-watch times 4, 8, 12, 16 minutes etc., for the subsequent LHAs. The intercept is plotted from the point on the time scale corresponding to the stop-watch time of the sight and laid off in the direction of the true bearing of the heavenly body (or its reciprocal). The position line is then drawn, after allowing for the ship's run in the usual manner.

For any heavenly body the tabulated altitudes can be obtained from *Sight Reduction Tables* (NP 401 and AP 3270, Vols. 2 and 3). However, when stars are being observed much time and labour are saved by using AP 3270, Vol. 1, which tabulates the altitudes and true bearings of seven selected stars as described in Chapter 10.

In the Standard Method the sextant altitude, corrected for index error, is then corrected for dip and refraction to give the true altitude. In the Rapid Method these corrections, with their signs reversed, are applied to the tabulated altitude which, compared with the sextant altitude, gives an intercept.

As the rate of change of LHA Aries is referred to sidereal time, a stop-watch adjusted to read sidereal time should be used. If mean solar time is used, the maximum errors introduced would be 1·2 miles at the equator or 0·6 miles in latitude 60 degrees over a period of half an hour.

If a sidereal stop-watch is not available, the error introduced by using an accurate mean solar time stop-watch may be overcome by correcting the times as follows:

Interval in Minutes	*Seconds to be added to Mean Solar Time to give Sidereal Time*
0–4	0
4–8	1
8–12	2
12–16	2
16–20	3
20–24	4
24–28	4
28–32	5

Advantages of using the Rapid Method

An observed position can be plotted within two minutes of observing the final heavenly body. To achieve this, about 15 minutes of preparatory work must be done at any convenient time beforehand.

Errors, such as badly observed or incorrect altitudes, wrongly applied index errors and personal errors can be detected immediately as each position line is plotted. Additional shots can then be taken in order to confirm or disprove doubtful results.

It is valuable as a training aid. When the DR is known accurately, junior officers' sights can be checked at the time of observation, both for accuracy and consistency, thereby ensuring correct sextant operation. Junior officers can gain confidence in making accurate observations.

Disadvantages

Only seven stars are available in AP 3270 for any one set of sights. When the sky is partially clouded this may prove a disadvantage.

The accuracy of the tables in AP 3270 is 0'·5, whereas that of NP 401 is 0'·1. The accuracy of an observed position derived from AP 3270 is considered to be within 2'·0.

An error in computing the time to start the stop-watch will cause the resultant observed position to be shifted E or W by 1 minute of longitude for every 4 seconds of error. A small error, therefore, may not be detected.

PRACTICE

Equipment required

NP Item Number	Name
99(1)	*Sight Reduction Tables for Air Navigation* (AP 3270, Vol. 1).
99(4)	Rapid Sight Reduction Form (H 494).
314	*Nautical Almanac.*
Patt. HS7	Sidereal Stop-watch.
	Diagram to facilitate obtaining a ship's position from stars by Rapid Reduction Method (Diagram 5035), *or*
Patt. 0552/85	Astroplot, *or*
	Appropriate mercatorial plotting sheet.

Outline of procedure

The LHA Aries for the DR or chosen longitude is found for a time shortly before Civil Twilight and the time (GMT) determined at which the LHA Aries will be a whole number. This time forms the basis for all observations. To this GMT deck-watch error is applied and a two-minute correction to make the DR or chosen longitude the central meridian of the time scale. (By so doing the lengths of the intercepts, which would otherwise be inconveniently large if the time of the observation was near the western end of the time scale, are reduced.) This gives the deck-watch time to start the stop-watch.

The tabulated altitudes and bearings of the seven selected stars are now extracted from AP 3270, Vol. 1, for arguments of chosen latitude and LHA Aries (increasing by 1° for every 4 sidereal minutes) for the period of observation. Corrections for dip, refraction and index error are applied, with signs reversed, to the tabulated altitudes. The sextant altitude may now be compared directly with the corrected tabulated altitude to produce an intercept.

A plotting sheet is prepared showing the intersection of the DR or chosen longitude with the chosen latitude (the nearest whole degree of latitude to the DR position). On either side of the centre are plotted 30 minutes of longitude corresponding to the scale of the chosen latitude. The point 30 minutes of longitude to the east is called the Zero Point from which is drawn, in a 270°

direction, the time scale from 0 to 4 minutes corresponding to one degree of longitude; hence the DR or chosen longitude will always lie on the two-minute mark. The advantage of using a chosen longitude (nearest whole degree to DR longitude) is that, if plotting on a mercatorial plotting sheet (or chart), the longitude scale, converted into time, can conveniently be used. If using a chosen longitude, it is recommended that the DR position be marked for direct comparison with the observed position.

The stop-watch is started at the calculated time, and the times of observations are now referred to as Stop-Watch Times. As each four-minute period ends, the next degree of LHA Aries crosses the Zero Point and the time scale starts again from the point on a 'fly-back' principle. As each sight is taken, the time is marked on the time scale; the sextant altitude is compared with the corrected tabulated altitude for the appropriate LHA Aries; an intercept is obtained and plotted from the mark on the time scale; and the position line is drawn.

Since all position lines must be related to a common time to obtain a position, they must all be adjusted to the time of starting the stop-watch. This can best be done by displacing the time point from the time scale by an amount equal to the ship's run since Zero time in a direction reciprocal to the ship's course. The intersection of these adjusted position lines is the observed position.

AP 3270, Vol. 1, is designed to cover a number of years. A small adjustment (applicable only to the selected seven stars) should now be made to the observed position for the precession and nutation of the year in question. The correction sheet for surface navigation gives this as a direction and distance to be applied to the observed position.

DETAILED INSTRUCTIONS AND EXAMPLE

Preparation (H 494 – *see* Fig. 149)

1. Insert DR for time of Civil Twilight, chosen latitude, date, height of eye, dip, course, speed and index error. Preparatory data for the example are as follows:

   DR at morning twilight on 4th July 1971 was 10° 14'N, 41° 42'W. Course 140°, speed 15 knots. Index error −0'·5. Height of eye 10 m (33 ft). Deck watch error 38ˢ slow on GMT.

2. Insert LMT Civil Twilight at the chosen latitude from the *Nautical Almanac*.

3. Insert the interval from Civil Twilight at which observations can start. This will vary with latitude and will be found from experience. It is suggested that 10 minutes should be subtracted for both morning and evening stars.

4. With the time from (3) enter GMT column in the *Nautical Almanac* and

RAPID SIGHT REDUCTION FORM

H.494
(REVISED JUNE 1958)

MORNING—TWILIGHT—EVENING

CO. AND SP. 140.°. 15 Knots

DATE 4th July 1971. HT. OF EYE 10m.(33ft.) DIP -5.6

S.W. TIME	L.H.A. ARIES	Mirfak BG	Mirfak ALT +7.7	Hamal BG	Hamal ALT +6.7	Acamar BG	Acamar ALT +8.0	Achernar BG	Achernar ALT +8.7	Fomalhaut BG	Fomalhaut ALT +7.0	Altair BG	Altair ALT +8.1	Deneb BG	Deneb ALT +7.5
0-4	359	037°	32°00'.7	063°	56°28'.7	144°	24°39'.0	166°	19°39'.7	199°	47°48'.0	275°	29°22'.1	319°	35°32'.6
4-8	000	045°	15°13'.2	076°	23°22'.1	144°	25°14'.0	166°	19°53'.7	201°	47°27'.0	275°	28°23'.1	319°	34°54'.6
8-12	001	045°	15°55'.2	076°	24°20'.1	145°	25°48'.0	167°	20°00'.7	202°	47°06'.0	275°	27°24'.1	319°	34°15'.6
12-16	002	045°	16°36'.2	076°	25°17'.1	145°	26°22'.0	167°	20°20'.7	203°	46°43'.0	275°	26°25'.1	318°	33°35'.6 / D1 1345 33°41'.0 / D2 1411 33°37'.3 / D3 1441 33°31'.3
16-20	003	045°	17°18'.2	076°	26°15'.1	146°	26°56'.0	168°	20°33'.7	204°	46°20'.0	275°	25°27'.1 / A1 1821 25°16'.1 / A2 1848 25°08'.9 / A3 1908 25°04'.8	318°	32°56'.6
20-24	004	045°	18°00'.2	077°	27°12'.1 / A1 2013 26°55'.3 / A2 2048 27°03'.2 / A3 2115 27°11'.0	146°	27°29'.0	169°	20°45'.7	205°	45°55'.0	275°	24°28'.1	318°	32°16'.6
24-28	005	045°	18°41'.2	077°	28°10'.1	147°	28°01'.0	169°	20°56'.7 / Ac1 2420 20°47'.3 / Ac2 2452 20°48'.6	206°	45°29'.0 / F1 2802 45°07'.0 / F2 2828 45°04'.6	275°	23°29'.1	317°	31°37'.6
28-32	006	045°	19°25'.2	077°	29°07'.1	148°	28°33'.0	170°	21°07'.7	207°	45°03'.0	275°	22°30'.1	317°	30°56'.6

Capella +9.2   Aldebaran +8.1

D.R. 10°14' ... N/S ... 41°42' .. E/W

CHOSEN LAT ... 10° ... N/S

TIME DATA

L.M.T. CIVIL TWILIGHT	05h 20m	
INTERVAL	-10	05h 10m
G.H.A. ARIES (FROM L.M.T.)	356° 33.5'	05h
INCREMENT	2° 30.4'	
	359° 03.9'	
CHOOSE L.H.A. ARIES	359°	
D.R. LONG W+ E-	41° 42'	
G.H.A. ARIES	40° 42'	26° 38.4'
HOUR 07		
MIN 56 SEC 05	14° 03.6'	
G.M.T. (DATE 4 July)	07h 56m 05s	
ADJUSTMENT TO CENTRE TIME SCALE	-2 00	
ZERO TIME	07 54 05	
D.W.E. SLOW - FAST +	38	
D.W.T. START WATCH	07 53 27	
ZONE TIME (FROM ZERO TIME ± ZONE)	04 54 (+3)	

PRECESSION AND NUTATION CORRECTION 1'.3 - 065°   INDEX ERROR -0.5   OBSERVED POSITION 10°12.5 N/S 41°37.0 E/W AT 0454 ZONE TIME

Fig. 149

extract GHA Aries (remembering the increment). This GHA Aries may be regarded as LHA Aries without serious error.

5. Choose the nearest whole number of degrees to (4) and enter it opposite '∴ choose LHA Aries'.

   Note. The symbol '∴' has been inadvertently omitted from Fig. 149.

6. Insert DR or chosen longitude in degrees and minutes; add or subtract as indicated to obtain GHA Aries.

7. Enter the *Nautical Almanac* with this GHA Aries to determine the exact hours, minutes and seconds (i.e., the normal procedure reversed). Insert this time opposite GMT. Insert GMT date.

8. Subtract 2 minutes to obtain Zero time and then apply error as indicated to obtain 'DWT start watch', which is the time at which the sidereal stop-watch must be started.

9. Apply the Zone description to the Zero time to obtain Zone time. This is the time of the observed position.

10. Insert the chosen LHA Aries (from (5)) opposite 0–4 minutes. As LHA Aries increases by 1° every 4 sidereal minutes, complete the rest of the LHA Aries column by adding 1° successively.

11. Enter AP 3270, Vol. 1, with the arguments of chosen latitude and the mean LHA Aries (chosen LHA +4°), extracting the names and approximate altitudes of each selected star. Enter the *Nautical Almanac* with each altitude in turn to obtain a refraction correction to which is applied the dip correction and finally the index error (with sign reversed), the sum being inserted in the space marked 'Total Correction' (sign +).

12. Enter AP 3270 with arguments of chosen latitude and Aries for 0–4 minutes. Insert the bearings of the seven selected stars and the altitudes, corrected for total correction, in the form. Repeat for the remaining LHA Aries.

   Note Insert these figures at the top of each box to leave room for the times and sextant altitudes of the sights.

13. Insert the Precession and Nutation correction (surface navigation version) from AP 3270, Vol. 1, in the space provided.

Preparing the plotting sheet (Diagram 5035 — *see* Fig. 150)

14. Choose a convenient scale for latitude and distance.

15. Determine the length of 1° of longitude at the chosen latitude and mark off 30′ of longitude on each side of the chosen longitude. This is the time scale; the centre point is the 2-minute mark; the eastern extremity is the Zero Point; the western extremity is the 4-minute mark. Graduate the time scale in convenient intervals of seconds. This is much simplified if a chart, or mercatorial plotting sheet, or Diagram 5035, is used. Instructions for the Diagram 5035 are printed on it.

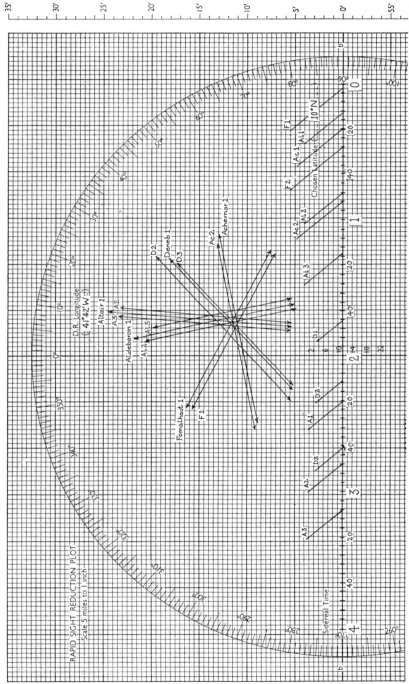

Fig. 150

Taking observations and plotting

1. Start the stop-watch at the calculated DWT.

2. Note the stop-watch time and sextant altitude of each observation in the appropriate space on the form.

3. Compare the sextant altitude with the corrected tabulated altitude to obtain the intercept. True bearing is that already entered in the appropriate space.

   In the example the following observations were taken:

Star	Stop-watch Time	Sextant Altitude
Deneb (D1)	13ᵐ 45ˢ	33° 41'·0
Deneb (D2)	14ᵐ 11ˢ	33° 37'·3
Deneb (D3)	14ᵐ 41ˢ	33° 31'·3
Altair (A1)	18ᵐ 21ˢ	25° 16'·1
Altair (A2)	18ᵐ 48ˢ	25° 08'·9
Altair (A3)	19ᵐ 08ˢ	25° 04'·8
Aldebaran (Al 1)	20ᵐ 13ˢ	26° 55'·3
Aldebaran (Al 2)	20ᵐ 48ˢ	27° 03'·2
Aldebaran (Al 3)	21ᵐ 15ˢ	27° 11'·0
Achernar (Ac 1)	24ᵐ 20ˢ	20° 47'·3
Achernar (Ac 2)	24ᵐ 52ˢ	20° 48'·6
Fomalhaut (F1)	28ᵐ 02ˢ	45° 07'·0
Fomalhaut (F2)	28ᵐ 28ˢ	45° 04'·6

4. From the point on the time scale corresponding to the stop-watch time of the observation, plot the ship's run (reciprocal), then the intercept and the position line.

   After plotting the first position line of a star, a second shot is taken which, if it lies within one mile of the first, confirms the reliability of the first. In this way mistakes can be eliminated.

   In dealing with random errors such as those resulting from a poor horizon it is well to remember that the evaluation of three position lines is more accurate than one. In the example the slightly greater spread of the position lines of Deneb was probably due to the poor horizon at the time.

   To assist plotting, a device consisting of a scale in miles (2 degrees graduated in minutes of latitude/miles) may be used. By setting the dividers with one point on the basic altitude for the four-minute 'window' and the other point adjusted to the sextant altitude, the actual value of the intercept is set on the dividers and need not be evaluated.

5. Select the observed position from the position lines and adjust it for precession and nutation.

The team

Experience has shown that the best results can be obtained by employing a junior officer as astro-plotter and a seaman (navigator's yeoman) as recorder; observations can then be plotted the moment they are made.

Good teamwork between observer and plotter should ensure that each string of sights is taken in a single 'window' (i.e. in a 4-minute period) and, if possible, two strings.

Time factor

The approximate time required for the preparation of the plotting sheet and sight form is 15 minutes. The plotting sheet, once prepared, can be used again when the chosen latitude is the same. If the sheet and form are prepared by an assistant, the Navigating Officer must check the preparation of the time data.

The time between observation and plotting a position line is about 15 seconds. The observed position is available as soon as the last sight is plotted.

Use in very high latitudes

Above 69°N or S when the time movement is very much less, the time scale can be based on 8-minute intervals (every 2° LHA Aries) and the star data prepared accordingly.

THE ASTROPLOT

The Astroplot has been designed to assist rapid plotting of the results of Rapid Sight Reduction without the aid of a parallel ruler or dividers. It may be considered as time-stabilized, since the Earth's rotation and ship's movement are compensated in the instrument.

Description (*see* folding plate)

The Astroplot is engraved on a scale of 5 miles = 1 inch, and comprises the following parts.

The Baseplate, constructed of Bexoid and containing a rotatable disc engraved in degree steps from 0° to 359° around its circumference. The face of the disc is engraved with 2-mile squares.

The Plotting Surface. A Perspex plotting surface is secured above, and proud of, the baseplate.

The Time Scale. A Bexoid strip, on which a time scale can be drawn, is provided for insertion between the plotting surface and the baseplate. It is adjustable, passing through slots on the East and West sides of the plotting surface. Engraved parallel index marks are provided at the slots to ensure that the strip is orientated accurately along the East–West axis.

Altitude Ruler: a Perspex ruler, engraved in minutes of altitude, is supplied separately. A cursor enables the controlling altitude for any selected four-minute period from Form H494 to be accurately set.

Setting up

The information required for setting up the Astroplot is compiled and recorded on Form H494. The folding plate at the end of the text shows the Astroplot set for the last observation (Fomalhaut 2) of the example on page 299.

Time Scale. A time scale for four minutes must be marked on the Bexoid strip to the scale of the Astroplot and for a chosen latitude. (The time scale on Diagram 5035 may be used.) The centre of the time scale (two-minute mark) must be lined up so that it coincides with the centre of the Astroplot at the time of 'start watch,' and subsequently it must be kept lined up for ship's movement.

Ship's Movement. The reciprocal of the ship's course can be drawn on the plotting surface and marked away from the centre of the plot in any convenient manner (e.g. in minutes of time) for ship's speed. Throughout the period of observation the two-minute mark on the time scale must be lined up to the appropriate point on the ship's movement line, care being taken to ensure that it lies on a true East–West line. This lining-up can be continuous or the time scale can be moved at convenient intervals consistent with the accuracy required. The ship's course can be obtained by lining up the baseplate to the ship's head, and any alterations of course can be allowed for by realigning the baseplate and using one of the parallel lines engraved on the baseplate to draw the course from the point of alteration along the old course.

DR Position. The North–South centre line of the Astroplot is the DR longitude position, chosen for the DWT of 'start watch' (*see* Form H 494). The East–West line represents the chosen latitude from which the DR position may be plotted.

Plotting procedure

1. At the time of 'start watch' or beginning of observations, the observer will choose the first star for observation. The plotter must line up the rotatable disc to the star's azimuth and set up the cursor on the altitude ruler to the appropriate altitude tabulated in Form H494.

2. At the moment of observation, the time and the observed altitude will be recorded. The plotter then lines up the cursor on the altitude ruler to the point in time along the time scale. The ruler is orientated with the aid of the parallel engraved lines on the rotatable disc so that its engraved arrow points directly towards the azimuth of the star observed. The observed altitude is then marked on the plotting surface as a dot (the J-point) at the altitude on the ruler corresponding to the observed altitude.

3. Further shots of the same star are taken until the J-points obtained are observed to lie on or nearly on a line at right angles to the star's azimuth. Stability is thus established and a position line can be drawn through the mean of the J-points.

4. This procedure is repeated for each star until a position is obtained which will be for the time of 'start watch.' It may be taken from the plot as a

bearing and distance from the DR position or as d.lat. and departure from the chosen latitude and DR longitude respectively.

Other techniques

When time is not of paramount importance, many variations of plotting procedures may be employed and Navigating Officers will doubtless develop methods to suit their own requirements. These may include:

observing in conjunction with Form H494 and subsequent plotting by astroplot or Diagram 5035; or
using AP 3270 and the standard intercept technique.

Conning the observer on to a selected heavenly body

By assuming the DR to be accurate to within a few miles, the astroplotter can set up his astroplot to determine the sextant altitude to bring the selected body into the observer's horizon field of view. This is particularly useful for early evening observations in cloudy conditions.

A Summary of Plane Trigonometry and Elementary Spherical Trigonometry

PLANE TRIGONOMETRY

Trigonometry is the science of finding the angles and sides of a triangle when certain of these angles and sides are given. Plane trigonometry is the science applied to plane triangles. Spherical trigonometry is the science applied to the triangles marked on the surface of a sphere by planes through its centre.

The degree

The angle between two lines is the inclination of one line to the other, and this inclination is commonly measured in degrees and sub-divisions of a degree.

In one complete revolution there are 360 degrees (Fig. 151). When the two arms of the angle are perpendicular, the angle is said to be a right angle, in which there are 90 degrees.

The sub-divisions of the degree are the minute and second, the relation between them being:

$$1° = 60 \text{ minutes } (')$$
$$1' = 60 \text{ seconds } ('')$$

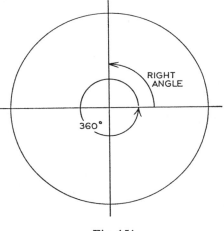

Fig. 151

The radian

The degree is an arbitrary unit. The principles of trigonometry would not be altered if its size were chosen so that one hundred degrees formed a right angle. The mathematical unit is the radian, which is defined as the angle subtended at the centre of a circle by a length of arc equal to the radius.

The ratio of the circumference of a circle to its diameter is constant and equal to 3·14159..., a number denoted by π. From this it follows that:

1. The angle subtended by an arc equal to the radius is also constant and equal to $360° \div 2\pi$, or approximately $57°$ $17'$ $45''$.

2. The number of radians in a right angle is $\frac{1}{2}\pi$.

3. The length of any arc is equal to the radius multiplied by the angle in radians.

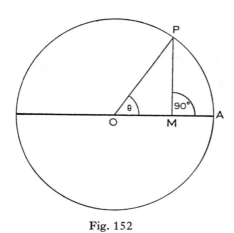

Fig. 152

Trigonometrical functions

There are six of these functions; only two of them are of fundamental importance, the other four being derived from them. These two are known as the sine and cosine of the angle.

In Fig. 152 *POM* is an angle θ where θ lies between $0°$ and $90°$, and *PM* is the perpendicular from *P* on to the arm *OA*, so that *OP*, *MP* and *OM* form a triangle right-angled at *M*.

The six trigonometrical functions are the sine and cosine, tangent and cotangent, secant and cosecant; and they are defined and abbreviated thus:

$$\sin \theta = \frac{\text{side opposite the angle}}{\text{hypotenuse}} = \frac{MP}{OP}$$

$$\cos \theta = \frac{\text{side adjacent to the angle}}{\text{hypotenuse}} = \frac{OM}{OP}$$

$$\tan \theta = \frac{\text{side opposite}}{\text{side adjacent}} = \frac{MP}{OM}$$

$$\cot \theta = \frac{OM}{MP} = \frac{1}{\tan \theta}$$

$$\sec \theta = \frac{OP}{OM} = \frac{1}{\cos \theta}$$

$$\operatorname{cosec} \theta = \frac{OP}{MP} = \frac{1}{\sin \theta}$$

The last three functions are thus reciprocals of the first three and:

$$\tan \theta = \frac{MP}{OM} = \frac{MP}{OP} \times \frac{OP}{OM} = \frac{\sin \theta}{\cos \theta}$$

The sign of the six functions

The sign of the six trigonometrical functions just defined varies with the size of the angle.

In Fig. 153 XOX' and YOY' are two straight lines cutting at right-angles in O and forming two axes along which all lengths are measured. The convention is that along OX or OY – to the right or towards the top of the page, that is – measurements are made in a *positive* direction and carry a plus sign; and along

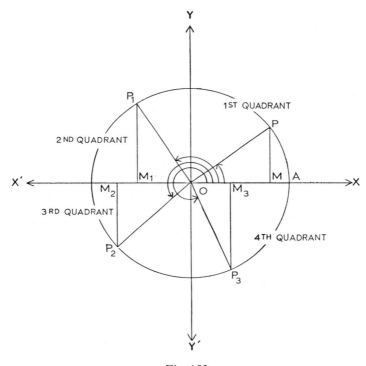

Fig. 153

OX' or OY' – to the left or towards the bottom of the page – they are made in a *negative* direction and carry a minus sign.

The radius OP is considered always to be positive and to move anti-clockwise round the circle occupying successive positions P, P_1, P_2 and P_3 in the four quadrants into which the axes divide the circle, and forming the angles AOP, AOP_1, AOP_2 and AOP_3.

1. *First Quadrant.* In this quadrant OM and MP are measured in positive directions, and since OP is positive, all the trigonometrical functions must be positive.

2. *Second Quadrant.* In this quadrant M_1P_1 is positive, but OM_1 is negative; sin AOP_1 is therefore positive, and cos AOP_1 is negative. Hence the tangent, cotangent and secant of angles in this quadrant are negative, and the cosecant is positive.

3. *Third Quadrant.* In this quadrant both M_2P_2 and OM_2 are negative, and both sin AOP_2 and cos AOP_2 are negative. The tangent is therefore positive.

4. *Fourth Quadrant.* In this quadrant M_3P_3 is negative, but OM_3 is positive. Hence the sine is negative, the cosine is positive, and the tangent is negative.

In summary these facts may be stated thus:

First Quadrant – all functions positive.
Second Quadrant – only the sine and cosecant positive.
Third Quadrant – only the tangent and cotangent positive.
Fourth Quadrant – only the cosine and secant positive.

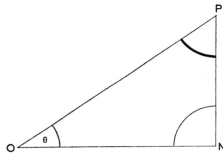

Fig. 154

Complementary angles

Angles that, when added together, make 90° are said to be 'complementary'. Thus, if one angle is 34° the complementary angle is 56°.

In any right-angled triangle the two acute angles are complementary, since the sum of the three angles, of which one is 90°, must be 180°. Fig. 154 shows this fact and also that:

$$\sin \theta = \frac{MP}{OP} = \cos (90° - \theta)$$

$$\cos \theta = \frac{OM}{OP} = \sin (90° - \theta)$$

Supplementary angles

Angles that, when added together, make 180° are said to be supplementary. Thus, if one angle is 34° the supplementary angle is 146°.

In Fig. 155 *MOP* and *MOP'* are supplementary angles. Then, since the angle *M'OP'* is numerically equal to the angle *MOP*:

$$\sin (180° - \theta) = \frac{M'P'}{OP'} = \frac{MP}{OP} = \sin \theta$$

$$\cos (180° - \theta) = \frac{OM'}{OP'} = \frac{- OM}{OP} = - \cos \theta$$

$$\therefore \tan (180° - \theta) = - \tan \theta$$

By reference to a geometrical figure, or by remembering the signs that the various functions take in the separate quadrants, it can be seen that:

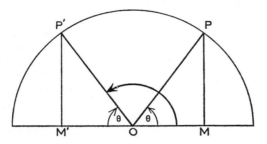

Fig. 155

$$\sin (\ 90° + \theta) = \cos \theta \qquad \cos (\ 90° + \theta) = -\sin \theta$$
$$\sin (180° + \theta) = -\sin \theta \qquad \cos (180° + \theta) = -\cos \theta$$
$$\sin (360° - \theta) = -\sin \theta \qquad \cos (360° - \theta) = \cos \theta$$

Since $(360° - \theta)$ is, in effect, the negative angle, $-\theta$, the last formulae may be written:

$$\sin (-\theta) = -\sin \theta \qquad \cos (-\theta) = \cos \theta$$

Connection between the sine and cosine

It has been shown that the tangent, cotangent, secant and cosecant can be expressed in terms of the sine and cosine. The sine and cosine are themselves connected by a relation which can be established geometrically.

By the Theorem of Pythagoras, the square on the hypotenuse of a right-angled triangle is equal to the sum of the squares on the other two sides. Therefore in Fig. 154:

$$MP^2 + OM^2 = OP^2$$

i.e. $$\frac{MP^2}{OP^2} + \frac{OM^2}{OP^2} = 1$$

or $$\sin^2 \theta + \cos^2 \theta = 1$$

This relation may be written:

$$\tan^2 \theta + 1 = \sec^2 \theta$$

$$1 + \cot^2 \theta = \mathrm{cosec}^2 \theta$$

These formulae hold for all values of θ, because the square of the trigonometrical function is always positive, although the angle may be such that the function itself is negative.

The plane triangle

There are several formulae connecting the sides and angles of a triangle, and the choice of formula is governed, as a rule, by convenience.

The convention adopted in order to distinguish the sides and angles of a triangle ABC (Fig. 156) is that A shall denote the angle at A where AB cuts AC, and that a shall denote the side BC opposite the angle A. A like significance attaches to B, b, C and c.

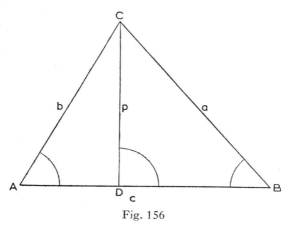

Fig. 156

The sine formula

This formula is established by dropping a perpendicular from any vertex on to the opposite side. In Fig. 156, the perpendicular is CD, denoted by p. Then:

$$\sin A = \frac{p}{b} \qquad\qquad \sin B = \frac{p}{a}$$

i.e.
$$p = b \sin A \qquad\qquad p = a \sin B$$

$$\therefore \quad b \sin A = a \sin B$$

or
$$\frac{a}{\sin A} = \frac{b}{\sin B}$$

If a perpendicular is dropped from A to BC, it can be shown that:

$$\frac{b}{\sin B} = \frac{c}{\sin C}$$

Hence:
$$\frac{a}{\sin A} = \frac{b}{\sin B} = \frac{c}{\sin C}$$

If two angles and one side of the triangle are given, the third angle is known to be $180° - (A + B)$, and the sine formula gives the remaining sides.

The formula is true for an obtuse-angled triangle.

Fig. 157 shows that ambiguity arises if the formula is used for solving the triangle when two sides and an angle other than the included angle are given, the given angle being opposite the smaller side. If, for example, the sides b and c and the angle C are given, the angle found from the formula is either ABC or its supplement $AB'C$, because the sine of an angle is equal to the sine of its supplement.

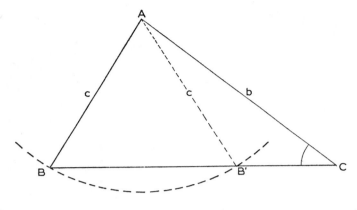

Fig. 157

The cosine formula

This formula is established by applying the Theorem of Pythagoras to the right-angled triangles ADC and BDC in Fig. 156. Thus:

$$b^2 = p^2 + AD^2 \qquad\qquad a^2 = p^2 + BD^2$$

$$\therefore \quad a^2 = (b^2 - AD^2) + BD^2$$
$$= b^2 - AD^2 + (c - AD)^2$$
$$= b^2 - AD^2 + c^2 - 2cAD + AD^2$$
$$= b^2 + c^2 - 2cAD$$
$$= b^2 + c^2 - 2bc \cos A$$

In the same way it can be established that:

$$b^2 = c^2 + a^2 - 2ca \cos B$$
$$c^2 = a^2 + b^2 - 2ab \cos C$$

This formula is true for any triangle, but it must be remembered that, if the angle A, B or C is greater than 90°, the angle lies in the second quadrant and its cosine is negative.

The formula gives the third side when two sides and the included angle are known.

The tangent formula

The sine formula can be adjusted algebraically and written:

$$\frac{a + b}{a - b} = \frac{\tan \tfrac{1}{2}(A + B)}{\tan \tfrac{1}{2}(A - B)}$$

There are similar formulae in b and c, and in c and a.

The area of a triangle

It is known that the area of a triangle is equal to half the base multiplied by the perpendicular height. The area of the triangle ABC (Fig. 156) is therefore given by:

$$\tfrac{1}{2}\, ab \sin C \qquad \cdot \qquad \cdot \qquad \cdot \qquad (1)$$
$$\tfrac{1}{2}\, bc \sin A \qquad \cdot \qquad \cdot \qquad \cdot \qquad (2)$$
$$\tfrac{1}{2}\, ca \sin B \qquad \cdot \qquad \cdot \qquad \cdot \qquad (3)$$

Functions of the sum and difference of two angles

It can be shown that the following trigonometrical relations connect the sum and difference of two angles A and B:

$$\sin (A + B) = \sin A \cos B + \cos A \sin B \qquad \cdot \qquad \cdot \qquad (1)$$
$$\cos (A + B) = \cos A \cos B - \sin A \sin B \qquad \cdot \qquad \cdot \qquad (2)$$
$$\sin (A - B) = \sin A \cos B - \cos A \sin B \qquad \cdot \qquad \cdot \qquad (3)$$
$$\cos (A - B) = \cos A \cos B + \sin A \sin B \qquad \cdot \qquad \cdot \qquad (4)$$

Functions of the half-angle

If A is equal to B, then it follows from formulae (1) and (2) that:

$$\sin 2A = 2 \sin A \cos A$$
$$\cos 2A = \cos^2 A - \sin^2 A$$
$$= 1 - 2 \sin^2 A$$
$$= 2 \cos^2 A - 1$$

In terms of the half-angle these formulae are:

$$\sin A = 2 \sin \tfrac{1}{2}A \cos \tfrac{1}{2}A$$
$$\cos A = \cos^2 \tfrac{1}{2}A - \sin^2 \tfrac{1}{2}A$$
$$= 1 - 2 \sin^2 \tfrac{1}{2}A$$
$$= 2 \cos^2 \tfrac{1}{2}A - 1$$

Sum and difference of functions

Formulae (1), (2), (3) and (4), which relate to *the sines and cosines of sums and differences,* may be combined to give other formulae which relate to *the sums and differences of sines and cosines.*

By adding (1) and (3), and writing P for $(A + B)$ and Q for $(A - B)$ so that A is equal to $\tfrac{1}{2}(P + Q)$ and B to $\tfrac{1}{2}(P - Q)$:

$$\sin (A + B) + \sin (A - B) = 2 \sin A \cos B$$
i.e. $$\sin P + \sin Q = 2 \sin \tfrac{1}{2}(P + Q) \cos \tfrac{1}{2}(P - Q)$$

By subtracting (3) from (1):

$$\sin (A + B) - \sin (A - B) = 2 \cos A \sin B$$
i.e. $$\sin P - \sin Q = 2 \cos \tfrac{1}{2}(P + Q) \sin \tfrac{1}{2}(P - Q)$$

By using formulae (2) and (4), it can be shown that:

$$\cos P + \cos Q = 2 \cos \tfrac{1}{2}(P + Q) \cos \tfrac{1}{2}(P - Q)$$
$$\cos P - \cos Q = -2 \sin \tfrac{1}{2}(P + Q) \sin \tfrac{1}{2}(P - Q)$$

The sine and cosine curves

Fig. 153 shows that as an angle increases from 0° to 90°, the perpendicular opposite to it, MP, increases from 0 to the length of the radius of circle described, and that the projection of this radius, OM, decreases from the given length to 0. Sin θ therefore increases from 0 to 1 and cos θ decreases from 1 to 0.

Between 90° and 180°, sin θ decreases from 1 to 0, and cos θ from 0 to -1.
Between 180° and 270°, sin θ decreases from 0 to -1, and cos θ increases from -1 to 0.
Between 270° and 360°, sin θ increases from -1 to 0, and cos θ from 0 to 1.
After 360°, the cycle is repeated.

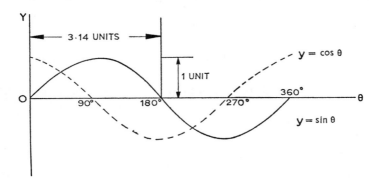

Fig. 158

Fig. 158 shows the curves $y = \sin \theta$ and $y = \cos \theta$, plotted for values of θ between 0° and 360°.

The sine of a small angle

Certain approximations suggest themselves when the angle is small.

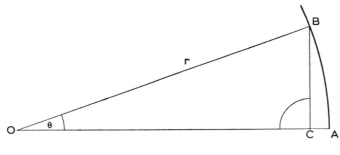

Fig. 159

In Fig. 159, AOB is a small angle θ, measured in radians. AB is the arc of a circle which subtends this small angle. The radius of the circle is r, and BC is perpendicular to OA at C.

On page 303 it was stated that the length of arc of a circle is equal to the radius multiplied by the angle subtended in radians. That is:

$$AB = r \times \theta$$

or
$$\theta = \frac{AB}{r}$$

But
$$\sin \theta = \frac{BC}{r}$$

Therefore, when θ is sufficiently small for AB to approximate to BC:

$$\sin \theta = \theta$$

If there are x' in this small angle of θ radians, then there must be $\left(\dfrac{x}{\theta}\right)$ in one radian. But one radian is equal to $57° \ 17' \ 45''$, or approximately 3,438'.

Hence:
$$\frac{x}{\theta} = 3{,}438$$

i.e.
$$\theta = \frac{x}{3{,}438}$$

The relation, $\sin \theta = \theta$, therefore becomes:

$$\sin x' = \frac{x}{3{,}438}$$

Since this relation holds for any value of x that is small:

$$\sin 1' = \frac{1}{3{,}438}$$

$$\therefore \qquad \sin x' = x \sin 1'$$

These adjustments are important when practical results have to be obtained from theoretical calculation, as in the construction of the ex-meridian tables described in Volume III.

The cosine of a small angle

Fig. 159 shows that when θ is small, OC approximates to OA, which is the same as OB. But:

$$\cos \theta = \frac{OC}{OB}$$

Therefore, when θ is small cos θ is equal to 1.

A second approximation can be obtained if cos θ is expressed in terms of the half-angle, for then:

$$\cos \theta = 1 - 2 \sin^2\tfrac{1}{2}\theta$$

i.e. $$\cos \theta = 1 - 2 \left(\tfrac{1}{2}\theta\right)^2$$

∴ $$\cos \theta = 1 - \tfrac{1}{2}\theta^2$$

ELEMENTARY SPHERICAL TRIGONOMETRY

The sphere

A sphere is defined as a surface every point on which is equidistant from one and the same point, called the *centre*. The distance of the surface from the centre is called the *radius* of the sphere.

Great circle

The intersection of the spherical surface with any plane through the centre of a sphere is known as a *great circle*.

Small circle

When a plane cuts a sphere but does not pass through its centre, its intersection with the spherical surface is called a *small circle*.

Spherical triangle

A three-sided figure formed by the arcs of three great circles on the spherical surface is known as a *spherical triangle*.

The side of a spherical triangle is the angle it subtends at the centre of the sphere and may be measured in degrees and minutes.

In Fig. 160, ABC is a spherical triangle formed by the arcs of three great circles, AB, AC and BC. The length of the side BC is the angle subtended at the centre of the sphere, that is, BOC.

Spherical angles

These, in a spherical triangle, correspond to the angles at the vertices of a plane triangle, and they are the angles between the great circles forming the sides. The planes of the great circles, of which AB and AC are arcs, cut the tangent plane at A in LA and MA. These lines are therefore tangents to the two great circles, and the angle between them, LAM, measures the angles between the two great circles.

The solution of the spherical triangle

There are six things to be known about a spherical triangle: the sizes of its three angles and the lengths of its three sides. Various formulae connect these angles and sides so that, if sufficient of them are given, the rest can be found. The common problems are those of finding the third side when two sides and their included angle are known, and finding a particular angle when the three sides are known.

The fundamental, or cosine, formula

Fig. 160 shows any spherical triangle ABC. It is customary to refer to its angles as A, B and C, and to the sides opposite these angles as a, b and c.

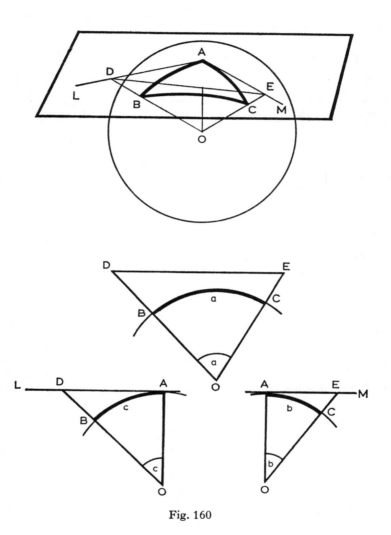

Fig. 160

The angle between any two curves is the angle between their tangents at the point of intersection. The angle A is therefore the angle between the tangents to the great circles BA and CA at their point of intersection A.

Since both these tangents AL and AM are at right angles to the same radius OA, the plane in which they lie is the tangent plane at A and the angle A in the spherical triangle is equal to the angle LAM in the tangent plane. But AL, being a tangent to AB, must also lie in the plane through the centre O, cutting the surface of the sphere in AB. Therefore, if OB is produced, it must cut AL in D. Similarly OC produced cuts AM in E.

There are thus four plane triangles, ADE, ODE, OAD and OAE, the last two of which are right-angled. Also, since a great-circle arc is measured by the angle it subtends at the centre, the angle DOE is a, the angle EOA is b, and the angle DOA is c.

The two right-angled triangles give:

$$\frac{AD}{OD} = \sin c \qquad\qquad \frac{AE}{OE} = \sin b \qquad \cdot \qquad \cdot \qquad \cdot \qquad (1)$$

$$\frac{OA}{OD} = \cos c \qquad\qquad \frac{OA}{OE} = \cos b \qquad \cdot \qquad \cdot \qquad \cdot \qquad (2)$$

$$OD^2 = OA^2 + AD^2 \qquad\qquad OE^2 = OA^2 + AE^2$$

i.e. $OD^2 - AD^2 = OA^2 \qquad\qquad OE^2 - AE^2 = OA^2 \qquad \cdot \qquad \cdot \qquad (3)$

The other two triangles give:

$$DE^2 = AD^2 + AE^2 - 2\,AD\,.\,AE \cos A$$

$$DE^2 = OD^2 + OE^2 - 2\,OD\,.\,OE \cos a$$

(For proof of these statements, *see* page 309 et seq.)

Hence, by subtraction and substitution:

$$AD^2 + AE^2 - 2\,AD\,.\,AE \cos A = OD^2 + OE^2 - 2\,OD\,.\,OE \cos a$$

i.e. $2\,OD\,.\,OE \cos a = (OD^2 - AD^2) + (OE^2 - AE^2) + 2\,AD\,.\,AE \cos A$

$$\cos a = \frac{OA}{OE} \times \frac{OA}{OD} + \frac{AE}{OE} \times \frac{AD}{OD} \cos A$$

This, from equations (1) and (2), may be written:

$$\cos a = \cos b \cos c + \sin b \sin c \cos A$$

Similarly, by working from the vertices B and C instead of A:

$$\cos b = \cos c \cos a + \sin c \sin a \cos B$$

$$\cos c = \cos a \cos b + \sin a \sin b \cos C$$

Thus if any two sides and their included angle are given, the third side can be found, this side being the one opposite the only spherical angle in the formula.

The haversine

As they stand, the above formulae are not suitable for logarithmic work because the cosine of an angle between 90° and 180° is negative. To make them suitable a function called the *haversine* of the angle is used.

This function is half the versine – hence the name haversine – and the versine of an angle is defined as the difference between its cosine and unity, that is:

$$\text{versine } \theta = 1 - \cos \theta$$

and it follows that:

$$\text{haversine } \theta = \tfrac{1}{2} (1 - \cos \theta)$$

The haversine of an angle is thus always positive, and it increases from 0 to 1 as the angle increases from 0° to 180°. Fig. 161 shows the haversine

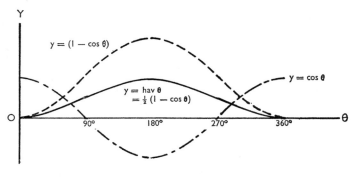

Fig. 161

curve in relation to the cosine curve from which it is derived. *Norie's Tables* give the values of the haversine for angles between 0° and 360°.

The haversine is used because (i) between 0° and 180° it is a continuously increasing (and therefore a 'single valued') function, and there is thus no ambiguity in deciding whether an angle is greater or less than 90°; and (ii) it is always positive and therefore suitable for logarithmic calculation.

The haversine formula

To express the fundamental formula in terms of haversines instead of cosines, substitute for the appropriate cosines their values in terms of the haversine. Thus $\cos A$ can be written $(1 - 2 \text{ hav } A)$, and the formula becomes:

$$\cos a = \cos b \cos c + \sin b \sin c (1 - 2 \text{ hav } A)$$

i.e. $\cos a = \cos b \cos c + \sin b \sin c - 2 \sin b \sin c \text{ hav } A$

$$= \cos (b \sim c) - 2 \sin b \sin c \text{ hav } A$$

Similar substitutions for $\cos a$ and $\cos (b \sim c)$ give:

$$1 - 2 \text{ hav } a = 1 - 2 \text{ hav } (b \sim c) - 2 \sin b \sin c \text{ hav } A$$

i.e. $\text{hav } a = \text{hav } (b \sim c) + \sin b \sin c \text{ hav } A$

This is the 'haversine formula' or, as it is sometimes called, to distinguish it from its logarithmic counterpart, the 'natural haversine formula'. As already shown, it is suitable for logarithmic work since all the quantities involved are positive and less than unity. The term (sin b sin c hav A) is therefore less than unity, and this further simplifies the use of the formula because the anti-logarithm of the term can be found immediately from the haversine tables where natural and logarithmic values are printed side by side. (Line 5 in the working of the example that follows is simply the anti-logarithm of line 4.) The formula is thus conveniently arranged in two parts, one using logarithmic functions and the other natural haversines.

EXAMPLE

It is required to find b when a is 40°, c 75° and B 56° (Fig. 162).

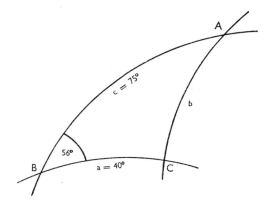

Fig. 162

The appropriate formula is:

$$\text{hav } b = \text{hav } (c \sim a) + \sin c \sin a \text{ hav } B$$

and in the evaluation of it *the known angle is written down first.* The actual work is arranged as shown:

$B = 56°$	log hav B	9·343	22
$c = 75°$	log sin c	9·984	94
$a = 40°$	log sin a	9·808	07
	log sin c sin a hav B	9·136	23
	sin c sin a hav B	0·136	84
$c \sim a = 35°$	hav $(c \sim a)$	0·090	42
	hav b	0·227	26

The side b is therefore equal to 56° 56'·5.

APPENDIX 2

Extracts from Nautical Almanac 1971

1971 JULY 3, 4, 5 (SAT., SUN., MON.)

G.M.T.	ARIES G.H.A.	VENUS −3.3 G.H.A.	VENUS Dec.	MARS −1.8 G.H.A.	MARS Dec.	JUPITER −2.0 G.H.A.	JUPITER Dec.	SATURN +0.4 G.H.A.	SATURN Dec.
3 00	280 22.0	195 34.0	N23 01.6	314 47.8	S18 58.0	45 07.5	S18 42.0	220 24.9	N18 38.3
01	295 24.5	210 33.2	01.8	329 49.9	58.1	60 10.2	41.9	235 27.1	38.4
02	310 27.0	225 32.3	02.0	344 52.1	58.2	75 12.8	41.9	250 29.3	38.4
03	325 29.4	240 31.5 ..	02.2	359 54.2 ..	58.2	90 15.4 ..	41.9	265 31.4 ..	38.5
04	340 31.9	255 30.6	02.4	14 56.4	58.3	105 18.1	41.9	280 33.6	38.5
05	355 34.4	270 29.8	02.6	29 58.5	58.4	120 20.7	41.8	295 35.8	38.6
S 06	10 36.8	285 28.9	N23 02.8	45 00.7	S18 58.5	135 23.3	S18 41.8	310 38.0	N18 38.6
07	25 39.3	300 28.1	03.0	60 02.8	58.6	150 26.0	41.8	325 40.2	38.7
S 08	40 41.7	315 27.2	03.2	75 05.0	58.7	165 28.6	41.8	340 42.3	38.7
A 09	55 44.2	330 26.4 ..	03.4	90 07.2 ..	58.8	180 31.2 ..	41.7	355 44.5 ..	38.8
T 10	70 46.7	345 25.5	03.6	105 09.3	58.9	195 33.8	41.7	10 46.7	38.8
U 11	85 49.1	0 24.7	03.8	120 11.5	58.9	210 36.5	41.7	25 48.9	38.9
R 12	100 51.6	15 23.9	N23 04.0	135 13.6	S18 59.0	225 39.1	S18 41.6	40 51.1	N18 38.9
D 13	115 54.1	30 23.0	04.2	150 15.8	59.1	240 41.7	41.6	55 53.2	39.0
A 14	130 56.5	45 22.2	04.4	165 18.0	59.2	255 44.4	41.6	70 55.4	39.0
Y 15	145 59.0	60 21.3 ..	04.6	180 20.1 ..	59.3	270 47.0 ..	41.6	85 57.6 ..	39.1
16	161 01.5	75 20.5	04.8	195 22.3	59.4	285 49.6	41.5	100 59.8	39.1
17	176 03.9	90 19.6	05.0	210 24.5	59.5	300 52.2	41.5	116 01.9	39.2
18	191 06.4	105 18.8	N23 05.2	225 26.6	S18 59.6	315 54.9	S18 41.5	131 04.1	N18 39.2
19	206 08.9	120 17.9	05.4	240 28.8	59.7	330 57.5	41.5	146 06.3	39.3
20	221 11.3	135 17.1	05.6	255 31.0	59.8	346 00.1	41.4	161 08.5	39.3
21	236 13.8	150 16.2 ..	05.8	270 33.1 ..	59.9	1 02.7 ..	41.4	176 10.7 ..	39.4
22	251 16.2	165 15.4	06.0	285 35.3	18 59.9	16 05.4	41.4	191 12.8	39.5
23	266 18.7	180 14.5	06.2	300 37.5	19 00.0	31 08.0	41.4	206 15.0	39.5
4 00	281 21.2	195 13.7	N23 06.3	315 39.7	S19 00.1	46 10.6	S18 41.3	221 17.2	N18 39.6
01	296 23.6	210 12.8	06.5	330 41.8	00.2	61 13.2	41.3	236 19.4	39.6
02	311 26.1	225 12.0	06.7	345 44.0	00.3	76 15.9	41.3	251 21.6	39.7
03	326 28.6	240 11.1 ..	06.9	0 46.2 ..	00.4	91 18.5 ..	41.3	266 23.7 ..	39.7
04	341 31.0	255 10.3	07.1	15 48.4	00.5	106 21.1	41.2	281 25.9	39.8
05	356 33.5	270 09.4	07.3	30 50.6	00.6	121 23.7	41.2	296 28.1	39.8
06	11 36.0	285 08.6	N23 07.4	45 52.7	S19 00.7	136 26.4	S18 41.2	311 30.3	N18 39.9
07	26 38.4	300 07.7	07.6	60 54.9	00.8	151 29.0	41.2	326 32.5	39.9
S 08	41 40.9	315 06.9	07.8	75 57.1	00.9	166 31.6	41.1	341 34.6	40.0
U 09	56 43.3	330 06.0 ..	08.0	90 59.3 ..	01.0	181 34.2 ..	41.1	356 36.8 ..	40.0
N 10	71 45.8	345 05.2	08.1	106 01.5	01.1	196 36.8	41.1	11 39.0	40.1
11	86 48.3	0 04.3	08.3	121 03.7	01.2	211 39.5	41.1	26 41.2	40.1
D 12	101 50.7	15 03.5	N23 08.5	136 05.9	S19 01.3	226 42.1	S18 41.0	41 43.4	N18 40.2
A 13	116 53.2	30 02.6	08.7	151 08.1	01.4	241 44.7	41.0	56 45.6	40.2
Y 14	131 55.7	45 01.8	08.8	166 10.3	01.5	256 47.3	41.0	71 47.7	40.3
15	146 58.1	60 00.9 ..	09.0	181 12.5 ..	01.6	271 49.9 ..	41.0	86 49.9 ..	40.3
16	162 00.6	75 00.1	09.2	196 14.7	01.7	286 52.6	40.9	101 52.1	40.4
17	177 03.1	89 59.2	09.3	211 16.8	01.8	301 55.2	40.9	116 54.3	40.4
18	192 05.5	104 58.3	N23 09.5	226 19.0	S19 01.9	316 57.8	S18 40.9	131 56.5	N18 40.5
19	207 08.0	119 57.5	09.7	241 21.2	02.0	332 00.4	40.9	146 58.6	40.5
20	222 10.5	134 56.6	09.8	256 23.4	02.1	347 03.0	40.8	162 00.8	40.6
21	237 12.9	149 55.8 ..	10.0	271 25.7 ..	02.2	2 05.7 ..	40.8	177 03.0 ..	40.6
22	252 15.4	164 54.9	10.1	286 27.9	02.3	17 08.3	40.8	192 05.2	40.7
23	267 17.8	179 54.1	10.3	301 30.1	02.4	32 10.9	40.8	207 07.4	40.7
5 00	282 20.3	194 53.2	N23 10.5	316 32.3	S19 02.5	47 13.5	S18 40.7	222 09.5	N18 40.8
01	297 22.8	209 52.4	10.6	331 34.5	02.6	62 16.1	40.7	237 11.7	40.8
02	312 25.2	224 51.5	10.8	346 36.7	02.7	77 18.7	40.7	252 13.9	40.9
03	327 27.7	239 50.7 ..	10.9	1 38.9 ..	02.8	92 21.4 ..	40.7	267 16.1 ..	40.9
04	342 30.2	254 49.8	11.1	16 41.1	02.9	107 24.0	40.6	282 18.3	41.0
05	357 32.6	269 49.0	11.2	31 43.3	03.0	122 26.6	40.6	297 20.5	41.0
06	12 35.1	284 48.1	N23 11.4	46 45.5	S19 03.1	137 29.2	S18 40.6	312 22.6	N18 41.1
07	27 37.6	299 47.3	11.5	61 47.7	03.2	152 31.8	40.6	327 24.8	41.1
M 08	42 40.0	314 46.4	11.7	76 50.0	03.3	167 34.4	40.5	342 27.0	41.2
O 09	57 42.5	329 45.5 ..	11.8	91 52.2 ..	03.5	182 37.1 ..	40.5	357 29.2 ..	41.2
N 10	72 45.0	344 44.7	12.0	106 54.4	03.6	197 39.7	40.5	12 31.4	41.3
11	87 47.4	359 43.8	12.1	121 56.6	03.7	212 42.3	40.5	27 33.6	41.3
D 12	102 49.9	14 43.0	N23 12.3	136 58.8	S19 03.8	227 44.9	S18 40.5	42 35.7	N18 41.4
A 13	117 52.3	29 42.1	12.4	152 01.1	03.9	242 47.5	40.4	57 37.9	41.4
Y 14	132 54.8	44 41.3	12.6	167 03.3	04.0	257 50.1	40.4	72 40.1	41.5
15	147 57.3	59 40.4 ..	12.7	182 05.5 ..	04.1	272 52.7 ..	40.4	87 42.3 ..	41.5
16	162 59.7	74 39.5	12.8	197 07.7	04.2	287 55.4	40.4	102 44.5	41.6
17	178 02.2	89 38.7	13.0	212 10.0	04.3	302 58.0	40.3	117 46.7	41.6
18	193 04.7	104 37.8	N23 13.1	227 12.2	S19 04.4	318 00.6	S18 40.3	132 48.8	N18 41.7
19	208 07.1	119 37.0	13.2	242 14.4	04.5	333 03.2	40.3	147 51.0	41.7
20	223 09.6	134 36.1	13.4	257 16.7	04.7	348 05.8	40.3	162 53.2	41.8
21	238 12.1	149 35.3 ..	13.5	272 18.9 ..	04.8	3 08.4 ..	40.2	177 55.4 ..	41.8
22	253 14.5	164 34.4	13.6	287 21.1	04.9	18 11.0	40.2	192 57.6	41.9
23	268 17.0	179 33.6	13.8	302 23.4	05.0	33 13.6	40.2	207 59.8	41.9
Mer. Pass.	5 13.7	v −0.9	d 0.2	v 2.2	d 0.1	v 2.6	d 0.0	v 2.2	d 0.1

STARS

Name	S.H.A.	Dec.
Acamar	315 42.3	S 40
Achernar	335 50.0	S 57
Acrux	173 45.0	S 62
Adhara	255 37.7	S 28
Aldebaran	291 25.9	N 16
Alioth	166 48.0	N 56
Alkaid	153 23.3	N 49
Al Na'ir	28 22.7	S 47
Alnilam	276 18.7	S 1
Alphard	218 27.3	S 8
Alphecca	126 37.4	N 26
Alpheratz	358 16.2	N 28
Altair	62 38.6	N 8
Ankaa	353 46.5	S 42
Antares	113 04.6	S 26
Arcturus	146 24.3	N 19
Atria	108 34.4	S 68
Avior	234 31.7	S 59
Bellatrix	279 06.1	N 6
Betelgeuse	271 35.7	N 7
Canopus	264 10.7	S 52
Capella	281 21.5	N 45
Deneb	49 52.6	N 45
Denebola	183 05.8	N 14
Diphda	349 27.4	S 18
Dubhe	194 30.2	N 61
Elnath	278 52.8	N 28
Eltanin	91 00.2	N 51
Enif	34 17.8	N 9
Fomalhaut	15 58.4	S 29
Gacrux	172 36.4	S 56
Gienah	176 24.8	S 17
Hadar	149 32.7	S 60
Hamal	328 36.5	N 23
Kaus Aust.	84 25.1	S 34
Kochab	137 17.5	N 74
Markab	14 09.6	N 15
Menkar	314 48.2	N 3
Menkent	148 44.7	S 36
Miaplacidus	221 47.5	S 69
Mirfak	309 26.0	N 49
Nunki	76 36.9	S 26
Peacock	54 08.0	S 56
Pollux	244 06.5	N 28
Procyon	245 33.0	N 5
Rasalhague	96 35.4	N 12
Regulus	208 17.2	N 12
Rigel	281 42.6	S 8
Rigil Kent.	140 34.7	S 60
Sabik	102 48.4	S 15
Schedar	350 16.8	N 56
Shaula	97 04.3	S 37
Sirius	259 01.9	S 16
Spica	159 04.4	S 11
Suhail	223 16.1	S 43
Vega	80 59.9	N 38
Zuben'ubi	137 40.2	S 15

	S.H.A.	Mer.
Venus	273 52.5	11 0
Mars	34 18.5	2 5
Jupiter	124 49.4	20 5
Saturn	299 56.0	9

1971 JULY 3, 4, 5 (SAT., SUN., MON.)

SUN and MOON — G.M.T.

d h	SUN G.H.A.	Dec.	MOON G.H.A.	v	Dec.	d	H.P.
3 00	179 00.7	N23 02.0	69 16.9	13.7	S18 03.9	10.7	54.8
01	194 00.6	01.8	83 49.6	13.6	18 14.6	10.7	54.9
02	209 00.4	01.7	98 22.2	13.4	18 25.3	10.7	54.9
03	224 00.3	.. 01.5	112 54.6	13.4	18 36.0	10.5	54.9
04	239 00.2	01.3	127 27.0	13.4	18 46.5	10.5	54.9
05	254 00.1	01.1	141 59.4	13.2	18 57.0	10.4	54.9
06	269 00.0	N23 00.9	156 31.6	13.1	S19 07.4	10.4	55.0
07	283 59.9	00.7	171 03.7	13.1	19 17.8	10.3	55.0
08	298 59.7	00.5	185 35.8	12.9	19 28.1	10.1	55.0
09	313 59.6	.. 00.3	200 07.7	12.9	19 38.2	10.2	55.0
10	328 59.5	23 00.1	214 39.6	12.8	19 48.4	10.0	55.0
11	343 59.4	22 59.9	229 11.4	12.7	19 58.4	9.9	55.1
12	358 59.3	N22 59.7	243 43.1	12.6	S20 08.3	9.9	55.1
13	13 59.2	59.5	258 14.7	12.5	20 18.2	9.8	55.1
14	28 59.0	59.3	272 46.2	12.4	20 28.0	9.7	55.1
15	43 58.9	.. 59.2	287 17.6	12.3	20 37.7	9.6	55.1
16	58 58.8	59.0	301 48.9	12.3	20 47.3	9.6	55.2
17	73 58.7	58.8	316 20.2	12.1	20 56.9	9.4	55.2
18	88 58.6	N22 58.6	330 51.3	12.1	S21 06.3	9.4	55.2
19	103 58.5	58.4	345 22.4	11.9	21 15.7	9.2	55.2
20	118 58.4	58.2	359 53.3	11.9	21 24.9	9.2	55.2
21	133 58.2	58.0	14 24.2	11.7	21 34.1	9.1	55.3
22	148 58.1	57.8	28 54.9	11.7	21 43.2	9.0	55.3
23	163 58.0	57.6	43 25.6	11.6	21 52.2	8.9	55.3
4 00	178 57.9	N22 57.3	57 56.2	11.5	S22 01.1	8.8	55.3
01	193 57.8	57.1	72 26.7	11.3	22 09.9	8.7	55.4
02	208 57.7	56.9	86 57.0	11.3	22 18.6	8.6	55.4
03	223 57.6	.. 56.7	101 27.3	11.2	22 27.2	8.6	55.4
04	238 57.4	56.5	115 57.5	11.1	22 35.8	8.4	55.4
05	253 57.3	56.3	130 27.6	11.0	22 44.2	8.3	55.5
06	268 57.2	N22 56.1	144 57.6	10.9	S22 52.5	8.2	55.5
07	283 57.1	55.9	159 27.5	10.8	23 00.7	8.1	55.5
08	298 57.0	55.7	173 57.3	10.7	23 08.8	8.0	55.5
09	313 56.9	.. 55.5	188 27.0	10.6	23 16.8	7.9	55.6
10	328 56.8	55.3	202 56.6	10.5	23 24.7	7.8	55.6
11	343 56.6	55.1	217 26.1	10.4	23 32.5	7.7	55.6
12	358 56.5	N22 54.9	231 55.5	10.3	S23 40.2	7.6	55.6
13	13 56.4	54.6	246 24.8	10.2	23 47.8	7.4	55.7
14	28 56.0	54.4	260 54.0	10.1	23 55.2	7.4	55.7
15	43 56.2	.. 54.2	275 23.1	10.1	24 02.6	7.2	55.7
16	58 56.1	54.0	289 52.2	9.9	24 09.8	7.1	55.7
17	73 56.0	53.8	304 21.1	9.8	24 16.9	7.0	55.8
18	88 55.9	N22 53.6	318 49.9	9.7	S24 23.9	6.9	55.8
19	103 55.8	53.4	333 18.6	9.7	24 30.8	6.8	55.8
20	118 55.6	53.1	347 47.3	9.5	24 37.6	6.6	55.8
21	133 55.5	.. 52.9	2 15.8	9.4	24 44.2	6.6	55.9
22	148 55.4	52.7	16 44.2	9.4	24 50.8	6.4	55.9
23	163 55.3	52.5	31 12.6	9.2	24 57.2	6.2	55.9
5 00	178 55.2	N22 52.2	45 40.8	9.2	S25 03.4	6.2	55.9
01	193 55.1	52.0	60 09.0	9.1	25 09.6	6.0	56.0
02	208 55.0	51.8	74 37.1	8.9	25 15.6	5.9	56.0
03	223 54.9	.. 51.6	89 05.0	8.9	25 21.5	5.8	56.0
04	238 54.8	51.4	103 32.9	8.8	25 27.3	5.7	56.1
05	253 54.6	51.2	118 00.7	8.7	25 33.0	5.5	56.1
06	268 54.5	N22 50.9	132 28.4	8.6	S25 38.5	5.4	56.1
07	283 54.4	50.7	146 56.0	8.5	25 43.9	5.2	56.1
08	298 54.3	50.5	161 23.5	8.4	25 49.1	5.1	56.2
09	313 54.2	.. 50.3	175 50.9	8.4	25 54.2	5.0	56.2
10	328 54.1	50.0	190 18.3	8.2	25 59.2	4.9	56.2
11	343 54.0	49.8	204 45.5	8.2	26 04.1	4.7	56.3
12	358 53.9	N22 49.6	219 12.7	8.1	S26 08.8	4.5	56.3
13	13 53.8	49.4	233 39.8	7.9	26 13.3	4.5	56.3
14	28 53.7	49.1	248 06.7	8.0	26 17.8	4.3	56.3
15	43 53.6	.. 48.9	262 33.7	7.8	26 22.1	4.1	56.4
16	58 53.4	48.7	277 00.5	7.7	26 26.2	4.0	56.4
17	73 53.3	48.4	291 27.2	7.7	26 30.2	3.9	56.4
18	88 53.2	N22 48.2	305 53.9	7.6	S26 34.1	3.7	56.5
19	103 53.1	48.0	320 20.5	7.5	26 37.8	3.5	56.5
20	118 53.0	47.7	334 47.0	7.4	26 41.3	3.5	56.5
21	133 52.9	.. 47.5	349 13.4	7.4	26 44.8	3.2	56.5
22	148 52.8	47.3	3 39.8	7.3	26 48.0	3.1	56.6
23	163 52.7	47.0	18 06.1	7.2	26 51.1	3.0	56.6
	S.D. 15.8	d 0.2	S.D. 15.0		15.2		15.3

(Left-margin day labels: July 3 = SATURDAY, July 4 = SUNDAY, July 5 = MONDAY)

Twilight, Sunrise and Moonrise

Lat.	Twilight Naut.	Civil	Sunrise	Moonrise 3	4	5	6
N 72	□	□	□	■	■	■	■
N 70	□	□	□	19 01	■	■	■
68	□	□	□	18 31	■	■	■
66	////	////	00 37	17 59	■	■	■
64	////	////	01 45	17 25	19 29	■	■
62	////	////	02 20	17 00	18 44	20 30	21 51
60	////	01 09	02 45	16 41	18 14	19 44	20 55
N 58	////	01 52	03 04	16 25	17 52	19 14	20 22
56	////	02 19	03 20	16 11	17 33	18 52	19 57
54	01 03	02 41	03 34	16 00	17 18	18 33	19 38
52	01 43	02 58	03 46	15 49	17 05	18 18	19 21
50	02 09	03 12	03 56	15 40	16 53	18 04	19 07
45	02 52	03 41	04 18	15 21	16 29	17 36	18 38
N 40	03 22	04 03	04 36	15 05	16 10	17 14	18 15
35	03 45	04 21	04 50	14 52	15 54	16 56	17 57
30	04 03	04 36	05 03	14 41	15 40	16 41	17 41
20	04 31	05 00	05 25	14 21	15 17	16 15	17 13
N 10	04 53	05 20	05 43	14 05	14 57	15 52	16 50
0	05 12	05 38	06 01	13 49	14 38	15 31	16 28
S 10	05 29	05 55	06 18	13 33	14 20	15 11	16 06
20	05 44	06 12	06 36	13 17	14 00	14 48	15 43
30	05 56	06 30	06 56	12 58	13 37	14 23	15 16
35	06 09	06 40	07 08	12 47	13 24	14 07	15 00
40	06 18	06 52	07 22	12 35	13 08	13 50	14 41
45	06 28	07 05	07 39	12 20	12 50	13 29	14 19
S 50	06 39	07 21	07 59	12 02	12 28	13 03	13 51
52	06 44	07 28	08 08	11 54	12 17	12 50	13 37
54	06 50	07 36	08 19	11 45	12 05	12 35	13 20
56	06 56	07 45	08 31	11 34	11 51	12 18	13 01
58	07 02	07 54	08 45	11 22	11 35	11 58	12 38
S 60	07 09	08 06	09 02	11 08	11 16	11 32	12 07

Sunset, Twilight and Moonset

Lat.	Sunset	Twilight Civil	Naut.	Moonset 3	4	5	6
N 72	□	□	□	■	■	■	■
N 70	□	□	□	20 46	■	■	■
68	□	□	□	21 48	■	■	■
66	23 26	////	////	22 23	22 03	■	■
64	22 21	////	////	22 49	22 49	22 55	23 34
62	21 47	////	////	22 59	23 04	23 18	24 02
60	21 23	22 57	////	23 09	23 19	23 41	24 30
N 58	21 04	22 15	////	23 26	23 42	24 11	00 11
56	20 48	21 48	////	23 40	24 01	00 01	00 34
54	20 34	21 27	23 03	23 52	24 16	00 16	00 53
52	20 22	21 10	22 24	24 03	00 03	00 30	01 09
50	20 12	20 55	21 59	24 12	00 12	00 42	01 23
45	19 50	20 27	21 16	24 31	00 31	01 07	01 51
N 40	19 32	20 05	20 46	00 19	00 49	01 27	02 13
35	19 18	19 47	20 23	00 30	01 03	01 43	02 31
30	19 05	19 32	20 05	00 40	01 16	01 58	02 47
20	18 43	19 08	19 37	00 57	01 37	02 22	03 14
N 10	18 25	18 48	19 15	01 11	01 55	02 43	03 37
0	18 08	18 30	18 56	01 25	02 12	03 03	03 58
S 10	17 51	18 14	18 40	01 39	02 29	03 23	04 20
20	17 33	17 57	18 24	01 54	02 48	03 45	04 43
30	17 12	17 38	18 08	02 11	03 09	04 09	05 10
35	17 00	17 28	18 00	02 21	03 22	04 24	05 26
40	16 46	17 17	17 51	02 32	03 36	04 41	05 44
45	16 30	17 03	17 40	02 46	03 54	05 01	06 06
S 50	16 10	16 48	17 29	03 02	04 15	05 27	06 34
52	16 00	16 41	17 24	03 10	04 25	05 40	06 48
54	15 50	16 33	17 19	03 19	04 37	05 54	07 04
56	15 37	16 24	17 13	03 29	04 50	06 11	07 24
58	15 23	16 14	17 06	03 40	05 06	06 31	07 47
S 60	15 06	16 03	16 59	03 53	05 24	06 57	08 18

SUN and MOON data

Day	SUN Eqn. of Time 00h	12h	Mer. Pass.	MOON Mer. Pass. Upper	Lower	Age	Phase
	m s	m s	h m	h m	h m	d	
3	03 57	04 03	12 04	20 00	07 37	11	◗
4	04 08	04 14	12 04	20 51	08 25	12	
5	04 19	04 24	12 04	21 45	09 17	13	

1971 DECEMBER 9, 10, 11 (THURS., FRI., SAT.)

G.M.T. d h	ARIES G.H.A.	VENUS −3.4 G.H.A.	VENUS Dec.	MARS +0.1 G.H.A.	MARS Dec.	JUPITER −1.3 G.H.A.	JUPITER Dec.	SATURN −0.2 G.H.A.	SATURN Dec.
9 00	77 05.1	153 34.5	S 24 21.6	87 04.5	S 5 09.6	180 58.9	S 22 24.0	16 45.5	N 18 28.4
01	92 07.6	168 33.6	21.3	102 05.5	08.9	196 00.7	24.1	31 48.1	28.4
02	107 10.1	183 32.6	21.1	117 06.6	08.2	211 02.6	24.1	46 50.8	28.3
03	122 12.5	198 31.7 · ·	20.9	132 07.7 · ·	07.5	226 04.4 · ·	24.2	61 53.5 · ·	28.3
04	137 15.0	213 30.8	20.6	147 08.7	06.8	241 06.3	24.3	76 56.1	28.3
05	152 17.4	228 29.8	20.4	162 09.8	06.2	256 08.2	24.3	91 58.8	28.2
T 06	167 19.9	243 28.9	S 24 20.2	177 10.9	S 5 05.5	271 10.0	S 22 24.4	107 01.5	N 18 28.2
H 07	182 22.4	258 28.0	20.0	192 11.9	04.8	286 11.9	24.4	122 04.1	28.2
U 08	197 24.8	273 27.0	19.7	207 13.0	04.1	301 13.7	24.5	137 06.8	28.1
R 09	212 27.3	288 26.1 · ·	19.5	222 14.1 · ·	03.5	316 15.6 · ·	24.5	152 09.5 · ·	28.1
S 10	227 29.8	303 25.2	19.3	237 15.2	02.8	331 17.4	24.6	167 12.1	28.1
D 11	242 32.2	318 24.2	19.0	252 16.2	02.1	346 19.3	24.7	182 14.8	28.0
A 12	257 34.7	333 23.3	S 24 18.8	267 17.3	S 5 01.4	1 21.1	S 22 24.7	197 17.5	N 18 28.0
Y 13	272 37.2	348 22.4	18.5	282 18.4	00.7	16 23.0	24.8	212 20.1	28.0
14	287 39.6	3 21.4	18.3	297 19.4	5 00.1	31 24.8	24.8	227 22.8	27.9
15	302 42.1	18 20.5 · ·	18.0	312 20.5	4 59.4	46 26.7 · ·	24.9	242 25.5 · ·	27.9
16	317 44.6	33 19.6	17.8	327 21.6	58.7	61 28.6	24.9	257 28.1	27.9
17	332 47.0	48 18.6	17.6	342 22.6	58.0	76 30.4	25.0	272 30.8	27.8
18	347 49.5	63 17.7	S 24 17.3	357 23.7	S 4 57.3	91 32.3	S 22 25.1	287 33.5	N 18 27.8
19	2 51.9	78 16.8	17.1	12 24.8	56.7	106 34.1	25.1	302 36.1	27.8
20	17 54.4	93 15.8	16.8	27 25.8	56.0	121 36.0	25.2	317 38.8	27.7
21	32 56.9	108 14.9 · ·	16.6	42 26.9 · ·	55.3	136 37.8 · ·	25.2	332 41.5 · ·	27.7
22	47 59.3	123 14.0	16.3	57 27.9	54.6	151 39.7	25.3	347 44.1	27.7
23	63 01.8	138 13.0	16.1	72 29.0	53.9	166 41.5	25.3	2 46.8	27.6
10 00	78 04.3	153 12.1	S 24 15.8	87 30.1	S 4 53.3	181 43.4	S 22 25.4	17 49.5	N 18 27.6
01	93 06.7	168 11.2	15.6	102 31.1	52.6	196 45.2	25.5	32 52.1	27.6
02	108 09.2	183 10.3	15.3	117 32.2	51.9	211 47.1	25.5	47 54.8	27.5
03	123 11.7	198 09.3 · ·	15.0	132 33.3 · ·	51.2	226 49.0 · ·	25.6	62 57.5 · ·	27.5
04	138 14.1	213 08.4	14.8	147 34.3	50.5	241 50.8	25.6	78 00.1	27.5
05	153 16.6	228 07.5	14.5	162 35.4	49.9	256 52.7	25.7	93 02.8	27.4
F 06	168 19.0	243 06.5	S 24 14.3	177 36.5	S 4 49.2	271 54.5	S 22 25.7	108 05.5	N 18 27.4
R 07	183 21.5	258 05.6	14.0	192 37.5	48.5	286 56.4	25.8	123 08.1	27.4
I 08	198 24.0	273 04.7	13.7	207 38.6	47.8	301 58.2	25.8	138 10.8	27.3
D 09	213 26.4	288 03.8 · ·	13.5	222 39.7 · ·	47.1	317 00.1 · ·	25.9	153 13.5 · ·	27.3
A 10	228 28.9	303 02.8	13.2	237 40.7	46.5	332 01.9	26.0	168 16.1	27.3
Y 11	243 31.4	318 01.9	12.9	252 41.8	45.8	347 03.8	26.0	183 18.8	27.2
12	258 33.8	333 01.0	S 24 12.7	267 42.9	S 4 45.1	2 05.6	S 22 26.1	198 21.5	N 18 27.2
13	273 36.3	348 00.1	12.4	282 43.9	44.4	17 07.5	26.1	213 24.1	27.2
14	288 38.8	2 59.1	12.1	297 45.0	43.7	32 09.4	26.2	228 26.8	27.2
15	303 41.2	17 58.2 · ·	11.8	312 46.0 · ·	43.1	47 11.2 · ·	26.2	243 29.4 · ·	27.1
16	318 43.7	32 57.3	11.6	327 47.1	42.4	62 13.1	26.3	258 32.1	27.1
17	333 46.2	47 56.3	11.3	342 48.2	41.7	77 14.9	26.4	273 34.8	27.1
18	348 48.6	62 55.4	S 24 11.0	357 49.2	S 4 41.0	92 16.8	S 22 26.4	288 37.4	N 18 27.0
19	3 51.1	77 54.5	10.7	12 50.3	40.3	107 18.6	26.5	303 40.1	27.0
20	18 53.5	92 53.6	10.5	27 51.4	39.7	122 20.5	26.5	318 42.8	27.0
21	33 56.0	107 52.6 · ·	10.2	42 52.4 · ·	39.0	137 22.3 · ·	26.6	333 45.4 · ·	26.9
22	48 58.5	122 51.7	09.9	57 53.5	38.3	152 24.2	26.6	348 48.1	26.9
23	64 00.9	137 50.8	09.6	72 54.5	37.6	167 26.0	26.7	3 50.8	26.9
11 00	79 03.4	152 49.9	S 24 09.3	87 55.6	S 4 36.9	182 27.9	S 22 26.7	18 53.4	N 18 26.8
01	94 05.9	167 48.9	09.0	102 56.7	36.2	197 29.8	26.8	33 56.1	26.8
02	109 08.3	182 48.0	08.7	117 57.7	35.6	212 31.6	26.9	48 58.7	26.8
03	124 10.8	197 47.1 · ·	08.5	132 58.8 · ·	34.9	227 33.5 · ·	26.9	64 01.4 · ·	26.7
04	139 13.3	212 46.2	08.2	147 59.9	34.2	242 35.3	27.0	79 04.1	26.7
05	154 15.7	227 45.3	07.9	163 00.9	33.5	257 37.2	27.0	94 06.7	26.7
S 06	169 18.2	242 44.3	S 24 07.6	178 02.0	S 4 32.8	272 39.0	S 22 27.1	109 09.4	N 18 26.6
A 07	184 20.6	257 43.4	07.3	193 03.0	32.2	287 40.9	27.1	124 12.1	26.6
T 08	199 23.1	272 42.5	07.0	208 04.1	31.5	302 42.7	27.2	139 14.7	26.6
U 09	214 25.6	287 41.6 · ·	06.7	223 05.2 · ·	30.8	317 44.6 · ·	27.2	154 17.4 · ·	26.5
R 10	229 28.0	302 40.6	06.4	238 06.2	30.1	332 46.4	27.3	169 20.1	26.5
D 11	244 30.5	317 39.7	06.1	253 07.3	29.4	347 48.3	27.4	184 22.7	26.5
A 12	259 33.0	332 38.8	S 24 05.8	268 08.3	S 4 28.7	2 50.2	S 22 27.4	199 25.4	N 18 26.4
Y 13	274 35.4	347 37.9	05.5	283 09.4	28.1	17 52.0	27.5	214 28.0	26.4
14	289 37.9	2 37.0	05.2	298 10.5	27.4	32 53.9	27.5	229 30.7	26.4
15	304 40.4	17 36.0 · ·	04.9	313 11.5 · ·	26.7	47 55.7 · ·	27.6	244 33.4 · ·	26.4
16	319 42.8	32 35.1	04.6	328 12.6	26.0	62 57.6	27.6	259 36.0	26.3
17	334 45.3	47 34.2	04.3	343 13.6	25.3	77 59.4	27.7	274 38.7	26.3
18	349 47.8	62 33.3	S 24 04.0	358 14.7	S 4 24.6	93 01.3	S 22 27.7	289 41.4	N 18 26.3
19	4 50.2	77 32.4	03.7	13 15.8	24.0	108 03.1	27.8	304 44.0	26.2
20	19 52.7	92 31.5	03.4	28 16.8	23.3	123 05.0	27.8	319 46.7	26.2
21	34 55.1	107 30.5 · ·	03.0	43 17.9 · ·	22.6	138 06.8 · ·	27.9	334 49.3 · ·	26.2
22	49 57.6	122 29.6	02.7	58 18.9	21.9	153 08.7	28.0	349 52.0	26.1
23	65 00.1	137 28.7	02.4	73 20.0	21.2	168 10.5	28.0	4 54.7	26.1
Mer. Pass. 18 44.6		v −0.9 d 0.3		v 1.1 d 0.7		v 1.9 d 0.1		v 2.7 d 0.0	

STARS

Name	S.H.A.	Dec.
Acamar	315 41.5	S 40 25.0
Achernar	335 49.3	S 57 22.8
Acrux	173 44.7	S 62 56.4
Adhara	255 36.7	S 28 55.8
Aldebaran	291 24.8	N 16 27.4
Alioth	166 48.0	N 56 06.4
Alkaid	153 23.5	N 49 26.9
Al Na'ir	28 22.7	S 47 06.0
Alnilam	276 17.6	S 1 13.0
Alphard	218 26.5	S 8 32.1
Alphecca	126 37.7	N 26 48.3
Alpheratz	358 15.8	N 28 56.4
Altair	62 38.9	N 8 47.6
Ankaa	353 46.1	S 42 27.6
Antares	113 04.9	S 26 22.3
Arcturus	146 24.3	N 19 19.5
Atria	108 35.4	S 68 58.8
Avior	234 30.5	S 59 24.9
Bellatrix	279 05.1	N 6 19.7
Betelgeuse	271 34.7	N 7 24.3
Canopus	264 09.5	S 52 40.6
Capella	281 20.1	N 45 58.4
Deneb	49 53.1	N 45 11.0
Denebola	183 05.4	N 14 43.6
Diphda	349 26.9	S 18 08.4
Dubhe	194 29.4	N 61 53.8
Elnath	278 51.6	N 28 35.2
Eltanin	91 01.2	N 51 29.5
Enif	34 17.9	N 9 44.8
Fomalhaut	15 58.2	S 29 46.4
Gacrux	172 36.1	S 56 57.2
Gienah	176 24.5	S 17 23.1
Hadar	149 32.9	S 60 14.2
Hamal	328 35.8	N 23 20.1
Kaus Aust.	84 25.5	S 34 24.1
Kochab	137 19.3	N 74 15.9
Markab	14 09.4	N 15 03.4
Menkar	314 47.4	N 3 59.0
Menkent	148 44.7	S 36 13.9
Miaplacidus	221 46.1	S 69 35.8
Mirfak	309 24.7	N 49 46.0
Nunki	76 37.2	S 26 20.1
Peacock	54 08.5	S 56 49.8
Pollux	244 05.4	N 28 05.7
Procyon	245 32.0	N 5 17.9
Rasalhague	96 35.7	N 12 34.7
Regulus	208 16.5	N 12 06.2
Rigel	281 41.7	S 8 13.9
Rigil Kent.	140 35.1	S 60 43.1
Sabik	102 48.6	S 15 41.6
Schedar	350 16.1	N 56 23.4
Shaula	97 04.7	S 37 05.2
Sirius	259 00.9	S 16 40.5
Spica	159 04.3	S 11 00.9
Suhail	223 15.2	S 43 18.9
Vega	81 00.5	N 38 45.4
Zuben'ubi	137 40.3	S 15 55.6

	S.H.A.	Mer. Pass.
Venus	75 07.9	13 48
Mars	9 25.8	18 09
Jupiter	103 39.1	11 52
Saturn	299 45.2	22 45

1971 DECEMBER 9, 10, 11 (THURS., FRI., SAT.)

SUN / MOON

G.M.T. d h	SUN G.H.A.	SUN Dec.	MOON G.H.A.	v	MOON Dec.	d	H.P.
9 00	182 01.4	S 22 44.0	277 40.0	16.1	N 5 42.4	13.5	55.0
01	197 01.1	44.3	292 15.1	16.0	5 28.9	13.5	55.0
02	212 00.9	44.5	306 50.1	16.2	5 15.4	13.4	55.0
03	227 00.6	·· 44.8	321 25.3	16.1	5 02.0	13.5	55.0
04	242 00.3	45.1	336 00.4	16.2	4 48.5	13.5	54.9
05	257 00.0	45.3	350 35.6	16.3	4 35.0	13.5	54.9
06	271 59.8	S 22 45.6	5 10.9	16.3	N 4 21.5	13.5	54.9
T 07	286 59.5	45.8	19 46.2	16.3	4 08.0	13.6	54.9
H 08	301 59.2	46.1	34 21.5	16.3	3 54.4	13.5	54.9
U 09	316 58.9	·· 46.3	48 56.8	16.4	3 40.9	13.5	54.8
R 10	331 58.7	46.6	63 32.2	16.5	3 27.4	13.5	54.8
S 11	346 58.4	46.8	78 07.7	16.4	3 13.9	13.6	54.8
D 12	1 58.1	S 22 47.1	92 43.1	16.5	N 3 00.3	13.5	54.8
A 13	16 57.8	47.3	107 18.6	16.5	2 46.8	13.5	54.8
Y 14	31 57.5	47.6	121 54.1	16.5	2 33.3	13.5	54.7
15	46 57.3	·· 47.8	136 29.6	16.6	2 19.8	13.6	54.7
16	61 57.0	48.1	151 05.2	16.6	2 06.2	13.5	54.7
17	76 56.7	48.3	165 40.8	16.6	1 52.7	13.5	54.7
18	91 56.4	S 22 48.6	180 16.4	16.7	N 1 39.2	13.5	54.7
19	106 56.1	48.8	194 52.1	16.6	1 25.7	13.6	54.7
20	121 55.9	49.1	209 27.7	16.7	1 12.1	13.5	54.6
21	136 55.6	·· 49.3	224 03.4	16.7	0 58.6	13.5	54.6
22	151 55.3	49.6	238 39.1	16.8	0 45.1	13.5	54.6
23	166 55.0	49.8	253 14.9	16.7	0 31.6	13.5	54.6
10 00	181 54.8	S 22 50.1	267 50.6	16.8	N 0 18.1	13.5	54.6
01	196 54.5	50.3	282 26.4	16.8	N 0 04.6	13.5	54.6
02	211 54.2	50.5	297 02.2	16.8	S 0 08.9	13.4	54.5
03	226 53.9	·· 50.8	311 38.0	16.8	0 22.3	13.5	54.5
04	241 53.6	51.0	326 13.8	16.8	0 35.8	13.5	54.5
05	256 53.3	51.3	340 49.6	16.8	0 49.3	13.4	54.5
06	271 53.1	S 22 51.5	355 25.4	16.8	S 1 02.7	13.4	54.5
F 07	286 52.8	51.7	10 01.2	16.9	1 16.1	13.5	54.5
R 08	301 52.5	52.0	24 37.1	16.8	1 29.6	13.4	54.4
I 09	316 52.2	·· 52.2	39 12.9	16.9	1 43.0	13.4	54.4
D 10	331 51.9	52.4	53 48.8	16.9	1 56.4	13.4	54.4
I 11	346 51.7	52.7	68 24.7	16.8	2 09.8	13.3	54.4
D 12	1 51.4	S 22 52.9	83 00.5	16.9	S 2 23.1	13.4	54.4
A 13	16 51.1	53.1	97 36.4	16.9	2 36.5	13.3	54.4
Y 14	31 50.8	53.4	112 12.3	16.9	2 49.8	13.4	54.4
15	46 50.5	·· 53.6	126 48.2	16.8	3 03.2	13.3	54.4
16	61 50.2	53.8	141 24.0	16.9	3 16.5	13.3	54.3
17	76 50.0	54.1	155 59.9	16.9	3 29.8	13.3	54.3
18	91 49.7	S 22 54.3	170 35.8	16.8	S 3 43.1	13.2	54.3
19	106 49.4	54.5	185 11.6	16.9	3 56.3	13.3	54.3
20	121 49.1	54.7	199 47.5	16.9	4 09.6	13.2	54.3
21	136 48.8	·· 55.0	214 23.4	16.8	4 22.8	13.2	54.3
22	151 48.5	55.2	228 59.2	16.8	4 36.0	13.2	54.3
23	166 48.3	55.4	243 35.0	16.9	4 49.2	13.1	54.3
11 00	181 48.0	S 22 55.6	258 10.9	16.8	S 5 02.3	13.2	54.3
01	196 47.7	55.9	272 46.7	16.8	5 15.5	13.1	54.3
02	211 47.4	56.1	287 22.5	16.8	5 28.6	13.1	54.2
03	226 47.1	·· 56.3	301 58.3	16.8	5 41.7	13.0	54.2
04	241 46.8	56.5	316 34.1	16.7	5 54.7	13.1	54.2
05	256 46.6	56.7	331 09.8	16.8	6 07.8	13.0	54.2
06	271 46.3	S 22 57.0	345 45.6	16.7	S 6 20.8	13.0	54.2
S 07	286 46.0	57.2	0 21.3	16.7	6 33.8	13.0	54.2
A 08	301 45.7	57.4	14 57.0	16.7	6 46.8	12.9	54.2
T 09	316 45.4	·· 57.6	29 32.7	16.7	6 59.7	12.9	54.2
U 10	331 45.1	57.8	44 08.4	16.7	7 12.6	12.9	54.2
R 11	346 44.8	58.0	58 44.1	16.6	7 25.5	12.9	54.2
D 12	1 44.5	S 22 58.3	73 19.7	16.6	S 7 38.4	12.8	54.2
A 13	16 44.3	58.5	87 55.3	16.6	7 51.2	12.8	54.2
Y 14	31 44.0	58.7	102 30.9	16.6	8 04.0	12.7	54.2
15	46 43.7	·· 58.9	117 06.5	16.5	8 16.7	12.8	54.2
16	61 43.4	59.1	131 42.0	16.5	8 29.5	12.7	54.2
17	76 43.1	59.3	146 17.5	16.5	8 42.2	12.6	54.2
18	91 42.8	S 22 59.5	160 53.0	16.4	S 8 54.8	12.7	54.2
19	106 42.5	59.7	175 28.4	16.5	9 07.5	12.6	54.1
20	121 42.2	22 59.9	190 03.9	16.4	9 20.1	12.6	54.1
21	136 42.0	23 00.1	204 39.3	16.3	9 32.7	12.5	54.1
22	151 41.7	00.3	219 14.6	16.3	9 45.2	12.5	54.1
23	166 41.4	00.6	233 49.9	16.3	9 57.7	12.4	54.1
	S.D. 16.3	d 0.2	S.D. 14.9		14.8		14.8

Twilight / Sunrise / Moonrise

Lat.	Naut.	Civil	Sunrise	Moonrise 9	10	11	12
N 72	08 10	10 26	■	24 07	00 07	02 00	04 01
N 70	07 52	09 35	■	24 07	00 07	01 52	03 42
68	07 37	09 03	■	24 07	00 07	01 45	03 27
66	07 25	08 40	10 13	24 07	00 07	01 40	03 15
64	07 14	08 21	09 36	24 07	00 07	01 35	03 04
62	07 05	08 06	09 10	24 08	00 08	01 31	02 56
60	06 57	07 53	08 50	24 08	00 08	01 28	02 49
N 58	06 50	07 42	08 33	24 08	00 08	01 25	02 42
56	06 43	07 32	08 19	24 08	00 08	01 22	02 36
54	06 38	07 23	08 07	24 08	00 08	01 20	02 31
52	06 32	07 16	07 56	24 08	00 08	01 17	02 27
50	06 27	07 08	07 46	24 08	00 08	01 15	02 23
45	06 16	06 53	07 27	24 08	00 08	01 11	02 14
N 40	06 06	06 40	07 10	24 08	00 08	01 07	02 06
35	05 57	06 28	06 56	24 09	00 09	01 04	02 00
30	05 48	06 18	06 45	24 09	00 09	01 02	01 55
20	05 33	06 00	06 24	24 09	00 09	00 57	01 45
N 10	05 17	05 43	06 06	24 09	00 09	00 53	01 37
0	05 00	05 26	05 49	24 09	00 09	00 49	01 29
S 10	04 42	05 09	05 32	24 09	00 09	00 45	01 21
20	04 20	04 49	05 13	24 10	00 10	00 41	01 13
30	03 51	04 24	04 52	24 10	00 10	00 37	01 04
35	03 33	04 10	04 39	24 10	00 10	00 34	00 59
40	03 11	03 52	04 25	24 10	00 10	00 31	00 53
45	02 41	03 30	04 07	24 10	00 10	00 28	00 46
S 50	01 58	03 02	03 45	24 11	00 11	00 24	00 38
52	01 33	02 47	03 35	24 11	00 11	00 22	00 34
54	00 55	02 30	03 23	00 02	00 11	00 20	00 30
56	////	02 09	03 10	00 04	00 11	00 18	00 25
58	////	01 42	02 54	00 07	00 11	00 16	00 20
S 60	////	01 00	02 34	00 10	00 11	00 13	00 15

Sunset / Twilight / Moonset

Lat.	Sunset	Civil	Naut.	Moonset 9	10	11	12
N 72	■	13 18	15 34	12 25	11 57	11 29	10 53
N 70	■	14 09	15 52	12 21	12 01	11 39	11 14
68		14 41	16 07	12 18	12 03	11 48	11 31
66	13 31	15 05	16 20	12 15	12 06	11 56	11 45
64	14 08	15 23	16 30	12 13	12 07	12 02	11 56
62	14 35	15 38	16 39	12 11	12 09	12 07	12 06
60	14 55	15 51	16 47	12 09	12 11	12 12	12 14
N 58	15 12	16 03	16 55	12 08	12 12	12 16	12 22
56	15 26	16 13	17 01	12 06	12 13	12 20	12 28
54	15 38	16 21	17 07	12 05	12 14	12 24	12 34
52	15 49	16 29	17 13	12 04	12 15	12 27	12 39
50	15 58	16 37	17 18	12 03	12 16	12 30	12 44
45	16 19	16 52	17 29	12 01	12 18	12 36	12 55
N 40	16 35	17 05	17 39	11 59	12 20	12 41	13 04
35	16 48	17 16	17 48	11 57	12 21	12 45	13 11
30	17 01	17 27	17 57	11 56	12 22	12 49	13 18
20	17 21	17 45	18 13	11 53	12 25	12 56	13 29
N 10	17 39	18 02	18 28	11 51	12 27	13 02	13 39
0	17 56	18 19	18 45	11 48	12 28	13 08	13 49
S 10	18 13	18 36	19 03	11 46	12 30	13 14	13 59
20	18 32	18 56	19 26	11 44	12 32	13 20	14 09
30	18 53	19 21	19 54	11 41	12 34	13 27	14 21
35	19 06	19 36	20 12	11 39	12 36	13 31	14 27
40	19 21	19 53	20 34	11 38	12 37	13 36	14 35
45	19 38	20 15	21 04	11 35	12 39	13 41	14 44
S 50	20 00	20 44	21 48	11 33	12 41	13 48	14 55
52	20 11	20 59	22 13	11 32	12 41	13 51	15 01
54	20 23	21 16	22 52	11 30	12 42	13 54	15 06
56	20 36	21 37	////	11 29	12 44	13 58	15 13
58	20 52	22 04	////	11 27	12 45	14 02	15 20
S 60	21 12	22 48	////	11 26	12 46	14 06	15 28

SUN / MOON

Day	Eqn. of Time 00h	12h	Mer. Pass.	Mer. Pass. Upper	Lower	Age	Phase
9	08 06	07 53	11 52	05 39	17 59	21	
10	07 40	07 26	11 53	06 19	18 39	22	
11	07 12	06 59	11 53	06 59	19 19	23	◐

46ᵐ   INCREMENTS AND CORRECTIONS   47ᵐ

46ᵐ

s	SUN PLANETS	ARIES	MOON	v or Corrⁿ d	v or Corrⁿ d	v or Corrⁿ d
00	11 30.0	11 31.9	10 58.6	0.0 0.0	6.0 4.7	12.0 9.3
01	11 30.3	11 32.1	10 58.8	0.1 0.1	6.1 4.7	12.1 9.4
02	11 30.5	11 32.4	10 59.0	0.2 0.2	6.2 4.8	12.2 9.5
03	11 30.8	11 32.6	10 59.3	0.3 0.2	6.3 4.9	12.3 9.5
04	11 31.0	11 32.9	10 59.5	0.4 0.3	6.4 5.0	12.4 9.6
05	11 31.3	11 33.1	10 59.8	0.5 0.4	6.5 5.0	12.5 9.7
06	11 31.5	11 33.4	11 00.0	0.6 0.5	6.6 5.1	12.6 9.8
07	11 31.8	11 33.6	11 00.2	0.7 0.5	6.7 5.2	12.7 9.8
08	11 32.0	11 33.9	11 00.5	0.8 0.6	6.8 5.3	12.8 9.9
09	11 32.3	11 34.1	11 00.7	0.9 0.7	6.9 5.3	12.9 10.0
10	11 32.5	11 34.4	11 01.0	1.0 0.8	7.0 5.4	13.0 10.1
11	11 32.8	11 34.6	11 01.2	1.1 0.9	7.1 5.5	13.1 10.2
12	11 33.0	11 34.9	11 01.4	1.2 0.9	7.2 5.6	13.2 10.2
13	11 33.3	11 35.1	11 01.7	1.3 1.0	7.3 5.7	13.3 10.3
14	11 33.5	11 35.4	11 01.9	1.4 1.1	7.4 5.7	13.4 10.4
15	11 33.8	11 35.6	11 02.1	1.5 1.2	7.5 5.8	13.5 10.5
16	11 34.0	11 35.9	11 02.4	1.6 1.2	7.6 5.9	13.6 10.5
17	11 34.3	11 36.2	11 02.6	1.7 1.3	7.7 6.0	13.7 10.6
18	11 34.5	11 36.4	11 02.9	1.8 1.4	7.8 6.0	13.8 10.7
19	11 34.8	11 36.7	11 03.1	1.9 1.5	7.9 6.1	13.9 10.8
20	11 35.0	11 36.9	11 03.3	2.0 1.6	8.0 6.2	14.0 10.9
21	11 35.3	11 37.2	11 03.6	2.1 1.6	8.1 6.3	14.1 10.9
22	11 35.5	11 37.4	11 03.8	2.2 1.7	8.2 6.4	14.2 11.0
23	11 35.8	11 37.7	11 04.1	2.3 1.8	8.3 6.4	14.3 11.1
24	11 36.0	11 37.9	11 04.3	2.4 1.9	8.4 6.5	14.4 11.2
25	11 36.3	11 38.2	11 04.5	2.5 1.9	8.5 6.6	14.5 11.2
26	11 36.5	11 38.4	11 04.8	2.6 2.0	8.6 6.7	14.6 11.3
27	11 36.8	11 38.7	11 05.0	2.7 2.1	8.7 6.7	14.7 11.4
28	11 37.0	11 38.9	11 05.2	2.8 2.2	8.8 6.8	14.8 11.5
29	11 37.3	11 39.2	11 05.5	2.9 2.2	8.9 6.9	14.9 11.5
30	11 37.5	11 39.4	11 05.7	3.0 2.3	9.0 7.0	15.0 11.6
31	11 37.8	11 39.7	11 06.0	3.1 2.4	9.1 7.1	15.1 11.7
32	11 38.0	11 39.9	11 06.2	3.2 2.5	9.2 7.1	15.2 11.8
33	11 38.3	11 40.2	11 06.4	3.3 2.6	9.3 7.2	15.3 11.9
34	11 38.5	11 40.4	11 06.7	3.4 2.6	9.4 7.3	15.4 11.9
35	11 38.8	11 40.7	11 06.9	3.5 2.7	9.5 7.4	15.5 12.0
36	11 39.0	11 40.9	11 07.2	3.6 2.8	9.6 7.4	15.6 12.1
37	11 39.3	11 41.2	11 07.4	3.7 2.9	9.7 7.5	15.7 12.2
38	11 39.5	11 41.4	11 07.6	3.8 2.9	9.8 7.6	15.8 12.2
39	11 39.8	11 41.7	11 07.9	3.9 3.0	9.9 7.7	15.9 12.3
40	11 40.0	11 41.9	11 08.1	4.0 3.1	10.0 7.8	16.0 12.4
41	11 40.3	11 42.2	11 08.3	4.1 3.2	10.1 7.8	16.1 12.5
42	11 40.5	11 42.4	11 08.6	4.2 3.3	10.2 7.9	16.2 12.6
43	11 40.8	11 42.7	11 08.8	4.3 3.3	10.3 8.0	16.3 12.6
44	11 41.0	11 42.9	11 09.1	4.4 3.4	10.4 8.1	16.4 12.7
45	11 41.3	11 43.2	11 09.3	4.5 3.5	10.5 8.1	16.5 12.8
46	11 41.5	11 43.4	11 09.5	4.6 3.6	10.6 8.2	16.6 12.9
47	11 41.8	11 43.7	11 09.8	4.7 3.6	10.7 8.3	16.7 12.9
48	11 42.0	11 43.9	11 10.0	4.8 3.7	10.8 8.4	16.8 13.0
49	11 42.3	11 44.2	11 10.3	4.9 3.8	10.9 8.4	16.9 13.1
50	11 42.5	11 44.4	11 10.5	5.0 3.9	11.0 8.5	17.0 13.2
51	11 42.8	11 44.7	11 10.7	5.1 4.0	11.1 8.6	17.1 13.3
52	11 43.0	11 44.9	11 11.0	5.2 4.0	11.2 8.7	17.2 13.3
53	11 43.3	11 45.2	11 11.2	5.3 4.1	11.3 8.8	17.3 13.4
54	11 43.5	11 45.4	11 11.5	5.4 4.2	11.4 8.8	17.4 13.5
55	11 43.8	11 45.7	11 11.7	5.5 4.3	11.5 8.9	17.5 13.6
56	11 44.0	11 45.9	11 11.9	5.6 4.3	11.6 9.0	17.6 13.6
57	11 44.3	11 46.2	11 12.2	5.7 4.4	11.7 9.1	17.7 13.7
58	11 44.5	11 46.4	11 12.4	5.8 4.5	11.8 9.1	17.8 13.8
59	11 44.8	11 46.7	11 12.6	5.9 4.6	11.9 9.2	17.9 13.9
60	11 45.0	11 46.9	11 12.9	6.0 4.7	12.0 9.3	18.0 14.0

47ᵐ

s	SUN PLANETS	ARIES	MOON	v or Corrⁿ d	v or Corrⁿ d	v or Corrⁿ d
00	11 45.0	11 46.9	11 12.9	0.0 0.0	6.0 4.8	12.0 9.5
01	11 45.3	11 47.2	11 13.1	0.1 0.1	6.1 4.8	12.1 9.6
02	11 45.5	11 47.4	11 13.4	0.2 0.2	6.2 4.9	12.2 9.7
03	11 45.8	11 47.7	11 13.6	0.3 0.2	6.3 5.0	12.3 9.7
04	11 46.0	11 47.9	11 13.8	0.4 0.3	6.4 5.1	12.4 9.8
05	11 46.3	11 48.2	11 14.1	0.5 0.4	6.5 5.1	12.5 9.9
06	11 46.5	11 48.4	11 14.3	0.6 0.5	6.6 5.2	12.6 10.0
07	11 46.8	11 48.7	11 14.6	0.7 0.6	6.7 5.3	12.7 10.1
08	11 47.0	11 48.9	11 14.8	0.8 0.6	6.8 5.4	12.8 10.1
09	11 47.3	11 49.2	11 15.0	0.9 0.7	6.9 5.5	12.9 10.2
10	11 47.5	11 49.4	11 15.3	1.0 0.8	7.0 5.5	13.0 10.3
11	11 47.8	11 49.7	11 15.5	1.1 0.9	7.1 5.6	13.1 10.4
12	11 48.0	11 49.9	11 15.7	1.2 1.0	7.2 5.7	13.2 10.5
13	11 48.3	11 50.2	11 16.0	1.3 1.0	7.3 5.8	13.3 10.5
14	11 48.5	11 50.4	11 16.2	1.4 1.1	7.4 5.9	13.4 10.6
15	11 48.8	11 50.7	11 16.5	1.5 1.2	7.5 5.9	13.5 10.7
16	11 49.0	11 50.9	11 16.7	1.6 1.3	7.6 6.0	13.6 10.8
17	11 49.3	11 51.2	11 16.9	1.7 1.3	7.7 6.1	13.7 10.8
18	11 49.5	11 51.4	11 17.2	1.8 1.4	7.8 6.2	13.8 10.9
19	11 49.8	11 51.7	11 17.4	1.9 1.5	7.9 6.3	13.9 11.0
20	11 50.0	11 51.9	11 17.7	2.0 1.6	8.0 6.3	14.0 11.1
21	11 50.3	11 52.2	11 17.9	2.1 1.7	8.1 6.4	14.1 11.2
22	11 50.5	11 52.4	11 18.1	2.2 1.7	8.2 6.5	14.2 11.2
23	11 50.8	11 52.7	11 18.4	2.3 1.8	8.3 6.6	14.3 11.3
24	11 51.0	11 52.9	11 18.6	2.4 1.9	8.4 6.7	14.4 11.4
25	11 51.3	11 53.2	11 18.8	2.5 2.0	8.5 6.7	14.5 11.5
26	11 51.5	11 53.4	11 19.1	2.6 2.1	8.6 6.8	14.6 11.6
27	11 51.8	11 53.7	11 19.3	2.7 2.1	8.7 6.9	14.7 11.6
28	11 52.0	11 53.9	11 19.6	2.8 2.2	8.8 7.0	14.8 11.7
29	11 52.3	11 54.2	11 19.8	2.9 2.3	8.9 7.0	14.9 11.8
30	11 52.5	11 54.5	11 20.0	3.0 2.4	9.0 7.1	15.0 11.9
31	11 52.8	11 54.7	11 20.3	3.1 2.5	9.1 7.2	15.1 12.0
32	11 53.0	11 55.0	11 20.5	3.2 2.5	9.2 7.3	15.2 12.0
33	11 53.3	11 55.2	11 20.8	3.3 2.6	9.3 7.4	15.3 12.1
34	11 53.5	11 55.5	11 21.0	3.4 2.7	9.4 7.4	15.4 12.2
35	11 53.8	11 55.7	11 21.2	3.5 2.8	9.5 7.5	15.5 12.3
36	11 54.0	11 56.0	11 21.5	3.6 2.9	9.6 7.6	15.6 12.4
37	11 54.3	11 56.2	11 21.7	3.7 2.9	9.7 7.7	15.7 12.4
38	11 54.5	11 56.5	11 22.0	3.8 3.0	9.8 7.8	15.8 12.5
39	11 54.8	11 56.7	11 22.2	3.9 3.1	9.9 7.8	15.9 12.6
40	11 55.0	11 57.0	11 22.4	4.0 3.2	10.0 7.9	16.0 12.7
41	11 55.3	11 57.2	11 22.7	4.1 3.2	10.1 8.0	16.1 12.7
42	11 55.5	11 57.5	11 22.9	4.2 3.3	10.2 8.1	16.2 12.8
43	11 55.8	11 57.7	11 23.1	4.3 3.4	10.3 8.2	16.3 12.9
44	11 56.0	11 58.0	11 23.4	4.4 3.5	10.4 8.2	16.4 13.0
45	11 56.3	11 58.2	11 23.6	4.5 3.6	10.5 8.3	16.5 13.1
46	11 56.5	11 58.5	11 23.9	4.6 3.6	10.6 8.4	16.6 13.1
47	11 56.8	11 58.7	11 24.1	4.7 3.7	10.7 8.5	16.7 13.2
48	11 57.0	11 59.0	11 24.3	4.8 3.8	10.8 8.6	16.8 13.3
49	11 57.3	11 59.2	11 24.6	4.9 3.9	10.9 8.6	16.9 13.4
50	11 57.5	11 59.5	11 24.8	5.0 4.0	11.0 8.7	17.0 13.5
51	11 57.8	11 59.7	11 25.1	5.1 4.0	11.1 8.8	17.1 13.5
52	11 58.0	12 00.0	11 25.3	5.2 4.1	11.2 8.9	17.2 13.6
53	11 58.3	12 00.2	11 25.5	5.3 4.2	11.3 8.9	17.3 13.7
54	11 58.5	12 00.5	11 25.8	5.4 4.3	11.4 9.0	17.4 13.8
55	11 58.8	12 00.7	11 26.0	5.5 4.4	11.5 9.1	17.5 13.9
56	11 59.0	12 01.0	11 26.2	5.6 4.4	11.6 9.2	17.6 13.9
57	11 59.3	12 01.2	11 26.5	5.7 4.5	11.7 9.3	17.7 14.0
58	11 59.5	12 01.5	11 26.7	5.8 4.6	11.8 9.3	17.8 14.1
59	11 59.8	12 01.7	11 27.0	5.9 4.7	11.9 9.4	17.9 14.2
60	12 00.0	12 02.0	11 27.2	6.0 4.8	12.0 9.5	18.0 14.3

Index